INSIGHT GUIDES

Series Created by Hans Höfer

Japan

Update Editor: Bill Williams
Executive Editor: Scott Rutherford

Editorial Director: Brian Bell

APA PUBLICATIONS

It's no small task assembling a book about Japan. Not only is it a complex and layered country, but it lends itself too easily to cliches and stereotypes, all of them shallow and of not much use. We first arrive in Japan expecting some sort of Zen-like ambiance and pristine environments, and we're assaulted, instead, with a clutter of unplanned urban design and loudspeakers scolding and informing and pestering. A ride on the subway or a visit to a famous tourist spot – even one the Zen temples – quickly dissipates most stereotypes.

It's also no easy task getting into the Japanese psyche. There's a lot going on beneath the outer graciousness, and much of Japanese communication involves not words and hand gestures, but rather subtle nuances of sentence structure, choice of words and context.

Moreover, there's the dilemma of interpreting how Japanese feel about events and situations. The past decade has not been easy for the Japanese as a group. The 1980s were an invigorating time, when the Japanese promoted themselves as the next superpower, even to the point of claiming that Japanese would be the next international language.

Things have changed. The economy not only slowed down, it imploded. Scandals peppered the headlines. A severe earthquake and domestic terrorism shook national confidence in the mid 1990s. Needless to say, these events will define how the Japanese see themselves and their international role, and how they respond to global events, in the next century.

Rutherford

This revamped edition of *Insight Guide: Japan* was handled by Apa's executive editor based in Singapore, **Scott Rutherford**, who lived in Tokyo and Japan for several years before heading south. Rutherford first came to Japan on a three-month photographic assignment for National Geographic; many of the pictures in this new edition, from Hokkaido to Okinawa, were taken by him on numerous assignments over the years.

Working with Rutherford was writer and editor **Bill Williams**, based in Osaka and a frequent contributor to publications around the world. For this edition, Williams reworked the Osaka, Kobe and Kyoto chapters, and reviewed many of the other regions.

Contributing to the updating work was **Matsutani Yuko**, a professional translator of books and magazines, and, most recently, an interpreter for the Nagano Olympic Committee.

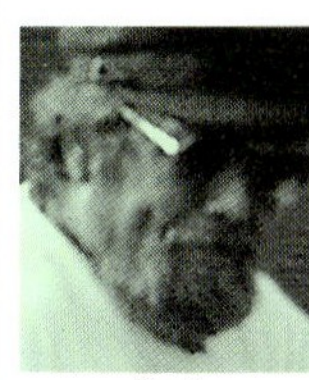

Davis

The original edition of *Insight Guide: Japan,* published in the early 1990s, was edited by **Malcolm B. Davis**. Having written for and edited travel books and magazines in Japan for three decades, including the in-flight monthly for All Nippon Airways and the quarterly magazine for Nikko Hotels, Davis had the knowledge and contacts to pull together a writing team.

One of the first to join Davis was author, book editor and craft specialist **Kim Schuefftan**, who contributed to the extensively researched sections on history, festivals, architecture, and traditional arts and crafts.

Carroll

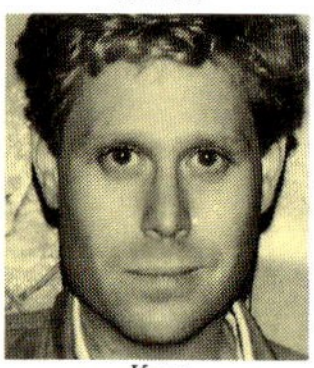
Kerr

Almost by accident, **Steve Usdin** became the next to heed the call, having dropped by to pitch Davis a series of travel stories on southern Japan. Davis sent him there.

Also armed with some impressive academic credentials (USC, Waseda, University of Hawaii, Doshisha University) came **John Carroll**, pitching in to handle the sections on Okinawa, Yokohama and Kamakura, as well as a knowledgeable essay on Japanese religion. **Alex Kerr** brought with him a number of Yale and Oxford degrees in things Oriental. Kerr grew up in Japan and has renovated a traditional farmhouse deep in Shikoku. Kerr is now a writer and essayist.

Other contributors to the first edition – all residents of Japan for years – included **Davis Barrager**, **Mark Schreiber**, **David Benjamin**, **Anthony J. Bryant**, **Bruce Leigh**, **Rich Blumm**, **Peter Ujlaki**, **Peter Hadfield** (*60 Seconds That Will Change the World – The Coming Tokyo Earthquake*), **Arturo Silva**, **Gail Feldman**, **Evelyn Corbett**, sports writer **Wayne Graczyk**, and **Jeanette Amano**.

Photography is, of course, an identifying hallmark of all Insight Guides. Despite being a nation of dedicated if obsessesed photographers, Japan can be problematic in capturing on film, especially when trying to illustrate those out-of-the-way places.

Sourcing the photography for the original edition was **Robert McLeod**, who has a journalistic and editorial background as a photographer. His tireless efforts to secure not only the most visually interesting but also the freshest and most revealing photography greatly enhanced the book.

Vilhar

Gorazd Vilhar's discerning photographic eye and unique perspective on Japanese culture and people first came to our attention in the original *Insight Guide: Tokyo*. **Jean Kugler** lived in Kyoto, and has also contributed to several other Insight Guides.

Carol Jopp, of Hong Kong, demonstrates the fine art of landscape photography. **Miguel Rivas-Micoud** and his *Insight Guide: Tokyo* team of photographers proved to be a natural resource for photos.

Others who helped in this revamped edition of *Insight Guide: Japan* include **Nakamura Yutaka**, **Itonaga Masayuki**, **Otani Eiho**, and **Oguro Kazumi**.

In Apa's Singapore office, overseeing the design and layout work – and Rutherford's compulsive but cogent last-minute changes of text – was **Suriyani Ahmad**. New maps were created by **Kathy Wee**, also on Apa's Singapore staff.

CONTENTS

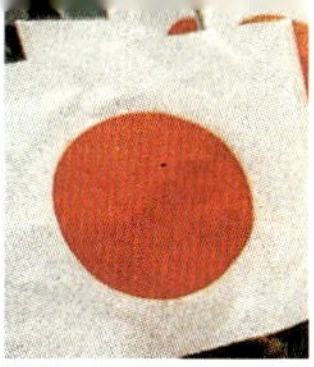

History

Features

Places

Maps

TRAVEL TIPS

Getting Acquainted

Planning the Trip

Practical Tips

Getting Around

Where to Stay

Attractions

Festivals

Shopping

Sports and Leisure

Language

Further Reading

3
ホテル

Dainaha
CITY COURT

INTRODUCTION

A traveler roaming amongst the islands of Japan is usually seeking the exotic, or the wondrous, or the unconventional. And indeed, Japan is often so, in both the cities and along the back roads. Often what's encountered seems illogical or of dubious purpose, but that is a distinction of culture and outlook. The traveler will inevitably compare Japan with the West, considering the obvious examples such as the suits and ties on Japan's *sarariman* – the "salary man" or white-collar worker. Fast-food franchises nearly everywhere, and the near-cult status of Western pop icons can lull the outsider into believing that East has met West. (Even the Japanese language, as different as it is, uses English loan words, an estimated ten percent of all words used in daily conversion.) The traveler thinks, *Japan has become like the West.*

Big mistake. In its history, Japan has adopted many things, taking what it wants or needs, adapting it, and discarding that which is of no use. Over the centuries, the Japanese have adopted Chinese writing and philosophy, Korean art and ceramics, and most recently, Western technology, clothes and fast-food. Indeed, since it yielded to Perry's Black Ships in 1853, Japan has adopted things foreign with gusto. Yet that which it adopts from the West or elsewhere becomes distinctly Japanese, somehow. Foreign words are taken, chopped in half, one half recombined with the half of another bisected foreign word, and – *voilà*, a new word in the Japanese language.

Although Japan derives most of its culture from its Asian neighbors, and most of its modernity from the West, the Japanese continue to cultivate a self-image of an almost divine uniqueness. The Japanese repeatedly refer to Japanese things – including themselves – as "special" or "unique" and thus beyond an outsider's understanding. That is something Japanese, they will say, and so you cannot understand it. The special Japanese snow once kept out French skis, as did the special and unique Japanese digestive system keep out American beef. A Japanese photographer once asked an American photographer, "I imagine that you don't have such a blue sky in America, do you? This type of blue sky is only in Japan."

Japan is special, of course. It has become the world's second-strongest economy while evenly – and in comparison with most of the world, uniquely – distributing a growing wealth, but generating no significant lower class. But having done so, it has made itself into a uniquely expensive place. And while Japan radiates an international image of sophistication and efficiency, the home country is oddly behind the times. Just two-thirds of Japanese dwellings are connected to a modern sewage system, for example. Bureaucrats in the Kasumigaseki district of Tokyo issue vague, and verbal, suggestions for guidance that somehow become the equivalent of regula-

Preceding pages: Sea of Japan coast, Honshu; harvesting rice the old way, Tohoku; urban life, Naha; the Emperor's birthday is a flag-waving occasion; Sakura-jima smolders, Kyushu. Left, flower picking, Tohoku.

tory edicts. Japanese companies understand the system, and the nuances, but foreign companies trying to start business in the country are like turtles out of water.

There is the nagging legacy of World War II, not to mention the uniquely Japanese forgetfulness regarding it. Other than of the atomic bombings of Nagasaki and Hiroshima, the Japanese don't talk about it much. Yet, increasingly, neighboring countries do, and Japan's relations with Korea and China, for example, are often rich with the undercurrents of the past. And most recently, national self-confidence has weakened under a collapsing superheated economy, followed by the 1995 Kobe earthquake that killed over 5,000 people and destroyed a supposedly earthquake-proof infrastructure, and a poison gas attack on its subways, right in the heart of the government district in downtown Tokyo.

Nonetheless, the Japanese are rightly proud of both their country – self-doubts aside – and of the sophistication and depth of its heritage. Much of its progress and advances have been the result of an inward-looking dedication and spirit. As an island nation, Japan is often focused inwardly in its approach to the world, as when the evening television news leads off with a cherry-blossom story, and the remainder of the world is shoved to the end. Yet the Japanese are perhaps more attuned to the subtleties of the changing seasons than any other people. Rural people will know if the dragonflies that appear in late spring are three days early this year, or if the *tsuyu*, the rainy season, is dragging on a bit longer than normal, say by two days. There is a delicate charm in such observations. It is a quality that says the people know their land.

There are those, Japanese and foreigners alike, who retain an image of a Japan of Zen-like serenity. It is a wistful image, a nostalgic retreat. The novelist and nationalist Mishima Yukio, who revered the old Japan and chose to kill himself for those old-guard principles, wrote that "Japan will disappear, it will become inorganic, empty, neutral-tinted; it will be wealthy and astute."

Who knows. Cultures change, shift, disappear. On its surface, Japan appears to be changing. Underneath, one wonders if it is capable of doing so, or if it wants to change. Does it need to change? Who knows.

Notes: Wherever possible, we use Japanese terms for geographical identifications. These appear as suffixes to the proper name. For example, Mount Fuji is referred to as Fuji-san. Mountains may also appear with other suffixes, including *-zan*, *-yama*, and for some active volcanoes, *-dake*. Islands are either *-shima* or *-jima*, lakes are *-ko*, and rivers are *-gawa*. Shinto shrines usually end in *-jinja*, *-jingu*, or *-gu*. Temples are Buddhist, with names usually ending in *-tera*, *-dera*, or *-ji*. When referring to individuals, we follow the Japanese style: family name first, given name second.

Proud harvesters of yams, Kyushu.

キン肉マン

The lands that are now the Japanese archipelago have been inhabited by human beings for at least 30,000 years, and maybe for as long as 100,000 to 200,000 years. The shallow seas separating Japan from the Asian mainland were incomplete when these people first settled on the terrain. However, it is certain that significant changes in the geography took place after people arrived, including rising sea levels that eventually covered land bridges.

Whether or not these settlers are the ancestors of the present Japanese remains a controversy. (Archaeological excavations of prehistoric sites in Japan only began in the 1960s, so a clear picture of the earliest human habitation has yet to emerge.) It is generally agreed that Japan was settled by waves of people coming from South Asia and the northern regions of the Asian continent, and that this migration very likely occurred over a long period.

Jomon Period (ca 10,000–300 BC): The earliest millennia of Neolithic culture saw a warming in worldwide climate, reaching peak temperature levels between 8000 and 4000 BC. In Japan, this phenomenon led to rising sea levels, which cut any remaining land bridges to the Asian mainland.

At the same time, the local waters produced more abundant species of fish and shellfish. New types of forest took root, sprang up and thrived. These natural developments in the environment set the stage for the Early Jomon Period.

Japan's earliest pottery – belonging to the Jomon culture – has been dated at about 10,000 BC, possibly the oldest known in the world, say some experts.

The Early Jomon people were mostly coastal-living, food-gathering nomads. Dietary reliance on fish, shellfish, and sea mammals gave rise to the community refuse heaps known as shell-mounds, the archaeologist's primary source of information about these people. The Early Jomon people also hunted deer and wild pig. Artifacts include stone blade tools and the first cord-marked pottery (*jomon,* in fact, means cord-marked).

In the Middle Jomon Period (from about 3500 to 2000 BC), the locus of life shifted away from coastal settlements toward inland areas. By this time, fish and shellfish may have been depleted by lower sea levels, or perhaps more reliance may have been placed on plants as dietary staple. Grinding stones, capped storage jars, and other Middle Jomon artifacts indicate a much more intense in-

volvement with plant cultivation. Middle Jomon came to an end when tree crops in inland hilly areas failed to provide sufficient sustenance. Late Jomon, from about 2000 BC, is marked by a resurgence of coastal fishing along the Pacific seaboard.

Yayoi Period (ca 300 BC–AD 300): Named after an archaeological site near Tokyo University, in the Hongo area, the Yayoi Period was a time of significant cultural transition, ushered in by peoples who migrated from rice-growing areas of the Asian mainland, starting around 300 BC, into northern Kyushu via Korea and, most likely, Okinawa. (Northern Japan, in fact, lingered behind the rest of

Preceding pages: an old illustration from the classic story *Tale of the Genji*. Left, clay figure from the Jomon Period. Above, earthenware pot from the Jomon Period.

the archipelago, with the Jomon culture persisting well into northern Japan's early historic periods.)

In a brief 600 years, Japan was transformed from a land of nomadic hunting-and-gathering communities into one of stationary farming villages. The growth of tight-knit, autonomous rice-farming settlements was so rapid in Kyushu and western Honshu that, by AD 100, such settlements were found in most parts of the country, except for the northern regions of Honshu and Hokkaido.

Kofun Period (ca AD 300–710): The break with Yayoi culture is represented by the construction of huge tombs of earth and stone in coastal areas of Kyushu and along

the shores of the Inland Sea. Hollow clay human and animal figures and models of houses called *haniwa* decorated the perimeters of these tombs. These were made, some experts have speculated, as substitutes for the living retainers and possessions of the departed noble or leader.

Political and social institutions developed rapidly. Each of the community clusters that defined itself as a "country" or "kingdom" had a hierarchical social structure, subjected to increasing influence by a burgeoning central power based in the Yamato Plain, what is now the area of Osaka and Nara. The imperial line, or the so-called Yamato Sun Line, was most likely formed out of a number of powerful *uji* (family-clan communities) that had developed in the Late Yayoi Period.

The Yamato uji that eventually became the imperial line claimed direct descent from Amaterasu Omikami, the Sun Goddess. (Today, this claim is made by only a few Japanese, notably right-wing nationalists; it has been officially denied both by the government and – more importantly – by the Imperial Household Agency, which administers the imperial family.)

Buddhism came to Japan in the sixth century from Korea. Although it is said that writing accompanied the religion, it may be that Chinese writing techniques preceded the religion by as much as 100 to 150 years. In any case, it was literacy that made the imported religion accessible to the nobility, also exposing them to the Chinese classics, and to the writings of sages such as Confucius. Social and political change naturally followed an increase in literacy.

With the advent of Buddhism, an aggressive clan – the Soga – strove to establish the faith as the official state religion. Their efforts met with some success, as all succeeding emperors would adopt the Buddhist faith.

The power of the Soga clan was enhanced by exclusive control of the imperial treasury and granaries, and by the clan's monopolistic role as sponsor for new learning brought in from the Asian mainland. Their consolidation of political power culminated with Soga daughters being chosen exclusively as the consorts of emperors, with Soga clansmen filling important court positions.

Reforms were aimed primarily at strengthening the central government and reducing the power of other clans at the imperial court. The reforms were radical and far-reaching, including changes in social structure, economic and legal systems, provincial boundaries, bureaucracy, and taxes.

As it has several times in history, location of the capital was changed twice before the end of the seventh century.

Nara Period (710–794): An empress in the early eighth century again constructed a new capital, this one in the northwest of the Yamato Plain and named Heijokyo, on the site of present Nara City.

The century that followed, comprising the Nara Period, saw the full enforcement of the system of centralized imperial rule based on

Chinese concepts (the *ritsuryo* system), as well as flourishing arts and culture.

With the enforcement of the ritsuryo system, the imperial government achieved tight control, placing administrative control in a powerful grand council. All land used for rice cultivation was claimed to be under imperial ownership, which later led to heavy taxation of farmers.

Heian Period (794–1185): In the last decade of the eighth century, the capital was relocated yet again. As usual, the city was built on the Chinese model, and was named Heiankyo and was the core around which the city of Kyoto developed.

Its completion in 795 marked the beginning of the glorious 400-year Heian Period; it remained the imperial capital until 1868, when the imperial court moved to Edo, shortly thereafter to be renamed Tokyo.

The strength of the central government continued for several decades, but later in the ninth century the ritsuryo system gradually began to crumble. The central government was interested in expanding the area of its influence farther and farther from the capital, but provincial government became harder to manage under the bureaucratic system. This was modified so that aristocrats and powerful temple guardians could own large estates (*shoen*). Farmers, working imperial lands but faced with oppressive taxation, fled to these estates in large numbers. Thus the estate holders began to gain political – and military – power in the provinces.

Provincial areas were neglected by the imperial court. Banditry became widespread, and local administrators were more interested in personal gain than in enforcing law and order. The result was that the lords of great estates continued to develop their own military power, engaging in struggles amongst themselves. The fighting ended the Heian Period dramatically and decisively.

Kamakura Period (1185–1333): The victor of the struggles, Minamoto no Yoritomo, was granted the title of shogun. He established his base at Kamakura, far from Kyoto and south of where Edo Tokyo would arise. There he established an administrative structure as well as military headquarters, creating ministries to take care of samurai under his control. He had, in effect, come to dominate the country by assuming control of justice, imperial succession and defense of the country. He remained in Kamakura, refusing to go to the imperial capital for any reason.

Nevertheless, he convinced the emperor to sanction officials called *shugo* (military governors) and *jito* (stewards) in each province. The former were responsible for military control of the provinces and the latter for supervising the land, plus collecting taxes. Both posts were answerable directly to the shogun himself. Government by the warrior class, located at a distance from the imperial capital, was created. This governing system was based on obligation and dependency,

not unlike that of medieval Europe, and thus it can be called a true feudal system, known as *bakufu*, or shogunate.

The imperial court was, in effect, shoved into a corner and ignored. The court remained alive, however, though subsequent centuries saw its impoverishment. Still, it kept an important function in ritual and as symbol until 1868, when the emperor again became the acting head of state.

Although the Kamakura Period was relatively brief, there were events and developments that profoundly affected the country. A revolutionary advance of agricultural techniques occurred, allowing greater produc-

Left, bronze vessel, Yayoi Period. Above, bodhisativa, Kofun Period.

tion of food. Consequently, there was an increase in population and economic growth, with more intense settlement of the land, better commerce and trade, the growth of local markets, and the beginnings of a currency system. Contact with China resumed, but on a private basis.

Strong Buddhist leaders arose, preaching doctrines that appealed to the samurai and the common people, and Buddhism became a popular religion, whereas in the past it had been the monopoly of the aristocracy.

The complexities of civil rule became top-heavy; the system of military governors and stewards started to crumble. More strain was added by the defense of the country against the two Mongol invasions in 1274 and 1281, both of which were unsuccessful due in great measure to the fortuitous occurrence of typhoons, which destroyed the invading Mongol fleet.

Muromachi Period (1333–1568): A subsequent shogun, Ashikaga Takauji, returned the capital to Kyoto, bringing the shogunate nose to nose with the imperial court and effectively eclipsing any power, political or economic, that the court may have retained. At the same time, the Ashikaga shogun and vassals, in the age-old pattern of conquering warriors anywhere, caught aristocratitis and actively delved into such effete pursuits as connoisseurship and cultural patronage after the manner of the old aristocracy.

The name of the period, Muromachi, comes from the area of Kyoto in which a later Ashikaga shogun, Yoshimitsu, built his residence. His life represents perhaps the high point of the Ashikaga shogunate. Yoshimitsu took an active role in court politics as well as excelling in his military duties as shogun.

Overall, the Muromachi Period introduced the basic changes that would assure the economic growth and stability of the coming Edo Period. Agricultural techniques were improved, new crops were introduced, irrigation and commercial farming expanded. Guilds of specialized craftsmen appeared, a money economy spread, and trade increased markedly. Most important, towns and cities arose and grew, and such development was accompanied by the appearance and flourishing of merchants and a service class.

A later Ashikaga shogun was assassinated in 1441, which started the decline of the shogunate; the relationship between the shogun and the military governors of the provinces broke down.

A decade of war and unrest marked the total erosion of centralized authority and a general dissolution of society. It ushered in the Age of Warring States, a century of battle that lasted from 1467 until 1568. The almost total decentralization of government that occurred in the Age of Warring States saw the development of what might be called a true type of feudal lord, the *daimyo*. The need to defend territory by military might meant that the political unit became contiguous with its military potential.

Up until this time, decisions regarding the provinces and land holdings were made by a central bureaucracy. No longer. The daimyo became what he was by right of conquest and might, backed up by vast armies.

During this century of warfare, with its ethic of ambition and expansion by force of arms, it is not surprising that the idea of unifying – or subduing – the entire country occurred to a few of the warriors, leaders of vision and ability.

Momoyama Period (1568–1600): This short period is somewhat of a historian's artifact, more the climaxing of the Muromachi Period. But it has been accorded a name, perhaps, because the Ashikaga shogunate ended in 1573 (the Muromachi Period is when the Ashikaga shogun ruled), notably when Oda Nobunaga (1534–82), the first of three leaders to go about the business of unifying the country, overran Kyoto. The other leaders were Toyotomi Hideyoshi (1536–98) and Tokugawa Ieyasu (1542–1616).

Nobunaga conquered the home provinces in a rigorous manner. He eliminated rivals in the usual military fashion, and is known particularly for razing the temples of militant Buddhist sects around Kyoto that opposed him. Temple burning aside, he had a flair for culture. Although he had only brought about one-third of the country under his control, Nobunaga laid the foundation for the unification that followed. He was assassinated by a treacherous general in 1582.

Hideyoshi, Nobunaga's chief general, did away with Nobunaga's murderer, and set himself up as Nobunaga's successor. With military brilliance, statesmanship and brass, he proceeded vigorously with the job of unifying Japan. By 1590, all territories of the country, directly or by proxy, were essentially under his control.

But although the country was unified under the power of one man, the government was still decentralized, a complex network of feudal relationships. Hideyoshi's hold on the country, based on oaths of fealty, was slippery at best. Though he could, and did, act as head of state, the administration of the land, resources and population was in the hands of the various regional daimyo.

Still, he effected sweeping domestic reforms. The action that perhaps had the longest-lasting social impact on Japanese history was his "sword hunt", in which all non-samurai were forced to give up their weapons. (To this day, there are strict regulations on weapons of any sort in Japan, whether knives or guns.)

A class system was also introduced. In some areas, this meant that rich landlords had to make a difficult choice: declare themselves to be samurai, thereby susceptible to the demands of the warrior's life, or remain as commoners and thus subservient to the samurai class.

Hideyoshi even tried to make his ambitions felt on the Asian mainland with two attempts to conquer Korea in 1592 and 1597, with the aim of taking over China thereafter. His death in 1598 brought this megalomanic effort to a swift end.

The cultural achievements of this tiny slice of Japanese history – a mere three decades – were astonishing. The country was in political ferment and war was rife, yet the most glorious textiles, ceramics, lacquer ware, screen paintings and tea utensils were produced. Such artistic achievement has never happened again in Japan.

Significant, too, was the economy's growth, the expansion of domestic and foreign trade, and the lifestyles of the daimyo. Nobunaga and Hideyoshi were cultural swashbucklers, and the great regional lords emulated them to some extent. Hideyoshi, in particular, seems to have had a penchant for gold and glitter and ostentatious splendor. In addition to the wealth of one's treasury, castle architecture encouraged the use of large areas of gold, in part to relieve the gloom of these mainly military structures.

The tea ceremony, as it is known today, attained its fundamental character under Hideyoshi's tea master, Sen no Rikyu, and the aesthetics he espoused resulted, both directly and indirectly, in the production of ceramics and tea utensils that have never been surpassed, much less copied by even the finest artisans of today.

Far left, Minamoto no Yorimoto, Kamakura Period. Left, *sumi-e* (ink painting), Muromachi Period.

靱負尉碓井貞光

In his eloquent essay *In Praise of Shadows*, Tanizaki Junichiro, one of the giants of Japanese literature, wrote that the quality that we call beauty "must always grow from the realities of life, and our ancestors, forced to live in dark rooms, presently came to discover beauty in shadows, ultimately to guide shadows towards beauty's ends."

Although he was discussing the aesthetics of Japanese architecture, this passage could just as easily refer to the daily lives of the common people of Edo, Tokyo's name when it was the capital of the Tokugawa shoguns. Compelled to live within a social straitjacket that bound their every move, they stole for themselves a certain kind of freedom that allowed them to develop a culture unique in human history.

The political, economic, social, religious, and intellectual facets of the Edo Period (1600–1868) are exceedingly complex. One often-cited general characteristic of this time is an increasingly prosperous merchant class, simultaneous with the development of urban centers. Edo itself became one of the world's great cities and is thought to have had a population in excess of one million at the beginning of the 18th century, greater than London or Paris at the time.

Tokugawa shogun: For many years, the shogun Hideyoshi had bemoaned his lack of a male heir. When in the twilight of Hideyoshi's years an infant son, Hideyori, was born, he was ecstatic and became obsessed with founding a dynasty of warrior rulers. So he established a regency council of leading vassals and allies, foremost of whom was Tokugawa Ieyasu (1542–1616), who controlled the most territory in the realm after Hideyoshi. Members of the council swore loyalty to the infant; the boy was five at the time of Hideyoshi's death.

The death of Hideyoshi was, naturally, an opportunity for the ambitions of restless warlords to surface. Tokugawa Ieyasu had about half of the lords who were allied with Hideyoshi's son sign pledges to him within a year of Hideyoshi's death. In 1600, however, he was challenged by a military coalition of lords from western Japan. He won that encounter, in the Battle of Sekigahara, and became the de facto ruler of the country.

In 1603, Tokugawa Ieyasu was given the title of shogun by the subservient, but symbolically important, emperor. He established his capital in Edo (now Tokyo), handed his son the shogun title in 1605, and then retired to a life of intrigue and scheming aimed at consolidating the position of his family. (Ieyasu himself would die in 1616.)

The primary problem facing Ieyasu was how to make a viable system out of the rather strange mix of a strong, central military power and a totally decentralized administrative structure.

Eventually, he devised a complex system that combined feudal authority and bureaucratic administration, with the Tokugawa shoguns as supreme authority from whom the various lords, or daimyo, received their domains, and to whom they allied themselves by oath.

While the military emphasis of the domain was curtailed, each daimyo had considerable autonomy in the administration of his do-

Left, relaxing days of leisure, ukiyo-e from Edo Period. Above, helmet of the Edo samurai.

main. The system sufficed to maintain peace and a growing prosperity for over two centuries. Its flaws were in its inability to adapt well to social and political change. Whether this fragile conservatism was inherent in the system or in the people who ran the system can be argued endlessly.

Ieyasu was Napoleonic in his passion for administration, and he thought of every device possible to assure that his descendants would retain power. Wanting to keep an eye on the daimyo in 1635 he established the *sankin kotai* system, which required staggered attendance in Edo for the close to 300 independent feudal lords. The shogunate set up a rigid class hierarchy – warriors, farmers, artisans, merchants – and adopted a school of neo-Confucianism as the theoretical basis for social and political policy.

Whether in Edo or the countryside, every individual knew exactly what his or her position in society was, and of how they were to behave. Sometimes encouraged with the sword, the emphasis on Confucian obedience and proper relations between superior and inferior filtered down to the lowest strata of society. People in a daimyo's domain had little recourse if their lord was autocratic, unprincipled or arbitrary.

As with today's Japan, there seems to have been a predisposition towards xenophobia, yet it was somehow coupled with an attraction toward things foreign. The xenophobia won, however, and the result was brutal and bloody for those tainted by the outside world. Indeed, for most of the Tokugawa years, Japan's doors were closed to the outside.

The long years of isolated peace slowly replaced the warrior's importance with that of the merchant. Standards of living for all classes increased greatly, and, at times, the shogunate felt compelled to quell the conspicuous consumption of wealthy merchants.

Growth of Edo: When Ieyasu first settled down in what eventually would become modern Tokyo, the area was little more than a collection of scattered farming and fishing villages. The little town of Edojuku, at the mouth of the Hirakawa River, contained only about 100 thatched huts in the shadow of a dilapidated castle, built in 1457 by the minor warlord Ota Dokan. A sophisticated poet and scholar, in 1485 he was betrayed and butchered at the behest of his own lord.

Ieyasu brought with him to Edo a ready-made population of considerable size. Huge numbers of peasants, merchants and *ronin* (masterless samurai) poured into the new capital of the shogun, laboring in the construction of the castle, mansions, warehouses and other infrastructure required to run the giant bureaucracy. The courses of rivers were changed, canals were dug, and Hibiya Inlet, which brought Tokyo Bay lapping at the base of the castle hill, was filled in.

When the major daimyo and their entourage were in town, the samurai portion of the city's population probably topped 500,000, maybe even outnumbering the commoners. The samurai allotted themselves more than 60 percent of the city's land. Another 20 percent went to hundreds of shrines and temples, which formed a spiritually-protective ring around the outer edges of the city.

By the early 1700s, an estimated 1 to 1.4 million people lived in Edo, making it by far the largest city in the world at the time. During the same period, Kyoto had a population of 400,000, and Osaka, 300,000. In 1801, when Britain's navy dominated the seas, Europe's largest city, London, had less than a million inhabitants. Japan's population hovered around 30 million for most of the Edo era; less than two million belonged to the samurai families.

In general, the samurai gravitated to the hilly parts of the city, or *yamanote,* while the townspeople congregated – or were forced to do so – in the downtown lowlands, or *shitamachi,* especially along the Sumida River. Over half of Edo's residents were crammed into the 15 percent of the city comprising Shitamachi, with a population density of about 70,000 people per square kilometer. Almost from the start, both Yamanote and Shitamachi began to encroach, through land-fill, onto Tokyo Bay.

Edo castle: The grounds of Ieyasu's huge castle, including the defensive moat system, were extensive. The complex was not actually completed until 1640, and was razed by fire seven years later.

Like everything else in Edo Tokyo, the castle underwent many resurrections following fires and earthquakes. Little of the Tokugawa castle remains today; in fact, there are no visual representations of the castle itself to tease our curiosity.

But the shogun's capital must have been a truly impressive city, backed by Mount Fuji and laced with canals. It is often forgotten nowadays that most of Edo's supplies came by sea, especially from Osaka. In fact, one of the reasons Ieyasu had chosen the area for his capital was its easy access to the sea. But the swampy shore of Tokyo Bay itself was unsuitable for building docks and wharves; instead, canals and rivers threading inland from the bay served as ports.

That is not to say that the five great highways from the provinces, and Kyoto, con-

Left, shoguns Hideyoshi and Ieyasu. Above, woodblock print of Nihom-bashi and Mt Fuji.

verging on the city were not also important. They were, especially the famous Tokaido, or East Sea Road, along which most of the feudal lords traveled to Tokyo for their periodic and mandated stays in Edo, and which also formed the central artery of the city itself between Shinagawa and Nihombashi.

Edo delights: The dichotomy between the refined – albeit somewhat constipated – culture of Yamanote and the robust, plebeian art and drama of Shitamachi (which Edward Seidensticker aptly dubbed respectively as the "high city" and "low city") has been a consistent feature of life in Edo.

The *Edokko* (Children of Edo) took delight in delight, and this sense of pleasure is grandly reflected in the popular culture of the time – the color and splash of *kabuki;* the *bunraku* puppet drama; *ukiyo-e* woodblock prints depicting the world of actors, sumo stars, courtesans and geisha; the pleasure quarters, licensed and unlicensed; the vigorous publishing world of both scholarship and trashy novels. All reflected the Edo pleasure in the material world and in a kind of high consumerism. The fact that men outnumbered women – two to one as late as 1721 – probably contributed to making the male population more than a bit rowdy and cantankerous. It would certainly explain the emphasis on catering to the sensual pleasures of men.

The shogunate unsuccessfully tried banning both kabuki and prostitution several times. Eventually, the shogunate simply moved them to less desirable locations, which in turn became desirable – and popular – locations. (Too, the government tried banning tobacco as early as 1610, but as a fire, not a health, hazard.)

Rise of merchants: The establishment of the shogunate caused many economic changes. After the seclusion orders eliminated international trade, the merchants and *zaibatsu* turned their attention to domestic distribution and marketing systems. The highways built by the Tokugawas, along with their standardization of weights, measures and

coinage, helped with the rise of the zaibatsu.

Just north of Nihom-bashi, the bridge from which all distances in Japan were then measured, stood the major dry-goods stores, including the Echigoya (now Mitsukoshi), established in 1673. Mitsukoshi, along with Mitsui, Sumitomo and the other major zaibatsu that were to have such a tremendous impact on the Japanese economy, got its start during the Edo period.

The samurai received their stipends in rice, but the economy was increasingly dependent upon money – not to the shogunate's liking, with its economic foundation based upon rice taxes. The result: the samurai borrowed from the merchants and increasingly went into debt.

By the 1800s, Japan was a wildly different country that of the 1600s. It was now a nation of relative prosperity, with well-developed domestic commerce, a budding manufacturing potential, flourishing cities and towns – yet it was still controlled with rigid social and governmental systems.

Internal pressures demanded change. Moreover, the world itself was not about to allow Japan to keep its doors closed. The industrial revolution was gaining momentum in Europe. The Western powers were casting about for countries into which to expand economic influence.

While others had tried rattling Japan's doors, it was the United States that yanked them open, in 1853, with Commodore Perry and America's East India Squadron – the famous Black Ships. He reappeared the following year to back up the demand, and was successful. Many in Edo were not especially giddy with delight in the shift of tides. When the first American consul, Townshend Harris, was allowed to enter Edo in 1857, he was greeted by a crowd of thousands – and absolute silence. Nevertheless, in 1858, a treaty of friendship and trade was signed with the United States, followed shortly by treaties with other Western powers.

Left, street life, Edo Tokyo. Above, Perry's American fleet at Uragawa, Kanagawa.

The turmoil and tumult of the 15 years from 1853 to 1868 have been well-documented in many books. The sense of Japan afloat in a sea of hostile powers, who possessed more technology and had voracious ambitions, may have acted to direct domestic energies away from internal wrangling.

The shogun was in a tight squeeze with the arrival of the Black Ships. His domestic response – seeking a consensus with the daimyo of how to respond to the Black Ships, and then encouraging them to individually strengthen defenses in their own domains – eventually diluted his control over them. His position of absolute authority dissipated.

At the same time, an anti-Tokugawa movement amongst lower-level daimyo was stewing down near Osaka and Kyoto. Rebel daimyo captured the emperor and declared the restoration of imperial rule. Shogunate forces sought to reverse the situation in Kyoto, but were defeated. The shogun yielded power to the imperial court in 1868 – the Meiji Restoration – and the emperor ascended once again to head of state. The reign of the Meiji emperor, lasting from 1868 until 1912, would cast a new Japan that the shoguns could never have imagined.

The Meiji Restoration of 1868, in which the ascension of the Meiji emperor as the nation's leader returned Japan to imperial rule, was a revolution of considerable proportions. Yet it was accomplished with surprisingly little bloodshed; the last shogun, Yoshinobu, in statesman-like fashion, retired and gave up the Edo castle rather than precipitate a full-scale civil war. Power was officially returned to the emperor in the fall of 1867. But shogunate residue remained in Edo; not all the samurai left town. (The samurai class would be abolished by imperial decree in 1872.)

It was at the Tokugawa family temple of Kan'ei-ji, most of which is now Ueno Park, that 2,000 die-hard Tokugawa loyalists, the Shogitai, chose to make a last stand in a bloody one-day battle. During this Battle of Ueno, the Shogitai burned most of the Kan'ei-ji complex to the ground. Hundreds of the Shogitai were killed, their bodies left rotting by the victors. (Days later, with the emperor's permission, monks released their souls with a funeral pyre.) Such was the end of Tokugawa Ieyasu's 250-year legacy. (Kan'ei-ji, a huge Buddhist temple complex with nearly 100 buildings, had been a mausoleum temple for all three generations of the Tokugawa family. Only Ieyasu and his grandson Iemitsu are entombed elsewhere, in Nikko, to the north.)

Meiji Period (1868–1912): In 1868, an imperial edict stripped Edo of its name and replaced it with Tokyo, or Eastern Capital. Moreover, Emperor Meiji moved his court from the imperial capital of Kyoto to Tokyo.

Before leaving Kyoto, the emperor issued an extremely important document. Among other things, it said, "Knowledge shall be sought throughout the world so as to strengthen the foundations of imperial rule." Moreover: "Evil customs of the past shall be broken and everything based upon the just laws of Nature." Japan was thus ready to enter the world, and ambitiously.

Because the office of emperor at the end of the Edo Period no longer was tied to a political system, the emperor's "restoration" could be used as a symbol and vehicle for choosing from a wide range of governmental structures. The quality of the nation's new leadership, and the political, economic, and cultural choices they made, can be seen as nothing less than spectacular.

The tremendous support the government gave to the corporate *zaibatsu* and other favored companies would appear to indicate it was really state capitalism, but such an assessment can be deceiving. There was, in fact, a dual economic structure: the huge industrial-and-trade zaibatsu conglomerates, and the small cottage industries. (To a certain extent, this dual structure of manufacturing continues to this day.)

Left, attempting to emulate high-brow European trends. Above, print of exposition in Ueno Park, Meiji Period.

In a few decades, Japan effectively restructured itself as a political entity. In retrospect, this seems astonishingly radical. Yet it did not happen overnight, but rather by a series of incremental modifications to the political system. The first new governmental structure was a compromise between old and new. It cleverly borrowed names from archaic imperial institutions to give an aura of tradition to what was hardly traditional. Meeting the Western powers as an equal was one of the guiding concerns of the Meiji years. This meant adopting anything and everything Western, from railroads to ballroom dancing. The pendulum first swung to extremes, from a total rejection of all native things (including a mindless urge to abandon the Japanese language) to an emotional nationalism after the excesses of initial enthusiasm for foreign imports.

Japan took to Western industrialization with enthusiasm. But the employment of numerous foreign advisors (upwards of 3,000) was ended as soon as the Japanese sensed that they could continue perfectly well on their own.

During both the Meiji and subsequent Taisho periods, an important factor in bringing Japan into the modern world was the prescience of Shibusawa Eiichi, entrepreneur and businessman. From a small farming village north of Tokyo (on his old estate is an international language school), Shibusawa became a retainer in a branch of the Tokugawa family. On a trip to Europe with the shogun's brother, Shibusawa was enchanted with Western industrial and economic systems. Returning to Japan shortly after the 1868 Meiji Restoration, Shibusawa joined the new government and was pivotal in the introduction of a modern banking system in Japan. Later, he founded over two dozen corporations, in shipping, manufacturing, textiles and insurance. His later years were consumed by social philanthropy and promotion of international relations, particularly with the United States.

An urgent need of the Meiji leaders was modification of the unequal treaties with the West, which had been negotiated by the shogunate. This issue alone was not resolved until the 1890s and saw the fall of several highly competent leaders.

After a number of unsuccessful drafts over the years, the new constitution of the country was promulgated in 1889. This Meiji Constitution was one of the major steps in Japan being recognized as an advanced nation. The next was Japan's success in the Sino-Japanese War of 1894–95, which proved the country's ability to wage modern warfare, at the same time emphasizing Japan's arrival as a major power in the Orient.

The clincher in making Japan a true world power was winning the Russo-Japanese War of 1904–06, the first time that an Asian nation had defeated a European power. It didn't stop there, however. In 1910, Japan annexed Korea, ostensibly by treaty but actually under military threat. Only Japan's surrender in World War II would restore Korea's independence.

Emperor Meiji died in 1912. By then, Japan had consolidated its economy, defined a political system, changed its social structure, and become one of the world's more advanced nations.

Taisho Period (1912–26): The short reign of Emperor Taisho saw the 20th century catch Japan in its grasp and carry it off on a strange

and sometimes unpleasant odyssey.

World War I proved an enormous economic boom, since Japan seized the chance to enter Asian markets vacated by the European powers. But the inevitable deflation hit hard and there were major rice riots in Tokyo, in 1918. The following year, politics became extremely polarized as the labor movement and leftists gained momentum. A new right, which believed in the politics of assassination rather than the ballot box, emerged from the political shadows.

A series of political murders, including of prime ministers and former prime ministers, followed over the next 15 years, helping to create the climate of violence that would let the military intervene in politics.

The big event of the 1920s was the Great Kanto Earthquake. It struck around noon on 1 September 1923, when a good percentage of the city's charcoal and gas stoves were lit. Fire, not the quake itself, caused the most damage. Ninety percent of Yokohama was also wiped out.

During the Taisho Period, Japan began to bubble intellectually. The growing prosperity (and the accompanying problems), the shrinking size of the world, and the relative youth of Japan as a world power contributed to the "Taisho Democracy." It was little more than a time of good, healthy intellectual ferment, when ideas of all kinds were welcome. It was an attitude important both as a precursor to Japan's plunge into the dark period of militarism and war, and as a foundation for the country's emergence from the violent darkness.

Showa Period (1926–89): With the death of the Taisho emperor in 1926, Hirohito succeeded to the throne to begin the Showa Period. Japan's isolation from World War I had kept the nation free of Europe's war-weary cynicism, and, too, of the horrors of such war. Within a decade, Japan itself would be sliding into world war.

Historians' analyses of why and how militarism developed in the 1930s has produced a rash of theories, some of which argue a conspiracy going back to Meiji days. Whatever the political, economic and social forces that produced the military government and the aggressive war effort, some observations can be made.

The distribution of wealth was still very uneven. The establishment factions included big business (the zaibatsu), the upper crust of government, and the military interests.

Political power within the country favored establishment interests; suffrage was not universal. Non-establishment interests were weak because they had little recourse for expression, other than through imported political concepts – that is, socialism and communism – which were distrusted and feared. The non-establishment interests never received adequate representation in government until after World War II.

Japan, sensitive to Western righteousness regarding Asia, felt insecure. This, and domestic economic and demographic pressures, made military hegemony seem a viable alternative, at least to the military. Indeed, the military and its supporters were increasingly frustrated by what they saw as ineffectual

Left, bestseller for Westernization from Meiji Period. Above, financial institutions in the 1930s.

and compromising civilian policies. They acted to make the government their own.

Militarism's rise and fall: The pivotal point was the Manchurian Incident of 1931, in which Japanese military forces occupied Manchuria and set up the state of Manchukuo. Protest over this action by the League of Nations resulted in Japan leaving the League and following a policy of isolation. Within the military itself, extremist factionalism grew, and during the 1930s, several plots of one kind or another sought to take over power. The most famous is the 26 February Incident of 1936, a bloody military uprising that might have been a coup d'etat had it not been based on vague, romantic ideas that did not include a practical plan of how to use power. This bolstered the civilian resistance to military involvement in politics. But in the summer of 1937, hot war erupted in China.

Seeking to discourage Western intervention in Japan's Asian expansion, the Japanese military launched pre-emptive attacks not only on Pearl Harbor in December of 1941, but against European colonial holdings throughout Asia.

In less than a year, Japan possessed most of East Asia and the western Pacific. Japanese occupation was savage and brutal. But by early 1945, Japan was on the defensive, its major cities (except Kyoto and Nara, because of their historical heritage) leveled by bombing raids.

Despite Germany's defeat in May of 1945, Japanese military leaders would not yield. The Allies and most Asians say it was necessary, the Japanese say not, but in mid-August of the same year, atomic bombs were dropped on Hiroshima and Nagasaki. A week later, the war was over.

On 15 August 1945, Emperor Hirohito spoke on the radio – the first time commoners had heard his voice – and declared an unconditional surrender. Japan lost its empire, its right to independent foreign policy, its emperor's claim to divinity, and its army. Over six million soldiers and civilians returned home to Japan. War-crime trials convicted several thousand Japanese; 920 of them were executed.

A new 1946 constitution issued under the mandate of Gen. MacArthur's occupation government guaranteed western-style liberties, established a British-style parliamentary system, dismantled the prewar industrial zaibatsu, and renounced war as national policy. With the signing of the 1952 San Francisco Peace Treaty, the American occupation ended. Japan was sovereign.

The sun rises again: Three significant characteristics help define postwar Japan: government-coordinated industrialization and spectacular economic growth; the mocking of parliamentary democracy by politicians; and modern Japan's collective inability to recall any Asian history involving Japan between 1910 and 1945.

The decades following the war were of well-coordinated corporate and bureaucratic efforts to revive both themselves and the country. Protected by the American military umbrella, Japan funneled full resources into its economy.

Meanwhile, the provincial millions who continued to flow into Tokyo – its population more than doubled after 1950 – often found homes along the rail lines leading out from the main terminals of Shibuya, Shinjuku and Ikebukuro. These rail lines were usually constructed by department store firms, which had major stores near the station and branches at most stations along their private lines. Real estate firms grabbed up land along the tracks and sold prefabricated "rabbit hutches" to the *sarariman* ("salaryman"), or male white-collar workers, who had not yet abandoned the dream of owning their own home. In the process, a nightmare of suburbia at its worst was created. Few can deny that urban Japan today is an aesthetic catastrophe.

With urban population's explosive rise, farming's importance dropped to a fraction of the nation's GNP. (Its political power, however, increased.) The new national wealth was evenly distributed, leaving almost no one in an economic lower class; unemployment remained low. Industrial labor disputes and strikes were minimal.

During postwar reconstruction, government regulation had served Japan's interests well. But as Japan joined the advanced economies, the one-way nature of Japan's markets strained relations with others, especially the US, its largest market, and Europe. Over-regulation and chummy business-government relationships saddled consumers with ridiculously high prices (¥70,000-plus for a phone line, domestically-sold televisions costing twice their export price) for nearly everything except umbrellas, unaccountably cheap in this rainy land.

High rates of household savings created excess capital, and the banks loaned it out. The economy accelerated with uncanny momentum, surpassing every other country except the United States. Japan became the new global paradigm for success and potency. The stock market was on a trajectory that, in the late 1980s, momentarily exceeded the New York Stock Exchange in volume and vigor. Real estate in Japan became the

Left, blessings for the warrior, 1945. Above, Japan's world re-entry, 1964 Tokyo Olympics.

planet's most valuable and banks dished money out secured by overvalued land. (These loans came back to haunt the banks in the mid 1990s, when several banks collapsed, while others had to be propped up by government support.)

Japan's rising sun seemed, for the moment, to outshine most of the world.

Heisei Period (1989–): Emperor Hirohito died in 1989, the longest reigning emperor (62 years) in Japanese recorded history. His son, Akihito, took the throne and adopted the period name of *Heisei,* which means "attainment of peace". He and his family have made sustained efforts to humanize the imperial family, and to tangentially deal with Japan's

brutal past. But as a politically-neutered figurehead, the emperor is not permitted to address history, nor his father's place in it. Every public utterance is controlled by either the Imperial Household Agency, the imperial family's reactionary nanny, or the bureaucrats of Kasumigaseki.

Japan's "bubble economy" superheated in the late 1980s, bursting in 1990. The stock market lost half its value in a matter of days, banks lost still-unspeakable amounts on loans secured by hyper-inflated land values, and a blossoming Japanese self-righteousness as economic superpower took a cold shower. The country went into a deep recession lasting throughout the 1990s, a financial stagnation recognized by everybody except the bureaucrats at the Ministry of Finance and Bank of Japan officials.

But in politics, life at the very top remained very good.

For nearly four decades, one political party has dominated Japan – the dubiously-named Liberal Democratic Party, or LDP. Conservative, unprogressive, and decidedly undemocratic by western standards, the LDP seemingly serves only to make its leaders wealthy; national leadership and governing are inconsequential and inconvenient sidelines.

Agriculture accounts for just 15 percent of Japan's GNP, but the LDP has subsidized and coddled the farmers, ignoring the welfare of the urban majority. Through arcane electoral laws, rural voters have twice the voting weight of city dwellers. Nobody complains, not entirely unexpected. (Indeed, in the times of sword-swinging samurai, a wayward opinion or complaint was lopped off along with the speaker's head. Best to remain obscure.)

Institutionalized and often immune to legal redress, *seiji fuhai,* or political corruption, festered unimpeded at the highest corporate and governmental levels. By the 1980s, *The Economist* opined, the LDP was "choking on its own corruption."

In 1992, the last of the LDP's omnipotent kingpins was caught not only in one of the scandals that sprouted regularly like the new rice crop, but prosecutors searching his house uncovered a stash of gold bullion worth millions. Like most politicians and corporate leaders seeking refuge from public scrutiny, he retreated to a hospital to rest and recover from unknown illnesses, a tradition in Japan.

The LDP fell from grace in 1993, replaced by a coalition government led by Hosokawa Morihiro. With a head of thick young hair, Hosokawa invigorated the nation with calls for substantial reform. Seven months later, he resigned because of scandal. Succeeding him was a coalition led by the socialist party and a well-meaning but impotent prime minister. In the meantime, the LDP has resuscitated itself by returning to control in 1996.

Doldrums of the 1990s: The collapse of the economic bubble was a shocking flame-out for the Japanese, who had thought themselves atop the fastest rocket around. Perhaps even worse than the economy's rapid flattening was the subsequent half decade or more of economic stagnation, if not recession. Nothing, it seemed, not even a series of economic jolts by the government, could get the economy accelerating. Banks started sinking beneath massive amounts of bad loans left over from the bubble economy. An increasingly strong yen – severely overvalued – quenched corporate profits as exports plummeted. And at home, where manufacturers had for decades overpriced consumer goods so as to subsidize low export prices (and thus gain market share), discounters started bypassing Japan's inefficient distribution system and buying foreign goods direct from American and European manufacturers. By 1996, Japan was the only country on earth, in every 60 to 70 years. The last was in 1923.

For decades, and most recently after the California earthquakes of the early 1990s, the Japanese people were constantly reassured by government, corporate and academic experts that Japan's design and construction techniques were unsurpassed in the world, and that collapses of expressways and high-rises in an earthquake could simply not happen in Japan. In fact, *would* not happen.

In January of 1995, an earthquake hit Kobe, an important coastal port near Osaka. The Great Hanshin Earthquake, as it has been named, killed nearly 6,000 people and left 300,000 homeless. Fires from igniting gas mains (said to be earthquake-proof) incinerated entire neighborhoods of poorly-constructed residences; elevated expressways and *shinkansen* rails toppled over like putty. Subway tunnels collapsed. Moreover, the government's response, both on the local and national level, was nothing short of inept and irresponsible. In the days that followed, the Japanese people were shocked by their government's inability to respond to a long-anticipated – and prepared for – disaster.

One wonders what might happen in Tokyo should a similar 7.2-Richter scale earthquake hit it. It's an ominous thought: the Kobe quake was considerably more powerful than the devastating 1923 Great Kanto Earth-

the history of the world, to undergo a substantive – and permanent – deflation of consumer prices. Corporate profits took a tumble into the toilet.

Shaky foundations: Two events within two months further evaporated Japanese self-confidence.

One in ten of the world's earthquakes occurs in Japan. Tokyo and the Kanto Plain, and the urban areas directly south, sit atop geologically unstable ground. Devastating earthquakes have hit Tokyo on an average of

Left, Akihito and Michiko, emperor and empress, in 1959. Above, the 1995 Kobe earthquake.

quake that destroyed Tokyo. By some geophysical measurements, the Kobe quake was twice as strong. And what of the building codes – and preparedness training – upon which modern Tokyo is constructed?

City government studies in the early 1990s estimated around 10,000 deaths and over half a million buildings destroyed in Tokyo if the 1923 earthquake were repeated. (The studies were annotated with a footnote: casualty estimates did not take into account subways. Three million people move in and out of Tokyo daily, mostly by train and subway, and should tunnels collapse, deaths in subways could reach tens of thousands alone.) The government has now amended estimates; should a Kobe-strength earthquake hit Tokyo, casualties could approach 100,000.

Safe and secure no more: Two months after the Kobe earthquake, another event further undermined Japanese confidence.

In the heart of Tokyo, in the center of the government district, 12 people died and thousands were injured when the Tokyo subway system was flooded with sarin, a nerve gas. It was rush-hour, and the prime target was Kasumigaseki Station, *the* subway stop for the national government offices. Elsewhere in central Tokyo, 16 other stations on the Chiyoda, Marunouchi and Hibiya lines were hit with sarin, simultaneously.

The effect on the Japanese psyche cannot be described. The Japanese have long prided themselves on having perhaps the safest nation in the world, believing that Japanese could simply not inflict horrors on other Japanese. The deaths and injuries from the nerve gas had been seemingly-spontaneous and random – the perfect terrorist attack. In the days that followed, the chief of the National Police Agency was shot in front of his Tokyo home. Mysterious fumes sickened people at Yokohama Station and in nearby department stores. Shinjuku Station was literally seconds away from the release of enough hydrocyanic gas to kill 10,000 people. A passer-by found the gas package in a restroom. It was rush-hour at the station.

The sarin gas attack – and other deadly deeds uncovered by investigators – were traced to a religious cult, Aum Shinrikyo. On the day that its guru leader was arrested at the cult's main compound near Mount Fuji, a parcel addressed to the governor of Tokyo exploded in the room next to his office; an aide's hand was blown apart.

Imperial imperative: In the 1990s, one bright ray of hope in an otherwise dismal decade was the imperial family. Of prime interest were the marriage possibilities (or, as it often seemed, lack thereof) for Crown Prince Naruhito, heir to the throne and still single at 30 years of age.

To the relief of every Japanese, he finally married the quite eligible Owada Masako, who had been heading for a brilliant career in the diplomatic corps. Many younger Japanese women saw in her the New Japanese Woman – stylish, worldly, educated in America and England, and on a career track of her own choosing. She, if anybody, it was believed, could liberate the Japanese woman for the 21st century.

It seems, however, that the Imperial Household Agency, made up of reactionary and conservative old men who strictly control the activities of the imperial family, have quenched Masako's individuality and spunk. Masako's mother-in-law, Empress Michiko, reportedly was poorly treated by the agency in the early years of her marriage to Emperor Akihito. A commoner like Masako, it is said that she has suffered severe mental distress.

Above, where's Mifune Toshiro when you need him? Right, affluence for these trying times.

Nihon-retto, the islands of the Japanese archipelago, were formed from the tears of a goddess. Where each tear fell into the Pacific, there arose an island to take its place.

So goes the legend. But no less poetic – and dramatic – is the scientific view of the origins of this huge archipelago, stretching from the subtropical waters of Okinawa – not far from Taiwan – to the frozen wastes of northern Hokkaido. The islands were born of massive crustal forces acting deep underground, and shaped by volcanos spitting out mountains of lava.

The results seen today are impressive. Japan has long been regarded as one of the more scenic places on the planet, with snow-capped mountain ranges and 27,000 kilometers (16,800 mi) of indented coastline.

The archipelago consists of four main islands – Kyushu, Shikoku, Honshu and Hokkaido – and about 3,900 smaller islands, which stretch from southwest to northeast over a distance of 3,800 kilometers (2,365 mi) off the east coast of Asia.

Honshu is by far the largest and most populous of all the islands. The main islands are noted for their rugged terrain, with 70 to 80 percent of the country being extremely mountainous. Most of the mountains were uplifted over millions of years as the oceanic crust of the Pacific collided with the continental plate of Asia. The oceanic crust submerged beneath the thicker continental crust, buckling the edge of it and forcing up the mountain chains that form the backbone of the Japanese archipelago, and too that of the Philippines to the south.

Other singular peaks in Japan – including Fuji, the highest – are volcanic in origin. They were formed from molten lava that originated far below the earth's surface, as the oceanic crust sank into the superheated depths of the upper mantle. The molten rock was forced up through fissures and faults, exploding onto the surface. Ice, wind, rain and glacial action did the rest.

Preceding pages: Sakura-jima seen from Osumi Hanto. Left, Iwo-yama, on Hokkaido's Shiretoko Hanto. Above, ocean caves, Miyako-jima, Okinawa.

Volcanoes and earthquakes: One of the attractions of a visit to Japan is the possibility of seeing these forces in action. About 60 of Japan's 186 volcanos are still active in geological terms, and occasionally they make their presence felt. Mihara on Oshima, one of the isles of Izu near Tokyo, exploded as recently as 1986, forcing thousands of residents to evacuate the island. A few years later, Unzen-dake on Kyushu violently erupted and devastated hundreds of kilometers of agricultural land. Sakura-jima, also

on Kyushu and just a few kilometers from the city of Kagoshima, regularly spews ash – and an occasional boulder – onto the city.

Earthquakes are a far more frequent than volcanic eruptions, especially around the more seismologically-active areas near Tokyo. They are also a more serious threat, and the Japanese government currently spends billions of yen annually on earthquake detection – not that it works particularly well. Complacency is a common problem anywhere, and certainly was in Kobe, which was declared outside of any significant earthquake zone. Nevertheless, in 1995 a massive quake hit the city, killing 6,000 people.

Most Japanese, however, tend not to dwell on the more morbid aspects of geological activity, preferring to enjoy its pleasures instead. *Onsen*, or hot springs, are a tangible and sensual result of the massive quantities of heat released underground, and for centuries have occupied a special place in Japanese culture.

Mountains: Despite the dominance of mountains in these islands, the Japanese are not a mountain people, preferring instead to squeeze onto the coastal plains, or into the valleys of the interior. Thus separated from each other by mountains, which once took days to traverse, the populated areas tended to develop independently, with distinct dialects and other social peculiarities; at the same time, isolation, along with the challenge of making maximum use of available land, meant that agriculture, land management and even communications evolved early in the country's history.

The highest non-volcanic peaks are in the so-called Japan Alps, of central Honshu. Many of the landforms in these mountain ranges were sculpted by glaciers during an ice age more than 27,000 years ago. Cirques, or depressions left where the glaciers formed, are still a common sight on some higher slopes. Debris brought down by melting ice can also be seen in lower regions.

Urban zones: By far the largest of these flat lands is the Kanto Plain, an area centered on Tokyo Bay and formed by a build up of sediments resulting from Ice Age-induced changes in sea level. Other extensive areas of flat land occur in the Tohoku region of northern Honshu, in Hokkaido, and along the Nagoya–Osaka industrial belt.

Such is the concentration of resources in these plains that most of Japan's people, factories, farmland, housing and public facilities are all crowded onto approximately 20 percent of Japan's total land area.

Thus, very little of what one might call countryside exists on the plains. Cities, towns and villages tend to merge into an indistinct urban blur that stretches endlessly across the flat land, with fields and farms dotted in between. In general, the plains are monochromatic and less than aesthetic.

The main industrial regions are the Kanto and Kansai areas, centering on Tokyo and Osaka respectively. The Kanto area alone produces nearly a third of Japan's entire gross domestic product. If it were an independent nation, it would produce more goods and services than the whole of Great Britain.

Once again, it is the Kanto region, and Tokyo in particular, that has benefitted from Japan's prosperity. Metropolitan Tokyo now has a nominal population of over 10 million, but in fact the city spreads beyond its political boundaries north, south and west, forming a massive urban complex that stretches across the entire Kanto Plain. The actual population of this megalopolis is estimated at around 30 million people.

Metropolitan Tokyo and Yokohama are the first and second cities of Japan, respectively. Third in size is Osaka, with a population of 3.2 million, followed by Nagoya with a little over 2 million.

These cities have experienced phenomenal growth since World War II, as Japan's urban industrialization and rural mechanization drew people off the farms and into the cities. Many rural communities are now suffering from an increasingly-aged population, and some have become virtual ghost towns as young people have literally fled the rural life-style. (A shortage of women in the countryside results in male farmers going on organized urban field trips in search of mates.) Farming on the garden-size Japanese farms is amazingly inefficient and backward, made profitable only by heavy and politically-motivated subsidies from the government.

This demographic problem is not one that will in future be restricted to the countryside. Japan as a whole has one of the slowest population growth rates in the world, at less than one percent annually, and many analysts believe that the problem of an aging population will, more than anything else, eventually lead to Japan's demise as a world economic leader.

The reasons for this low growth rate are not hard to find. The average Japanese enjoys the longest life expectancy in the world. But the overcrowded condition of the cities, which forces couples to live in cramped two- or three-room apartments, is not conducive to large families, nor are the phenomenal costs of education and urban life.

The concentration of employment opportunities in the cities is mirrored by a lack of job prospects in the countryside. Unlike most other modern, industrial nations, Japan has few natural resources and has depended heavily upon its manufacturing industry as a source of wealth and employment.

<u>Left</u>, **Showa Shinzan, born 1943, from Usu-dake.** <u>Above</u>, **farmhouse in Honshu mountains.**

Natural resources: There are coal mines in Hokkaido and Kyushu, but coal production peaked in 1941, and many coal-mining communities are now in serious decline. Nearly all of Japan's other raw materials, such as oil, minerals and metal ores, are imported.

Timber is one resource Japan has in abundance, as most of the country's mountains are covered in natural or plantation forest.

The natural cover varies from sub-arctic conifers in Hokkaido to deciduous and evergreen temperate broad-leafed trees throughout the other three main islands. Yet despite a soaring demand for timber, used in the construction industry and for paper and disposable chopsticks, domestic production has actually fallen. The Japanese prefer to buy cheap, imported timber from the tropical rain forests of Southeast Asia, a practice which is causing considerable concern among many environmentalists as the rain forests of Borneo, Burma and Thailand are reduced to barren slopes.

Fishing is another rural occupation that has declined in activity, mainly because of a decline in fish stocks as a result of overexploitation. Japanese fleets now operate in international waters far away from home, and ports that once supported fishing fleets are turning towards other endeavors.

One of the most lucrative of these is tourism. As the urban Japanese become more affluent and seek recreation outside the cities, ports and harbors are becoming leisure marinas, hotels and resorts are springing up all over the countryside, and mountains are being leveled in order to make way for golf courses. This has damaged the natural environment and an increase in pollution. Here, it is worth noting a paradox. It has always been one of the proud boasts of the Japanese that they live close to and in harmony with nature, always a strong theme in Japanese poetry, and, too, in the Japanese preoccupation with the weather.

Fauna and flora: To the Japanese, people are a part of nature, and therefore anything people have constructed is considered part of the environment. A Japanese can look upon a garden – moulded, cut, sculptured and trimmed to perfect proportions – and still see it as a perfect expression of nature.

The result of this philosophy has been disastrous for the wildlife and ecosystems of Japan. The crested ibis, for example, once considered to be a representative bird of Japan and common throughout the archipelago 100 years ago, is reduced today to less than a dozen individuals.

The Japanese crane (*tancho*) is also close to extinction, though the bird was once common in Hokkaido. Fish such as salmon and trout are no longer able to survive in Japan's polluted rivers and lakes. Brown bears have been hunted almost to extinction, and only recently have hunting laws been amended and the animal recognized as an endangered species. A few hundred wild bear remain on Hokkaido; the rest are in confinement in amusement parks, with dozens of bears often confined to small, single concrete pits.

Of the other land mammals, the Japanese monkey, or *macaca*, is by far the most common in Japan. Originally a creature of the tropical rain forests, the macaca has adapted to the more temperate climates of these islands and can now be found throughout Kyushu, Shikoku and Honshu, although its numbers have been sharply reduced since the 1950s. During the winter months, macaca in Nagano and Hokkaido take to bathing in local hot springs in order to keep warm.

In the far south of Japan, the islands of Okinawa have a distinctive fauna and flora of their own. Here, the natural forests are subtropical, but many of the indigenous species of fauna have now become rare or even extinct. The most spectacular characteristic of these islands is the marine life. Most of the islands are surrounded by coral, home to a rich and colorful variety of warm-water fish. Yet here again, the rapid growth of the tourist and leisure industry – especially that of scuba diving – has led to the destruction of much of this natural coral.

In Hokkaido, the greater availability of space and natural moorland vegetation have led to the growth of the cattle and dairy industries. Meat is gradually becoming a more important part of the Japanese diet, just as rice is declining in popularity. In a sense, this is symptomatic of the way Japanese culture is changing over the years. The new generations are gradually turning away from the traditional fish-and-rice diet to eat more meat and bread, as Japan becomes more affluent, more urbanized, and, one suspects, increasingly more "advanced" in outlook.

Left, autumn harvest, northeast Hokkaido. Above, storm along Sea of Japan, Honshu.

Climate: As any visitor will soon discover, an obsessive past-time with Japanese is talking – or listening – about the weather. People, as a matter of routine, nearly always greet each other by commenting on the weather, and the changing seasons still attract an unwarranted amount of attention by the television and print media in what is, after all, a largely urban society.

The two extremities of Japan, from the coral reefs of Okinawa to the ice floes of northern Hokkaido, are in very dissimilar climatic zones. Because of the high mountain ranges running along the spine of Honshu, there are also major climatic differences between the Sea of Japan coast and the Pacific Ocean coast of Honshu.

A northern hemisphere country, in Japan the seasons are, of course, similar to those of Europe and North America. The coldest months are December through February, when the Sea of Japan side of Hokkaido and

Honshu experience heavy falls of snow, the cold air from Siberia picking up moisture over the Sea of Japan. The Pacific Ocean side, by contrast, is very dry during the winter months. This is accentuated in Tokyo by urban growth, which has tended to reduce evaporation and therefore is the cause of a further drop in winter precipitation. Winter water shortages are now becoming a serious annual problem in the capital.

The southern areas of Kyushu and Okinawa have a relatively mild winter, and are the first to experience the coming of spring. This manifests itself with the flowering of the cherry blossom, an event which the Japanese like to celebrate with a festival called *hanami*.

Like the weather, the blossoming of *sakura* (and the autumn changing of leaves) are followed in the national media like the advance of an attacking army. The cherry trees flower in Kyushu towards the end of March, and the phenomenon moves slowly northwards, finally reaching Hokkaido about the second week in May.

Alas, the burst of spring that follows is all too short. Soon after the cherry blossoms have fallen, about a week after they opened, they are blown around by strong, southerly winds, which bring with them occasional rain and precede the start of *tsuyu*, the rainy season. Temperatures rise quickly, and continuous but moderate rains begin to fall about two months after the end of the cherry-blossom season. (The Japanese are very definitive about their seasons. One weather forecaster once announced on television: "The rain you are now experiencing is not the rainy season rain – the rainy season will start as soon as this rain finishes.")

Once again, the central mountains of Japan define the boundaries of the rain fronts. On the Pacific Ocean coast of Honshu, the tsuyu rain is soft and drizzly. Further south and on the Japan Sea coast, it is hard and much more tropical in nature, and in the southern areas, especially, the rain is often accompanied by typhoons. Hokkaido, however, has a very indistinct rainy season.

The rains ease around late June on the Pacific Ocean side and make way for the hot, humid summer. Temperatures reach a peak in August, when many city dwellers escape to the cool comfort of the mountains. The city of Yamagata, for example, which is buried under one meter of snow in the winter, once recorded Japan's highest-ever summertime temperature: 41°C (105°F).

The warm body of water around Japan causes the heat of summer to linger into September, with occasional balmy days in October. But as the warm air mass moves south, the rains return, this time on the backs of devastating typhoons.

Typhoons: Generally three or four typhoons hit Japan during the season, smaller ones in August building up to larger ones in September. The southern, Pacific side of Japan bears the brunt of these ferocious winds, which are quite capable of knocking down houses and wrecking ships. Fortunately for Japan, however, most typhoons have expended their energy in the Philippines or Taiwan before reaching the archipelago. While more frequent than Atlantic hurricanes or the Indian Ocean's cyclones, the Asian typhoons are also considerably smaller in size and strength.

When the typhoon season ends, the Japanese islands once again relax to a relatively placid autumn. October and early November are the best times to visit Japan, not only because of the mild weather, but also because the autumn foliage turn the mountains into a spectacular blaze of color.

Above, autumn show. Right, first snow, Rishiri Island.

Of whatever size or purpose, the group defines for the Japanese their individual purpose and function. And the group known as the Japanese – *nihonjin*, or if especially nationalistic, *nipponjin* – is the mother of all groups. (Not exactly an irreverent comment, given that Amaterasu Omikami, or Great Heaven-Shining Mother, is the foremother of the Japanese themselves.) Television commentators and musing politicians repeatedly refer to *ware-ware Nipponjin,* or "we Japanese", and the implicit definition of what "we Japanese" are or aren't, do or don't do, believe or not believe. The compulsion to define identity even shows up in advertising.

"Don't understand us too quickly," the Japanese will warn visitors, by definition outside of any group of which the Japanese feel themselves a part. Indeed, they often seem to prefer that foreigners not understand too much about them at all. There is a certain pride amongst Japanese in their collective feeling that outsiders simply don't understand – so they'll proclaim – simply because they are not Japanese.

Origins: The Japanese sense of uniqueness extends down to a basic racial identity, of a race and culture distinct from others – if not superior. But the objective evidence strongly points to origins from the mainland.

From the third century BC, waves of human migration from the Asian continent entered the Japanese archipelago, accompanied by rice cultivation (including the use of tools), metallurgy, and different social structures. These migrations are now considered to have brought the ancestors of today's Japanese people, the Yamato, who displaced and pushed the resident – and different – Jomon population into the northern regions, or into other less desirable areas.

Theories regarding the racial origins of the Japanese cite both the north and the south – Manchuria and Siberia, and the South China or Indochina regions – as likely possibilities. Students of the subject differ as to which origin to favor. The southern physical type is, of course, the Malay; the northern type is the Mongolian. Today, both north and south Asia are considered equally valid as likely origins of the Japanese. Still, the precise configuration of the migrations and the cultural traits associated with areas of origin are subject to argument. (Toss in, too, other theories about migrations from Polynesia or Micronesia.)

There was considerable human immigration later – in addition to cultural and artistic influences – from Korea, a point vehemently denied by Japanese nationalists and racial purists, despite the overwhelming archaeological and anthropological evidence. Whereas archaeology in many countries is considered the most neutral of disciplines, without political overtones of any kind, in Japan it is rife with factions and hot-tempered rivalries. One group of "experts" in Japan has steadfastly refuted and rejected most modern dating methods, particularly when used to authenticate theories proposing a Japan–Korea connection.

(Some observers have dared to suggest that Japan's brutal occupation of Korea from 1910 through 1945 was an attempt to erase

Preceding pages: carrying the omikoshi; painting seascapes north of Tokyo. Left, Tokyo fishing expedition. Above, Kyoto temple smiles.

that historical Korean link – the Japanese forced Koreans to take Japanese names, speak only Japanese, and tens of thousands of Koreans were brought to Japan as slaves to work in mines and factories. Even today, third-generation descendants of those imported Koreans are denied the rights of Japanese citizenship, even though they, and their parents, were born and raised in Japan.)

In any case, it may also be possible that the Korean and Japanese languages were mutually understandable, if not identical, some 2,000 years ago, and that a close affinity between the people on the Korean peninsula and the Japanese archipelago may have approached a common culture.

The question of the Ainu people in Hokkaido – with a population of less than 20,000 – is another explosive debate. Although Ainu cultural traits are undoubtedly circumpolar, some scholars maintain that, since the Ainu are Caucasian, they came from the south and picked up the Siberian-type traits after their arrival. This theory, however, runs counter to the conventional theory that the Ainu are directly related to Siberian groups.

Unique or arrogant?: Perhaps the most substantial insulator of Japanese from the outside is the language, spoken only in the islands. In fact, the grammar and syntax are considerably easier than most germanic or romance languages. The Japanese will retort, however, that it is one of the world's most difficult. The language isn't, but the context of usage can be confusing for those not brought up within the Japanese culture. To fully understand the Japanese and their ways, knowing the language is essential. An "expert" on Japan who doesn't speak the language fluently is a fraud.

There is much in the Japanese language that buttresses a fundamental notion: There is an undercurrent in Japanese thinking – and in Japanese traditions – that all things Japanese, including the race, are "special", if not unique, among the world's things. And most Japanese certainly believe that outsiders will never be able to fully appreciate, much less understand, the distinctions and nuances of *being* Japanese, and of Japanese ways. Stay in Japan long enough, listen to the conversation and media, and it seems that only Japan has earthquakes, typhoons, tasty rice, misery, hot weather, bad memories of war, trees that change color in autumn, snowfall and fast trains.

When French ski manufacturers first tried to export skis to Japan several decades ago, the Japanese government declared the skis unsuitable for the special and unique Japanese snow. Later, in the late 1980s, when

American beef producers were trying to open the Japanese market, a high-ranking official in the agriculture ministry argued that only Japanese beef was suitable for the special and unique digestive systems of Japanese people. In the 1990s, respected university researchers claimed that the Japanese were genetically special and unique in their ability to appreciate to the fullest the sounds of nature: crickets and cicadas, and waterfalls.

Every language has its ways of dealing with different situations. The way people speak at a funeral wake is different from old school friends at a class reunion. Depending on the language, these distinctions may be a speaker's choice of words and phrases.

without the use of expletives can nonetheless inject sarcasm or a devastating insult. Fortunately, foreigners are not expected to learn these niceties at the beginning, and the younger generation appears keen in dropping some of the complicated constructions.

Equally perplexing to outsiders are the distinctions between the talk of males and females. Consider the first-person pronoun. Men have the option of several forms, the use of each dependent upon the situation and the people involved: *watakushi, watashi, boku,* or *ore*, from most polite to exceedingly casual. Women, of course, have fewer options.

Modulation and tone of voice also tend to vary between the sexes. Men try to affect a

Linguistic tools: The Japanese *keigo*, or polite language, is a hold-over from the structured class system of feudal times, when politeness was reinforced with a sword. In the present century, keigo has been preserved as a key element in the deeply-rooted Japanese tradition of deference to one's superiors, and of courtesy to guests.

Proper speech is a source of pride for most Japanese, and the use of keigo can be an art in itself. Moreover, simply shifting the politeness level up a notch – or down one – and

Left, Shinto ceremony, Tohoku. Above, last harvest, Hokkaido.

deep rumble, which can approach theatrical proportions at times. Women, on the other hand, tend to inflect a high and nasalized pitch, said to be appealing and sexy to men. (Bilingual women will often drop their voice when speaking the second language, then shift into high gear when switching back to speaking Japanese.)

In informal speech, women tend to drop the copula and substitute the particle *wa* to end a sentence, such as *Shiranai wa* (I don't know). To get the same effect, a man might grunt *Shiran na.* Both expressions use the negative form of the verb *shiru* (to know), but it comes out slightly different.

Living on egg shells: In a country where physical crowding and complex interpersonal relationships have, over the centuries, shaped the language and social manners, even the slightest chance of offending, or disappointing, or inconveniencing someone else is couched in a shower of soft words, bows, and grave smiles. (Or worse, giggles, a sure signal of acute embarrassment.) To call such behavior insincere is, to the Japanese, simply ignorant, and hurtful. It doesn't have to be approved of by foreigners – *gaijin,* or if especially polite, *gaikokujin.* However, if one is to be effective in Japan, the special – and unique? – Japanese way must be learned and applied with grace and skill.

Notable, both for the linguistic hedging and for the insight into Japanese thinking, is the difference in how Japan and the rest of Asia, if not the world, remember history. If the past is not flattering, it is best forgotten, think the Japanese. But Japan's neighbors – especially Korea, Philippines and China – think differently. Collectively, the Japanese seem unable to recall five decades of brute Japanese aggression capped by a Pacific war killing 20 million people. But with the Imperial army's own documents magically appearing from hiding, and as aging veterans publicly purge their nightmares, forgetting is increasingly difficult to do. What rankles its Asian neighbors most, however, is the regularity with which Japan's conservative politicians denounce factual history. In 1994, Japan's minister of justice publicly declared that the 1937 Rape of Nanking – when between 100,000 and 300,000 Chinese were slaughtered by an out-of-control Japanese army – was merely an unsubstantiated fabrication. A myth.

Consider the observations of one Russian journalist: "From generation to generation, the Japanese have become accustomed to beating about the bush in order to avoid open conflicts of opinion and direct assertions that might hurt someone's feelings."

"The ability to express thoughts clearly, accurately and in a straight-line fashion," continues the Russian with marvelous understatement, "corresponds very little with the Japanese understanding of courtesy." Indeed, the Japanese language is excruciatingly indirect, requiring a finesse in extracting the proper message. Sometimes, the Japanese are able to use this to their advantage.

Recent prime ministers, especially since the 1993 election humiliation of the conservation Liberal Democratic Party, have made efforts to address the past, despite the vociferous views of right-wing politicians, nationalists and university scholars to the contrary. Yet the linguistic nuances, when properly translated and understood, reveal not the expected apology, but rather a promise of "reflection" or "remorse concerning unfortunate events," hardly an admission of wrong. And to this day, history books are censored by the ministry of education, and the media focus almost solely on Japanese suffering in the war; the impression is of only Japan as a victim of World War II.

Obligations: If apologies are linguistic puzzles, other expressions of social necessity too are interesting, if not curious.

Strangely, the very word for "thank you" – *arigato* – literally means, "You put me in a difficult position." *Oki no doku,* which is an expression of sympathy, means "poisonous feeling." And who but the Japanese would think of expressing regret or apology with *sumimasen,* which, in strictly literal translation, means, "This (situation/inconvenience) will never end"?

Then there is that virtually untranslatable word, *giri.* To violate it is simply unthinkable. Giri is often translated as a sense of duty and honor, but such a definition ignores the subtle communal and personal responsibilities behind giri. In Japan, there are unspoken responsibilities inherent in acceptance within a group, whether in a friendship or with coworkers in an office, or in the sharing of communal village life. When the responsibility beckons – and the member of any group will recognize it without articulating it – the individual must meet that responsibility, putting aside one's work or desires.

Giri is the theme of many tragedies in Japanese literature and drama. A plot might turn on a daughter's obligation to put aside *ninjo,* or human feeling, and marry someone of her parents' choosing. If unable to reconcile her own desires with the obligations of giri to her parents, suicide is an accepted recourse. Of course, such recourse is rare today, but it happens. Newspapers often report student suicides. A student's failures in school might be perceived by the student as a failure to meet giri to the family. (Another cause of student suicide, a significant problem in modern Japan, especially among boys, is peer bullying in school.)

Westerners may have an appreciation of what they think giri entails, but rarely do they understand the intrinsic depth of giri in the lives of Japanese. Not only is giri an obligation to another, but one has obligation to accept responsibility, if not shame, for an action committed by a distant relative, a coworker, even a close neighbor – all member's of one's various groups.

Left, untangling a line, Fukuoka. Above, kendo master, Naha.

Family: No doubt there's a proverb somewhere saying that obligation, like charity, begins at home. It's true, for example, that in Japan the eldest child (once only the male, but now the female as well) is expected to care for aged parents. Likewise, it is still true that the estate, if any, of a deceased parent automatically passes to that eldest child. In fact, these mutual obligations were once inviolable. Today, however, disputes over care for the aged and for inheritance of wealth are relatively common – and often decided in favor not of the parents or children, but of the national government because of prohibitively-high inheritance taxes.

Extended families – often cited as the core of Japan's traditional social stability – are nowadays as far flung from the original homestead as education, job opportunities and jet planes can take them. And although nostalgia for the *furusato* (hometown) and simpler living has taken on a trendy air in recent years, the urban nuclear family is increasingly defining the contours of Japanese life.

On the surface, the family appears both paternal – the man is still the household head – and maternal, as women still control the household budget and child rearing. Wider opportunities for women in business, however, along with increased affluence and broader appetites for the good life, are slowly challenging this status quo. But the inertia to any social change is considerable.

In the Japan of pre-World War II, a young man often got married about the time his parents reminded him that he had reached the *tekireiki*, or appropriate marriageable age. His parents would take an active role in the selection of his bride, making sure she bore the markings of a good wife, wise mother, and self-sacrificing daughter-in-law. They interviewed the woman's parents. Even birth records were checked (and often still are), assuring that the woman's family tree had no bad apples or embarrassing branches.

Love rarely entered the picture. Parents

knew that the couple would eventually become fond of each other; they might even become good friends.

The wife, having severed the ties to her own family through marriage, adhered to the customs and practices of her husband's family. After all, throughout her upbringing and education, she had been taught that a woman found her greatest fulfillment in marriage. The mother-in-law – and often the sisters-in-law – frequently added to the wife's burdens by complaining about her shortcomings as a housewife and mother. When the mother-in-law grew feeble, the wife would become her caretaker and provider.

Despite the hardships, the wife generally chose to stay married. To divorce meant she had to face the censure – blame for the marital break-up was all hers – of her own family, and that of the community. Outside of the cities, nothing has changed.

In many marriages today, the husband still maintains a higher status and exercises greater authority in the family by virtue of being the sole provider. He shows little inclination in helping around the house or taking care of the children, except when it suits him.

Yet some of the younger urban husbands, like their wives, have been exposed to Western lifestyles and trends, and so do make some effort at being liberated males.

The traditional wife follows a pattern that her grandmother followed in the prewar years. Getting up earlier than her husband and children, she prepares the breakfasts and makes sure everyone gets off to work or school on time. During the day, she does the housework, goes shopping, and manages the daily household accounts. Occasionally, she takes part in activities of the neighborhood association or of her children's school. She may also enjoy leisure activities such as learning a foreign language.

Left, rural mother and child, Honshu. Above, tradition versus pragmatism.

At night, she and the children will eat together, since her husband comes home much later in the evening. Upon his return, she will serve him his dinner and sit with him while he eats. The wife knows better than to discuss family matters at those times. She waits until the weekends or when he appears less drained.

Like her grandmother, she feels obligated to show appreciation to the family through acquiescence and service. Unlike her grandmother, she is more willing to regain control over her own life by getting a divorce.

Although comparatively low, rising divorce rates reflect the growing desire of spouses, particularly wives, to exert personal aspirations and concerns over those of the family.

Some wives file for divorce when husbands retire from their jobs, demanding half of the husband's severance pay. Increasingly, some couples divorce before they even get started on a proper married life. It's called a Narita Divorce. Modern Japanese women have often spent more time traveling overseas than their new husbands; their first joint jaunt overseas, usually the honeymoon, is ripe with tension and ends in disaster because the woman is more self-reliant than the man. After returning home to Narita, Tokyo's international airport, they divorce.

In the office: Postwar political and social reforms, a powerful economy, and demographic factors have given a woman choices that go beyond the imagination of her grandmother. Foremost, she wants a man not bound to his parents. She avoids forming relationships to elder sons, knowing that she might end up having to live with, and eventually to take care of, his mother – and having to put up with pushy and demanding sisters-in-law.

It used to be that a Tokyo woman with career plans was limited to the government bureaucracy, joining a foreign firm, or establishing her own business. For years, companies put new employees on one of two tracks, regardless of education and qualifications.

The managerial track led to decision-making responsibility and was largely reserved for men. The clerical track, which led nowhere at all beyond learning telephone manner (soft, high voices preferred) and salutations (a 30-degree forward bow for most people, a 45-degree bow for special guests and executives), was the one reserved for women. Unfortunately, many companies still force young women to quit their *OL* – "office lady" – jobs once they become married, the assumption being that they will shortly discover themselves to be pregnant and thus not of much use, or attractiveness. In spite of the equal employment opportunity law passed in 1986, many companies still discourage women from joining the managerial career track; the law carries no penalties. Yet, like a glacier, there is some movement regarding the woman's position in Tokyo.

Slowly, and from causes more economical than ideological, women have been restructuring their own opportunities; with increased travel and exposure to foreign media, they've seen the alternatives to a submissive role. The number of women subscribing to the standard pattern of a brief period of initial employment, followed by several decades of full-time devotion to a home and children, followed by a return to the job market as a part-time or temporary worker, is declining. Increasingly, women are demanding to be allowed to work after marriage and after giving birth to children – a remarkable transformation of attitudes.

Some 95 percent of Tokyo's women have been through high school, and over a third hold college degrees. But until the late 1980s, the vast majority of these highly qualified graduates may not have wanted careers, considering the working lives of men.

Education: In the sixth century, Japan adopted major elements of Chinese culture, including Chinese ideographs, Buddhism and Confucianism, and a heavily-bureaucratic system of government. Education was based on the meritocratic selection of talented individuals, later to be bureaucrats, who would then be taught to read and write the Analects of Confucius and works related to Buddhism. This Chinese system of education and civil service was absorbed into Japan.

With the rise of the Tokugawa clan to power in 1603, the pursuit of Western knowledge was strictly limited and controlled, and the study of Buddhist works declined in favor of Confucian ethics. Both actions were in part due to difficulties the shoguns had with religiously-motivated rivals for political power. More than one activist Buddhist temple was torched and the monks scattered to the winds by the shogun's samurai.

During the feudal period, education was available to common people in *terakoya.* (*Tera* means temple, and *koya* refers to a small room.) These one-room temple schools offered the masses instruction in the written language and certain practical subjects, such as the use of the abacus and elementary arithmetic. Texts were similar to the Chinese classics used by the samurai. Many teachers, of course, were monks.

Defeat in 1945 brought to Japan a total reformation of the educational system. The new model was essentially American in structure: six years of elementary school, three years of junior high school, and three years of high school. The first nine years were to be compulsory education.

Left, students on Kyoto excursion. Above, Meiji-era school boys (left), Tokyo University (right).

Approximately two kilometers northeast of Tokyo's central government district, Kasumigaseki, stands a red, double-doored wooden gate roofed with gray slate tiles. A low, amber-hued brick wall stretches northeast and southwest from the gate, hiding much of what lies beyond from the casual gaze of bypassers on the busy thoroughfare outside the wall. The upper stories of a number of buildings – some obviously post-1945, others from previous decades – can just be

glimpsed among the trees that line the inner edge of the wall.

The gate is called Akamon (Red Gate), and it stands at the entrance of Japan's premier institution of higher education, Tokyo University, or more commonly in Japanese, Todai. A degree from here, regardless of one's academic success within, is a guarantee of prestigious employment.

Japanese social institutions in general, and schools in particular, are arranged hierarchically in terms of their ability to bestow economic and social status. No institution ranks higher in this regard than Tokyo University. (The other two heavyweights are Keio University and Waseda University, both also in Tokyo.) Since its founding in 1877, Tokyo University has supplied most of the nation's political leaders and career bureaucrats, as well as the largest number of presidents of companies listed on the Tokyo Stock Exchange. The awe with which the Akamon is regarded is illustrated in tales of ambitious kimono-clad mothers taking their five-year-olds to visit the gate before packing them off to their first day at school, seeking to impress upon the youngster *the* goal for the next 15 years of their life.

Entrance to higher education is determined by dreaded examinations, which are administered by the individual universities; for each school applied to for admission, a complete set of entrance exams must be endured. The more prestigious a school is, the greater the number of applicants seeking admission and the more difficult the examination.

To help them reach this goal, parents will budget a considerable amount of their monthly income to send children to *juku,* private cram schools that are a multibillion-yen business. For the most disciplined of students, every night and weekend is spent at juku, having their brains crammed with exam-passing information.

There is no doubt that the Japanese are united in a consensus that education is essential for social cohesion, economic prosperity, and prestige in the international arena. Unfortunately, both in the primary and university levels, form and rote usually take precedence over function and knowledge. Students are taught not analysis and discourse, but rather only the information needed to pass exams for entrance into the next level of their schooling. There are exams for primary school, middle school, and high school. And there are the exams for the university, the whole point of life up to this point.

Perhaps, more importantly, schools reform undisciplined brats into socially-predictable, and responsible, persons. The schools pound down the nail that sticks out. From the earliest days of school, the educational system focuses on developing such basic Japanese values as harmonious relations with others and establishing group identity, through membership in a limited number of social and vocational groups.

Education is respected in Japan, and so are educators. In fact, the honorific for teacher – *sensei,* as in Nakamura-sensei – is the same as for physicians. Unfortunately, the responsibility and professional pressure is considerable upon teachers, especially at the high school level, when students are preparing for their university examinations. Holidays are rare for the teachers.

The concentration of so much of the nation's educational and cultural resources in Tokyo has its problems. Population growth is one. In fact, the expansion of schools within the city has been restricted.

Even the Japanese themselves admit their educational system's shortcomings. The excessive emphasis on entrance examinations is a cause of much national concern and debate. Because of the emphasis on conformity and passing exams, students lack initiative and creative abilities. As a result, Japanese corporations, for example, must go to America and Europe for original research-and-development work. Reforms are being considered. The rigidity of certain facets of the formal education system and the alienation of increasing numbers of young people, along with increased awareness of violence in the schools and bullying of some pupils, are also concerns.

Above, even rebels seek solace. Right, bamboo cutter, Honshu.

Polls asking Japanese in which religion they believe consistently yield results that total well over 100 percent – most say they are followers of both Shinto and Buddhism.

The average Japanese thinks nothing of marrying at a Shinto shrine, burying loved ones in a Buddhist cemetery or boisterously celebrating Christmas. Although the devout Christian or Muslim – each with a monotheistic god demanding unswerving fidelity – might find this religious promiscuity hard to fathom, if not slightly sinful, the typical Japanese sees no contradiction.

Ask a Japanese how many gods there are, and the answer may be one or one thousand. Ask about the nature of the *kamisama*, or deities, that are worshipped, and a confused silence may result.

There is no Japanese equivalent of the Bible or Koran, unless one counts the *Kojiki* (Record of Ancient Matters), which describes the mythological origins of the Japanese; even the most ardent ultranationalist does not completely accept the eighth-century chronicle as divine writ, however.

Until recently, nearly every home was equipped with a *kamidana* god-shelf with Shinto symbols, or else a *butsudan* Buddhist household altar containing memorials for the family's ancestors, before which offerings of flowers, food, drink or incense are made daily. Many had both. Likewise, people passing by any of the thousands of Shinto shrines or Buddhist temples throughout the country still tend to drop in for a brief devotion before going on their busy way again.

It is hard to attribute all this to simple custom; the Japanese definitely seem to have a sense of religious piety and spiritual yearning, although it is far different from that in the West. The main difference seems to be that the line between the sacred and the profane is much less clearly drawn in Japan. In many ways, community life and religion are one and the same. Similarly, the distinction between good and bad, or sinful and righteous, is less clear in Japanese society. It is said that the West considers most things as black or white; in Japan, there is a lot of gray.

First-time visitors to Japan are apt to overlook the important role that religion continues to play in the daily lives of the Japanese. In rushing from one temple to the next, visitors more often than not miss that little Shinto shrine perched on the top of a department store or between looming office buildings, or the purification-cum-exorcism being conducted by a Shinto priest at a new Seven-Eleven store.

Preceding pages: village Shinto shrine, Hokkaido. Left, Shinto priest reciting prayers to deities, Tohoku. Above, Buddhist tomb.

Shinto: A basic understanding of the Japanese religious sensibility must begin with Shinto – not a "national religion" in any current official sense (although it once was zealously nationalistic), but rather one that influences virtually every aspect of Japanese culture and society. It is hard to give any simple definition of Shinto (lit. way of the gods), since it is not a systematized set of beliefs. There is no dogmatic set of rules, nor any holy script. The term *shinto* was not even invented until after the introduction of Buddhism, a date traditionally given as AD 552, and then only as a way of contrasting the native beliefs with that imported faith.

In general, it can be said that Shinto shares with many other animistic beliefs the truth that all natural objects and phenomena possess a spiritual side. It is this animism, mixed with ancestor worship – a shared trait with Buddhism – that characterizes Shinto, then. A tree, for example, was revered by the ancient Japanese as a source of food in nuts and fruit, of energy in firewood, of shelter, and even of clothing. For that reason, when a great tree was felled to provide wood for the Buddhist temple complexes at Nara or Kyoto, it was not used for several years, in order to give the spirit within time to safely depart. Mountains, forests and even the oceans were also similarly revered.

As for ancestor worship, the Yamato "race" always believed that it had descended from heaven, and so worshiped Amaterasu Omikami – the sun goddess, she who ruled the heavens – as the ancestress of the imperial family, if not all the people. The *Kojiki* is basically a justification for their conquest of the "Middle Land Where Reeds Grow Luxuriously" and their rule over other apparently related groups, such as the inhabitants of Izumo on the Japan Sea, who were said to be descendants of Amaterasu's brother, the rowdy storm god, Susanoo no Mikoto.

It should be recognized that the term *kami*, although usually translated as "god," is quite different from the Western concept of divinity. The classic definition, as originally understood in Japan, was made by the eighteenth-century scholar Motori Norinaga: "Anything whatsoever which was outside the ordinary, which possessed superior power, or which was awe-inspiring, was called kami."

That goes for people, too. Today, in Japan one often hears expressions like "the god of baseball," or "the god of management." These expressions are not intended to be taken entirely tongue-in-cheek. The Japanese at least subconsciously still believe that their land and its air is filled with the presence of kamisama of all kinds.

In ancient Shinto there was also a belief in a kind of soul – *tamashii* – that lived on after death. An unrefined form of ancestor worship also existed, remnants of which can be seen in the observances of the spring and autumn equinoxes. It can also be seen in the *Obon,* which, although primarily Buddhist in other parts of Asia, has both Shinto and Buddhist overtones in Japan.

Primitive Shinto had concepts of heaven and hell, as well, although they were hazily conceived at best. To use electricity as an analogy, you might say this world is plus, while the after-world is minus. There was no concept of sin, nor of divine retribution, nor of absolution for offenses committed. Just about the worst thing that could happen was the pollution of a ritual. Otherwise, as far as the afterlife was concerned, it was commonly thought that the dead would eventually be reborn into this world, just as spring returns after winter.

The aforementioned plus-minus concept in Shinto suggests an affinity with Daoism, and indicates that the basis of the religion arose in China or even Korea. In fact, however, not much is known about the origins of Shinto; elements seem also to have come from Southeast Asia and Polynesia.

Some experts feel that prehistoric beliefs from as far back as the Jomon culture also have survived in Shinto. They look to remnants of the original beliefs of Ainu, the indigenous people of Hokkaido, and to the still-surviving Okinawan religion, for evidence of this. Specifically, the Ainu creation myth, as well as that found in Okinawa's *Omoro Soshi*, which was compiled in the mid-sixteenth century, have some interesting parallels to the ostensibly Shinto tale told in the *Kojiki*.

There are 13 mainstream Shinto sects and numerous sub-sects in Japan today, but since the American occupation following World War II, they have not been controlled by the government. In fact, it was only during the period from the Meiji Restoration of 1868 through the end of World War II that the government took any direct part in Shinto.

It was during the Meiji Restoration that the government introduced *kokka* (national) Shinto as a political tool for controlling the people through the policy of *saisei it'chi* – the "unity of rites and politics." Although the emperor was said in the Meiji constitution to be "sacred and inviolable," the nature of his sacredness was never officially defined; the most common interpretation, however, was that, through prayer, he became one with his divine ancestor Amaterasu and the other gods, and could therefore intercede on behalf of his people.

Yasukuni Jinja, a Shinto shrine just north of the Imperial Palace in central Tokyo, is an example (a particularly notorious one) of the national shrines set up by the authorities. It is here that the spirits of every soldier who died in the name of the emperor since 1853 are enshrined (including war criminals executed by the Allies after World War II). Visits made here – official or not – by the prime minister and other members of government are often violently opposed by those who believe the constitution now supports the

Left, schoolgirl, Heian-jingu, Kyoto. Above, Shinto shrine, Rishiri Island.

separation of church and state. Another national shrine is the impressive Meiji Jingu, not far away, whose majestic architecture reminds one that Emperor Meiji, enshrined therein, was thought of as divine.

In fact, none of the national shrines – state inventions all – has much to do with traditional beliefs. Dismissing them as unimportant in the modern scheme of things, however, would be a sociological, if not religious, mistake.

Buddhism: The traditionally-accepted date for Buddhism to have arrived in Japan is AD 552. While this may be true, it wasn't until centuries later that it ceased to be the exclusive province of aristocrats. This is somewhat ironic in view of the beliefs of the religion's founder, Sakyamuni – born a prince in eastern India (now part of Nepal) around 500 BC – who advocated a middle way between indulgence and asceticism.

The Buddha, as he came to be known (though this is a misnomer), blamed all the world's pain and discontent on desire, and claimed that through right living, desire could be negated and the "self" totally done away with through entry into the blissful state of *nirvana,* or Buddhahood.

Buddha's followers came to believe that one who really knows the truth, lives the life of truth, and thus becomes truth itself. By overcoming the conflicts of the ego, then, one can attain a universal, cosmic harmony.

Mahayana, meaning Greater Vehicle, was the form of Buddhism that became established throughout most of East Asia. It holds that every being, sentient or non-sentient, shares a basic spiritual communion, and that all are destined for Buddhahood. Although all beings are separate in appearance, they are one and the same in reality. Every person's present situation is determined by past deeds, Buddhists believe; this is the principle of *karma.*

Since the main Mahayana sutras only appeared around 100 BC, it is not known how closely they reflect the original thoughts of the Buddha. But by the time it reached Japan's shores through China, Buddhism had changed tremendously from Sakyamuni's simple message. It was to undergo even more radical change when it encountered the beliefs held in the Japanese archipelago.

As early as the sixth century, for example, *Ryobu* Shinto began to emerge as a syncretic compromise with Buddhism. In this hybrid belief system, kamisama were regarded as temporary manifestations of the Buddhist deities. In time, Buddhist thought became influenced by the indigenous beliefs, deviating so far from the original, that some scholars doubt whether the Japanese version really deserves to be called Buddhism. For example, although the goal of nirvana is to break the cycle of reincarnation, most Japanese Buddhists seem to believe that the souls of the dead are eventually reborn. As the famed folklorist Yanagida Kunio once pointed out, if asked where people go after they die, the typical Japanese will usually answer *Gokuraku*, which translates as Paradise. Contrast this with the more orthodox Buddhist belief in death as a permanent state; in fact, a euphemism expressing someone's death is *Hotoke ni natta* ("He became a Buddha").

In practice, however, Japanese usually return to their *furosato*, or ancestral home, for the two equinoxes, as well as during the midsummer Obon, or Feast of the Dead observances. The purpose of attending Obon is to be present when the family's ranking male ceremoniously offers food to the spirits of departed ancestors – spirits that supposedly return to earth for the occasion.

From where do they return? Yanagida says most people will answer "the mountains." This may derive from the special place mountains have always held in Japanese religious lore. Certain peaks – Omine near Nara, and, of course, Fuji – are especially sacred; each year, thousands of pilgrims dressed in white ascend them. Such considerations also lay behind the choice of the mounts of Koya and Hiei, near Kyoto, as the respective sites for the headquarters of the Shingon and Tendai Buddhist sects.

The contemporary Japanese concept of an afterlife, then, appears to be quite similar to that held before Buddhism arrived. Excepting those Japanese Buddhists whose particular sect specifically countermands such a concept, most seem to believe that the life force passed on from one generation to the next continues eternally, although little energy is spent in explaining exactly how.

Left, jizo images for protection of children, Kyoto. Above, sake and fruit offerings.

Amida Buddhism: There are today an estimated 56 main divisions, and 170 subdivisions, in Japanese Buddhism.

The single most popular sect is Jodo Shinshu, founded by Shinran (1173–1262), who preached an "easy road to salvation" by means of the *nembutsu* prayer to the Amida, a bodhisattva who made a vow eons ago to save all who placed faith in him or her, and to guide them to the Blissful Land of Purity in the West.

About half of the Japanese Buddhists belong to either Jodo Shinshu, or to Jodo, another form of Amidaism established by Honen (1133–1212). True believers of Jodo

Shinshu think that it is not even necessary to be "good" in order to be reborn into the Western Paradise, and that the laity can become Buddhas as easily as priests, even without the faith Honen claimed essential.

Amidaism is perhaps the form of Buddhism closest to the core Japanese beliefs, in its slight concern for moral judgement and exaltation of natural inclinations beyond considerations of good and evil. This, no doubt, helps account for its popularity.

Back in the Kamakura Period, when religion was a much more vital social force than it is today, the Amidaists directly contended for converts with the followers of the obstinate reformer Nichiren (1222–82). Nichiren

claimed that he was the man selected to spread the "True Word" that would lead men to the "Primeval Gateway". He gloried in street preaching, and neither exile nor the threat of execution could faze him.

His highly nationalistic thinking is well-known; he predicted the Mongul thrust at Japan and noted that Buddhism had constantly been spreading eastward toward the land where it would achieve its ultimate maturity: Japan.

Nichiren's followers have been called "Buddhist Calvinists," and are usually to be found among the *petite bourgeoisie* and lower classes. During the fourteenth century, they often engaged in pitched battles with Shinran's followers, usually farmers or townspeople.

Today, many of Nichiren's followers in Japan belong to the *Soka Gakkai,* a controversial organization whose political arm, the *Komei-to,* or Clean-Government Party, has considerable strength in the National Diet.

Zen emptiness: The impact of that particularly eclectic form of Buddhism called Zen on Japanese culture is considerable, reaching far beyond the temple and entering into cultural and social areas of all kinds, including interior decoration, gardening, ink painting, calligraphy, the tea ceremony, cuisine, and even military strategies.

Two Buddhist priests in the twelfth and thirteenth centuries – Eisai, founder of the Rinzai Zen sect, and his disciple Dogen, who established the Soto Zen sect – are given the lion's share of credit for bringing the principle of "emptiness" into Japanese Buddhism.

Soto sect followers rely almost solely on *zazen*, or sitting meditation; they reject scripture and seek to emulate Sakyamuni, who reached the state of enlightenment while meditating without conscious thought in such a position. In contrast, the Rinzai sect also utilizes *koan* riddles, such as the famous "What is the sound of one hand clapping?" Koan must be tackled with something beyond logic and non-logic, and the riddles' function is to stimulate (or perhaps divert) the mind into a similar state.

Zen was influenced by both Daoism and the Wang Yangming school of neo-Confucianism, which stressed the "prime conscience" and the importance of action. They would describe the "Great Ultimate" as being akin to the hub of a well: empty but the point from which all action flows. For various reasons, Zen sects proved better able than the others to satisfy the spiritual needs of the samurai.

Whether through zazen or the use of koan posed by the Zen master, the goal is for the disciple to be provoked, excited or irritated to the point where one makes a non-intellectual leap into the void and experiences reality and the unity of all things directly. If successful, one will then view everything anew with a light from within, and there will no longer be any contradictions or duality.

Buddhist beneath sacred waterfall.

SHRINES AND TEMPLES

Shrines are of the Shinto religion, and the names of shrines often end in the suffixes *-gu*, *-jinja* or *-jingu*. Temples, on the other hand, are Buddhist and usually end with *-ji*, *-tera* or *-dera*. Quite often, both temples and shrines will be found side by side, or a temple or shrine will have an adjunct opposite on the grounds.

Shrines: The thousands of Shinto shrines in Japan vary in size from tiny roadside boxes to large compounds, such as the Grand Shrines at Ise and the Tosho-gu at Nikko. But nearly all share certain features.

First, there is at least one *torii*, shaped somewhat like the Greek letter pi. This gateway may have evolved from a bird's perch – a certain kind of bird having been a religious symbol in many animistic cults – and it may be made of wood, stone or metal, or even concrete. Like the *shimenawa*, or sacred straw festoon, zigzag cuts of paper, mounts of salt and cleanly-swept gravel, the torii serves to mark off areas considered sacred from those thought profane.

Often the largest building of the shrine is the inner sanctum called the *honden*. This is the main dwelling of the deity. It is usually elevated above the other buildings and reached by a staircase. Unfortunately, it is likely to be off-limits to visitors, but other than a mirror or, on rare occasions, an image, there is little to see inside. These objects, by the way, are the *mitama-shiro* or *go-shintai*, serving as spirit substitutes for the deity, or *kami*, being worshiped.

In front of the honden is the often quite spacious *haiden* or worship hall, used for ritual ceremonies. Usually, this structure is merely a roof supported by pillars, open on all sides, and is used only by the priests and special guests.

There are no elaborate rituals or prescribed procedure involved in worshiping at a shrine. On entering the grounds there is a stone wash-basin, often with wooden, bamboo or tin ladles balanced across it. Here, one rinses mouth and hands in preparation for approaching the deity. Water, like salt, such as tossed at sumo matches, or the shreds of paper tied to the duster known as the *obarai*, are used for purification.

It is customary to toss a small offering into the cashbox at the foot of the haiden, before sounding the shaker to attract the attention of the god. Most devout worshipers also clap their hands twice, making doubly sure the god is listening. Then, a deep bow is performed, and held, while the prayer is offered.

Often, in the shrine office or in a nearby kiosk, there is usually an array of amulets of all kinds, "guaranteed" to ensure everything from automobile safety to success in school exams.

During *matsuri*, or festivals, the gods are taken out for rollicking rides through the streets in *mikoshi* (portable shrines) by tipsy bearers, so as to bring the blessings of the *kami-sama* to all the community. This one of the few times when Japanese collectively shed social inhibitions.

Temples: Under the Tokugawa shogunate, Japanese Buddhism lost much of its vigor, leading cynics to charge that priests were good for nothing else but buying people. An exaggeration, no doubt, but cemeteries still provide a good part of the income for most temples. (Cremation is the Buddhist choice.)

The main building (*hondo*), library (*bunko*), bell tower (*shoro*) and other buildings of a temple complex can be exquisite architectural creations. But the one most easily admired is the pagoda, or *to*. The form seen in Japan is the culmination

of a long evolution from the dome-shaped stupa (thought to represent an upside- down rice bowl), in which the bones of the Buddha and Buddhist saints were buried in India.

Statues that may be found in temples include Nyorai (Tathagata) Buddhas, such as Sakyamuni after Enlightenment (the lump on their foreheads, a reminder of Buddhism's roots in Hinduism, is a sign of wisdom), and Maitreya (Miroku) or Future Buddhas, distinguished by a pose with one leg crossed over the other.

Other images include the *nio*, fierce-looking images flanking the gates to many temples and derived from the Hindu gods Brahma and Indra, and Shi-Tenno, a Deva king, is often standing nonchalantly on the heads of demons at the four cardinal points. ■

The earliest preserved and distinctly Japanese works of art are those of the late Yayoi Period. These were small, tubular clay figurines called *haniwa*, some of which were set up like fences around imperial mausolea. Whatever their purpose may have been – substitutes for people buried alive in the tombs, or magical instruments to ward off evil spirits or bandits – their immediate interest lies in their utter simplicity and charm.

Although many of them are only cylinders, some of the haniwa (and there are hundreds) are figures of men and women (dancers, warriors, singers), horses, monkeys and birds. Most are very simple, with only a few details of decoration – a sword or a necklace, perhaps. They have large hollow spaces for the mouth and eyes, which prevented them from cracking when being fired, and which adds not only to their charm, but to their mystery, too. Who are they? What are they saying? Some emotion or song seems to have been eternally suspended here, and while the will to know them may be strong, the recognition of the eternally human, of the eternally here and now, is more compelling.

Aesthetic impulses: The haniwa figures are also important for another reason. We find in them – at the very beginning of the culture – many of the salient characteristics of almost all Japanese art. The haniwa are, so to speak, decorative; they are very much in this world (regardless of how much they may evoke the next). They are narrational – we want to create stories for them; as still in time as they are, we imagine a time before and after their eyes and mouths opened. And, with their soft modeling and indolent lines, they are recognizably human. These figures are not gods or angels: they smile, they shout, they gaze. In fact, there is little that is abstract about them. This is an "art of the real", which does not eliminate the fantastic or even the artificial.

It is easy to see that the haniwa possess a beauty that seems – almost uncannily – to come from a natural aesthetic impulse. They occur during a lull in Japanese absorption of outside influences, at a time when Japanese culture was developing its own native hues. It is possible to draw a parallel with another art: the haniwa are to later art what the slightly later poetry of the *Manyoshu* (compiled in AD 759) is in purity of diction and sentiment.

Decorative, narrative, human. The decorative extends from modest fence posts to elaborately gilded and painted screens and walls in palaces and castles, to pin-ups in a

swordsmith's shop. The narrational can range from rolls and rolls of scrolls illustrating one of the world's biggest (and greatest) novels – *Genji Monogatari*, or *Tale of the Genji* – to a single illustration of a young boy playing a flute before a warrior. As for the human: in Japanese art it embraces everything, from demons to gods, from animals to, well, people.

Nara and Kamakura sculpture: Before the Nara Period, there are some superb examples of sculpture (such as the Kuze Kannon and the Kudara Kannon, both at Horyu-ji, in Nara). To recommend only one, mention must be made of the Miroku in Koryu-ji, in Kyoto. This is a delicately-carved wooden

Preceding pages: Buddhist scriptures from Heian Period, 12th century; kabuki actor warms up. Left, *Fugen Bosatsu*, Heian silk painting. Above, creating nature, Kyoto's Daisen-in.

statue of the Buddha of the Future. The young person (gender is blurred in Buddhist art, but one assumes the figure is of a boy) has one leg crossed over the other, his chin rests on a couple of extended fingers, and one detects the slightest hint of the most gracious, lyrical smile imaginable. The Miroku is a hint of the greatness to come.

In the Nara Period (646–794), with Japan's full-scale welcome of things Chinese, the native response to the real is fused with its spiritual aspirations without ever abandoning the former. Work is done in wood, clay, bronze or by using the curious technique of hollow lacquer.

There are some fine early pieces to be seen in the Yakushi-ji, in Nara, but visits must especially be made to the Kofuku-ji and the Todai-ji to see some of the world's masterpieces of sculptures. There, one can see numerous sculptures of the Buddha, of guardian deities, and of monks. There is, for example, the somewhat awkwardly-modeled, three-headed, six-armed Ashura, a young demon (demoness?) that has all the charms of a sensitive youth.

All of these sculptures – gods and humans alike – are spiritually powerful because they are so real (they probably had real models). And though it cannot now be seen, they were originally colored. The patinas of age may lend them a spiritual depth, but one should not forget their original splendor. While the Buddha and some of the deities are ruled by convention (the beatific smile, various hand gestures for the former, terrifying gazes for the latter), the portraits of the blind monk Ganjin (Toshodai-ji) and of the Buddha's disciples (Kofuku-ji) are utterly remarkable for the realism of their portraiture.

It was also during this time that the 16-meter-high, bronze Daibutsu (the Great Buddha) was created. It is a sorry sight from what it must have originally looked like, housed as it is now in a much smaller hall and worn by age. It was originally gilded with bronze, and incised with designs that can now only be barely discerned on some of the lotus petals upon which the figure sits. This is the great tourist attraction at Todai-ji, in Nara, which should not be missed. The other Nara temples already mentioned are also worth visiting if one wants to look at the true genius of Japanese sculpture.

The Nara Period ended with the move of capital to Kyoto. With that, the beginning of the Heian Period (794–1185), Japanese sculpture declined as other arts ascended, and did not revive until the Kamakura Period, several centuries later. While Nara Period sculpture was both human and ideal, that of the Kamakura Period was wholly human, passionate, personal and emotional.

For example, the Kamakura Period (1185–1336) produced more portraits of monks and of demons (warriors, really) than of aloof gods. Many of these (of the priests Muchaku and Seshin, and of the Kongoo Rikishi, the Guardians of the Law), fortunately, can also be seen in Todai-ji and Kofuku-ji, in Nara. The Kamakura Period also produced its

Daibutsu, which, though somewhat smaller than that in Nara, is equally affecting. Now sitting uncovered in the Kamakura hills, its impressiveness has been enhanced by time and exposure to the ocean air.

Painting: In the Heian Period, life itself became an art, and works of art became its decorative attendant. Kyoto's Byodoin may have been meant as a model of the next world, but it only showed that life in this one was already exquisite.

(One last note on sculpture: when visiting the Byodoin, do not miss out on the many small, elegant Boddhisatva musicians floating around the statue of the Buddha.)

Japanese painting had long existed, but it had not flowered into great sophistication, particularly in the form of long, unfolding (and hand-held) scrolls. These paintings, called *Yamato-e*, might depict the changing seasons, famous beauty spots, or illustrate well-known stories. The best Yamato-e were of the latter type, depicting popular legends, warrior tales, or works of great literature, such as the *Ise Monogatari* and the *Tale of the Genji*. The popular legends might include a satirical look at pompous officials turned into battling frogs and rabbits, or a man who can't stop farting, or a look into the punishments that await evil-doers in hell. Post-Heian warrior tales drew on the many

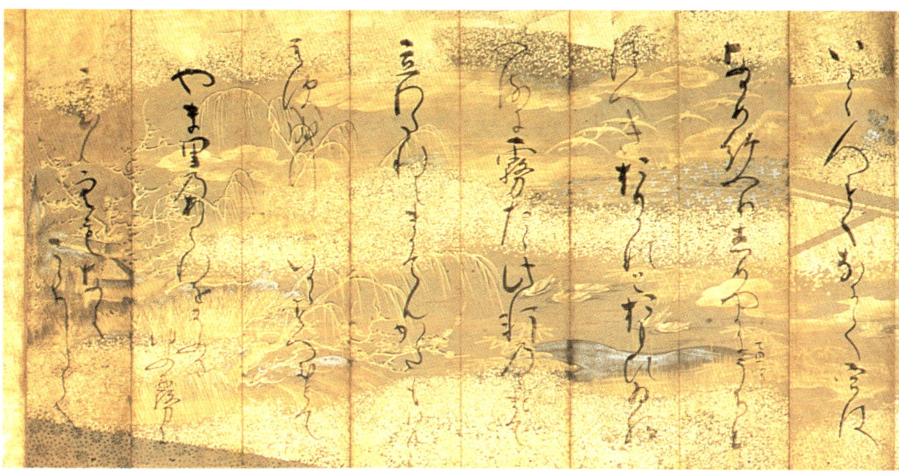

heroic or sentimental tales collected in the *Heike Monogatari* and other stories (as Western artists drew theirs on Homer and Virgil).

The scrolls are easy to follow, and with their delicacy of line reveal the Japanese gift of design. With the Genji scroll are the conventions of the removed roof, the "dash for the eye and a hook for the nose," and the floating, golden clouds that rhythmically lead the eye from scene to scene. It is a splendid example of the great Japanese graphic sensibility that is still seen today in advertising and comic art.

Left, standing boddhisattva, Nara Period. Above, excerpts from *Tale of the Genji*, by Konoe Nobutada, Momoyama Period, 17th century.

In the Kamakura Period, war and religion came together. This was the great period of Zen art, when *suiboku* (water-ink, painting with black *sumi* ink) comes to the fore. One of the world's masterpieces of *suiboku-ga* can be seen in the National Museum in Tokyo: Sesshu's *Winter Landscape*, a bold landscape of a traveler dwarfed by nature, a lonely town and mountain all around, and a vertical streak of ink that cuts the sky. Because of his line, his sense of composition, and the moods he can evoke, Sesshu seems at times to be a contemporary artist, though he died in 1506 at the age of 86; another of his masterpieces, the *View of Amanohashi-Date*, can be seen in the National Museum in Kyoto.

In addition to calligraphy, suiboku-ga includes portraiture and landscape. An example of the principal "the line is the man himself" in portraiture is the stark portrait of the priest Ikkyu, in the National Museum in Tokyo. In suiboku landscapes, the emphasis is, again, on the real, on the visually pleasurable (hence, Japanese landscape is rarely as profoundly mystical as that of Chinese), and quite often, on the grotesque, the curious and the fantastic.

The Momoyama Period (late 16th century) is Japan's age of Baroque splendor, when, as one scholar says, "The simper of the late Ashikaga court went down before the swagger of men like Nobunaga." It is the one of the high points of Japan's decorative genius. It is filled with gold and silver, with very bright, flat colors (no shading or outlining), with lush scenes painted on screens and walls of flower-viewing parties, of lovely women and sight-seeing spots.

This is not to imply that monochrome was abandoned during Momoyama. Far from it: there was a great deal of superb *sumi-e* (ink picture) screens and paintings done at this time. The overwhelming impression, however, is of gold, as one can see in the *Jodan-no-ma* and other ceremonial halls in the Nijo

Castle in Kyoto, with its painted walls and gilded ceilings, or at nearby Nishi Hongan-ji in its expansive *taimensho* (audience hall) and *Konoma* (stork room).

Floating world: The Edo Period (1603–1868) is the great age of popular art, even though much great decorative art was being made for the aristocracy or the military classes, especially by Koetsu, Sotatsu and Korin. The latter's gorgeous *Irises* – all violet and gold – is an excellent example and can be seen in the Nezu Museum of Art, in Tokyo.

The merchant class, however, was developing its own pleasures in fiction, drama (*kabuki*) and art, and mass appeal soon became more important than ever before in most of the disciplines.

The art most associated with Edo Tokyo is *ukiyo-e* (literally, "pictures of the floating world"). Once again, the sublunary, fleshy human existence was a key element. Although wood-block printing had been used to reproduce sutras, for example, the technique first began to be used in a more popular vein in the early eighteenth century; at first, the prints were either monochromatic or hand-colored with an orange-red. In time, two colors were used, then four, and so on.

Although the names of hundreds of ukiyo-e artists are known, it should be remembered that the production of these prints was a cooperative effort between many highly-skilled people. There was the artist who created the design and suggested colors, the carvers of the many blocks, the actual printers, and finally the publishers.

Early ukiyo-e, especially those by the first great master, Moronobu, are usually portraits of prostitutes from the Yoshiwara district of old Edo, or else illustrations for books; with polychrome printing, in ukiyo-e a number of "genres" became established. There were, for example, portraits of prostitutes (*bijin ga*), kabuki actors in famous roles, the ever-present scenes of renowned places, and of plant and animal life.

Ukiyo-e, suffice it to say, is one of the world's great graphic art forms, and in more ways than one. For example, the charmingly named *shunga* (literally, "spring pictures") represent pornographic art of stupendous imagination, and comprised a large part of every ukiyo-e artist's *oeuvre*. Unfortunately, *shunga* cannot be seen in Japan, but outside, most museums with an ukiyo-e collection are sure to have some examples.

The Japanese never considered ukiyo-e to be "art". It was a publishing form, and not art until foreigners started collecting them. Only in the past few decades have Japanese collectors begun to realize the value of ukiyo-e, long appreciated by outsiders.

In the rigid society of the Edo Period, the artisan was the third of the four social classes, one step above the merchant, who was at the bottom (in theory). This was the age of the unknown craftsman, whose tools, hands, and skills were part of a tradition, and who learned techniques as an apprentice.

Ceramics: Japan is a treasure house of ceramic techniques, a craft that has attracted many students from abroad over the years. There are famous wares (*yaki*), the names of which have a certain amount of currency in antique and crafts circles throughout the world. In general, pottery in Japan is stoneware or porcelain, that is, high-fired wares. Earthenware and low-fired pottery are found in small quantities, usually in the form of humble utensils, in Raku-yaki – a rustic style produced by hand and without the use of a potter's wheel – and in some of the enameled wares of Kyoto and Satsuma.

There are a number of unglazed wares, of which the most famous is Bizen, made from hard clay and with a bronze-like texture after firing. Traditional glazes are mainly iron glazes (ash glazes), though feld spathic glazes are used in some wares. The palette of the traditional folk potter is thus usually browns and black. Green from copper and iron, and a milky, streaked blue glaze made with rice bran ash are also found. Saturated iron glaze in thick application results in the deep-black *temmoku*; when thin, the same glaze fires a persimmon ocher. Stonewares also show iron and cobalt blue underglaze decoration.

Porcelains are decorated with underglaze cobalt and overglaze enamels. The decorated porcelains produced by numerous kilns in the Arita area of northern Kyushu, and shipped from the port of Imari from the seventeenth to the nineteenth century, are still avidly sought and collected by antique

Left, shunga erotic woodblock print. Above, making ukiyo-e, or woodblock print.

buffs, as is the Kutani porcelain of the Kanazawa area. The porcelain industry still thrives, and much of it is hand-painted, though modern transfer processes are able to capture all the shades and nuances of hand-painted wares.

Textiles: This craft includes weaving and dyeing, as well as braiding (*kumihimo*) and quilting (*sashiko*). Japan is a vast storehouse of textile techniques, one that Western craftspeople have yet to tap.

Of course, silks are the most famous and highly refined of Japanese textiles. The glorious brocades used in *noh* drama costumes, and in the apparel of the aristocracy and high clergy of bygone ages, are among the highest

achievements of textile art anywhere, as are the more humble but lyrical *tsujigahana* "tie-dyed" silks of the sixteenth century.

Japanese folk textiles are a world unto themselves. Cotton and hemp and ramie are the most common fibers, but the bark fibers of the *shina* tree, *kuzu* (kudzu), paper mulberry, plantain (in Okinawa), and other fibers were used in remote mountain areas. Indigo is the predominant color, and the *ikat* technique (known as *kasuri*) is the most popular for work clothes, quilt covers, and the like. These white-on-blue textiles are also found at flea markets and antique shops, and are durable and long-lasting.

Lacquer: Japanese lacquer (*urushi*) is the sap of a certain tree (*Rhus verniciflua*) that has been refined and which may or may not have pigment added. It is an organic, living substance, and has been used as a decorative coating on wood, leather, and cloth for 1,500 years. Actually, the earliest-known examples of lacquer in Japan – red and black lacquered earthenware pots – date back about 4,000 years, to the Jomon culture.

Lacquerware (*nurimono*) is a true community craft – no one person can do all of the 50 or so steps involved in just making a plain coating on a wooden bowl. Decoration techniques may involve another 30 steps.

Whereas in the West, "Japanese lacquer" evokes images of objects and panels opulently decorated with gold, often in relief, the Japanese popular image of lacquerware is of food bowls and serving trays – tableware known as *shikki* and simply decorated, if at all. It is doubtful if there is a household in Japan that does not possess lacquer bowls (or their plastic copies).

Bamboo: Generally, bamboo is split and made into baskets, screens, and the like, but on Kyushu, where the best bamboo grows, it is used to make bottles and containers. Japanese basketry, bamboo and otherwise, is unsurpassed anywhere in refinement and skill. Contemporary craftspeople have explored the abstract and light-capturing qualities of fine bamboo basketry. This substance also forms the frameworks of fans, umbrellas, kites and lanterns. In places such as Kamakura, one can find exquisite bamboo art and sculptures.

Metalcrafts: There are a number of alloys, particularly alloys of copper and gold, that are unique to Japan. Japanese carbon steel used for swords and knives also has never been surpassed. One of the best gifts a cook can receive is a set of fine Japanese kitchen knives – the vegetable knife (*nakiri-bocho*) and all-purpose knife (*deba-bocho*, really a fish knife) are sufficient, but a slicer (*yanagiba*) makes a complete set.

Although traditional work in metals is easily available in the antique market, contemporary work is somewhat limited and harder to come by. Japanese designers have been more active in jewelry design than in expanding traditional metallurgy.

Sixteenth-century silk noh costume.

SADO: THE WAY OF TEA

Whether you encounter it through one of the traditional crafts or even architecture, it is hard to explore Japanese culture without stumbling over the "tea ceremony."

One may be told that, at the higher levels of its mastery, the "ceremony" can impart all kinds of transcendent and spiritual rewards. Part of our initial surprise at the depth and seriousness of Tea could be avoided by a small change in vocabulary: in Japanese, the art is often called *sado* or even *chado*; the *do* in each case means way, and the *sa* and *cha* both mean tea. Translated into English, sado means the way of tea.

What makes sado so hard to achieve (and define) is that it is largely a state of mind. Making a bowl of tea is not the challenge; it is making it in the right spirit that consumes a lifetime of effort. As in Zen, implements, procedures and esoterica have value only as prods toward a higher objective, and in sado that higher objective, quite simply, is the ability to show sublime hospitality. The years of training are to make the motions second nature, so that the whole thing will appear casual and effortless.

Though some form of tea drinking was brought to Japan from China in the Heian period, it was not until the end of the twelfth century that the special strain of bush, and the technique for making the powdered green tea called *matcha,* were brought over by the founder of the Rinzai Zen sect, Eisai.

Eisai planted his first seeds on a hillside in Uji, near Kyoto – a region still boasting Japan's best buds – and then encouraged his monks to drink the frothy, bitter-tasting tea as a health potion, as a cure for hangovers (Rinzai monks are very worldly) and, most importantly, as a sleep inhibitor. Meditating monks need every possible aid to stay awake, and matcha – loaded with caffeine and vitamin C – provides an adequate jolt.

By the fifteenth century, matcha had evolved into the party stimulant of choice for the rich merchant class, particularly in the Osaka region. These merchants used these (often licentious) tea parties to show their rare porcelains.

The Zen connection was maintained, however, thanks to the nightly presence of eccentric monks such as Ikkyu (abbot of Daitoku-ji in Kyoto) and his disciple Murata Shuko. In a fateful conversation, Ikkyu told his student to forget Zen and concentrate only on making tea.

Two members of the Sakai merchant class, Takeno Jo-o (1504–55) and his student Sen no Rikyu (1522–91), are credited with elevating the tea party far above the category of rich pastimes. They rejected showy extravagance in favor of the uncontrived beauty in things simple, earthy, humble, uneven, sad, overlooked, rustic, old and imperfect. These are part of *wabi* and *sabi*, crucial sado concepts that are reflected in the look of the implements and in the tea house.

Rikyu helped liberalize thinking in other ways as well. "All people are equal in the tea room" is an important axiom, a rule actually built into tea house design. For example, the door is so small that all guests must bow equally low to enter. ■

For many of the traditional Japanese performing arts, the distinction between dance and drama is tenuous in the extreme. Most of the traditional Japanese drama forms extant today developed out of some form of dance, and all, accordingly, employ musical accompaniment. Several of the forms also involve vocal disciplines to some extent, but not enough to qualify as opera.

There are five major traditional performing art forms or genres in Japan – *bugaku*, *noh*, *kyogen*, *bunraku*, and *kabuki*. Often, visitors confuse traditional and classical Japanese performing arts. This is an unfortunate error, because it potentially limits the enjoyment of bunraku and kabuki.

Only bugaku, noh and kyogen could be called classical – all are tightly contained and formal entertainments performed originally for the aristocracy. Both bunraku and kabuki are traditional stage arts, too, but instead, welled up out of the vigorous common-folk culture of the Edo Period. Another form, *kagura,* needs to be mentioned as well. Although it falls within what could be called folk drama, there is no single form of kagura. Rather, these offertory dance-drama-story-religious performances, held on festival days before the deity, all differ greatly throughout the country, involving anything from religious mystery to heroic epics, to bawdy buffoonery and symbolic sexual enactments – or a combination of all these elements.

Bugaku: What the ancient indigenous dance and drama forms in Japan were is not known. There certainly must have been some such expression before the cultural imports from the Asian mainland, but whatever traces might remain have not been reconstructed. Concentrated and intelligent study might turn up some interesting results, however. During the seventh and eighth centuries, mainland culture from both Korea and China dominated the life of the archipelago's imperial court.

In 702, the court established a court music bureau to record, preserve, and perform the continental music forms (*gagaku*) and dance (bugaku). Influences include not only dance from China and Korea, but also from India and Southeast Asia.

These dances are so highly stylized and abstract that there is little or no sense of story or dramatic event. The choreography is very rigid and is usually symmetrical, since the dances are most often performed by two pairs of dancers. (An almost identical music-and-dance form has been preserved in Korea, as well.)

The bugaku stage is a raised platform erected outdoors, independent of other structures and ascended by steps at the front and back. The performance area is floored with

green silk, the stairs are lacquered black, and the surrounding railings and posts are in cinnabar lacquer. Given that the bugaku repertoire has been preserved for almost 15 centuries, it is amazing to consider that about 60 different dances are known and performed today. These dances are categorized into "right" and "left," as was the custom in China. Left dances are slow, flowing and graceful, while right dances are relatively more humorous and spirited. The costumes for left dances are long and full, while those for right dances are far less voluminous.

Masks are often part of a bugaku dance. Those used for the dances still performed, and many of those preserved in temples and other repositories (though the dances associated with them are no longer performed), closely resemble some of the masks employed in religious performances in the Himalayas, particularly in Bhutan.

Bugaku is further classified into four categories: ceremonial, military, "running," and children's dances. The Imperial Household Agency – keeper and administrator of the imperial family – maintains a bugaku section for the preservation and performance of this ancient form, and performances are held at certain times of year. Furthermore, some shrines and temples have kept up bugaku performances as part of festival and other yearly observances.

Noh and kyogen: What is called noh drama today dates from the early part of the fifteenth century. As an art form, its high degree of stylization, lack of overt action, and monotonous-sounding vocal declamation (*utai*, a cross between chanting and dramatic narrative) makes it a distinctly acquired taste. It is admired by many in Japan, but its hard-core devotees are few. Still, it is performed, and a modern noh theater was completed in Tokyo in the 1980s.

Such terms as classic dignity, grace and symbolism are used to describe the noh drama. It is said to have been developed from a dance-drama form called *sarugaku*. Little is known about sarugaku. There is evidence that would categorize it in the same way as kagura – a calling-down into physical manifestation and an offering to a deity or deities. Also, it seems there were wandering troupes who performed sarugaku. Considered part of the noh repertoire, the sprightly dance *sanbaso* is performed by tradition as part of the rituals to invoke a felicitous beginning, such as at the opening of New Year or the start of a new company. It is thought to be the closest in the noh-kyogen repertoire to any kind of ancestral form.

Whatever its origins, noh was perfected by Kan'ami Kiyotsugu (1333–84) and his son Zeami Motokiyo (1363–1443), who were playwrights, actors, and aesthetic theorists of the highest level. Between them they created about one-third of the 240 noh plays

Left, mask on noh performer. Above, noh stages are minimal.

that are known today. Zeami's writings of the aesthetics of the theater remains as some of the most profound thinking on the subject of its kind.

The *-ami* ending on the names of Kan'ami and Zeami indicates that they were both part of a Buddhist calling. This religion had a profound influence on the content and dramatic structure of noh. The veil of "illusion" that we perceive as everyday "reality" is, in a sense, pierced momentarily by noh to expose something more basic, something that subsumes the senses.

Masks, highly-stylized sets and props (when such things do appear), a tightly-controlled style of movement, a voice style that projects and declaims but does not entice, and musical accompaniment – *hayashi* – of a few types of drum and a piercing fife mean that this form of play relies mostly on imagery and symbolism for its dramatic impact. In contrast to the sparse and uncluttered form of drama, the textiles used for noh costumes are the diametric opposite. The world's most opulent and gorgeous gold and silver and polychrome brocades are what the noh actor wears on stage. And noh masks are an art form by themselves, one that ranks among the great arts of the world.

As with Greek drama, the heavy and sober noh is performed in tandem with the light farces of kyogen (lit. crazy words), itself thought to reflect more directly the sarugaku antecedents it shares with noh. Though the dramatic methods share something with noh, kyogen does not use masks and is more direct and active. Traditionally, it is performed during intermissions of a noh performance, but today it is often performed by itself. These farces are both part of and independent of noh. Their purpose is to be light-hearted, to deal with nonsense, and to be simple. By achieving this, they also say something about the human condition.

An American student of the art has been performing it in English for years, and other foreigners have undertaken serious studies.

Bunraku: Japan's glorious puppet drama is a combination of three elements, which, about 400 years ago, fused into a composite: *samisen* music, puppetry techniques, and a form of narrative or epic-chanting called *joruri*. The result is bunraku, the puppet drama that is considered to be an equal with live-stage theater performance. Though bunraku developed and matured in the two centuries after its creation, the origin of the puppetry techniques used is still shrouded in mystery. There are folk-puppet dramas scattered throughout Japan, but the center of bunraku puppet drama is in Osaka.

The samisen (a banjo-like instrument usually pronounced *shami-sen*) entered Japan from the kingdom of the Ryukyus (now known as Okinawa) sometime in the sixteenth century and, for whatever reason, was adapted and spread throughout the country very quickly. Although the instrument only has three strings, music produced by the samisen has great versatility and, in particular, lends itself well to dramatic emphasis – as a solo, in ensemble, and as accompaniment to narrative.

Unlike marionettes, bunraku puppets (*ningyo*) are manipulated directly by hand and are quite large – it takes three men to handle one of the major puppets in a play. The skills involved in this manipulation of bunraku puppets are considerable. The narrative style derives from classic epics of heroism chanted to accompaniment of the *biwa*, a form of lute that made its way to Japan from central Asia at an early date. One such epic dealt with Princess Joruri, and the narrative style took on the name, joruri.

Although there may be more than one samisen to give musical density to the accompaniment, there is only one chanter. He uses different tones of voice to project dialogue, distinguishing male from female characters, young from old, good from bad. Accent and intonation convey nuances of feeling and indicate shifts of scene.

At the end of the seventeenth century, a master joruri chanter named Takemoto Gidayu teamed up with playwright Chikamatsu Monzaemon to produce a brilliant series of puppet dramas, some of which were later made part of the kabuki repertoire. The narrative chanting is sometimes called *gidayu* as well, honoring the skill and innovations of Takemoto.

The name *bunraku* appeared in the nineteenth century, after the impressario Uemura Bunrakuken. It should be emphasized that, while bunraku and kabuki share many traits and have some plays in common, bunraku is the older of the two, and it was kabuki that adopted elements of the puppet drama, not the other way around, as one might naturally think. In some of the plays taken from bunraku, kabuki actors even imitate the stiff movements of bunraku puppets at certain points in the drama.

The important point is that both bunraku and kabuki are popular theater. Bunraku was written and produced for the people of the towns – Osaka in this case – not for aristocratic patronage. Its entire existence and content was as popular entertainment, much like the plays of Shakespeare in his own day.

Left, Okinawan samisen. Above, bunraku puppet and puppeteer.

Kabuki: Plays for kabuki are still being written. Not many, granted, but the genre is alive, and like bunraku, it is not "classical." Kabuki is the equivalent of cabaret spectacular, soap opera, morality play, religious pageant, and tear-jerker. It is music and dance and story and color and pathos and farce and everything any theater-goer could want.

The highly-stylized language of kabuki, the poses and posturing and eye-crossing for dramatic emphasis, the swashbuckling and acrobatics and flashy exits, instant costume changes and magic transformations – all are part of the fun. Any visitor who goes expecting to see "classic theater" is in for a dull time, but if one goes knowing that this is

unsurpassed high-camp, then everything opens up. Even the tear-jerkers are the soggiest for which one could hope.

Kabuki originated in the early years of the seventeenth century, with a troupe of women who performed what seems to have been a kind of dance, based on a dance performed at Buddhist festivals, and perhaps comic skits as well, on the river bank at Kyoto. Whether there was anything untoward in this performance probably will never be known, but the shogunal authorities seemed to think there was, and so, in 1629, they banned women from appearing on stage. Male performers took their place, and to this day, all kabuki performers are men, and the discipline of the actor who takes female parts (*onnagata*) is particularly rigorous.

The female troupes were supplanted in short order by itinerant troupes of young men, who too got into trouble with the authorities. These were disbanded, and the permanent theater companies developed in the cities of Kyoto, Osaka and Edo (now Tokyo) after the middle of the seventeenth century. Kabuki soon became the Edo Period's most popular entertainment.

The production of a kabuki play involves strict conventions: gestures and movements, colors, props, costumes, wigs and makeup. Even the types of textiles used for costumes are determined. (But there are places in a play left for spontaneous ad-libs.) Within this framework, an actor can bring a part to life and thrill the audience.

The audience directs much attention to the performer or performers. The story is secondary, and it will be well-known anyway. Kabuki devotees want to see favorite stars in familiar roles. Indeed, kabuki has been actor-centered since its beginning. The playwrights are recognized, but their role is more of a supporter in which performers can showcase talents and advance their prestige. There have also been some outstanding actor-playwrights, especially in the Danjuro lineage of star actors. Kabuki actors belong to professional acting families, and each family may contain lineages of a given name. For example, the Ichikawa family contains the Danjuro lineage. A Danjuro will train his son (actual or adopted) to take on the Danjuro tradition, and the name will be passed on whenever it is felt that the son has matured into the role (and the father is no longer in said role). The present Danjuro is the twelfth of his lineage.

Training of a kabuki actor starts at about the age of three, when actors leave their children backstage in order to do nothing other than internalize the ambiance and also the music and rhythms. With this kind of training, kabuki literally becomes part of one's body at an early age. This facilitates – but does not eliminate – the long years of rigorous apprenticeship and training that every kabuki actor must undergo.

The kabuki stage has a number of unique features. The most striking is the walkway that extends from the stage to the doors at the rear of the theater, at stage level. Actors enter and exit at this stage extension (*hanamichi*, or flower path), and it is sometimes used as a venue of action. Another is the classic draw curtain, which is in vertical stripes of black, green and persimmon, and is opened from stage right to left with the percussive sound of wooden clappers. It is closed in a similar fashion. The kabuki theater also featured a revolving stage long before the concept arose in Europe.

Both noh and kabuki show no clear-cut distinction between dance forms and stage movements. However, kabuki's grandiloquent gestures are a far cry from the austere containment of noh, although the latter had no small influence on the development of the kabuki genre. The kabuki technique called *mie* illustrates the formalized beauty of performance. A mie occurs at certain climactic moments, when the starring actor, projecting dramatic energy at top output, freezes into a statuesque pose with rigid stare and eyes crossed to emphasize a dramatic peak of intense emotional power. Glorious overkill, indeed. At such (and other) high points of a performance, shouts will ring out from the audience – the equivalent of "Do it, Eiho!" or "Kill 'em dead, Masayuki!".

Far left, kabuki. Left, koto ensemble.

There are two categories of kabuki play: *jidai-mono* and *sewa-mono*. The former deals with historical events, legends, heroes, magic and bigger-than-life episodes. These tend to be flamboyant, colorful, sometimes with incredible costumes and makeup, and may have lots of flashy stage effects. Sewa-mono deals with the lives of the townspeople and includes many of the tear-jerkers and soap operas. There are some 240 plays in the conventional kabuki repertoire, though by no means all are commonly performed. A kabuki performance usually is composed of famous scenes and pieces of longer plays. Both the morning and afternoon performances at the Kabuki-za in Tokyo last about four hours, but it is almost always possible to buy tickets for the "cheap seats" in the gallery. Performances are also held in Tokyo's National Theater, in Osaka and Kyoto and elsewhere in Japan.

Music: In addition to solo or small-ensemble musical forms, particularly those featuring the harp-like *koto,* the *shakuhachi* bamboo flute, and/or the samisen, and the numerous *taiko* (drum) and *minon* (folk singing) troupes, the most authentic (if not typical) form of Japanese music performed apart from drama or dance is *gagaku* (lit. elegant music). It is a kind of orchestral music developed in the ninth century, and little changed since. Quite unlike the popular entertainments described above, gagaku was strictly court music, almost never performed in public before World War II, and only occasionally now.

It employs esoteric instruments resembling (sometimes identical to) those used in India and China, long before high-tech instruments such as the koto or the sitar were developed – drums, nose-flutes and bowed, single-stringed droners, for example. These, together with a slow, "courtly" tempo, makes gagaku ideal for (and to most Japanese ears, synonymous with) funeral music. In fact, probably the first and only time the Japanese public has heard it recently was during the televised funeral of Emperor Showa (Hirohito), in 1989. True devotees, however, find tremendous excitement in gagaku's extended, soulful sounds and unrelieved tensions, and they may have a point. Fan or foe, however, one would agree that the ancient costumes worn by the musicians are interesting and colorful.

ARCHITECTURE

What kind of house would one build in Japan if one knew it might be blown away by winds or fall apart by movements of the earth? Besides typhoons and earthquakes, Japan also has severe rains, which often cause flooding and landslides. How would one make a palace or temple or hall, a farmhouse or gate to survive such destructive forces?

These questions had to be faced by the designers of buildings in Japan's remote past, and are still faced today.

The fact that Japan has the world's oldest wooden buildings (Horyu-ji, built about AD 670) and the world's largest wooden structure (at Todai-ji, some 50 meters (165 ft) high and said to have been rebuilt at only two-thirds its original size) seems to argue that the architectural system adopted by the Japanese was at least partially successful in creating structures to last. On the other hand, at least in contemporary times, the devastation of the 1995 Kobe earthquake – thousands of homes, office buildings and expressways simply collapsed, while thousands more burned down in a matter of seconds – suggests otherwise. Indeed, rather than wind, earth and water, it is fire that is the greatest destroyer of buildings.

It is also no coincidence that Japanese architecture has influenced architectural design throughout the world. Its concepts of fluidity, modularity, utilization of limited space, and use of light and shadow have a great power and appeal, both aesthetically and as solutions to architectural problems of the twentieth century.

Whatever factors determined how buildings were built and what they looked like in Japan – survival, tradition, aesthetic preference – there are some common characteristics that can be found, a bedrock of shared traits that define the tradition of Japanese architecture. Given the great range of climates, the complex topography of the archipelago – which has produced numerous local styles of building – and the long history of the islands, the persistence of such common architectural features is truly remarkable.

Preceding pages: open verandah. **Left**, rebuilding a shrine, Noto Hanto. **Above**, Karatsu-jo, Kyushu.

Materials: The favored material of building construction is wood. Walls, foundations of castles, the podia of some structures, and a few novel experiments saw stone in limited use, usually without mortar. Yet, undoubtedly because it was plentiful, wood remained the material of preference, particularly the wood of conifers. This is reflected in the reforestation laws of the shogunate and various feudal lords. The disappearance of certain types of large trees due to lumbering can be seen today in certain historical

changes in temple and shrine buildings.

This preference for wood is directly related to the fact that the basic structural system in Japanese architecture is post and beam. The structure is basically a box, on which a hat – the roof – rests. This system allows great freedom in the design of the roof, and the Japanese seemed to prefer large ones, sometimes exceeding one-half of the total height of a structure. Roofs also became elaborate, with generous eaves, and often are very heavy. (Building codes in some Western countries do not recognize this type of top-heavy structure. Getting a building permit for a traditional Japanese house in the

United States is not easy. Many of the homes destroyed in Kobe were the result of the heavy roofs collapsing earthward.)

The spectacular complex brackets upholding the eaves are one of the more arresting aspects of temple architecture. The preference for generous eaves has a chicken-and-egg relationship with the widespread use of veranda.

Straight lines dominate Japanese architecture, seemingly a natural result of using wood and the post-and-beam system. There are few curves and no arches. Barrel vaulting is unheard of. Curves, when they appear as an integral part of a structure, are gentle and used as aesthetic relief from the predominantly planar – that is, boxy – construction. The curves on gables and eaves are a good example. On the other hand, carved and nonstructural embellishment, especially on temple and other buildings that go in for opulent display, often shows wild proliferation of scrolls, volutes, and curvilinear motifs of many kinds, perhaps to offset the effect of this basic boxiness of the structure.

Post-and-beam boxes also may be combined and strung together in many ways to create fine aesthetic effects. The Katsura Imperial Villa outside of Kyoto represents the height of such architecture. Since posts or columns bear the weight of the roof, walls could be – and were – thin and non-supporting. This lightness of wall is another feature that makes traditional Japanese buildings top-heavy, and it was developed to the point that walls often ceased to be walls and became more like movable partitions instead. (The main exceptions were buildings that were meant to have a protective or defensive function – storehouses, go–downs, and castles – which had thick walls of clay or wood.) This is the origin of fluidity or modularity, perhaps the most noteworthy single aspect of Japanese buildings. Interior spaces were partitioned so that rooms could be expanded (combined, rather) or contracted. The former was accomplished through the

use of sliding door panels, which could be easily removed. A room could be divided by decorative standing screens. The use of such screens, especially those with gold backgrounds to act as a reflective surface and bring light into gloomy castle or palace interiors, gave birth to an entire genre of artistic expression.

This fluidity of interior space went hand in hand with the modularity of room size. Room area was measured in the number of *tatami* floor mats of standard size, and some combinations of mats became standard – specifically, three, four and one-half, six, eight, ten, twelve. (Rooms are still measured in this way today, even if of hardwood.) Veranda and corridor width came to be standardized as just the necessary width to allow two people carrying serving trays to pass.

Inside is outside: Also in this approach, the distinction between wall and door often disappears. This applies to outside walls – the "boundary" between interior and exterior – as well. Outside walls are often nothing more than a series of sliding wooden panels that can be easily removed, thus eliminating the solid border between inside and outside, a feature very much welcomed in Japan's humid summer. The veranda thus becomes a transitional space connecting interior with exterior of the building.

Since the floors of traditional Japanese buildings are generally raised, house floor and ground surface are not contiguous (except in the case of the packed-earth *doma*, the work and implement storage area of a farmhouse). In effect, this means that the indoor-outdoor fluidity is mainly visual and for circulation of air, not for movement of people. In rural areas, the veranda, when open, becomes a place to sit and have a good gossip with a neighbor or friend.

The ability to open up a house interior completely to external vistas led to the development of a heightened sensitivity to such vistas, and to their manipulation. Or perhaps it was a desire to view nature that led to the ability to remove the outer partitions of a house. Whatever the origin, the juxtaposition of building and nature without a clear dividing line is one origin of the Japanese garden – a manipulated or totally artificial vista, grand or miniature, "natural" or stylized and symbolic. The Japanese garden is an artifact open to the sun and rain, but clearly made to be seen and appreciated from within a building. Gardens for walking exist, but are rather exceptional.

The materials used in traditional Japanese room interiors are few and limited, reflecting an ambivalence between interior and exterior, or perhaps a pleasure in harmonizing rather than sharply demarking interior and exterior. Sliding door panels are either translucent *shoji* or the heavier, opaque *fusuma* paper screens, or of wood. Walls are of clay (wattle and daub, with a surface of fine-quality clay). Floors are of thick, resilient straw mats surfaced with woven reed (tatami mats), or of plain wood. Supporting wooden posts remain exposed, and ceilings are generally of wood or of woven materials of various kinds. Wooden surfaces remain unpainted (a fact that received little understanding from the American occupation forces housed in requisitioned Japanese homes). In the few areas of the country where wooden architectural surfaces are lacquered, the lacquer enhances the woodiness of the material, letting it speak; to cover it over would be seen as "cheap".

Because of the generous eaves of Japanese buildings, interiors tend to be dark and, often enough, may be gloomy. The use of translucent paper shoji screens to diffuse soft light helps, but the soft, natural colors of the room materials generally absorb rather than reflect light. The colors, lighting and textures of traditional Japanese rooms directly influenced the qualities of all objects that were made to be used in them, including clothing. A Japanese ceramic bowl and a kimono are very different when seen in a Japanese room and in a room with plaster walls and glass windows.

New principles: The artistic unity or harmony of a building extends to its properties, as well. Master carpenters, who were

Left, tea break during shrine construction. Above, Kyoto's Heian-jingu.

both the architects and the builders of traditional buildings, developed formulas of pleasing proportions that applied to all elements of a single structure, as well as to individual buildings in a complex. There are special and very sophisticated traditional carpenter's measures that apply this system of aesthetic proportion to new buildings.

And finally, Japanese architecture is united in the display of an astonishing degree of contrast and variety. The earth's oldest wooden buildings exist not too far from the Ise shrines, whose immortality is defined by their being ritually rebuilt exactly as the original every 20 years. The shrine is both ancient and new at the same time. Tiny tea houses and the world's biggest wooden building both show an equally awesome skill in building, but of varying scales and degrees. Gardens are contrived to draw in the vistas of distant mountains within their boundaries. Tiny "dry landscape" gardens – or rock gardens – may display such symbolic potency that they are both big and small at the same time – and their size ceases to have significant meaning.

Some of the finest tea houses, whose total lack of surface ornament is itself a purely ornamental statement, were built at roughly the same time as the Toshogu Shrine in Nikko, whose detail and color-crammed surfaces display a naive delight in complexity and brightness, and which seems to go so far beyond mere clutter as to define a new set of principles. Both the tea house and the ornate shrines, temples, and palaces shout out that they were built by skilled artists, the former emphasizing taste, but as a tool to contemplation and quiet, while the latter's primary message is loud flaunting of skill, effort, money and power.

Historically, Japanese architecture shows a dialectic between imported, continental styles (mainly Chinese, with some Korean) and native Japanese styles. The former was constantly being modified, adapted, and made into something clearly Japanese in taste, a process that demarks Japan's entire cultural history.

Historical summary: The oldest Japanese dwellings are the pit houses of the neolithic Jomon culture, but the oldest structure to which the term "architecture" might be applied are the Grand Shrines of Ise, mentioned earlier. First completed in the fifth century, the shrines have been ritually rebuilt 60 times, every 20 years. Each rebuilding takes years to accomplish, starting with the cutting of special cypress trees deep in the mountains, and involves special carpenter's techniques as well as time-honored rituals. The disappearance of carpenters with the necessary skills and the enormous cost of the project have resulted in the prediction that the 1993 rebuilding will also be the final one.

The introduction of Buddhism to Japan in AD 552 brought with it, in one sweep, many cultural and technical features, not the least of which was architecture in the continental manner. It is said that Korean builders came over to Japan and either built or supervised the building of the Horyu-ji (AD 607). The foundations of the vast temple that was the prototype of Horyu-ji can still be visited in Kyongju, South Korea.

In the seventh century at the capital in Nara, Chinese architectural influence became quite obvious, not only in the structures themselves, but in the adoption of the north–south grid plan of the capital, based on the layout of the Chinese capital. At this time, both secular and sacred architecture was essentially the same, and palaces were often rededicated as temples. Both displayed red-lacquered columns and green roofs with pronounced upswinging curves in the eaves. Roofs were tiled.

The mutability of residence and temple held true in the subsequent Heian Period as well, as evidenced by the villa of the nobleman Fujiwara no Yorimichi (990–1074), which became the Phoenix Hall of Byodo-in, in Uji, near Kyoto. The graceful *shinden-zukuri* style of this structure, utilized for the residences of Heian court nobles, is characterized by rectangular structures in symmetrical arrangement, linked by long corridors. The layout of Kyoto's Imperial Palace is similar, though it is a replica of this style.

When the imperial court at Kyoto lost the reins of power to the military government of the shogunate, located far to the west in Kamakura, the open and vulnerable *shinden* style was supplanted by a type of residential building more easily defended. This warrior style (*bukke-zukuri*) placed a number of rooms under one roof or a series of conjoined roofs, and was surrounded by a defensive device such as a fence, wall, or moat, with guard towers and gates. Tiled roofs gave way to either shingled or thatched roofs.

<u>Left</u>, temple roofs and pagoda, Kyushu. <u>Above</u>, Kinkaku-ji, Kyoto.

This period also saw the importation of Chinese Song dynasty architectural styles for temples, particularly the so-called Zen style, which is characterized by shingled roofs, pillars set on carved stone plinths, and the "hidden roof" system developed in Japan, among other features.

In the subsequent Muromachi Period, which saw the purest expression of feudal government and its breakup into the Age of

Civil Wars, Zen Buddhist influence transformed the warrior style into the *shoin* style.

This at first was little more than the addition of a small reading or waiting room (*shoin*), with a deep sill that could be used as a desk and decorative, built-in shelves to hold books or other objects. This room also displayed an alcove, the *toko-noma*, in which treasured objects could be effectively displayed. This shoin room eventually exerted its influence over the entire structure. Both the Golden Pavilion and the Silver Pavilion of Kyoto are examples of this early style.

At the end of the Age of Civil Wars, firearms became common in warfare. In response to this, massive castles were built. Few remain today; Himeji Castle, with white walls and soaring roof (nicknamed the "Heron") is the finest surviving example.

Political change brought the country into the Edo Period, and architecture saw a melding of the shoin style and tea house concepts to produce the *sukiya* style, the grandest example of which is the Katsura Imperial Villa outside of Kyoto.

This residential architecture displays an overall lightness of members, a simplified roof, and restrained, subtle ornamentation. By the end of the seventeenth century, it had achieved its mold.

Gardens: The unique beauty of the Japanese garden, which has been imitated all over the world, comes from a sensitive attention to combinations of natural elements and compositional harmony. Clearly enough, it is derived from the Japanese landscape itself, and as well as from the sharply-defined seasons of the archipelago.

Religion, particularly Zen, also plays a profound role in the design of the Japanese garden, especially the "dry landscape". It is said that viewing such a garden in the right conditions and with the appropriate mental preparation is a form of meditation, and may lead to a spiritual experience for which there are no words.

In the Heian Period, courtiers sought relief from the oppressive humidity of summer by having their residences and grounds landscaped to include little streams, small waterfalls, and ponds. This type of garden was situated on the south side of the residence and was often created as a simulation of the Buddhist Garden of Paradise. The garden of Byodo-in at Uji is an example of this style.

The military ethic of the Kamakura Period saw a modification of the garden plan to fit the needs and tastes of the warrior class. This period also saw the oldest Japanese writing on garden design and composition, Tachibana Toshitsuna's *Sakateiki*.

In the Muromachi Period, a further development occurred, with gardens becoming fashionable as objects for tranquil contemplation and as miniature representations of nature, to be savored and actively explored for their spiritual values. During this same period, considered the golden age of Japanese gardens, the tea garden developed in conjunction with the tea house.

Elements that these prototype tea gardens introduced to the art of garden-making include stepping stones, groves of trees, stone lanterns and washbasins, and rustic huts where tea is served. The splendid garden of the Katsura Imperial Villa is, in essence, a series of individual tea gardens.

The Momoyama and Edo periods saw numerous beautiful gardens built, and these must be included along with those of the Muromachi Period as being among Japan's supreme artistic achievements.

Above, Buddha and garden, Tokyo. Right, three-tiered pagoda, Kyoto.

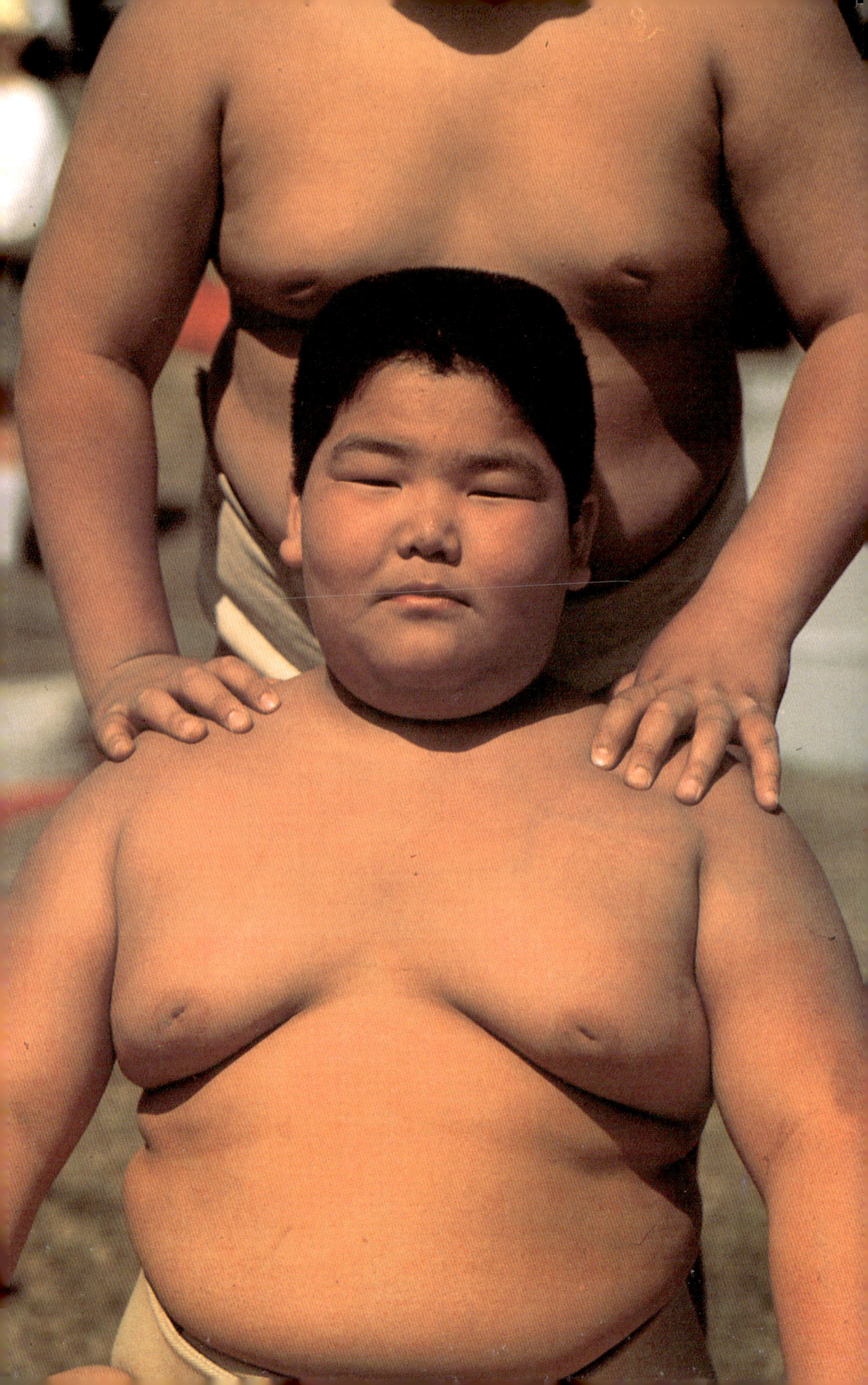

Baseball and *sumo* are the two perennial spectator sports, but in the early 1990s, professional soccer was introduced under the excessively-hyped "J-League" banner. For the first couple of years, it seemed the Japanese couldn't get enough of J-League or its stars, both Japanese and imported foreigners. But attendance slumped after two years, as did all the breathless enthusiasm, and wags are speculating as to if J-League was simply a fad or will have staying power.

Participatory sports are few within Tokyo. It's just too expensive. Golf, the world knows, is fanatically popular in Japan, but only the rich can afford to play a proper round of golf in Japan; the rest stand in cubicles at driving ranges and hit balls towards distant nets. Skiing is a fashionable sport, and Japan has the mountains. But like most activities in which the Japanese engage, there are crowds and blaring loudspeakers everywhere, even on the slopes, both of which leave skiing in Japan less than satisfying. (An alternative, of course, is the year-round refrigerated ski slope in a long and inclined enclosed tunnel, looking like an odd industrial "thing," just outside Tokyo, on the way to Disneyland.)

In this chapter, we'll look at sumo and baseball. Although baseball is truly the athletic obsession of Japan, occupying much more of the time and energy of the country's young athletes, sumo (pronounced *s'mo*) remains the "official" national sport. This is fitting, partly because of its history, dating back as far as the third century, and its hoary, quasi-religious ritualism – but mostly because, in Japan, it's a more exciting sport.

Sumo: Some people say sumo is the national sport, some say it's the national spirit. Sumo wrestlers, or *rikishi,* would probably say it's a long, hard grind to fleeting glory.

Sumo, as court entertainment, dates back to the 8th century, when wrestlers drawn from army ranks fought to amuse the imperial court in Kyoto. It evolved over the years, mainly as gladiatorial entertainment. Sumo was formalized as a sport during the 17th century, with matches held on the grounds of Shinto shrines. The parades, costumes and rituals preserve a long tradition.

Preceding pages: when push comes to a shove in the *sumo* ring. Left, budding star. Above, top rikishi in a pre-tournament ritual.

There was a period in the heady, decadent days of the Edo Period when there was women's sumo as well. At first they appeared just in loincloths like the men, until the law made them cover up; the engravers of popular woodblock *ukiyo-e* prints had to oblige by adding vests to cover breasts.

Traditionally, however, women are not allowed to step foot in the ring, called a

dohyo. This discrimination was challenged in January 1990 when Chief Cabinet Secretary Mayumi Moriyama expressed a wish to present the Prime Minister's Cup to the tournament winner. She was turned down by the conservative Sumo Association and withdrew her request.

Sumo is a fascinating phenomenon because it involves so many different things: physical strength, centuries-old ritual, a complicated code of behavior, religious overtones, a daunting hierarchy system, and feudalistic training regimes.

It's a long physical and emotional climb to the top, with little sleep, lots of dirt and sweat, constant humiliation, cooking, shopping, running errands, scrubbing backs, and the awesome task of accompanying 200-kilogram senior wrestlers to the restroom – all for just bed and board. Only those at the top receive a salary.

Six two-week tournaments are held each year, three in Tokyo's Kokugikan, in the Ryogoku area in the eastern part of the city. The Tokyo tournaments are held in January, May, and September. Each rikishi fights one match daily for the two weeks. Winning a tournament heaps upon the tournament champion an Emperor's Cup, a significant amount of cash, and sumo-sized awards of beef, a few tons of rice... In fact, enough commodities of all kinds to keep a "stable" of hearty wrestlers and their hangers-on flatulent for years.

In the old days before the construction of the new hall in 1985, it was possible to rub shoulders with the wrestlers outside, watch them exercising in the car park, and peep into the dressing rooms before tournaments. All that has gone. To do that now you will have to visit the *beya,* or stables, themselves, where practice starts at the crack of dawn. Some beya require introductions to enter, others are open to the public. Training takes place in a kind of hushed, largely humorless fashion, even though rikishi are immensely sociable off the job. Appearances to the contrary, rikishi are not slabs of flab. They are immensely strong, rigorously-trained athletes, with solid muscle often loosely covered in flab. The biggest rikishi in history (a Hawaiian named Salevaa Atisanoe, now a Japanese citizen and whose sumo name is Konishiki) has reached 253 kilograms (557 lbs) before slimming down a bit for his wedding. Most grand champions, however, have ranged in weight from 110 to 150 kilograms (220–330 lbs). There are active rikishi in sumo's upper two divisions as small as 90 kilograms (198 lbs).

The goal of newcomers to the sport is to one day reach proper *sekitori* status, to be in the top 50 or so wrestlers out of the more than 600 wrestlers. Doing so means a fancy topknot, assistants and a salary. Only one or two of those 50 will reach the very top, that of being a grand champion, or *yokozuna*.

The rikishi wrestle on a raised square of mud and sand, the dohyo. A circle within the square, the *tawara*, is made of rice-straw bales. Matches in the upper division present sumo's full suspense, with rikishi lumbering forth and sizing each other up as many as five times – each time throwing salt to purify the dohyo as they step out.

The wrestler's goal is to force his opponent to touch the surface of the dohyo with some part of his body other than the feet, or set foot out of the ring. This happens very fast. The average sumo bout lasts no longer than six seconds.

Just as they come in all sizes, rikishi come in a range of abilities. The top sumo rank is yokozuna, or grand champion, and there are rarely more than four active yokozuna at any time. Just below is the rank of *ozeki*. Both yokozuna and ozeki retain their rank, even after a losing record (less than half of the 15 matches per basho) in a basho. After two straight basho with a losing record, however, ozeki are demoted and yokozuna are pressured to retire.

The top division is called *makunouchi* (or "inside the curtain"). Here, the descending ranks below ozeki are *sekiwake*, *komusubi* and a large group of *maegashira*, the latter being the rank-and-file wrestlers. A rikishi who achieves *kachikoshi* – at least eight wins out of the 15 bouts he must fight during a given tournament – moves automatically up the ranks; *makekoshi* (eight or more losses) on the other hand means demotion.

There are no weight or size divisions; everyone fights everyone. Some bouts will have a rikishi wrestling another who weighs literally twice as much. Few holds are barred, but tradition frowns on below-the-waist attacks.

The waist itself is wrapped in sumo's only garment, a belt called the *mawashi*. The most dignified (and probably dullest) winning technique – called *yorikiri* – requires a two-handed grip on the mawashi, which allows the winner to lift and push his opponent out. *Tsuridashi* is a more dramatic cousin of yorikiri, in which the winner literally carries his foe (kicking and helpless) over the edge.

Arm throws are preferred among smaller rikishi, who compensate for their lack of size with cleverness and technical virtuosity.

Left, the objective is to force opponents out of the ring. Above, major league action, Tokyo.

Baseball: The real national sport, in terms of popularity and year-round interest, is the grand old Japanese game of baseball. It has been here since 1873 and is a major preoccupation for all ages. When American missionaries began teaching baseball to college students in Tokyo in 1912, they didn't realize how popular it was to become in Japan.

Yakyu, as baseball is called in Japanese, rivals sumo as the national sport. The two-league professional baseball system is a money-making industry, drawing more than 15 million spectators to stadiums.

Millions more watch on national television and train commuters devour the pages

THE MARTIAL ARTS

A general term for various types of fighting arts that originated in the Orient, most martial arts practiced today came from China, Japan and Korea. They all share common techniques, but there is no one superior style.

The use of weapons is often a part of advanced training in martial arts as a way to preserve ancient tradition. In some forms of martial arts, however, weapons are part of the basic training.

Two major martial arts evolved in Japan, the *bujutsu,* or ancient martial arts, and the *budo,* or new martial ways. Both are based on spiritual concepts embodied in Zen Buddhism. Bujutsu

emphasizes combat and willingness to face death as a matter of honor. It contains the philosophy and techniques of the samurai warriors and includes such arts as *jujutsu* and *karate-jutsu.* Budo, which started during the late 1800s, focuses on moral and aesthetic development of the student. *Karate-do, judo,* and *aikido* are all forms of budo. In short, understandably, Japanese martial arts have shifted from killing to both participant and spectator sport.

Most of the martial arts end in the suffix *-do,* usually translated as "way" or "path". Thus, *kendo* is the way of the sword. *Do* is also the root of *dojo,* the place where one studies and practices a martial art, and in budo.

Judo: The original form of judo, called jujutsu, was developed in the Edo period (1603–1868). It was made up of different systems of fighting and defense, primarily without weapons, against either an armed or bare-handed opponent on the battlefield.

The basic principle of the judo technique is to utilize the strength of the opponent to one's own advantage. It is because of this that a person of weaker physique can win over a stronger opponent. The best known judo hall in Japan is the Kodokan in Tokyo, where one can observe for free the judoists practicing in early evenings.

Karate: Karate, meaning "empty hand" in Japanese, is a form of unarmed combat in which a person kicks or strikes with the hands, elbows, knees, or feet.

In Japan, karate developed around the 1600s on the island of Okinawa. A Japanese clan had conquered the island and passed a strict law banning the ownership of weapons. As a result, the Okinawans – racially and culturally different from the Japanese – developed many of the unarmed techniques of modern karate.

Aikido: A system of pure self-defense, derived from the traditional weaponless fighting techniques of jujutsu, with its use of immobilizing holds and twisting throws, whereby an attacker's own momentum and strength are made to work against him.

Since aikido is primarily a self-defense system and does not require great physical strength, it has attracted many women and elderly practitioners.

By meeting, rather than blocking, a blow, one can redirect the flow of the opponent's *ki* (often translated as "mind" or "positive energy force"), dissipate it, and, through joint manipulation, turn it against the opponent until he or she is thrown or pinned down.

Kendo: Kendo ("the way of the sword") is Japanese fencing based on the techniques of the samurai two-handed sword. Kendo is a relatively recent term that implies spiritual discipline as well as fencing technique. It is taught to most upper-level school children. (At the end of World War II, the Occupation authorities banned kendo on the basis of its use before the war to cultivate militarism. But in 1957, the practice of kendo was returned to Japanese middle schools.

Ninjutsu: Another martial art form that developed in Japan is *ninjutsu,* which means "the art of stealing in," or espionage. People who practice ninjutsu are called *ninja.* Mountain mystics developed ninjutsu in the late 1200s. At that time, ninja were masters at all forms of armed and unarmed combat, including the use of disguises, bombs, and poisons.

Although the rulers of Japan banned ninjutsu in the 1600s, the ninja practiced it secretly and preserved its techniques. Today, ninja practice as a traditional martial art, with a non-violent philosophy. ■

of Japan's daily national sports newspapers on their way to work each morning, from April through October, for details of the previous night's baseball league action. To put it mildly, Japan is a baseball-crazy country, probably even more so than the United States.

One essential difference between North American and Japanese baseball is that baseball players in Japan are regarded as salaried men, just like anyone else and are, therefore, expected to train out of season as hard as they play during the April-October season.

Each team plays a 130-game season, as opposed to the 162-game US major league schedule, with opening day the first Saturday in April and the final regular season game played in mid October. The winners of each league pennant meet in Japan's version of the World Series, the best-of-seven Japan Series, beginning the third week of October.

There are two major leagues in Japanese professional baseball, with teams owned by big companies rather than being associated with cities, although a city's name often figures in the team's official name. For teams constantly on top, the advertising and promotional value for the parent company – department stores, media giants and food processing companies – is considerable.

The beautiful Seibu ball park just happens to be on a Seibu railway line next to the Seibu Amusement Park, to keep the whole family happy. Whenever a Seibu home-run is hit, the sky above the Seibu property around the ball park is lit up with fireworks. Display boards at the main Seibu station in Ikebukuro keep commuters informed of the latest scores as they hurry past the massive Seibu department store. And inside that store – and in every other Seibu store in Japan – if they've won the pennant, the team's fighting-spirit song is played repeatedly, over and over and over, all day, on the store's public address system. Over and over and over.

Interior of the Tokyo Dome, also called the "Big Egg" and Japan's first enclosed stadium.

The Japanese rule allowing *gaijin* players in its pro leagues is one of the most interesting aspects of the system. Each Japanese team can list three foreign players on its 60-man roster, which includes the "major league" team and one farm team. Most teams employ two former US major leaguers and one US minor leaguer, or a young player from Taiwan, who will be assigned to the farm team for development in the hope that he will become a big star in the future.

There are critics who believe the teams should be allowed to employ as many foreigners as they wish and that the limitation rule should be abolished. Others have said gaijin players are not good for Japanese baseball and should be banned.

Most, however, feel the situation is fine as is, since the colorful American players with their quirks – and occasional outbursts – make the Japanese game that much more interesting; the limit does, nonetheless, allows baseball in Japan to keep its identity as Japanese. Since the two-league system was begun in 1950, more than 300 foreign players have appeared in the Japanese leagues – some great, some mediocre, some who simply could not adjust to living in Japan or Japanese baseball.

Excessive, year-round workouts (including on the day of games) is the biggest gripe of American players who come and try their hand at the Japanese version (same rules, different attitudes): they all maintain that a short pre-season training period and the regular season games are enough for anyone, and that professionals shouldn't need to have to practice techniques all winter long. The argument the other way round is that Americans on salaries bigger than their Japanese counterparts should play the game the Japanese way.

Of how many foreigners should be permitted to play on Japanese teams, the debate remains unsettled. However, now that the Japanese are showing more power and speed – if not the sheer physical size – in the game, the chances of them becoming more active on the international baseball scene are good. In 1995, a Japanese player, Nomo Hideo, became a national sensation (in both Japan and America) when he joined the Los Angeles Dodgers as a pitcher, and then when he became one of the top pitchers in "American" baseball.

The farm system in Japan is simple and differs from the American "bush leagues" in that there is only one minor league team per organization, compared with four or five at various levels in North America. The 12 minor league teams in Japan are divided into two leagues and the games are played strictly for convenience and player development – not for profit.

The rules of Japanese baseball are generally the same as for those of its North American counterpart. There are, however, several peculiarities. For example, the ball-strike count is reversed in Japan, making a full count 2-3, rather than 3-2, which causes some confusion to the fan of American baseball who is observing Japanese baseball for the first time.

In Japan there are tie games, the result of a 12-inning or 4-hour time limit necessiated by the fact that most fans travel to and from the games by public transportation, which stops running shortly after midnight. If the games were allowed to continue until decided, as they are in North America, the crowds of spectators would have to leave early, or else risk missing a ride home in case of a 20-inning or 6-hour contest.

The largest of the baseball stadiums is Japan's first roofed stadium, the Tokyo Dome, nicknamed the "Big Egg" and holding up to 56,000 spectators. The Big Egg is part of the massive Korakuen Leisureland complex, which includes an amusement park and pool with artificial wave generators.

Teams have their own rooting sections, with trumpets, drums and tambourines, headed by cheerleaders paid by the team. Their job is to provide a monotonous din that shatters eardrums and clouds the thoughts. It's never a relaxing day at the ball game, at least not American-style.

Above, player for Daiei Hawks likes press coverage. Right, at bat, Seibu Stadium.

NISSAN
ライオンズ
SEIYU
SONY
Lions

Japan is a country of regional cuisines, and, too, of seasonal cuisines. In fact, sampling local dishes is a fundamental purpose of traveling for many Japanese, whether it be a local ekiben box lunch bought at the train station, or an exquisite dinner at a remote ryokan. It would be foolish for this book to try and cover the multitudinous regional and local cuisines. Even the Japanese don't try to know them all. But to sample them all, that would be a worthy life. Here, we offer just a glimpse of some foods.

There is some place to eat everywhere, and in the cities, there are almost too many places from which to choose. Two types of places that particularly deserve attention for their pure Japanese ambience are the *izaka-ya*, or pub, often with a string of red lanterns above its door, and the *taishu-sakaba*, a much larger tavern-like establishment that may also sport red lanterns. These red lanterns – *akachochin* – signify a traditional Japanese place for eating and drinking. Specialties include Japanese-style fried fish, shellfish, broiled dishes, *tofu* (bean curd) dishes, *yakitori* (skewered and broiled meat), fried rice-balls, and simple *sashimi* dishes.

Eating is expensive in Japan, if one goes to restaurants. Even the average restaurant, of whatever cuisine, can set the wallet back ¥5,000 to ¥10,000, triple what one might expect to pay in restaurants in other countries. However, it is quite possible to eat inexpensively in Japan.

Increasingly, for example, Japanese are buying meals at convenience stores like Seven-Eleven. Don't laugh. The competition amongst convenience stores is stiff, and the quality of the food is excellent, made fresh daily and using only top-quality rice (Japanese are finicky about their rice) for *bento*, and for *onigiri,* a rice ball with a dash of filling and wrapped in dried seaweed, a great snack or light meal.

Among the best bargains are *soba* restaurants and *ramen* shops. Both types of noodles usually come with meat or seafood, and they're popular with students, people in a hurry, and ordinary workers. But if money is not an issue...

Kaiseki ryori: At least one meal in Tokyo should be *kaiseki ryori*, a centuries-old form of Japanese cuisine served at restaurants, or in ryokan, in several elegant courses. Ingredients depend upon the season and region. One might spend a lifetime sampling every regional variation.

Fastidiously prepared, kaiseki ryori is so aesthetically pleasing that it's virtually an art form. Ideally, the food's visual appeal would be heightened by a proper setting for the meal, whether in the snow-blanketed mountains or on the sea shore. Some of the better restaurants serving kaiseki ryori have succeeded in creating exactly such an atmosphere regardless of outside environment, with brush works, flower arrangements, and views of waterfalls cascading over well-hewn rocks into placid pools. The effect at once elevates the senses and the pleasure of kaiseki ryori.

The ingredients must be as fresh as the dawn. That's a prime requisite of good food in general, of course, together with a good recipe and a good cook. Rejoice in the fact that Japan has plenty of all three.

Unlike in the West, relatively few Japanese dishes are submerged in sauces, doused with gravy, and seasoned beyond recognition. Granted, the Japanese often splash on soy sauce as impulsively as some Westerners do catsup.

Japanese cuisine focuses on flavor and its subtleties, and on the food's presentation. Rather than create distinctive flavors for their dishes, Japanese chefs seek above all to retain natural flavors. And rather than alter the appearance of their ingredients, they strive to enhance their visual appeal through artful arrangements.

In fact, the Japanese dining experience involves all the senses. Unlike the fork or spoon, for example, chopsticks, or *hashi*, convey to the hand a sense of tactile rapport with the food. Small soup bowls (*owan*) raised to the mouth with the free hand convey the warmth or coolness of their ingredients. Similarly, the slurping of hot udon imparts its own lusty ambience.

Many of Japan's most enjoyable and popular dishes are common and reasonably priced. Among them are such everyday dishes as *yakimono* (fried dishes), *nabemono* (pot dishes), *agemono* (deep fat fried dishes), *nimono* (boiled dishes) and a wide variety of noodle dishes. (The suffix *-mono* can be roughly translated here as "things", as in "fried things".)

Noodles: Noodles are eaten in Japan throughout the year and nearly throughout the day – and night.

Japanese noodles are of three main types: soba, *udon*, and *somen*. Soba noodles, made of buckwheat, are thin and brownish. Udon noodles, made of wheat, are usually off-white, and thick to very thick. Somen noodles, also made of wheat, are as thin as vermicelli. Udon is usually eaten in hot dishes, and soba and somen may be eaten hot or cold, depending upon season. Additionally, eaten only cold is a type called *hiyamugi* (iced noodles), made of the same ingredients as udon but much thinner.

Most common are soba, from buckwheat flour and particularly delicious if not overburdened with non-buckwheat flour extender.

Preceding pages: Kaiseki ryori, using only local and seasonal ingredients. Left, popular festival snack. Above, hashi, or bashi, or chopsticks.

It is usually served with *wasabi* (Japanese green horseradish), thinly sliced scallions, a dip made of *mirin* (sweet *sake*), and *katsuobushi* (shaved flakes of dried bonito). Soba noodles in this form, when served chilled on a *zaru*, a type of bamboo tray, are called *zarusoba,* a delicious summer meal. Soba is not only tasty, but extremely nutritious, the more so in proportion to its *sobako* (wheat flour) content, a rich source of vitamins B1 and C. Another hot weather favorite – just as soba is, but entirely different – is the

thin, off-white wheat noodle called somen, noted for its delicate flavor and adaptability to a variety of garnishes.

Somen can be served *gomoku* ("five-flavor") style with strips of omelette, chicken, and vegetables; *gomadare* style, with eggplant, fish, and *shiso* (beefsteak plant); with fruit and hard-boiled swallow eggs; or *hiyashi* style – cold, with nothing but soy sauce containing sesame oil. As a light, refreshing treat on a hot summer day, somen may have no filling rival.

One of Japan's great cold weather favorites is udon, a somewhat thick to very thick wheat noodle served in a hot soy-base broth with scallions, other vegetables, and an egg. Unlike soba and somen, udon is not placed in a dip before being eaten. Udon, a real body-warmer, is particularly appreciated for its excellent texture.

Not strictly a traditional dish, but one that is uniquely Japanese and that can be (one must admit) quite delicious, is *kare-udon*. As its name implies, it's udon served in the thick, somewhat-spicy gravy that passes for curry in Japan. (Another popular curry dish in *kare-risu,* or curry rice. Look for it at most large train stations.)

Unlike pasta that's turned around on a fork, Japanese noodles are drawn into the mouth with chopsticks and *slurped* down.

Noisily. In Japan that's how you do it, unabashedly, with total commitment. Noisily slurped down. Experts say the noodles taste better that way.

Although essentially Chinese, so-called ramen noodles are eaten so obsessively in Japan that to omit mentioning them would be remiss. Ramen is served very hot in soy-flavored broth with savory ingredients, most typically strips of bamboo and slices of scallion and roast pork. Instant ramen is a mainstay of home cuisine.

If short on time, drop into a stand-and-eat soba stand, a *tachiguisoba-ya*, "stand-and-eat soba". Train stations always have them, and a stand will sometimes be found even on the platform. Very cheap. Prices usually range from ¥200 or so for *kakesoba* (basic soba in broth) to somewhat higher for *tendama* (soba with raw-egg and mixed ingredients fried together, tempura-style). Priced in between are *tempura soba*, *kitsune* (with fried tofu), *tanuki* (with tempura drippings), *tsukimi* (with raw-egg), *wakame* (with kelp) and others. At the tachiguisoba-ya's low prices, the quality usually is average, but on a cold day, hot Japanese noodles are wonderfully warming.

Sushi and sashimi: Taste and visual pleasure converge in sushi and sashimi, both of uncooked seafood. Japanese simply adore sushi and sashimi, and knowing the Western bias against raw fish, will often ask visitors, simply out of sheer curiosity, if they can eat one or the other.

A good sushi shop, or *sushi-ya*, can be both expensive and confounding if one doesn't know what to ask for. Try, instead, a *kaiten sushi-ya,* where small dishes of sushi pass by on a conveyor belt along the counter. It lacks a certain elegance, but in a kaiten sushi-ya, the uninitiated can study the sushi offerings at leisure, and sample it for less cost. Then, later, armed with new-found expertise, visit a proper sushi-ya.

Good sushi requires the ingredients should be of good quality, that the rice be properly vinegared and steamed, and that the topping should be absolutely fresh. (Thawed-out frozen fish just doesn't cut it.)

Those who prefer raw fish and seafood without rice order sashimi, served in a lacquer tray or on a plate with characteristic attention to the appearance.

Nabemono: If hot-pot dishes are your pleasure, Japan is the place to be. Every part of Japan, without exception, has its own distinctive *nabe-ryori* (pot dishes). Nabemono are winter dishes, essentially, and include: *ishikari-nabe* (Hokkaido Prefecture), containing salmon, onions, Chinese cabbage, tofu, *konnyaku* (a jelly made of root starch), and *shungiku* (spring chrysanthemum); *hoto* (Yamanashi), containing handmade udon, *daikon* (white radish), *ninjin* (carrot), *gobo* (burdock), squash, onions, Chinese cabbage and chicken; and *chiri-nabe* (Yamaguchi), containing fugu white meat, Chinese cabbage, mushrooms, tofu and starch noodles.

Popular for a quick meal is Tokyo-style

oden-nabe, a potpourri containing potatoes, tofu, konnyaku, boiled eggs, octopus, carrots, daikon, kelp, and a wide variety of other ingredients. Make a note of oden, which are often presented as pick-and-chose in convenience stores. It is one of the better winter body-warmers and a hearty dish.

To dare to suggest that these few nabe-ryori dishes should be considered to the exclusion of others, of equal merit from all over Japan, would incur well-deserved local censure from regions far and wide.

Tsukemono: Never is one served a Japanese meal without *tsukemono*, or distinctive Japanese-style pickles. Historically, pickles probably owe their origins to the practice of pickling foods in anticipation of famines. So it was in Japan, where nearly every form of food was pickled long before agriculture became widespread.

Literature from the Nara period makes reference to the practice of pickling as a means of food preservation, and in the Muromachi period, pickling reached new heights of sophistication as a means of complementing and enhancing the flavors of other foods. For those returning from travels, pickles are a popular gift.

During the Edo period, pickles came into their own in Japan, increasing in variety and popularity, and the *tsukemono-ya* (pickle shop) emerged as a new type of business.

Ingredients used in Japanese pickles vary somewhat with the seasons and are of considerable variety. Common ingredients are Chinese cabbage, bamboo, turnips, *kyuri* (Japanese cucumbers), hackberry, daikon, ginger root, *nasu* (Japanese eggplant), *myoga* (Zingiber Mioga), *udo* (a type of asparagus), *gobo* and many others.

Besides taste and nutrition, tsukemono add color to a meal, and also offer a wide range of textures, from *crunch* to *squish,* that might be missing from the main dishes. Furthermore, pickles can serve to clear the palate for new tastes – such as in a round of sushi, in which a bite of pickled ginger root rids the mouth of the aftertaste of an oily, white-skinned fish such as *aji* (mackerel), and prepares it for the delicate sweetness of, say, an *ebi* (prawn).

Bento: Like most modern countries, Japan is increasingly a land of fast-food. The traditional Japanese box lunch, *bento*, or more respectfully, *obento,* has become a form of fast-food in itself, with both convenience stores and *bento-ya* offering wide selections to take out. A bento box is used, flat and shallow and with small dividers to separate

<u>Left</u>, warm welcome at a sushi-ya. <u>Above</u>, counter fare is economical, sort of, and fast, sort of.

rice, pickles, and whatever else might grace the inside. Just about anything can be used in bento, including Western imports like spaghetti and hamburger.

A special type of bento that has become an art in itself, not to mention a pursuit for the connoisseur, is the ekiben (from *eki* for train station and bento). Japan is a nation of travelers who have long been obsessed with domestic travel.

Of all transportation forms, the train is incontestably the most popular. Thus, some of Japan's most popular forms of food are those sold inside the stations. Trains often makes stops of just long enough duration to permit passengers to get off briefly and buy

some of their favorite *meisanbutsu* (local specialties), or the ubiquitous ekiben.

Travelers will encounter many other unusual dishes in Japan. Some fit in a category that Japanese commonly refer to as *stamina ryori*, or dishes intended to raise energy levels and staying power. Japan, and especially Tokyo, can be pretty enervating, so "stamina restaurants" (and drinks) are a common phenomenon.

A popular summer dish is *unagi*, or broiled eel served on rice. It's said to help one withstand the hot and humid days of the Japanese summer – *doyo no iri*. Usually served with a sweetish *tare* sauce, unagi is rich in vitamins E and A, and exceeds pork and beef in protein content, yet contains fewer calories.

With the drinks: At a traditional Japanese pub, the ubiquitous izaka-ya, try the likes of *saba* (mackerel), *sanma* (mackerel pike), *nijimasu* (rainbow trout), *nishin* (herring), *iwashi* (sardines) and *katei* (turbot). Try them *shioyaki*-style (salt broiled), with a good cold Japanese beer or a very dry sake. Japanese ginger-fried pork and beef are other simple but satisfying fried dishes enormously popular in any season.

In both izaka-ya and *koryori-ya*, small Japanese eateries featuring regional foods, such dishes are invariably served with rice. Izaka-ya, essentially drinking places, serve a wide variety of Japanese snack foods but not meals, whereas koryori-ya, being essentially eateries, serve light Japanese meals. Both types of establishments serve beer and sake, often *shochu* (a vodka-like spirit), and sometimes whisky.

Etiquette: Never wave chopsticks indecisively over food, considered bad manners. Likewise, never spear food (*sashi-bashi*) with the tips of the chopsticks. Some things may be a bit more difficult to pick up with chopsticks than others, but chopsticks are designed to pick food up, not to spear and stab it. Equally forbidden is *yose-bashi*, using chopsticks to pull a dish forward. Use only hands. Do not pass food back and forth with chopsticks (*hashi-watashi*).

For dishes that are dipped in sauce, such as tempura and sashimi, hold the sauce dish with one hand and dip the food into it with the chopsticks.

Japanese-style soups (*suimono*) and other liquid dishes should be sipped straight from the bowl. Whereas it is altogether acceptable form in Japan to slurp noodle dishes, such as udon or ramen, it is not required nor indeed is there any reason to slurp Japanese soups. Sip them directly from the bowl, without a spoon, as this the best way to savor their delicate nuances of flavor.

Soy sauce should not be splashed onto a dish. Rather, pour into the small soy sauce dish, only a little at a time and sparingly. Eat all the rice in the bowl, and when asking for more, take only what can be finished.

Above, plastic food is often perfection. Right, pickle stand for take-home souvenirs.

京
つ
け
西利
にし り
京つけもの
京都・西本願寺
京都・四条祇園町
ゆずの香り
はりはり漬
からし漬

1:46

If a poll were to be held among Japan's businessmen, the greatest inspiration would almost surely be Tokugawa Ieyasu, the man who united the country's warring domains in the 1590s and, as the shogun, founded a 250-year-long dynasty. The exploits of popular naval hero Admiral Yamamoto Isoroku, architect of the attack on Pearl Harbor, are given frequent media coverage.

What is it about the military mind that seems to capture the imagination of contemporary Japanese businessmen?

It is true that Japan's top management is guided to some degree by samurai-like discipline, which functions to maintain the hierarchical structure of the organization, and also to preserve harmony within the group.

But just as the duality of nature is explained by the concepts of *yin* and *yang*, there is another important attribute in Japanese business philosophy: *shokon*, translated into English as entrepreneurial spirit.

Looking back in history, the samurai – the feudal warrior class – had always held titular leadership to the country's domains. But once the Tokugawa clan ruled over a united and peaceful Japan, an urban merchant class began to flourish. The energy these men poured into their trade became exemplified in the word shokon, whose philosophy can be refined to the single maxim *o-kyaku wa kami*, or treat the customer like a god. It's a mixed bag. In a store, one is indeed treated like a god. But in regards to consumer rights, there are none.

Keiretsu: One word that unfailingly pops up when discussing Japanese business is *keiretsu*, which might be translated as corporate affiliation. Keiretsu ties have their origins in the days of the notorious *zaibatsu*, or family-owned industrial cliques, which held a near-pervasive influence over Japan's political and economic systems before World War II. The big zaibatsu names should be familiar: Mitsubishi, Mitsui, Sumitomo, Nomura and Yasuda. Except for Mitsubishi, which was controlled by the Iwasaki family, the others bear the names of their original founders.

Although the zaibatsu were forcibly broken up during the postwar occupation, the ties gradually returned, albeit in a less threatening form. Today, the keiretsu maintain their status as giant conglomerates, with each one having its own banks, manufacturers, construction companies, real estate firms and large trading houses. The Mitsubishi group, for example, includes the Mitsubishi

Bank, Mitsubishi Trading, Mitsubishi Mining & Cement, Mitsubishi Heavy Industries, Mitsubishi Chemical, *ad infinitum*. But some of the keiretsu affiliations are less transparent – also under the Mitsubishi corporate umbrella are such diverse firms as Kirin Brewery and Nikon.

Although it is obvious that this kind of financial integration gives a large business organization some amazing strengths, the Japanese insist that even within a given keiretsu, company management functions independently, and members on occasion even compete with other members. It's confusing – unless you're Japanese.

Preceding pages: a relatively calm day on the Tokyo Stock Exchange. Left, young businessman in Naha, Okinawa. Above, missing the good old days, Tokyo.

Seniority: The deferential treatment to one's elders clearly stems from Confucian traditions, which place importance on social order. Confucius' message was that society ran most smoothly by everyone knowing, and keeping, one's proper place.

On a day-to-day basis, it is middle management that carries the lion's share of the corporate burden. To be a *kacho*, or the chief of a section (*ka*) of a Japanese company, places a great demand on one's ability to perform assigned tasks, demonstrate organizational skills, and communicate well with both one's superiors and subordinates.

A kacho spends a great deal of time nurturing personal relationships, cultivating consensus and developing cooperative effort among the members of the group. And it is a very demanding role indeed, extending beyond normal working hours to socializing with co-workers.

Short-term performance is less of a concern to the Japanese manager than the Western manager. Top management – more secure in their own roles thanks to the security of the seniority system – is willing to let the kacho make a few mistakes, and hope that he will listen to advice and sort things out later.

The seniority system remains well-entrenched in Japanese corporate life, and there are few signs that this is changing. Impatient, strong-willed young men who feel they want to buck the system of promotion by "escalator" have always had the freedom to strike out on their own. Many have done so, and gone on to found their own business dynasties – Sony's Morita Akio, Honda Soichiro and Matsushita Konosuke. All three were, above all, men who personally embodied the spirit of shokon.

The office: Here are gray and small metal desks, jammed together in a long row; folders and documents piled in disarray; overflowing ashtrays; and a bank of lockers that often resemble a sports gym. Computers are rare, and usually laptops because of no free desk space.

The desks are arranged to reflect the order of the organizational chart. In the building's coziest corner is the *shacho*, the company president. He is, as often as not, the only member of the organization accorded the honor of a private room.

The president's office, however, is invariably equipped with sofa and chairs, a practical move that performs a dual purpose: making visitors feel welcome and for use as a conference room. (While the president is treated with deference, the practical side of Japanese efficiency dictates that precious space should not go unused.)

The desk layout in the center of the office

has rank-and-file members facing one another in a long, double row of desks. The head of each section flanks them, almost always on the side of the building nearest the window. And behind him is the division head, closer yet to the window.

A seat right near the window is not necessarily coveted, however. The term *madogiwa-zoku*, or window-gazing tribe, refers to middle managers who have reached the end of their corporate usefulness. They are promoted one notch above their level of competence, moved out of the mainstream to their window-side desks, with meaningless work.

Much has been written about *kaigi*, or group discussion. It is interesting to note that once the meeting starts, the demand not to be interrupted "under any circumstances" is seldom heard. Thus, the meeting room, invariably wreathed in clouds of cigarette smoke, is one of comings and goings, as participants are called out to check documents, sign papers or receive telephone calls.

The company man: Students, recruited for white-collar jobs while still in the university and hired right after graduation, have traditionally chosen to ride the corporate escalator, remaining with the same company – or group – throughout their entire career. But after the collapse of the superheated bubble economy in the early 1990s, Japanese corporations have been retrenching with vigor, much like their Western counterparts did in the 1980s. Unlike before, life-time employment is no longer a certainty. Nonetheless, the idea of a life-long company man is deeply institutionalized.

Group psychology is an important factor here, as each year, a new "class" arrives at the company on the first of April. In later years, being of the same class at a company instills a group bonding, much as an Ivy League university graduating class. There is no disputing the fact that the Japanese tend to place a high value on close loyalty to one's employer, and the commitment by the company in return is mutual.

But the notion of a monolithic lifetime employment system is a far cry from the reality. Like everywhere else, people in Japan quit their jobs every day. The reasons range from personal disputes with co-workers to refusing a transfer that would create economic hardship for the family.

Many small companies lead a marginal existence and have little to offer their workers in the way of fringe benefits. As soon as they get experience or find a better opportunity, these workers leave. The worker turn-

Left, pleasures of the salaryman. Above, morning male bonding, Fukuoka.

over rate among small manufacturers and service businesses is far higher than keiretsu-affiliated companies.

In the past, one reason why workers held onto their jobs come hell or high water was the strong perception that job-hoppers were losers. But much has happened to alter this situation. The large influx of foreign firms in banking and securities has introduced head-hunters and loyalty to the most yen and best package of benefits. Needless to say, job specialization in such areas as computers – where a huge shortage of competent staff current exists – means that talented individuals can find better paying employment elsewhere with ease.

Another change in the work place has been evolutionary. The younger generation, having grown up knowing nothing but peace and prosperity, is regarded by older Japanese as having less willingness to endure intolerable situations. The growing number of thirty-something dropouts at top companies, quitting within the first three months of service, has become a serious concern among personnel managers.

Payday and bonuses: At one time, it used to be that the assembled workers, upon hearing their name called by the division head, went forward to receive their bonus, in cash, one by one. Now, the bonus is automatically deposited into a bank account. Today, the expectation of twice-yearly bonuses (*bonasu*) to company employees is virtually automatic, to the point that workers and companies negotiate the exact details of the bonus. Since it is paid out to one and all, a bonus can hardly be viewed as a reward for outstanding performance on the job. Rather, these twice-a-year remunerations, on top of a worker's regular salary, can best be understood as the withholding of a portion of the worker's salary for payment every six months.

How much is in the bonus? The usual practice is to pay out the equivalent of two to four months of an employee's base pay. The amount might be boosted depending on business conditions, which means the bonus does incorporate elements of profit-sharing. On the other hand, the size of bonuses is announced publicly; the amounts paid out to workers in a given industry (such as automotive or electronics) tend to adhere closely to within certain norms, whether a particular company is enjoying high profits or not.

The bonus system has a major impact on household finances in savings, credit and spending. Japanese workers have traditionally maintained a high savings rate compared to workers in Western countries, and much of their bonuses go into savings accounts, interest-bearing life insurance policies, or perhaps securities.

When Japanese take out loans to purchase a house or car, the financing plan invariably incorporates two extra installments at the time of bonus. Thus, in terms of consume -credit spending, the twice-a-year bonus i counted on to relieve what would otherwise be much heavier monthly payments. And not to receive a bonus, therefore, could spell possible disaster for the household budget.

The advantage of the Japanese system is that, when the wife works out the family budget (as she invariably does), she adjusts household expenditures according to the monthly wage. The bonus, when it comes, is usually apportioned into savings and outlays for consumer durables. For younger salaried workers, especially women, bonuses are a windfall that can be spent on flashy and expensive overseas travel. Men, on the other hand, refuse to take vacations.

Left, office decor. Right, Japanese women must define their own professional futures.

千社札広告札等の
浅草寺
みくじ 五十円

お札 お守

止まれ
40
40

PLACES

Spread like cultured pearls in the western Pacific, the islands of the Japanese archipelago lie off the coast of China, Russia and Korea. There are nearly 4,000 of these islands, strung out for over 2,800 kilometers (1,700 mi) – from the remote mountains of the north, which look out across small stretches of water to Russian islands, to the southwest in Okinawa and nearly within sight of Taiwan. Covering a total of 380,000 square kilometers (147,000 sq. mi), Japan's land area is the size of Montana, and a little larger than Italy, but twice as populous with more than 120 million residents – half the population of the entire United States.

The main islands of Hokkaido, Honshu, Shikoku and Kyushu are mountainous, cut through with narrow valleys. Fuji-san, the snow-capped 3,776-meter-high (12,388-ft) landmark, remains dormant and within sight of downtown Tokyo on a clear winter day. Overall, there are some 60 mountains on the island considered to be active.

The transportation system of Japan is known throughout the world, both for its efficiency and punctuality and for its rush-hour congestion within the train. The trains will take travelers nearly anywhere on the four main islands, even to the smallest villages and with a punctuality by which to set chronometers.

The nation's capital, Tokyo, is on the main island of Honshu, which has the country's 10 largest cities, including the sprawling megalopolis of Tokyo-Kawasaki-Yokohama. The next largest city, Fukuoka, is far to the south on Kyushu.

It is expensive to travel within Japan. Trains aren't cheap and accommodation is rather expensive. Indeed, it is cheaper for Japanese to take vacations in Hawaii or Sydney instead of within their own country. Yet they do travel within Japan, and they have made an art of travel that is often a bit too hierarchical and dogmatic for Westerners. Nevertheless, regardless of where one ends up, there are exquisite and delightful pleasures for the traveler, whether the *ekiben* box lunches at train stations or the precision with which a traditional *ryokan* pampers guests.

Notes: Wherever possible, we use Japanese terms for geographical identifications. These appear as suffixes to the proper name. For example, Mount Fuji is referred to as Fuji-san. Mountains may also appear with other suffixes, including *-zan*, *-yama*, and for some active volcanoes, *-dake*. Islands are either *-shima* or *-jima*, lakes are *-ko*, and rivers are *-gawa*.

Shrines are Shinto, and proper shrine names usually end in *-jinja*, *-jingu*, or *-gu*. Temples are Buddhist, with names usually ending in *-tera*, *-dera*, or *-ji*.

Preceding pages: agriculture in northern Hokkaido; Osaka skyline; Asakusa Kannon, in Tokyo; shinkansen and Fuji-san. Left, autumn within a shrine, Kyoto.

Japan
250 km / 155 miles
RUSSIA
CHINA
NORTH KOREA
SOUTH KOREA
JAPAN
SEA OF OKHOTSK
SEA OF JAPAN
EAST CHINA SEA
PACIFIC OCEAN
SAKHALIN
Juzno-Sahalinsk
Aniva Bay
REBUN I.
RISHIRI I.
Wakkanai
KUNASHIRI I.
Abashiri
Asahikawa
HOKKAIDO
Nemuro
Kushiro
SAPPORO
Muroran
Uchiura Bay
OKUSHIRI I.
Hakodate
O I.
Mutsu
Aomori
Hachinohe
Akita
AWA I.
SENDAI
SADO I.
NIIGATA
Sanjo
Iwaki
HONSHU
Utsunomiya
Kashima Bay
Kanazawa
Wakasa Bay
TOKYO
CHIBA
Fuji-san
3776 m
NAGOYA
Tateyama
O ISLAND
NII ISLAND
KOZU ISLAND
MIYAKE ISLAND
MIKURA ISLAND
HACHIJO ISLAND
KYOTO
OSAKA
Matsue
HIROSHIMA
DOGO I.
DOZEN I.
ULLUNG-DO
(S. KOREA)
Vladivostok
Ch'ongjin
Kimch'aek
SEOUL
Pusan
KAMINO I.
SHIMONO I.
Kitakyushu
IKI I.
Matsuyama
Kochi
SHIKOKU
FUKUOKA
CHEJU-DO
NAKADORI I.
FUKUE I.
Nagasaki
KYUSHU
KAMI-KOSHIKI I.
SHIMO-KOSHIKI I.
Miyazaki
KAGOSHIMA
TANEGA I.
YAKU I.
NAKANO I.
SUWANOSE I.
AMAMI-O I.
TOKUNO I.
OKINO-ERABU I.
IHEYA I.
YORON I.
OKINAWA I.
Naha
N

Hokkaido
100 km / 62 miles
RUSSIA
JAPAN
SEA OF OKHOTSK
KUNASHIRI ISLAND
Shiretoko P.
KURIL ISLANDS
SHIIBOTSU I.
Rausu
Nemuro
Wakkanai
REBUN ISLAND
RISHIRI ISLAND
SEA OF JAPAN
Mombetsu
Abashiri
Bihoro
Kitami
Kussharo-ko
Akan-ko
Nayoro
Shibetsu
YAGISHIRI ISLAND
TEURI ISLAND
Rumoi
Asahikawa
HOKKAIDO
Kushiro
Takikawa
Furano
Obihiro
Ishikari Bay
Iwamizawa
Otaru
Eniwa
SAPPORO
Tomakomai
Toya-ko
Date
Noboribetsu
Uchiura Bay
Hakodate
Kamiiso
OKUSHIRI ISLAND
PACIFIC OCEAN
Tsugaru Strait
Mutsu
N

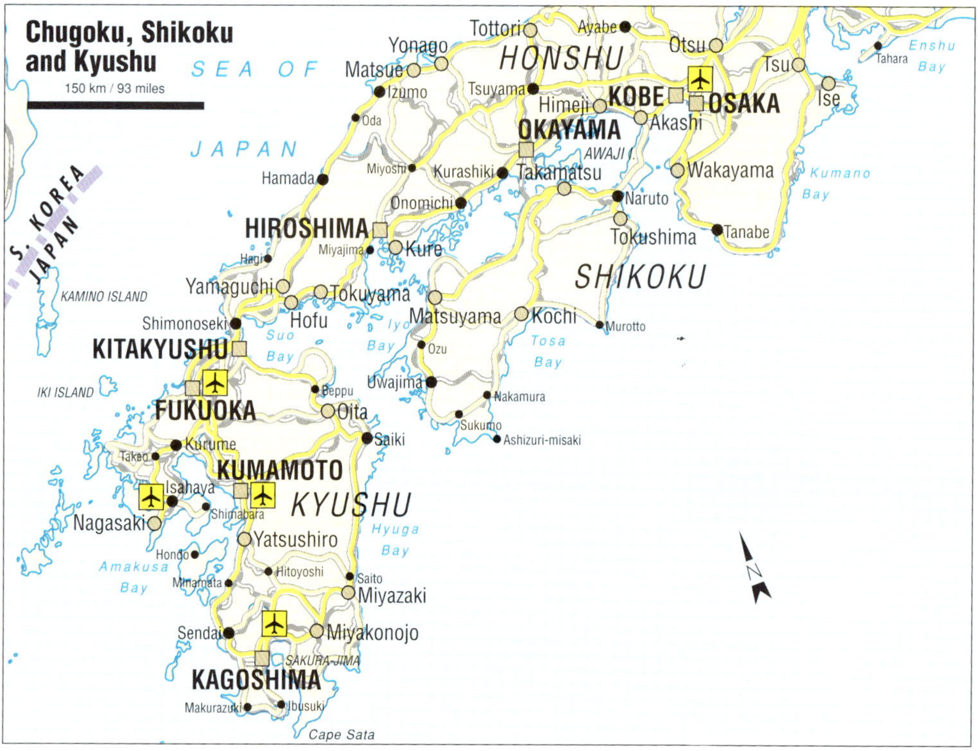
Chugoku, Shikoku and Kyushu
150 km / 93 miles
SEA OF JAPAN
Tottori
Ayabe
Yonago
HONSHU
Otsu
Tahara
Enshu Bay
Matsue
Tsu
Izumo
Tsuyama
Himeji
KOBE
OSAKA
Ise
Oda
Akashi
OKAYAMA
AWAJI I.
Miyoshi
Kurashiki
Takamatsu
Wakayama
Kumano Bay
Hamada
Onomichi
Naruto
S. KOREA
JAPAN
HIROSHIMA
Tokushima
Tanabe
Miyajima
Kure
Hagi
SHIKOKU
KAMINO ISLAND
Yamaguchi
Tokuyama
Hofu
Shimonoseki
Matsuyama
Kochi
Murotto
Suo Bay
Iyo Bay
Tosa Bay
KITAKYUSHU
Ozu
IKI ISLAND
Beppu
Uwajima
Nakamura
FUKUOKA
Oita
Sukumo
Ashizuri-misaki
Kurume
Saiki
Takeo
KUMAMOTO
Isahaya
KYUSHU
Shimabara
Nagasaki
Hyuga Bay
Yatsushiro
Hondo
Amakusa Bay
Hitoyoshi
Minamata
Saito
Miyazaki
Sendai
Miyakonojo
SAKURA-JIMA
KAGOSHIMA
Makurazuki
Ibusuki
Cape Sata
N

Honshu
100 km / 62 miles
HOKKAIDO
Mutsu
Mutsu Bay
Aomori
Misawa
Hachinohe
Hirosaki
Ninohe
Odate
Noshiro
Iwate 2047 m
Miyako
Morioka
Shiwa
SANRIKU COAST
Akita
Omagari
Kitakami
Yokote
Honjo
Mizusawa
Yuzawa
Ichinoseki
Sakata
Shinjo
Furukawa
Ishinomaki
Tsuruoka
Matsushima
Tendo
SENDAI
SEA OF JAPAN
AWA ISLAND
Shiroishi
Murakami
Nanyo
Yonezawa
Nakajo
Fukushima
SADO ISLAND
Sado Strait
NIIGATA
Koriyama
Sanjo
Aizu-Wakamatsu
Sukagawa
Iwaki
Nagaoka
Ojiya
Kuroiso
Muikamachi
Nikko
Joetsu
Utsunomiya
Wajima
Toyama Bay
Mito
NOTO
Kashima Bay
Maebashi
Ishioka
Nanao
Oyama
Kashima
Kurobe Uozu
Nagano
Hakui
Fujioka
Choshi
Narita
Toyama
Komoro
Kasukabe
Kanazawa
Matsumoto
TOKYO
CHIBA
Matto
Shiojiri
Okaya
Komatsu
YOKOHAMA
Takayama
Kisarazu
Kaga
Maruoka
HONSHU
Kamakura
Fukui
Miura
Fuji-san 3776 m
Iida
Tateyama
Sagami Bay
Nakatsugawa
Numazu
Tsuruga
Wakasa Bay
Gifu
Izu Peninsula
O ISLAND
SHIZUOKA
Nagahama
NAGOYA
Suruga Bay
TO ISLAND
Miyazu
Biwa-ko
NII ISLAND
Fukuchiyama
SHIKINE ISLAND
Tottori
Moriyama
HAMAMATSU
KOZU ISLAND
KYOTO
Suzuka
Tahara
Tsu
Yamasaki
Kasai
Toba
PACIFIC OCEAN
Kobe
Nara
Himeji
Ise
OSAKA
Akashi

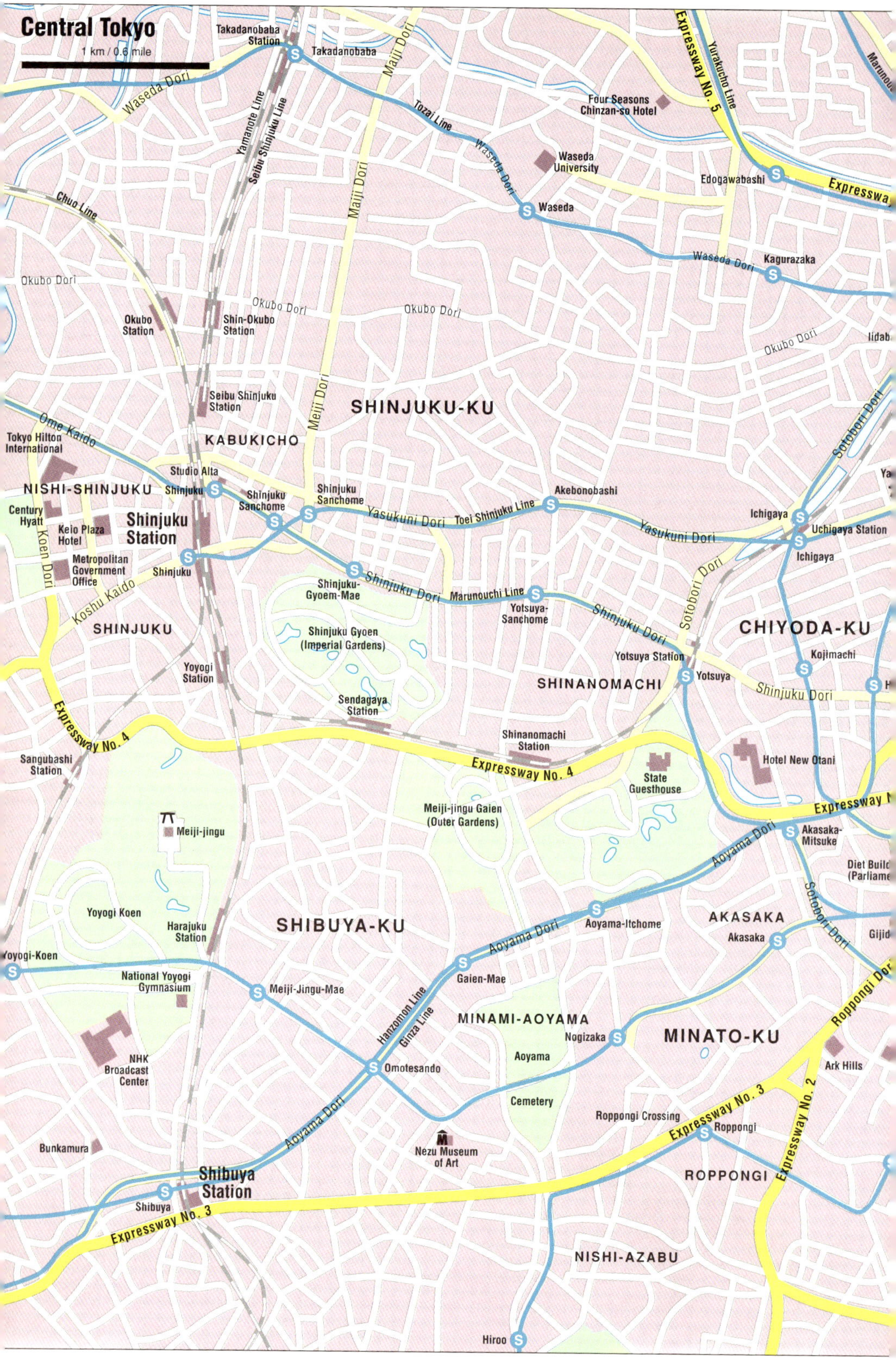

Central Tokyo
1 km / 0.6 mile
Takadanobaba Station
Takadanobaba
Waseda Dori
Maiji Dori
Yamanote Line
Seibu Shinjuku Line
Tozai Line
Four Seasons Chinzan-so Hotel
Expressway No. 5
Yurakucho Line
Waseda University
Edogawabashi
Waseda
Chuo Line
Maiji Dori
Kagurazaka
Okubo Dori
Okubo Station
Shin-Okubo Station
Iidab
Seibu Shinjuku Station
SHINJUKU-KU
Meiji Dori
Ome Kaido
Tokyo Hilton International
KABUKICHO
Sotobori Dori
Studio Alta
NISHI-SHINJUKU
Shinjuku
Shinjuku Sanchome
Akebonobashi
Century Hyatt
Keio Plaza Hotel
Shinjuku Station
Yasukuni Dori
Toei Shinjuku Line
Ichigaya
Uchigaya Station
Koen Dori
Metropolitan Government Office
Shinjuku-Gyoem-Mae
Shinjuku Dori
Marunouchi Line
Yotsuya-Sanchome
Koshu Kaido
SHINJUKU
Shinjuku Gyoen (Imperial Gardens)
CHIYODA-KU
Kojimachi
Yoyogi Station
Yotsuya Station
Yotsuya
SHINANOMACHI
Sendagaya Station
Expressway No. 4
Shinanomachi Station
Hotel New Otani
Sangubashi Station
State Guesthouse
Meiji-jingu
Meiji-jingu Gaien (Outer Gardens)
Akasaka-Mitsuke
Aoyama Dori
Diet Build (Parliame
Yoyogi Koen
Harajuku Station
SHIBUYA-KU
Aoyama-Itchome
AKASAKA
Akasaka
Yoyogi-Koen
National Yoyogi Gymnasium
Meiji-Jingu-Mae
Gaien-Mae
Hanzomon Line
Ginza Line
MINAMI-AOYAMA
Nogizaka
MINATO-KU
Roppongi Dori
NHK Broadcast Center
Omotesando
Aoyama Cemetery
Ark Hills
Roppongi Crossing
Expressway No. 3
Roppongi
Expressway No. 2
Bunkamura
Nezu Museum of Art
Shibuya Station
Shibuya
ROPPONGI
NISHI-AZABU
Hiroo

Tokyo National Museum
Nezu
Ueno Koen
Shinobazuno-ike
Ueno Station
Expressway No. 1
Hibiya Line
Kiyosubashi Dori
Kappabashi Dori
Kokusai Dori
Kototoi Dori
Asakusa Kannon
Hakusan Dori
Toei Mita Line
Hongo Dori
Chiyoda Line
Tokyo University
Keisei Ueno Station
Inarichio
ASAKUSA
Kasuga
Shitamachi Museum
Ueno
Asakusa Dori
Asakusa
Tawaramachi
Chuo Dori
Korakuen
Kasuga Dori
Yushima
Koishikawa-Korakuen
Hongo-Sanchome
Ueno-Hirokoji
Naka-Okachimachi
Kasuga Dori
Kappabashi Dori
Asakusa
Edo Dori
Tokyo Dome
Sotobori Dori
UENO
Suehirocho
OKACHIMACHI
Kokusai Dori
Toei Asakusa Line
Expressway No. 6
Suidobashi
Kuramaebashi Dori
Showa Dori
Iidabashi
Suidobashi Station
Hongo Dori
Kuramaebashi Dori
Kuramae
Ochanomizu
Chuo Dori
Kiyosbashi Dori
Sotobori Dori
Ochanomizu Station
Akihabara Station
Edo Dori
Shin-Ochanomizu
Kudanshita
Jimbocho
Akihabara
Asakusabashi
Fukagawa Edo Tokyo Museum
Kokugikan (Sumo)
Ogawamachi
Awajiche
Iwamotocho
Yasukuni Dori
Ryogoku Station
Ryogoku Bashi
Kinomaru Koen
Kanda
Hibiya Dori
Bakuro
SUMIDA-KU
Expressway No. 5
Kanda Station
Expressway No. 1
KANDA
Higaashi-Nihonbashi
Expressway No. 7
Takebashi
Sotobori Dori
Kodenmacho
Kokyo Higashi Gyoen
Communications Museum
Edo Dori
Otemachi
Bank of Japan
Hamacho
Morishita
Shin Ohashi Bashi
Uchibori Dori
OTEMACHI
Mitsukoshimae
Currency Museum
Ningyocho
Otemachi
Mitsukoshimae
NIHOMBASHI
Shin Ohashi Dori
Palace Hotel
KOKYO (Imperial Palace)
Tokyo Station
Nihombashi
Nihom-bashi (Bridge)
Suitengumae
Tokyo
Sotobori Dori
YAESU
Nihombashi
Royal Park Hotel
Nijubashi-Mae
Eitai Dori
TCAT (Tokyo City Air Terminal)
Nijo-bashi
MARUNOUCHI
Kayabacho
Kokyo Gaien
Hibiya Dori
Chuo Dori
Showa Dori
Kiyosumi Garden
Shin Ohashi Dori
Tozai Line
KOTO-KU
Yurakucho
Harumi Dori
Kyobashi
Expressway No. 1
Sakurada Dori
Yurakucho
Uchibori Dori
Takaracho
Eitai Bashi
Hibiya
Expressway No. 9
Hibiya Koen
Yurakucho Station
Hotel Seiyo Ginza
Hatchobori
Kasumigaseki
Tozai Line
Ginza
Ginza-Itchome
CHUO-KU
GINZA
Sony Building
Ginza
Imperial Hotel
Monzen-Nakacho
Toranomon
Ginza 4-chome
Eitai Dori
Sotobori Dori
Uchisaiwaicho
Higashi-Ginza
Shintomicho
Yurakucho Line
TSUKUDA
Chuo Dori
Harumi Dori
Dori
Kiyosumi Dori
Shimbashi
Showa Dori
Tsukuda Ohashi
Tsukiji
Nishi Hongan-ji
Shimbashi
Shin Ohashi
Hibiya Dori
SHIMBASHI
Expressway No. 1
Tsukishima
TSUKIJI
TSUKISHIMA
Onarimon
Kachidoki Bashi
Kiyosumi Dori
Hama Rikyu Gaien
Dori
Hibiya Dori
Sumida-gawa
Harumi Dori
Daimon
Shiba Rikyu Garen
Kiyosumi Dori
Shiba-Koen
Chuo
Toyosu

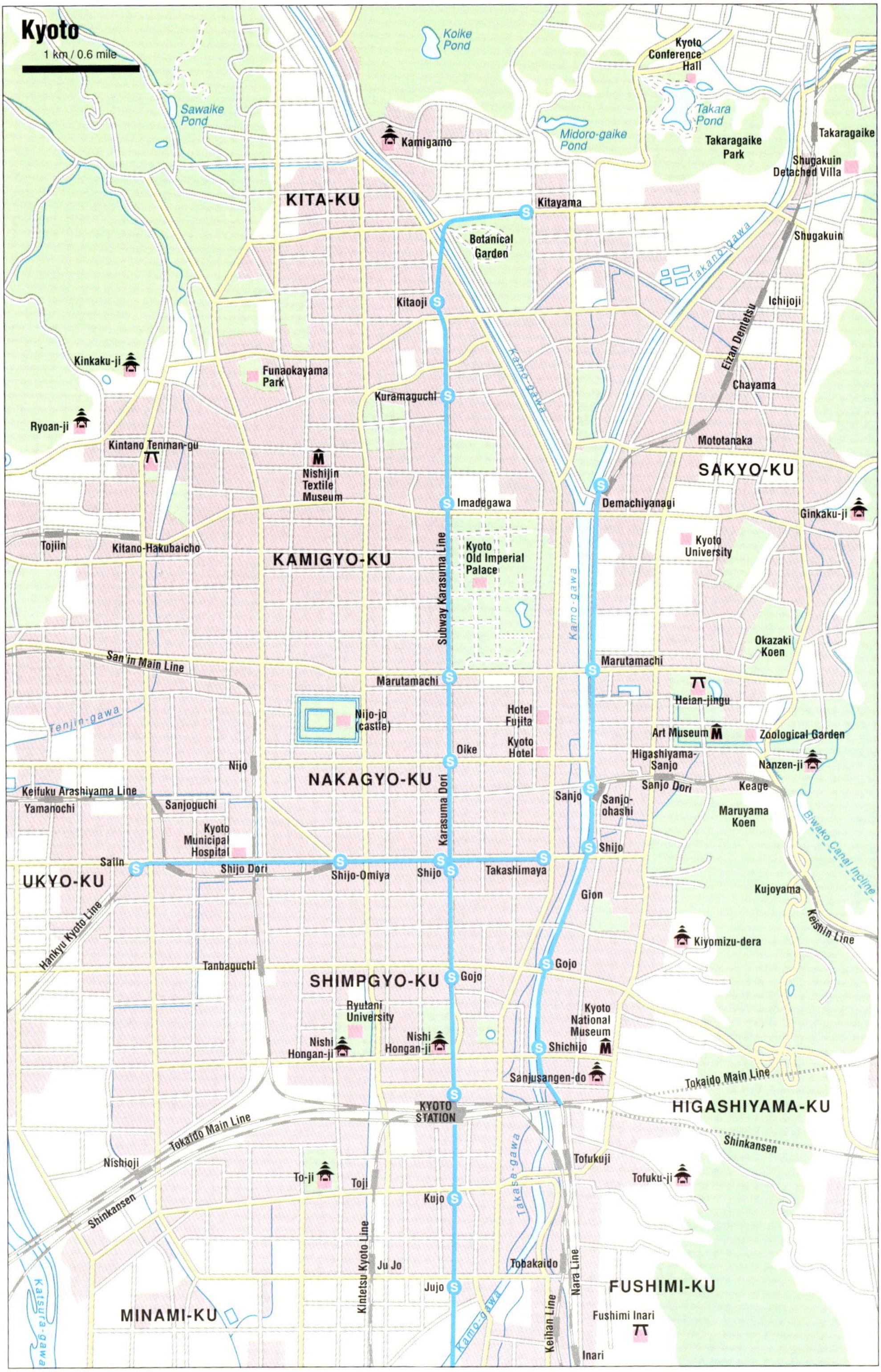
Kyoto
1 km / 0.6 mile
Koike Pond
Kyoto Conference Hall
Sawaike Pond
Takara Pond
Kamigamo
Midoro-gaike Pond
Takaragaike Park
Takaragaike
Shugakuin Detached Villa
KITA-KU
Kitayama
Botanical Garden
Shugakuin
Takano-gawa
Kitaoji
Ichijoji
Eizan Dentetsu
Kinkaku-ji
Funaokayama Park
Kamo-gawa
Chayama
Kuramaguchi
Ryoan-ji
Kintano Tenman-gu
Mototanaka
Nishijin Textile Museum
SAKYO-KU
Imadegawa
Demachiyanagi
Ginkaku-ji
Tojiin
Kitano-Hakubaicho
KAMIGYO-KU
Kyoto Old Imperial Palace
Kyoto University
Subway Karasuma Line
Kamo-gawa
Okazaki Koen
San'in Main Line
Marutamachi
Marutamachi
Heian-jingu
Tenjin-gawa
Nijo-jo (castle)
Hotel Fujita
Art Museum
Zoological Garden
Kyoto Hotel
Oike
Higashiyama-Sanjo
Nanzen-ji
Nijo
NAKAGYO-KU
Keifuku Arashiyama Line
Sanjo Dori
Keage
Karasuma Dori
Sanjo
Yamanochi
Sanjoguchi
Sanjo-ohashi
Maruyama Koen
Kyoto Municipal Hospital
Biwako Canal Incline
Shijo
Saiin
Shijo Dori
Takashimaya
UKYO-KU
Shijo-Omiya
Shijo
Kujoyama
Gion
Hankyu Kyoto Line
Keishin Line
Kiyomizu-dera
Tanbaguchi
Gojo
SHIMPGYO-KU
Gojo
Ryukoku University
Kyoto National Museum
Nishi Hongan-ji
Nishi Hongan-ji
Shichijo
Sanjusangen-do
Tokaido Main Line
KYOTO STATION
HIGASHIYAMA-KU
Tokaido Main Line
Shinkansen
Nishioji
Tofukuji
To-ji
Toji
Tofuku-ji
Takase-gawa
Kujo
Shinkansen
Kintetsu Kyoto Line
Ju Jo
Tobakaido
Nara Line
Katsura-gawa
Jujo
FUSHIMI-KU
Kamo-gawa
MINAMI-KU
Fushimi Inari
Keihan Line
Inari

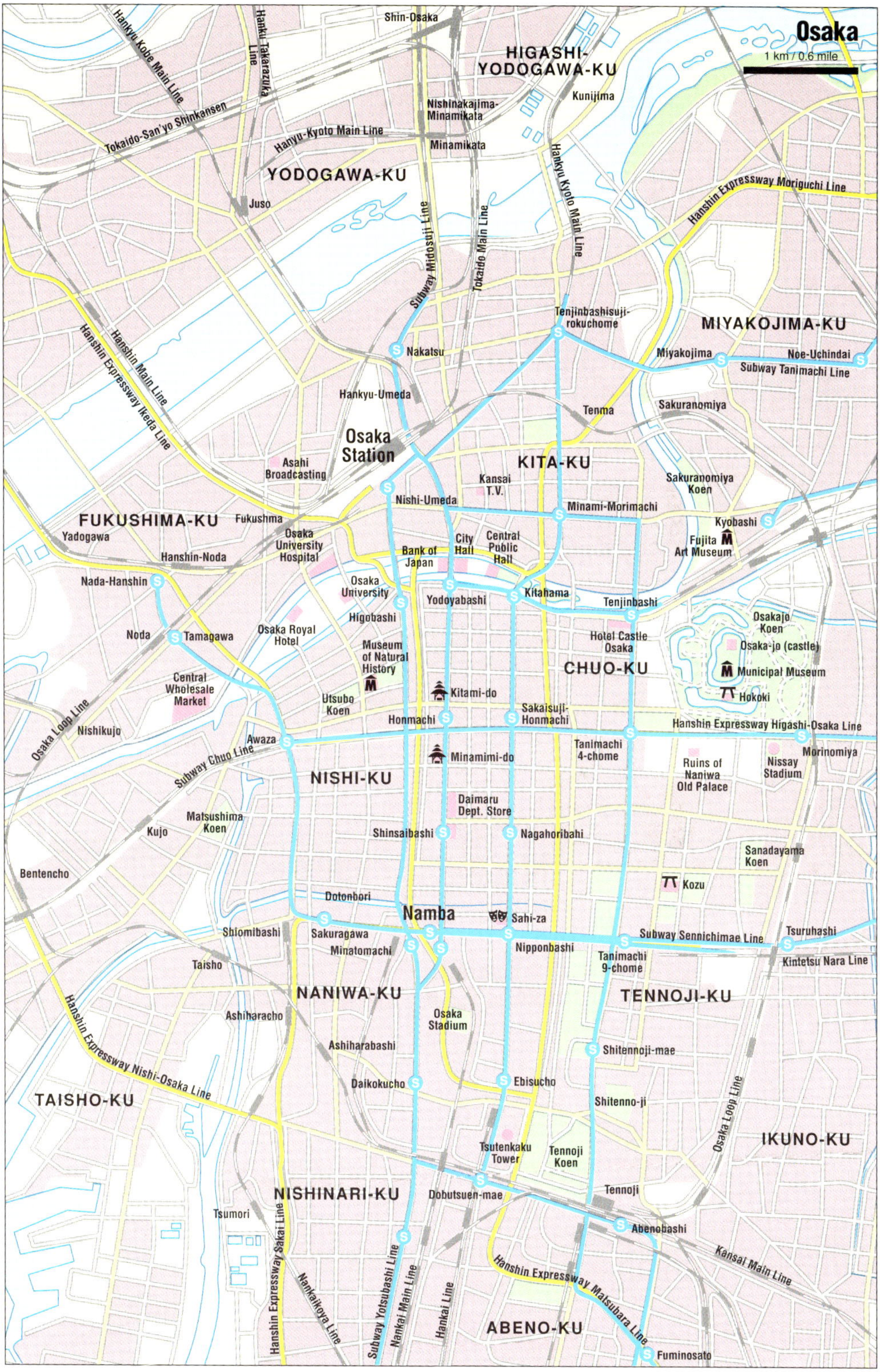
Osaka
1 km / 0.6 mile
HIGASHI-YODOGAWA-KU
YODOGAWA-KU
MIYAKOJIMA-KU
KITA-KU
FUKUSHIMA-KU
CHUO-KU
NISHI-KU
NANIWA-KU
TENNOJI-KU
TAISHO-KU
IKUNO-KU
NISHINARI-KU
ABENO-KU
Osaka Station
Namba
Shin-Osaka
Kunijima
Juso
Nakatsu
Hankyu-Umeda
Nishi-Umeda
Tenjinbashisuji-rokuchome
Miyakojima
Noe-Uchindai
Tenma
Sakuranomiya
Sakuranomiya Koen
Minami-Morimachi
Kyobashi
Fujita Art Museum
Yodoyabashi
Kitahama
Tenjinbashi
Osakajo Koen
Osaka-jo (castle)
Municipal Museum
Hokoki
Hotel Castle Osaka
Kitami-do
Minamimi-do
Honmachi
Sakaisuji-Honmachi
Tanimachi 4-chome
Morinomiya
Nissay Stadium
Ruins of Naniwa Old Palace
Daimaru Dept. Store
Shinsaibashi
Nagahoribahi
Sanadayama Koen
Kozu
Dotonbori
Sahi-za
Nipponbashi
Tanimachi 9-chome
Tsuruhashi
Sakuragawa
Minatomachi
Shiomibashi
Taisho
Ashiharacho
Ashiharabashi
Osaka Stadium
Daikokucho
Ebisucho
Shitennoji-mae
Shitenno-ji
Tsutenkaku Tower
Tennoji Koen
Tennoji
Dobutsuen-mae
Abenobashi
Tsumori
Fuminosato
Yadogawa
Fukushma
Hanshin-Noda
Nada-Hanshin
Noda
Tamagawa
Central Wholesale Market
Nishikujo
Awaza
Kujo
Matsushima Koen
Bentencho
Asahi Broadcasting
Osaka University Hospital
Osaka University
Higobashi
Osaka Royal Hotel
Museum of Natural History
Utsubo Koen
Bank of Japan
City Hall
Central Public Hall
Kansai T.V.
Nishinakajima-Minamikata
Minamikata
Hankyu Kobe Main Line
Hanku Takarazuka Line
Tokaido-San'yo Shinkansen
Hanyu-Kyoto Main Line
Subway Midostuji Line
Tokaido Main Line
Hankyu Kyoto Main Line
Hanshin Expressway Moriguchi Line
Subway Tanimachi Line
Hanshin Main Line
Hanshin Expressway Ikeda Line
Osaka Loop Line
Subway Chuo Line
Hanshin Expressway Higashi-Osaka Line
Subway Sennichimae Line
Kintetsu Nara Line
Hanshin Expressway Nishi-Osaka Line
Kansai Main Line
Hanshin Expressway Matsubara Line
Hanshin Expressway Sakai Line
Nankaikoya Line
Subway Yotsubashi Line
Nankai Main Line
Hankai Line

THE NORTHLANDS

"I might as well be going to the ends of the earth."

That's how Basho, Japan's great seventeenth-century *haiku* poet, put it on the eve of his departure into the north, in 1689. Back then, when Basho decided to prowl the back country, the roads were narrow and minimal, or nonexistent. Today, Sendai, Tohoku's predominant city and north from Tokyo along the Pacific coast, is only two hours from Tokyo via *shinkansen*. Moreover, it is often mentioned as a new site for Japan's capital, should it be decided that Tokyo is just too big and too expensive and too congested.

Even the large island of Hokkaido, forcibly settled during the Meiji Restoration in the late nineteenth century, is but nine hours from Tokyo by train, or two hours by plane. (In fact, the Tokyo–Sapporo air route is the world's busiest.)

The north has always been perceived as remote and strange, existing outside the normal sphere of Japanese life. Even imagining that such a place as Hokkaido exists, for example, is difficult, as it is so different from the rest of Japan. But perhaps this is not so much a matter of distance as of psychology – there is a seemingly-limitless amount of open space and nature untouched by people, of which both impressions are quite false.

Undoubtedly, the northern mountains have a lot of to do with perceptions of remoteness. There are mountains everywhere in Japan, but those in the north tend to be bigger, more imposing and, from late autumn to mid-spring, not especially accommodating.

Then, too, the people of the north bear some responsibility. Tohoku was originally settled by itinerant warlords and soldiers, who constructed castle fortresses to keep out potentially unfriendly neighbors, mostly from the south. These castle towns developed into insular communities with their own unique lifestyle, crafts, cottage industries and language. The famous *Tohoku-ben*, still spoken by many people here, is actually a series of subdialects with numerous variations. For people from elsewhere in Japan, it is a foreign language requiring, literally, a dictionary.

It is perhaps no longer an easy matter to find ourselves – as Basho was able to do – alone in some idyllic spot.

Yet it is possible, and for the adventurous at heart, for a little while anyway, losing oneself in the mysterious back-country of the north is bliss.

Preceding pages: Hokkaido's first snowfall against autumn's last colors. Left, waterfall at Tenninkyo, Hokkaido.

HOKKAIDO

"Boys, be ambitious!" These were the parting words of Dr. William S. Clark, first president of Hokkaido University, in 1876. This injunction still applies to the traveler venturing to Japan's northern island, where the temples and castles of the south give way to mountains, forests and farms. Hokkaido has only been part of the Japanese nation since it was settled in the nineteenth century, as an example of the Meiji Restoration development.

The roots of Hokkaido's people are in farming, fishing, hunting and shark trading. The visitor will find the residents here more direct and friendlier than their southern counterparts, and due to the Meiji-era Westernization, quite sophisticated. Hokkaido is also home to Japan's last indigenous people, the Ainu, of Caucasian ancestry and with no genetic connection to today's Japanese. With a population of only 20,000, the Ainu are today a phantom culture with a forgotten language, looked upon by Japanese as a sightseeing curiosity and whose main occupation – besides fishing and farming – is dressing up and posing for photographs at tourist sites. A brutal statement, but unfortunately true.

Hokkaido offers all the standard overdeveloped and tacky tourist traps and loudspeaker-enhanced "scenic" places so common throughout Japan. But add Dr. Clark's dose of ambition, and Hokkaido can be high adventure in the rustic northland. Its climate parallels Quebec and Finland. In winter, icebergs scrape its shores. In summer, hills and fields are riotous with wildflowers and tranquil with dairy cows. (In fact, because of American agricultural experts brought to Hokkaido in the first decades of this century, the farms look nearly identical to those in Iowa or Vermont. Likewise, Hokkaido's urban streets have a broad American look, spacious by Japanese standards.)

Transportation around the island by bus or train is spotty. Most Japanese tourists visit via the tour-bus route.

Hakodate: To the south of Sapporo – and just across the Tsugaru Strait from Aomori and Honshu's northern tip – is Hakodate. Wait until dark and take the rope-way up the nearby mountain. From there, gape at one the region's most beautiful night views. Somewhere there lies Goryokaku, a star-shaped bastion where loyalists of the Tokugawa shogunate lost the last battle against the Meiji imperial army, in 1869.

Hakodate is Hokkaido's historic city, with Japanese settlers as early as the thirteenth century, Russian visitors around 1750, and a foreign enclave, at Motomachi, in 1854. Don't miss the fish market at dawn, when the squid fleet and the crab trappers return to port. Whereas Sapporo is a night city, Hakodate is, at heart, a morning city.

Use the streetcar system to explore. For dinner, have Japan's freshest seafood. *Ika somen* – thinly-sliced, noodle-like strips of raw squid – is the city's specialty. Crab and salmon are also abundant and delicious. A unique salmon stew (*shake nabe*) called *sanpei-jiru* is

Left, sunrise, Kussharo-ko. Right, Sapporo.

truly remarkable. In early August, join in the historical pageant that is part of Hakodate's annual Port Festival.

West of the city are a Trappist convent, famous for its cookies, and **Yunokawa** onsen, comfortable and rural. From Hakodate, buses and trains go south to **Matsumae**, Hokkaido's only castle town.

Shikotsu-Toya: Between Hakodate and Sapporo, near Sapporo's Chitose Airport, the Shikotsu-Toya area is Hokkaido's most accessible national park. Closest to Sapporo is **Shikotsu-ko**, a huge caldera lake. **Shikotsu Kohan**, a fishing village, provides lodgings and tour boats. As in all of Hokkaido's national parks, youth hostels are landmarks where anyone – young or old – can get help in renting a bike, locating a trail, getting directions. There are numerous youth hostels and camping sites in the area.

Toya-ko, south of Shikotsu, is round and a popular lake. Tour boats visit its four islands, where the view of **Yotei-zan** at 1,890 meters (6,200 ft) due north is best. Climbers can attack Yotei, or three other peaks: Eniwa, Fuppushi and Tarumae. The latter, on the south shore of Shikotsu-ko and rising 1,040 meters (3,400 ft), is a volcano that still steams and fumes, and is probably the best climb. The route to Tarumae from Shikotsu-ko passes through the eerie and deep beauty of **Koke no Domon** (Moss Gorge).

Toya-ko resort is boisterous in summer, with fireworks during the August festival season. There are many *ryokan*, whose hot-spring baths have lake views. The "must" here is **Showa Shinzan**, a small volcano just south that emerged from the earth in 1944. **Usu-zan**, Showa Shinzan's papa, stands nearby. (The view is excellent from the cable car up to the summit of Usu-zan.) It blew up in 1977, wreaking havoc on the resort. See it on film in the Volcanic Museum.

The best route from Toya-ko east to the tourist mecca of **Noboribetsu** is by bus through gorgeous Orofure Pass. Noboribetsu's weirdest sight is at the Dai-Ichi Takimoto-kan Hotel, where 40

Dairy farm, central Hokkaido.

indoor hot-spring baths can hold 1,000 bathers simultaneously. There is nothing else like it.

Here, tour the volcanic **Jigokudani** (Hell Gorge) and go up to the summit of Shihorei. There are two festivals in August at Noboribetsu, recommended only if you love crowds. For a gourmet treat, in season, ask for *kegani koramushi*, or small freshwater crabs.

Sapporo: In southwest Hokkaido, Sapporo is the island's capital and its largest city with 1.7 million people. The city's downtown revolves around Japan's liveliest, most charming boulevard, **Odori Koen** (Odori Park), running east and west through downtown.

In the first week of February, this broad avenue of parks and fountains contains Sapporo's world-famous Snow Festival. (Book accommodation months in advance.) This festival includes snow statues and ice sculptures made by corporate, professional and amateur teams. In summer, beer gardens spring up on the lawn, and people linger outdoors long into the night. After visiting Sapporo's other tourist musts, take a breath. Return to Odori Koen.

A tour of Sapporo is easy – it is a new city, laid out in a grid, so uncommon amongst Japan's villages, towns and cities. Just northwest of Sapporo Station, itself a few blocks north of Odori Koen, is Hokkaido University, and the Sapporo Brewery is due east. Otherwise, go south from Sapporo Station – to the botanic garden (detour west), the **Tokeidai** (clock tower, detour east), and then Odori Koen.

Farther south is **Tanuki-Koji**, a vibrant strip of restaurants and shops. The market of Nijo serves every dining and household need for locals, and purveys souvenirs in abundance for eager first-time visitors. Finally, south of Odori Koen is **Susukino**, Sapporo's night life and strip-joint district, where Ramen Yokocho is a circus of Sapporo-style "fast-food."

Other Sapporo sites include the Snow Dairy and Asahi Brewery, two restored historical sites – the Kotani Tondenkei Oku (Settlers House) and Hokkaido

Sapporo's snow festival.

Settlers Village – the Sapporo Art Forest, and Sheep Hill Tower. But for many, Sapporo is the staging point for trips beyond, including such nearby attractions as the onsen at Jozankei and Koganeyu, and the ski areas.

Otaru-Shakotan: West of Sapporo is **Otaru**, once a fishing and trading center, and where the buildings are an eclectic blend of Western and nineteenth-century Japanese influence.

Otaru is gateway to the **Shakotan Hanto**, a peninsular microcosm of Hokkaido, with its rugged coastlines, abundant campsites, ski areas, boating and fishing in the Sea of Japan, and glorious sunsets from **Shakotan-misaki** and **Kamui-misaki**. This area's proximity to Sapporo makes sightseeing hectic at times, especially on holidays and weekends. But along the side roads and in quiet villages, there is always an inn with a room, if not a view.

Akan National Park: To the east along the southern coast of Hokkaido is the port city of **Kushiro**, where ultramodern architecture contrasts with one of Japan's most congenial dockside scenes. Kushiro itself is noted mostly for the migrating cranes that put on mating displays in the fields outside the city.

In the east, **Nemuro Hanto** and the marshlands that stretch north from Kushiro along the eastern coastline are a recluse's paradise. None of these forays are on the standard tourist itinerary, which means the discoveries you make, the people you meet, will be unique.

North of Kushiro are the virgin forests, volcanoes, and lakes that draw tens of thousands of visitors every year to Akan National Park, whose best staging point is Kushiro.

Akan-ko is famous with the Japanese for *marimo*, odd and green algae balls – also known as "God's fairies" – that will either delight, or bore, you. Tour buses dominate this park, which makes a car or a bicycle a plus.

Akan Kohan, the main town, has ten ryokan, and the park has six youth hostels, and campsites aplenty. Two volcanoes, **Oakan-dake** and **Meakan-dake**, tempt climbers, with Meakan the pre-

Ice cream at Io-san.

ferred jaunt, partly because an onsen awaits the weary climber. North of Akan Kohan, **Bokke** features bubbling, hot mud. Ainu are abundant in Akan National Park; they dance and sing on schedule when the tour buses arrive. The smiles evaporate into the vapor when the tourists do.

The bus ride between Akan-ko and Mashu-ko, to the northeast, features wonderful views at **Sogakudai** – overlooking Meakan and Oakan. **Mashu-ko** is a landmark. Called Devil's Lake by the Ainu, its 200-meter-high cliffs, towering over misty waters, have often served as leaps for lovers.

Also on the Akan circuit, and less touristy, is **Kussharo-ko**, the largest inland lake in Hokkaido (80 sq km) and home to Kusshi, Japan's very own "Nessie." Three congenial onsen surround Kussharo: Kawayu, Wakoto, and Sunayu, whose hot sands provide a welcome novelty. **Io-san**, or Mount Sulphur, steams and reeks impressively. **Bihoro Pass**, above Kussharo's west shore, is a breathtaking vista.

Taisetsuzan: Wilder and colder than Akan and Shikotsu-Toya, Taisetsuzan is the biggest national park in Japan (230,900 hectares/570,500 acres), anchored directly in the center of Hokkaido and to the west of Akan. It is cool here even in summer.

This is a landscape of volcanic peaks and steep highlands, magnificent gorges, carpets of alpine wildflowers and inevitable sightings of the park's rich wildlife – deer, fox, bears and exotic birds. A car, again, is ideal transportation to the interior. A bike is ideal for sightseeing, but there is much climbing and hard work along the way.

In the park, there are several good youth hostels and a series of campsites. They are useful because, once inside rugged Taisetsuzan, hiking is the preferred recreation. Start at **Sounkyo**, a busy village near Sounkyo Gorge (Gorges Reaching to the Clouds), chiseled walls of volcanic rock – punctuated with feathery waterfalls – more than 100 meters high. From Sounkyo, one of the park's two main ropeways ends near

Ainu posing with tourists.

the peak of Kuro, jumping-off point for hiking territory. The goal is Hokkaido's highest peak, **Asahi-dake**, at 2,290 meters (7,500 ft). Along the way, hikers come across vast tracts of creeping pine and virgin forests, timberline barrens, small lakes and side trails, volcanic vents, flower-covered hillsides, patches of year-round snow – and the inevitable friendly mosquitoes.

There are many hot springs in Taisetsuzan, the most sought-after atop Asahi-dake, to soothe the hiker. Onsen at Sounkyo and **Tenninkyo** lie at both ends of the Asahi-dake trail, while to the south lie onsen at **Tomuraushi** and **Taisetsu Kogen**. To the north is Aizankei onsen. All can be reached by trail, and are much more rustic than their more civilized counterparts elsewhere in Hokkaido.

Among the best festivals in Hokkaido are Sounkyo's Kyokoku Himatsuri, an authentic Ainu fire-festival in late June, and Sounkyo's Ice Festival in winter.

Shiretoko Hanto: A beautiful, barely-civilized finger of volcanic peninsula jutting into the **Sea of Okhotsk**, Shiretoko Hanto is nearly the end of the earth, and that sensation can be vividly felt in places like **Seseki**, a south-coast hot spring that steams on a rocky shore. There are no hotels in sight, no tourist shops, nor any place to eat. A car or bike is necessary for exploring most of Shiretoko, and many places require backpacks and sleeping bags for overnight stays.

Starting from the fishing and onsen village of **Rausu**, a trip along the south coast is rugged and lonely, but adequately relieved by the pleasures of scenic seaside *rotemburo* (outdoor bath).

The north shore, starting from the mundane spa town of **Utoro**, offers more visitors' amenities. From Utoro, there are sightseeing boats and roads east. **Iwaobetsu** is a lovely and unspoiled onsen, from which one can hike to the top of **Rausu-dake**, the peninsula's highest mountain at 1,660 meters.

From here, hikers can descend southward to Rausu, or turn eastward along a ridge of mountains toward 1,560-meter-high (5,100 ft) **Iwo-yama**, a steaming and active volcano. Just north of Iwo-yama, boasting a waterfall, a hot spring, and a breathtaking view of mountain and ocean, is **Kamuiwakka no Taki**, which for many travelers to Japan is the jewel of Shiretoko.

North coast: The best route away from the Shiretoko is west along the northern coast, through the village of Shari and towards **Abashiri**, with its interesting but quirky prison museum, pleasant walks along Tofutsu-ko, and the Natural Flower Gardens.

Abashiri, best of all, is at the beginning of Hokkaido's easiest long-distance bicycle trip, popular with youths on summer holiday. This route involves riding north alongside the Sea of Okhotsk, through the attractive Abashiri Quasi-National Park, to **Wakkanai**, which lies at the northernmost tip of Hokkaido. In spring, the break-up of the ice to the north of Wakkanai is a mainstay of national television news.

Rishiri and Rebun: The small volcanic islands of Rishiri and Rebun are just west of Wakkanai, but before boarding the ferry, visit **Sarobetsu alpine wildflower refuge**, a rainbow of color as far as the eye can see, especially in July. This is one of Hokkaido's real wonders, remote, natural, uncrowded.

Across the water, both Rishiri and Rebun offer delights for the biker, hiker, camper and fisherman. It's possible lodge at a *minshuku* (home-style inn) on either island and get up early in the morning with your host to go fishing in the Sea of Japan.

Hiking is excellent, with Rishiri the best with a climb up **Rishiri-san**, poking up from the ocean 1,720 meters (5,620 ft), like Neptune's elbow. On Rebun, which is comparatively flat, hike from Sukotan-misaki to Momiwa, or bike from Kabuka to Funadomori to make the most of the rewarding coastline scenery. Joining a youth hostel group is good insurance against getting lost.

Accommodations on these northern islands are adventurous. There is a hotel, the Kitaguni Grand, but staying in a hostel (there are three on Rishiri and one on Rebun), or else a minshuku, is a more down-to-earth choice.

Rishiri-san on the island of Rishiri.

YAMAHA

TOHOKU

Perhaps as a way of explaining and coping with the difficult realities of weather and topography, the northern quarter of Honshu – Tohoku – is still filled with myths: clever foxes who turn into beautiful women and lure unsuspecting men to their doom; green-headed river creatures who snatch small children venturing too close to the water; devils and ghosts in great abundance.

By Japanese standards, the Tohoku region (*tohoku chiho*) is sparsely populated, with just 10 million people in an area just under 67,000 square kilometers (26,000 sq. mi). This northern quarter of Honshu comprises six prefectures: Aomori, Akita, Iwate, Miyagi, Yamagata and Fukushima. Its climate is comparable to New England in the United States, with the possible exception of the month of August, when certain parts of southern Tohoku slyly pretend they are on the equator. (In fact, the city of Yamagata holds the record for the highest recorded temperature in Japan, at 41°C or 104°F, in 1933.)

Long known for its natural beauty, rugged mountains, sometimes incomprehensible dialects, innumerable hot springs and – it cannot be denied – its harsh winters, Tohoku was once known as Michinoku, or interior or narrow road. The name was not as benign as it seems, implying someplace rather uncivilized, the lack of culture. In the old days, a barrier wall was constructed at Shirakawa, in southern Fukushima, to separate the civilized world of the south from the barbarians in the north. Although the name was eventually changed to the innocent *tohoku*, or northeast, the image of cultural immaturity lingers for many urban Japanese to the south.

There is a certain irony in this, since it is generally agreed that Tohoku is perhaps the last bastion of traditional Japanese culture. To a large degree, Tohoku has escaped the rapid modernization that the rest of Japan has undergone since the end of World War II. In the north, it is still possible to discover farms growing rice by methods used hundreds of years ago, tiny fishing villages nestled into cliffs overlooking unspoiled sea coasts, isolated hot-spring inns, and a people whose open friendliness is unstinting, even if their dialect an exclusive mystery. No longer unknown, Tohoku is still a place of spectacular beauty, and a must-see for any visitor.

Sendai: This coastal city was originally called Sentaijo, after the Thousand Buddha Statue Temple that once graced the top of Aoba-yama. The name was changed to Sendai, or Thousand Generations, by the Date clan during their reign of the area, possibly in the mistaken belief that they would reign supreme for that long.

Sendai is a cosmopolitan city of approximately 910,000 people, the capital of Miyagi Prefecture, and the preeminent city of the entire Tohoku region. It is known as the Green City and the City of Trees, and visitors arriving on the *shinkansen* from treeless urban points south will understand why. From the **Sendai Station**, considered one of the

Preceding pages: shellfish harvesting near Sendai. Left, Matsushima Bay. Right, captain of the boat, Matsushima.

most beautiful train stations in Japan, the main boulevards running east and west are all tree-lined.

Those wide, European-style avenues are a pleasure along which to stroll. If so inclined, the entire downtown area is small enough to cover in an hour or so of leisurely walking. From Sendai's tallest building, the brilliantly-named **SS-30 Building** with its 30 floors, one can relax in numerous top-floor restaurants that offer an excellent view of mountains to the north and west, the Pacific Ocean to the east, and the city below.

A 10-minute walk west up Aoba Dori from Sendai Station is **Ichiban-cho**, Sendai's main shopping arcade. Parts of it are covered in Plexiglass skylights, and all of it is vehicle-free.

Evenings suggest a walk a little further to **Kokobuncho Dori**, Sendai's main after-hours strip, where there are the usual (and seemingly endless) Japanese-style bars, nightclubs, discos, karaoke boxes and other entertainment.

Sendai's atmosphere is casually sophisticated, and the fuss of Tokyo is conspicuously missing. Just beneath the surface, the traditional ways of Tohoku remain: the visitor can still watch artisans and craftsmen making knives, *tatami* flooring and the famed *kayaki tansu*, or chests, in the traditional shops tucked into the shadows of much larger and more modern architecture.

Sendai didn't come into its own until Date Masamune, the great one-eyed warrior lord of the north, moved to his newly-constructed castle on Aobayama. Both Aoba-jo and the Date family collapsed during the Meiji era, but the castle walls remain. In addition, a small museum, souvenir shop, shrine and statue of the great Masamune himself now occupy the grounds. Looking northwards and down from the castle grounds, one can see the **Hirose-gawa**, unpolluted – and thus unusual in Japan – even today. Edible trout still swim downstream.

Zuihoden, the burial site of Date Masamune, sits atop Kyogamine Hill. There are several cemeteries along the way up, as well as a beautiful Rinzai Zen temple, **Zuiho-ji**. Above the temple are steps leading to the mausoleum at the very top, and nearby are the tombs of samurai who committed ritual suicide when Masamune died. There is also an exhibition room, displaying pictures taken when the mausoleum was opened during restoration, necessitated by bomb attacks near the end of World War II.

Osaki Hachiman Jinja was originally built in 1100, and later moved to its present location by Date Masamune. Dedicated to the god of war or of archery, this shrine is one of Japan's national treasures. Walk up the 100 or so steps to the top – reportedly, the count is never the same twice. Follow the stone-paved path lined with enormous cedar trees to the shrine, picturesquely set back in a small forest. It is done in the Momoyama style of gold, black lacquer and bright colors.

There are several more modern attractions worth a look, especially in **Aobayama Koen**, including a city museum, **Hakubutsukan**, and a prefectural fine-art museum. The museum is interesting architecturally, housing an extensive and permanent exhibition of the area's history. There is also a children's exhibit where everything on display can be touched. The prefectural fine-art museum has a sculpture wing with an outdoor sculpture garden.

If having the time and the energy, consider the **Tohoku University Botanical Garden**, a place to cool off on a hot summer afternoon, as well as to observe owls, bats and the region's flora and fauna. Sendai observatory is a relatively good place for constellation-viewing, if you don't mind waiting in line. Finally, there's Kotsu Koen, a "traffic park" for children, complete with roads, red lights, busy intersections and train tracks. Kids can cruise around in pedal-powered cars and get a taste for what real life is like on Japan's busy and claustrophobic roads.

On the northern outskirts of Sendai, near Kitayama Station and a delightful place for a mountain stroll, are two Zen temples, **Rinno-ji** and **Shifuku-ji**, both dating from the fifteenth century, and destroyed and rebuilt many times over the years. They offer beautiful Zen-inspired gardens, as well as azaleas and irises in the spring, brilliant foliage in autumn, and dazzling winter scenes.

Northward: Sendai is the logical jumping-off point for exploring the rest of Tohoku. A short ride to the northwest is **Naruko**, Tohoku's most popular hot-spring onsen. Once a sacred site to honor the gods of the hot springs, Naruko is known for its medicinal waters (the treatment of nervous tension is a specialty here), and the production of wooden *kokeshi* dolls, with ball-shaped heads and limbless cylindrical bodies. Now produced in many regions, kokeshi originated in Tohoku as a winter industry.

Follow the coast north to **Matsushima**, considered by Japanese to be one of the three officially-designated most-beautiful spots (*Nihon-sankei*) in Japan. The others are on Miyazu Bay, north of Kyoto, and Miyajima, near Hiroshima. (Be warned: such a banner guarantees crowds, tackiness and considerable noise.)

The bay is filled with beautiful pine-covered islets of all shapes and sizes, and a fleet of ferry boats cruises the islands, sometimes in the form of ridiculous peacocks and other gimmicks. The poet Basho couldn't get enough of this place, nonetheless, declaring his arrival in Matsushima as the happiest moment of his life. Try the *sasa-kamaboko* (molded fish paste) and squid-on-a-stick, two of the local delicacies.

Continuing north along the coast, the fishing port of **Ishinomaki** is noted for seafood of all kinds. Try the *hoya* (sea squirt) in vinegar sauce. Ferries from Ishinomaki skirt around **Ojika Hanto** to **Kinkazan** (Gold Flower Mountain), a once-mysterious place of bamboo groves, dense forest, and roaming wild deer and monkeys.

At the northeast tip of Miyagi and on the coast is the city of **Kesennuma** and its variety of shark dishes. Beyond Kesennuma begins Iwate Prefecture's famed **Rikuchu-kaigan Kokuritsu-koen** (a national park commonly called the **Sanriku Coast**), 200 kilometers (124 mi) of fantastic coastline, fishing villages and beautiful sandy beaches.

Matsushima cruise.

Jodogahama (Paradise Beach) was named by a visiting priest, who assumed that this was as close to heaven-on-earth as he would ever get.

Midway up the Sanriku Coast, inland over the mountains, is the town of **Tono**, offering a perfectly-preserved glimpse into feudal Japan. No modern trappings here. Farming is still done the old-fashioned way; note the *magariya*, traditional L-shaped farmhouses. The long side of the structure is for people, the short side for animals and ghosts. Do not go too near the rivers here – this is where the legendary *kappa* resides, beneath the waters and waiting to pull people and horses under. (The traditional way to defeat a kappa, if encountered, is to bow in greeting, forcing the kappa to return the bow and thus drain the depression atop its head of life-giving fluid, water.)

North lies Aomori Prefecture and the **Shimokita Hanto**. The world's northernmost community of wild monkeys can be found here, as well as the ominous **Osore-zan**, 870-meters (2,870 ft) high. With its bubbling, multicolored mud pits and clinging sulphur clouds, Osore's translation of "dread" seems apt. Here, in late July, the blind Itako female shamen contact the dead.

Aomori: Capital of Aomori Prefecture, the city of **Aomori** is a logical departure point for Hokkaido, or, if heading south again, Towada-Hachimantai National Park area. **Hirosaki**, an hour's ride southwest from Aomori, is an old castle town boasting the most elegant (some say most difficult) regional dialect in Tohoku, as well as what Japanese chauvinists claim are Japan's most beautiful women. (*Editor's note:* This guide will wisely pass on pronouncing judgements on such claims.)

To the southeast are the Hakkodo mountains, running down the middle of Aomori Prefecture to the valley of **Oirase-gawa**. Before entering this spectacular valley of steep cliffs, churning rapids and waterfalls, spend a night at **Sukaya** onsen. The waters here are thought to be curative, and the location is rustic and traditional.

Tohoku defies harsh winters with fertile soil.

The Towada-Hachimantai national park covers a vast area, touching the borders of three prefectures – Aomori, Akita and Iwate.

Tamagawa onsen, on the Akita side of Hachimantai Plateau, has hot, acidic and slightly radioactive water, considered to be one of the best in the area. Excluding Hokkaido, this is Japan's last area of untamed wilderness, with several volcanos (including **Iwate-san**, at 2,040-meters-high considered the Fuji of the north), bubbling mud pools, steam geysers and scenic splendor. South of **Towada-ko**, Iwate-san is one of eight active volcanoes in the Tohoku region.

Just to the southeast and at the base of Iwate-san is **Morioka**, Iwate's capital and famous for its competitions for eating *wanko soba*. Further south is the town of **Hiraizumi**, near Miyagi Prefecture. Its beautiful **Chuson-ji**, a temple dating from the twelfth century, contains the Konjiki-do (Golden Pavilion), Japan's first national treasure.

West from Hachimantai is Akita Prefecture, home of **Tazawa-ko** (reportedly Japan's deepest lake) and the spectacular **Oga Hanto**, home of the *namahage*, the devils of the New Year. These horrible creatures burst into the local homes on January 3 each year, and they are not appeased until fed sufficient quantities of sake and rice cakes.

Traveling south through Akita, Yamagata is a truly rustic and traditional prefecture.

The **Dewa Sanzan** are Yamagata's three holy mountains, where the ascetic mountain priests called *yamabushi* still perform their sacred rituals, and can be seen walking the trails dressed in checked jackets and baggy white pants, and carrying conch shells.

Join the other pilgrims and walk the 2,446 steps to the summit of Haguro. Afterwards, travel down the Mogami-gawa on a flat-bottomed boat, while the boatman sings of the area's legends. Towards the inland highlands is Tendo, an onsen town famous for its craftsmen who make *shogi* chess pieces. If time permits, follow any small valley road to its very end, to the old Japan.

Flower tending.

消火栓
東郷神社
東郷記念館
DANCE
PARIS KID'S
McDonald's
ハラク

THE KANTO

Descriptions of the Kanto region can be misleading. It is Japan's largest alluvial plain, but it is certainly not an area of wide-open spaces. None of the flat land extends far enough to offer a level, unbroken horizon. Most of Japan's longest rivers – the Tone, Naka, Ara, Tama, and Sagami – all pass through the Kanto and empty into the Pacific, but few would call these concrete-lined conduits, managed and contained into near-obscurity, rivers at all.

Kanto is home to Tokyo, perhaps the world's most populated urban area. The Kanto plain wraps itself around Tokyo and its equally-congested southern neighbor, Yokohama.

Encircling the two cities are Fuji-san in the west, Nikko in the north, southeast through Narita and Boso Hanto, across Tokyo Bay to Yokohama and Izu Hanto, and finally back to Fuji-san. There are six large prefectures in Kanto, not including Tokyo itself, which is a self-administrating entity. The area has a total population of well over 30 million persons, most of them within commuting distance of Tokyo-to, or Metropolitan Tokyo.

The average population density of the Kanto region is approximately 15,600 persons per square kilometer, three times that of Los Angeles, but not so bad in comparison with Hong Kong, Bombay, Jakarta or even Mexico City. Yet many people think that Tokyo has grown too big, and recently, talk has returned of relocating much of the national government's operations elsewhere, perhaps in Sendai, to the north in Tohoku.

Virtually nothing of interest about the region is recorded until Minamoto no Yoritomo, the first Kamakura shogun, endowed Tokyo's Asakusa-jinja with 90 acres of arable land, around 1180. Later, in 1456, a village called Edo (Estuary Gate) was recorded when the first Edo castle was built by a small-time *daimyo*, on the site of the present Imperial Palace. In 1600, a shipwrecked Englishman became the first foreign guest at Edo, tutoring Ieyasu Tokugawa. Three years later, Ieyasu started the 250-year Tokugawa dynasty.

Like all great cities, although perhaps even more so, Edo suffered its share of natural disasters, amongst them earthquakes and the last eruption of Fuji-san, in 1707, which covered Edo with 10 centimeters (4 in) of volcanic ash. (Fuji is still considered an active volcano.)

Changing Edo's name to Tokyo, or Eastern Capital, with the collapse of the shogunate and the 1868 revival of the imperial throne didn't slow the Kanto's steady climb. Nor did disasters. The Great Kanto Earthquake in 1923, which claimed 100,000 victims, and the bombing raids of World War II destroyed much of the old city. Tokyo was literally rebuilt from the ground up.

Preceding pages: Fuji-san rises above Tokyo. Left, weekend strollers, Takeshita Dori, Tokyo.

TOKYO

Japan has always been a country of villages. If Tokyo is the biggest village, then one can easily reduce Tokyo itself into a gathering of smaller villages, most of them anchored around major train stations. Indeed, these stations are the foundation for understanding Tokyo's layout. Most of Tokyo's smaller villages lie on a circular rail line called **Yamanote-sen**, or Yamanote Line. There are 29 stations on the Yamanote, and it takes about an hour to make the complete loop, actually an oval in shape. Look at the layout of the Yamanote-sen, and of the placement of the stations along the way, and orientation in Tokyo becomes so much easier.

The important stations on the line – and the ones with which to become most familiar – are Tokyo, Ueno, Shinjuku, and Shibuya.

In the center of the oval defined by the Yamanote-sen, a bit off-center to the east, are the grounds of what once was the Edo castle. The Imperial Palace has replaced the castle, but the old symmetry of the castle defenses – moats and gates – are evident still today.

In all cases, most of Tokyo is accessible by one station or another, by one train or subway line, or many. Use them. They're fast, cheap and utilitarian. Just stay off the trains during rush-hour, for obvious reasons. Or walk. Only then do the many of Tokyo's villages feel connected, giving a sense of the big village, Tokyo itself.

TOKYO STATION

While not Japan's busiest station – Shinjuku is quite possessive of the honor – **Tokyo Station** is nonetheless sizable, with 19 platforms side by side, including the terminus for the shinkansen, or bullet train. Deep beneath the station are additional platforms for more subway and JR lines.

The **Marunouchi** side is fronted by the original Tokyo Station, built in 1914 of red brick in an Old World, European style. Air raids in 1945 damaged the station, taking off the top floors; renovations, finished in 1947, left it somewhat lower.

Wedged between the western entrance of Tokyo Station and the present-day Imperial Palace, Marunouchi was once an inlet of Tokyo Bay, its waters extending almost up to where the Palace Hotel now sits. Marunouchi is old feudal land-fill; numerous shogunate engineering projects left a lot of excavated dirt. Atop this land-fill of Marunouchi – meaning "inside the wall" of the Edo castle fortifications – an exclusive residential area for Tokugawa samurai lords was created in the early seventeenth century. Known as *Daimyo Koji,* or the Little Lanes of the Great Lords, Marunouchi served not only as a buffer between the shogun's castle and the outside world of commoners, but also permitted the shogun to keep an eye on his provincial warlords, whom he required to live in Edo on a rotating basis.

From the Marunouchi entrance of Tokyo Station, a wide boulevard slices

Left, high-rises over west Shinjuku. Right, the old Tokyo Station.

through corporate buildings towards the grounds of the Imperial Palace.

Yaesu side: On the other side of Tokyo Station, the **Yaesu** entrance opens onto a boulevard of rather undistinguished office buildings, many of them banks and corporate headquarters. Extending from the Yaesu central exit is Yaesu Dori, which intersects the major arteries of Chuo Dori and Showa Dori, running south to Ginza and north to Ueno.

Chuo Dori crosses Nihombashi-gawa over **Nihom-bashi**, or Nihon Bridge. (The Nihom/Nihon variation is a phonetic one of pronunciation.) An infuriatingly ugly elevated **Shuto expressway** directly above was erected just before the 1964 Tokyo Olympics. Both the concrete-lined river and expressway diminish the significance of the original 1603 arched wooden bridge: the center of Edo Tokyo, and the zero point for the five main roads leading out of Edo. The present stone bridge, erected in 1911, retains little – actually none – of its Edo-era ambience. Nevertheless, embellishments such as bronze Chinese lions and granite sidewalks distinguish this bridge from most of Tokyo's sterile concrete-and-steel bridges.

Nihombashi, as the area came to be known and still is, was a stage of gossip, announcements, and public humiliation. Paul Waley relates how murderers, condemned to crucifixion, were allowed an alternative, whether they liked it or not. The condemned were buried in the ground near the bridge, with only neck and head exposed. Lines were drawn on the neck, and two saws left on either side. Any passers-by so inclined could saw off the murderer's head. Painful, perhaps, but quicker than crucifixion. If left with a head, the condemned was dug up and led off to crucifixion.

On the eastern periphery of Nihombashi, towards the Sumida-gawa, the **Tokyo City Air Terminal** is a downtown check-in facility for flights departing Narita. Not only can airline and baggage check-in be done here, but clearance of immigration, too. A nonstop limousine bus goes to Narita, with minimal hassles at immigration. (And the

Azaleas on bloom bring the crowds.

lines at Narita's immigration counters can get long at times.)

Ryogoku: The site of Tokyo's sumo arena, called the **Kokugikan**, is in the area called Ryogoku, on the other side of Sumida-gawa and northeast of Tokyo Station. A lot of very large people live in Ryogoku – it is the home of many of the *sumo beya*, or stables, as the training center/dormitories for the *rikishi,* or wrestlers, are called.

Near Ryogoku is the **Fukagawa Edo Tokyo Museum**, a spectacular hall that encompasses a massive reconstruction of a part of *shitamachi* Edo from the nineteenth century. It is like walking on to the set of a samurai drama: there is even a life-like dog relieving himself by the guard tower. Every 20 minutes, the lighting cycles through night and day. There are intricately-constructed models of villages, and a life-size reconstruction of Nihom-bashi, the Edo-period bridge. It is one of the finest museums in Japan, well-planned and meticulously thought out. A hall for concerts and public performances is attached.

IMPERIAL PALACE

The Imperial Palace, or **Kokyo**, is a functional palace, where the emperor and his family reside. Much of the palace grounds – including the palace itself – are closed to the public and secluded behind massive stone walls, old trees and Edo-period moats. (The best view of the grounds is from the observation windows on the 36th floor of the Kasumigaseki Building, a tall office tower about one kilometer south of the palace, in the government office district of Kasumigaseki.)

Most of the 110-hectare complex is forested or given to private gardens and small ponds. The Showa Emperor (Hirohito), who reigned from 1926 until early 1989, was a skilled biologist; much of the inner garden area is a nature preserve. The Imperial Palace building itself is an expansive, low building of concrete, veiled with a green roof. It was completed in 1970 to replace the wooden residence destroyed in a 1945 Allied air raid.

Fukagawa Edo Tokyo Museum.

Kokyo Gaien, the palace's outer garden to the southeast, is an expansive area of green and impeccably-sculpted pine trees planted in 1889. Approaching from Marunouchi, this is the area first encountered after crossing Hibiya Dori. A large gravel-covered area leads to a famous postcard scenic – literally – of **Niju-bashi**, a distinctive bridge across an inner moat and one of the most widely-recognized landmarks in Japan. Tourists come here by the bus-loads for a group portrait in front of the bridge and moat; behind, scenically placed, is Fushimi-yagura, a lookout turret of the original Edo castle.

While the bridge is rather elegant, it is a functional entrance into the palace grounds. In fact, it's the main gate, and definitely not open to the public, except on New Year's Day and the emperor's birthday. Then, the public (but not all of Japan) is allowed to cross Niju-bashi and stand near the imperial residence to receive greetings from the emperor.

Parts of the outer grounds were unpleasant places in 1945, immediately after the emperor announced Japan's surrender on the radio. (In fact, it was the first time that the people had heard his voice.) Numerous loyal soldiers, refusing to admit surrender or defeat to the Allies, disemboweled themselves outside the palace walls.

Visitors are also permitted in the **Kokyo Higashi Gyoen**, the East Imperial Garden of the palace. It is open most days and can be entered through Ote-mon, Hirakawa-mon and Kitahanebashi-mon, three of the eight gates into the palace grounds. Inside are remains of the defenses of Edo-jo, and the foundations of the castle's *donjon*, the primary lookout tower of the shogun's residence.

The castle itself was constructed of granite and basaltic rocks quarried at Izu Peninsula, a hundred kilometers south. Several thousand boats made the two-week round-trip carrying immense stones. Off-loaded near Kanda, the stones were dragged on sleds – often with seaweed laid underneath for lubrication – by oxen and men provided by the shogun's warlords, eager to impress.

Niju-bashi and Fushimi-yagura, Imperial Palace.

Half a century later, around 1640, the Edo castle was completed. But less than two decades later, it was reduced to ashes in a great fire. It was rebuilt.

Covering about two square kilometers, the castle's inner compound had four fortresses, or *maru*. Honmaru – or the inner citadel, and as the shogun's residence, the most important maru – was also the highest. Just below Honmaru was the second fortress, Ninomaru, intended as a pleasant (but secure) place of retirement for the shogun in his twilight years. Southwest was Nishinomaru, the western fortress, and where the Imperial Palace now stands. North was Kitanomaru, now a public park. Each fortress had its own defenses, which were buttressed by the adjacent fortress's defenses. In turn, the complex was protected by the moat system. Twenty-one guard towers, or *yagura*, lined the defenses; three still stand.

The Meiji emperor chose the shogunal castle to be the new imperial residence and moved there in 1869 from Kyoto, the city that had been the imperial capital for over a millennium. The new Imperial Palace was completed in 1889 of exquisitely-designed wood. The city was renamed Tokyo, or Eastern Capital. The palace has remained the residence of Japan's emperors ever since. (In 1945, the 1889 Meiji palace was destroyed in Allied bombing raids.)

Unfortunately, today nothing substantial remains of the old Edo castle – except for some turrets and donjon foundations, in addition to the moats and gates – nor do we have any surviving visual images of the castle.

GINZA

Of all places in Japan, **Ginza** has perhaps the greatest name recognition in the world, after Tokyo and Kyoto. During the super-heated bubble economy of the late 1980s, land in Ginza was literally priceless, the most expensive real estate anywhere. Likewise, an evening's entertainment in the exclusive and unmarked clubs of its back alleys too seemed nearly priceless.

Beginnings of a Ginza evening.

Ginza derives its name from *gin,* or silver. Japan had been using three different coinage systems, each based upon silver, gold and copper. Tokugawa Ieyasu decided to simplify the system, basing it upon silver. In 1612, he relocated the official mint from the countryside to Ginza. Two centuries later, the mint was once again shifted, to Nihombashi, but the name of Ginza stayed.

Chuo Dori, sometimes called Ginza Dori, is one of two main arteries through Ginza. A few blocks past the overpass separating Ginza from Nihombashi and Yaesu is a monument to the original site of Ginza. Further on, numerous fashionable boutiques and galleries line the wide boulevard. Immense department stores – including Matsuya (Ginza's largest) and Mitsukoshi (founded in 1673, the Ginza store from 1930) – cascade down onto the sidewalks.

The Mitsukoshi store anchors **Ginza 4-chome**, where Chuo Dori intersects Harumi Dori, the second main artery. (Most Tokyo districts are subdivided into *chome;* Ginza has eight.) **Harumi Dori** extends from Hibiya Koen, down through Ginza and Tsukiji and across the Sumida-gawa. Along Harumi Dori towards Tsukiji, just past Showa Dori, the **Kabuki-za** is clearly a venue of kabuki. The current building was built in 1925, in what is known as the Momoyama style, which has roots in the castles of the late 1600s.

Deeper into Tsukiji towards the Sumida-gawa is the famous **Tsukiji fish market**, where merchants arrive long before dawn to select the best of the day's fresh catch. Other produce is also auctioned here; in fact, there is a storage refrigerator here large enough to chill ten-days' food supply for the entire city.

Tsukiji means, simply, "built land." And indeed it is, Edo-period land-fill that pushed back the shoreline of Tokyo Bay. As with Marunouchi, another landfill area, the newly-created land was set aside for samurai estates, although of lower ranking than Marunouchi.

In the mid 1800s, a part of Tsukiji was set aside for foreigners, and a hotel was

Rain on Ginza 4-chome.

constructed. Apparently it was quite dapper, with over 100 rooms and a billiards parlour; a few years later, it burned to the ground and was left that way.

In the opposite direction on Harumi Dori from Tsukiji, back past Ginza 4-chome, Ginza's potential for shopping ecstasy abounds. A popular meeting place is the **Sony Building** – note the waiting and expectant faces outside; inside are the latest in electronics, and a Toyota showroom. In the alleys southwest of Harumi Dori are numerous art galleries, with offerings of the highest caliber. (Take the gold card.)

An elevated expressway over Harumi Dori defines the boundary between Ginza and **Yurakucho**. Towering on the opposite side of the expressway are the tall, curving exteriors of the Seibu and Hankyu department stores, anchored at the ground by a musical clock and a hard-to-miss (or ignore) police box. Just beyond are elevated train tracks extending from **Yurakucho Station**, constructed in 1910; the *shinkansen* and Yamanote-san trains snake along the overhead tracks. On the Yurakucho side of the tracks – directly across from the Yurakucho Denki Building, with the American Express office at street level – is the **Tourist Information Center**, or **TIC**. If expecting to travel in Japan, hit this place for extensive information about Japan, whether walking tours through Tokyo or lodging in Okinawa. The staff speaks English and offers more printed information than can be stuffed into a ragged backpack.

Along **Hibiya Dori** is the towering **Imperial Hotel** (or in Japanese, *teikoku hoteru*). Always a place of impeccable standards by which other hotels are measured, the first Imperial Hotel opened in 1890. Its modest structure was replaced by a wonderful Frank Lloyd Wright design. The day after it opened to the public in 1923, the destructive Great Kanto Earthquake hit Tokyo. The hotel was one of the few structures to escape destruction. The Wright building was replaced by the modern structure in 1970. It's indeed a shame the Wright building wasn't kept

Chuo Dori, Ginza.

in Tokyo; if going to Nagoya, there it is, relocated and reassembled as before.

Next to the hotel, down a busy side street leading back to Yurakucho and Ginza, is the **Tokyo Takarazuka Theater**, where a number of live stage revues are offered. Across from the Imperial Hotel, **Hibiya Koen** was Japan's first European-style plaza and garden, opened in 1903. It quickly became a popular venue for rallies and demonstrations against rises in rice prices during the early 1900s.

KANDA and AKIHABARA

If there is a book, however old and in whatever language, that seems unattainable, it can be found in the **Jimbocho** station area of **Kanda**. There are stores specializing in art books, second-hand books, comic books – in English, French, German, Russian... Anything and everything.

The bookshops have been in Kanda as long as the nearby universities, since around the 1880s. Many of the early book printers established their shops in Kanda, followed by several of the most famous publishers in Japan.

West along Yasukuni Dori leads to its namesake, **Yasukuni-jinja**, in the **Kudan** area. What is said to be Japan's largest *torii* – eight stories high, made of high-tension steel plates, and weighing 100 tons – boldly announces the shrine. Its entrance nipping the northern tip of the Imperial Palace grounds, at Kitanomaru Koen, this Shinto shrine is Japan's most controversial. Proponents say it honors those who died for Japan; opponents say it glorifies Japanese aggression, and that it honors convicted war criminals. Pincered between the two extremes are politicians, who must decide whether or not to attend annual ceremonies at the shrine.

The souls of over 2.5 million Japanese soldiers killed between 1868 (the shrine was founded in 1869) and World War II are enshrined at Yasukuni (lit. peaceful country). In the shrine's archives, the names, dates and places of death for each soldier are recorded.

Yasukuni-jinja.

Akihabara: The neighborhood of Akihabara epitomizes the old Edo tradition of merchants or craftsmen of a particular commodity congregating together. Indeed, Akihabara is singularly devoted to the sales of electrical and electronic things. Today, its prices may be the cheapest in Japan, but rarely do they beat prices of similar components for sale overseas.

Akihabara's fame for electrical things originated shortly after World War II. A black market for scarce electrical and radio components evolved near the station. Now, Akihabara accounts for around 10 percent of Japan's domestic electrical and electronic sales.

UENO

North of Tokyo Station and Akihabara, exactly eight minutes on the Yamanote train, is **Ueno Station**. It's a subjective and subtle impression, but the area around the station seems somehow more down to earth, if not grittier, than other parts of urban Tokyo. It was once the commoner's part of town, in what was called Shitamachi. Nowadays, there's an aspect of urban life around Ueno not typically noticeable in Japan – the homeless men that camp out in Ueno Koen; foreigners overstaying on expired visas, hustling passers-by with altered, counterfeit telephone cards; the park itself lacking the showcase polish expected of an urban park in one of the world's richest cities.

West of the station, **Ueno Koen** (Ueno Park) is perhaps Tokyo's most distinctly "park" park: sprawling grounds with trees, flocks of scrounging pigeons, monuments and statues, homeless Japanese (and until a few years ago, illegal immigrants from the Middle East), a zoo, a big pond with waterfowl, national museums. It's not quite as tidy and pristine as one might expect in Japan; the park seems tired and in need of scrubbing and a few more trash cans, always a scarce item in Japan.

But the park is a fine place for people-watching, especially on weekends when people take a few hours to play. In the

Akihabara shop, and Ueno Park.

spring, Ueno Koen is cherished amongst Japanese for its blossoming cherry trees. The idea of blossom viewing – *hanami,* a tradition extending back centuries – seems aesthetically appealing; in fact, it is often a claustrophobic, drunken party.

The **Tosho-gu**, a shrine adjacent to the Five-Storied Pagoda, was established in 1627 (the present buildings date from a 1651 renovation) by a warlord – on his own estate – to honor the first Tokugawa shogunate, Tokugawa Ieyasu. The walkway to Tosho-gu (lit. Illuminator of the East) is lined with dozens of large and symbolic stone or copper free-standing lanterns, all donated by warlords from throughout the land to cultivate a little merit with the shogun. (Lanterns such as these are simply symbolic and not used for illumination.)

Although not as embellished as it was in the Edo period, the main shrine building is still a magnificent, ornate building. The outer hall features murals painted by the famous Edo artist, Kano Tanyu. Also interesting is the Chinese-style Kara-mon, a gate decorated with dragons that are meant to be ascending to, and descending from, heaven. It's said that the dragons slither over to nearby Shinobazuno-ike under the cover of night to drink.

Behind the shrine and down a slope is a road that acts as a natural divider between the park and **Shinobazuno-ike**, once an inlet and now a pond *(ike)* dense with lily plants. A small peninsula juts into the pond, with a Buddhist temple to Benten – a goddess of good fortune and the only female amongst the Seven Deities of Good Luck – perched on the end. A promenade follows the pond's squarish two-kilometer circumference. The **Shitamachi Museum** (look for it in the cluster of buildings near the pond, at the park's south entrance) is a hands-on exhibit of Edo commoners' daily life in Shitamachi, as this part of Edo Tokyo was once known.

The **National Museum of Western Art** is anchored by a collection of nearly a thousand pieces, ranging from the Renaissance to the contemporary; the collection includes several sculptures

National Museum of Western Art.

by Rodin, and a sizeable collection of nineteenth-century French art. The **Tokyo National Museum** offers a superbly-displayed collection of Asian art and archeology. Holding the extensive Japanese collection, the main hall dates from 1937. Arching over the outside entrance to the museum grounds is an immense samurai estate gate.

West of Ueno is the most prestigious of Japanese universities, Todai, or **Tokyo University**, founded in 1869. The competition to enter is fearsome, devouring the childhood of many children and the youth of many teenagers.

ASAKUSA

From the mid 1800s until World War II, Asakusa was the center of all fine things in Tokyo, a cultural nucleus of theater and literature, and of cuisine and the sensual delights. Imagine today's Shibuya, Ginza, Roppongi and Shinjuku tossed together, countrified and without the benefit of neon, fast-food and loudspeakers.

Asakusa's cultural and social flowering began with exile. First, with the banishment to Asakusa of the Yoshiwara, or the licensed prostitution district (the name followed the ladies), in the 1600s, and then later with that of theater, especially *kabuki*, in the 1800s. Located to the northeast outside of the Edo gates, the Asakusa area along the Sumida-gawa became a vigorous commercial port, with wharfs on the Sumida's bank, including an important rice depot for the shogun.

The people of Asakusa (and of Nihombashi, Kanda and Ueno) were known as *Edokko,* people of Edo. Asakusa dripped with *iki*, a sense of style and urbane polish, and with *inase,* gallantry. It was *the* place to be seen in Edo Tokyo, reaching a critical mass in the 1800s.

Anchoring Asakusa was **Senso-ji**, or **Asakusa Kannon**, perhaps the oldest Buddhist temple in the region, and a draw for people from around Japan, who brought with them spending money to make Asakusa prosper.

Main gate to Asakusa Kannon.

Old places always start with a legend. Asakusa's legend has it that Senso-ji was founded in AD 628, when two fishermen – brothers, actually – netted a small statue of Kannon, the deity of mercy. (In Buddhism, Kannon is typically male or neuter, but exceedingly feminine in form and personality.) A temple was built by the village leader to house it. Around the time that the statue appeared, the legend continues, a great and golden dragon slithered its way down to earth from the heavens. The temple became a favorite of samurai and shoguns. It prospered, economically and politically.

The south entrance to the temple, on Asakusa Dori, is a large gate, **Kaminari-mon**, or Thunder Gate, dating from 1960. (It had burned down a century before.) Here begins **Nakamise Dori** (lit. inside the shops), where two rows of red buildings funnel temple-goers northwards through a shopping arcade before spilling out onto the temple grounds.

In the other direction, east of Senso-ji, is the **Sumida-gawa**, which empties into Tokyo Bay. The exit for the Ginza Line, Tokyo's first subway line that opened in 1927, surfaces near the **Azuma-bashi** (bridge). Just north of the bridge is **Sumida Koen**, a recent attempt to open up the river front.

Although the Sumida was an easily-accessed and well-used, if not commercially essential, river during the Edo period and well into the early 1900s, until recently, property along it was considered undesirable. It was not considered a proper place in which to live.

With the lack of interest in the river, especially as its commercial and transport importance faded with industrialization, most of the Sumida became inaccessible and hidden behind concrete. But as Japanese began traveling during the 1970s and 1980s, they returned with memories of romantic urban rivers in Europe. Only in the past few years have efforts started to bring the Sumida back. The park is a pleasant stroll, especially in spring when the cherry trees are blooming, but benches in the park are often draped with the homeless.

Sumida fireworks, and Asakusa festival.

SHIBUYA, HARAJUKU and ROPPONGI

Shibuya is one of the trendiest neighborhoods in Tokyo, although many resident foreigners might nominate Roppongi to the east, mostly because Roppongi caters to foreigners, and has done so with high style for decades. Shibuya, on the other hand, caters to Japanese youth with money to spend, and there's a lot of both here.

Shibuya was a rural but bustling stop along one of the great highways, built during the Tokugawa years, in and out of Edo Tokyo. Later, mulberry (for an abortive attempt at silk production) and tea fields surrounded Shibuya's first train station, which opened in 1885. Nearby, along the Shibuya-gawa were mills powered by water wheels.

Several private rail lines opened in the subsequent years, each with its own station. Finally, all the stations were consolidated at the current site in 1920.

The most popular exit of **Shibuya Station**, opening to the northwest, is named after a hound dog. And outside of that entrance, one will find a statue, erected in 1964, of said dog, an Akita named Hachiko. For a rendezvous in Shibuya, Hachiko's statue is the preferred rendezvous spot.

Every Japanese knows the story of Hachiko, *ad nauseam*, from movies, television, novels and an expanding legend. Stay in Tokyo long enough, and the story of this dog turns increasingly tedious and mushy. Nonetheless, the story goes like this: In the 1920s, Hachiko would follow his master, a professor at the Imperial University, to the station. In the evenings, Hachiko would meet his returning master. One day, the master returned no more. He had died. Yet Hachiko waited and waited, returning night after night, year after year, until he himself died. Japanese love the story, but there are some doubts about its authenticity. Enough of Hachiko.

Beyond the Hachiko entrance is an immense intersection. Looking straight ahead, note the tall cylindrical building: the **Shibuya 109** building, a good reference for orientation. The crowded road

Main crossing, Shibuya.

to its right leads up a gentle hill to Tokyu department store, and adjacent to it, the **Bunkamura**, a performance hall built during the roaring 1980s. Something's always going on inside – art, music, cinema, theater – and the interior spaces are a refreshing retreat on a hot day.

At the top of the hill, bearing to the left, is the huge **NHK Broadcast Center**, a 23-story building with two dozen TV studios and an equal number of radio studios. NHK is the government-run, viewer-subsidized (or taxed, more accurately) television and radio broadcaster. In addition to two subscription satellite channels, there is the standard NHK broadcast channel and an educational channel, with dowdy professors and chalkboards and charts of chemical molecules. Over 1,500 shows are produced in the broadcast center weekly.

Open to the public inside the center is the **NHK Studio Park**, a well-designed introduction to television broadcasting, with a number of interactive exhibits. Intriguing is a 3-D high-definition television presentation. Overhead observation windows look down upon sets for the ever-popular samurai dramas, which in fact rarely seem to be in production during visitor hours.

Yoyogi Koen served as the Olympic Village during the 1964 games. Before that, however, the area was a barracks, called Washington Heights, for the American army. Everything was eventually torn down, but rather than erecting something new, the site was turned into the park. It now includes a wild bird park, playground, and on weekends, some of the spunkiest Japanese anywhere. Too, there is some of the worst music, as wannabe rock groups give free "concerts," all at the same time, hoping to establish a following of adolescent girls that will cascade into Japan-wide popularity.

Yoyogi Koen is an extension of one of Japan's most famous Shinto shrines, **Meiji-jingu**. The shrine deifies Emperor Meiji and Empress Shoken. (Their remains, however, are in Kyoto.) The emperor, of course, was restored to rule in the 1868 Meiji Restoration, when the Tokugawa shogunate collapsed. The

Meiji-jingu at New Years, and Harajuku dusk.

emperor died in 1912, the empress, two years later. The original shrine, built in 1920, was destroyed during World War II; the current shrine buildings were reconstructed in 1958. The shrine itself is constructed of Japanese cypress from Kiso, said to be the best lumber in Japan.

The grounds of the shrine cover about 175 acres, and were a favorite retreat of the emperor. The park is populated by nearly every species of tree growing in Japan, donations to the shrine. The walk to the shrine passes through a tunnel of these trees, and beneath three large *torii* gates, said to include one of the largest wooden gates in Japan: 12 meters high with pillars over a meter in diameter. Cypress wood, over 1,700 years old, from Taiwan was used.

Harajuku: The entrance to Meiji-jingu is near **Harajuku Station**, architecturally interesting for a Japanese train station. Leading from the station are a number of hip, groovy and rad avenues. (Harajuku itself was once a post station on the road from Kamakura, in the less-hip eleventh century.)

For some reason, narrow **Takeshita Dori**, a small side street between the station and Meiji Dori, has become a teeny-bopper avenue of shops and eateries. Positively for the young, it is without breathing room on weekends.

More room is found instead on the wide and upscale **Omote Sando**, a boulevard running from the southern end of Harajuku Station, where one finds the entrance to Meiji-jingu. Omote Sando has a European feel about it, from the expansiveness of the boulevard (at least for Japan), to the zelkovea trees that line it, to the style of architecture in some of the buildings. In summer, outdoor cafes with suave-sounding French names offer expensive coffees and draw a decidedly cosmopolitan crowd.

Roppongi: In the lower middle of the oval defined by the Yamanote-sen, and just to the southwest of the Imperial Palace, is an area favoured by Tokyo's expatriate community: **Minato-ku**, a Tokyo ward made up of Aoyama, Akasaka, Roppongi, Azabu and Hiroo. The area is peppered with embassies

Roppongi expedition.

and high-priced expat (and company-subsidized) housing, and liberally spiced with nightclubs and restaurants.

Up on a hill served by the Hibiya-sen, **Roppongi** is the heart of the area's social life, and night life, and courting life. It crawls with both foreigners and Japanese on the prowl for the opposite sex. Its main avenues are bright and loud, the back alleys lined with drinking establishments laced by themes meant to nurture nostalgia, or homesickness, in strangers in a strange land. But don't confuse the activity here with the blatant sex trade of Shinjuku's Kabukicho. In Roppongi, it's only upscale food and drinks, buttressed by probing smiles.

Roppongi means six trees. There may have been six trees, perhaps pine, at one time. But if in fact there were, they disappeared in the early 1800s. Another possibility for the name are the six samurai lords who had estates here during the Edo period. Each of their names were related to trees: Aoki, or green tree, and Takagi, or tall tree, as examples. Roppongi later became a garrison town for the Meiji government, and later, after World War II, the American army established barracks here. With a steady turnover of hormonal young soldiers, together with the embassy staffs in nearby Azabu and Akasaka, Roppongi was a natural crossroads for nightlife. It still is. Probably always will be.

East of Roppongi, along the roadway towards the Imperial Palace, the **Ark Hills** complex of offices, apartments and stores is the work of Mori Taikichiro. Riding the real estate boom of the 1970s and 1980s, he advocated urban redevelopment, replacing some of the claustrophobic neighborhoods of Tokyo with modern complexes. He made most of his US$13 billion of wealth *after retiring* at age 55 from academia. At his death in 1993, he owned over 80 buildings in central Tokyo, and was considered the richest private citizen in the world. Most of his buildings he named after himself, such as Mori Building 25.

Check the horizon to the south, towards Shiba: the red-and-white **Tokyo Tower** juts skyward, looking industrial and out of place. Finished in 1958, its primary purpose was to broadcast television signals. Subsequent lyrical allusions to the Eiffel Tower or dynamic elegance were fabrications of creative writing. It's an ugly projection into the skyline, but the views from the observation decks are quite excellent.

Tokyo Tower.

SHINJUKU

After building Edo castle and settling down, Tokugawa Ieyasu had the **Shinjuku** area surveyed at the urging of some entrepreneurs. He then established a guard post – near today's Shinjuku 2-chome – along the Koshu Kaido, a road that led west into the mountains. Shinjuku (lit. new lodging) quickly became one of the largest urban towns in Edo, filled with shopkeepers, wholesale distributors, inns and tea houses. Shinjuku was also known for the male sensual delights, with over 50 "inns" catered by "serving girls". Unlike those in Asakusa, the women of Shinjuku were without licenses, and thus were considered as less than equals.

In its early days, when the line through Shinjuku was but 21 kilometers long, only about 50 people used the station at Shinjuku daily. Surrounding the wooden station was a forest of trees. The year was 1885. Nowadays, it's said by the Japanese that **Shinjuku Station** is the world's busiest train station. Maybe, maybe not, given the Japanese propensity for superlatives. Let there be no doubt, however: It is a furiously busy place – approaching three million people daily – and congested, and can test the traveler's patience.

Shinjuku Station is one of the most important stations in Japan, a major transfer point for both metropolitan and regional trains, and for subways.

As with most large urban stations in Japan, there are multitudinous shops and restaurants filling every unused space in the multi-level labyrinth, above and below ground. There are also four massive department stores within Shinjuku Station itself, two of which have their own private train lines leading from Shinjuku: Keio, with a line that opened in 1915, and Odakyu, its line beginning in 1927.

Japanese trains wait for no one. On busy lines, they are timed to the second. During Tokyo's morning rush hour that peaks around 8am, a ten-car train with 3,000 severely-compressed people stops at platforms for the Chuo and Yamanote lines every 90 seconds. Unloading and boarding times included, not to mention the time needed for the white-gloved handlers to push in the last passengers, thus permitting the doors to close, there is but a 10- to 20-second window between trains. (Evening rush hour is less congested, as it's staggered throughout the afternoon and into night.)

To the East: If the four department stores within the station are somehow lacking, tumble out the station's east entrance onto **Shinjuku Dori**, where there are more department stores, and thousands of regular stores, and tens of thousands of people. This entrance of Shinjuku Station is a popular meeting and rendezvous spot. A small open plaza tempts the idle to linger, especially when

Shinjuku Station's east entrance, Studio Alta.

there is something to watch on the immense outside television screen at **Studio Alta**. If a rendezvous has fizzled, or has the possibility of doing so, watching the television – with blaring sound – helps to mask any humiliation.

This side of the station is, of course, a superb rambling area, which one can do for hours with little purpose. Many of those who have a purpose enter **Kabukicho**, north of Yasukuni Dori. After World War II, residents of this area sought to establish a sophisticated entertainment area of cinemas and dance halls, and perhaps most importantly, a kabuki theater. Hence, Kabukicho. But somewhat optimistically, naming of the neighborhood preceded construction of the kabuki theater, which was in fact never built.

The cinemas were, however, and for many years Tokyo's best cinema-viewing was in Kabukicho; European films were very popular during the 1960s, especially with intellectuals, wannabe intellectuals, political radicals and radical wannabes. Eventually, they moved elsewhere, leaving Kabukicho to the *yakuza*. Kabukicho is most famous nowadays for its sexual entertainment, which tends towards voyeurism rather than participation or solicitation.

West Shinjuku: For more stately pursuits, follow Yasukuni Dori under the tracks to the west side of Shinjuku. (One could also exit the station directly to avoid the east side altogether.)

Of most immediate interest are the numerous tall buildings on this side. Much of Tokyo is either alluvial soil or land-fill; both are geologically unstable foundations during earthquakes. (On the east side of the Sumida-gawa, the soil is so unstable that it has settled up to three meters or more in some areas, due to the lowering of the groundwater level by industrial use.)

Given the shakiness of Tokyo's land, not to mention the experience of several devastating earthquakes, tall buildings in Tokyo have been limited. But Shinjuku sits atop rather solid ground, giving architects the confidence to build what they claim are earthquake-proof buildings that utilize sophisticated techniques for stress dissipation and structure stabilization.

Continue to the twin-towered building of the **Tokyo Metropolitan Government Office**. Conceived and started at the beginning of the so-called bubble economy in the 1980s, the buildings were designed to make a statement, simply put: Tokyo was now one of the world's great urban centers. (Still, it can be noted, only 85 percent of Tokyo residences have access to sewage systems.) Around 13,000 city employees fill the buildings each day.

At the base of the main building is the **Assembly Hall**, separated from the main building by a semicircular, 5,000-square-meter public plaza. Some interesting sculptures – mostly of naked women, a popular theme in Japan – grace the plaza. The main building has two twin upper towers. Finished in 1991, these two towers are 48 floors high, or 243 meters (797 ft). At the top of both towers, expansive observation windows offer without doubt the finest views in Tokyo, and they're free.

Left, Shinjuku alley. Right, Tokyo Metropolitan Government Building.

MARU YOKOHAMA

SOUTH OF TOKYO

YOKOHAMA

Yokohama – the very sound of it is exotic. And although the city today is both an integral part of the Greater Tokyo area and a major urban center in its own right, it has a personality, even a mystique, much of it stemming from its vital role as one of the greatest international seaports of the Far East.

With a population of over three million, Yokohama is second in size only to Tokyo. Happily, however, many of those areas worthy of exploring are concentrated in a relatively small area and can be covered, for the most part by foot, within a single day.

Another thing that makes Yokohama (only a 30-minute train ride from Tokyo) alluring is the fact that its broad, relatively uncrowded streets (except on weekends) and laid-back atmosphere provide a perfect antidote for Tokyo's claustrophobia and fast pace.

Start a walking tour of central Yokohama at **Sakuragicho Station**, which is the terminus for the Toyoko Line, originating at Tokyo's Shibuya Station. Other ways to get here from Tokyo are aboard the JR Yokosuka or Tokaido lines from Tokyo, or the Keihin Kyuko Line from Shinagawa. In both cases, you have to transfer onto the Negishi Line at Yokohama Station. Incidentally, Sakuragicho was also the last stop on Japan's first railroad, which began service to Shimbashi in Tokyo in September 1872.

Central Yokohama is in a state of great flux at the moment, as work proceeds down near the harbor on the massive **Minato Mirai 21** project, which will totally revamp the port area by the turn of the century.

Within its 190 square kilometers (75 sq. mi), it includes the 73-story **Landmark Tower**, at 296 meters (970 ft) one of the tallest buildings in Japan. The International Zone will feature a huge convention complex, and the Amenity Zone will be devoted to landscaped parks. Nearby are the *Nippon Maru*, a tall ship, and the neighboring **Maritime Museum**. Also close by is the **Yokohama Art Museum**, with its excellent collection of modernist sculpture.

The other side of the **Oka-gawa** from **Sakuragicho Station** is an area of old government buildings, banks and the like. Further on is a tree-lined street with red-brick sidewalks: **Basha-Michi Dori** (Street of Horse Carriages). Here is the **Kanagawa Prefectural Museum**. The building, built in 1904, was formerly the head office of a bank, and as one of the best surviving examples of the city's old commercial architecture, it has been designated a so-called Important Cultural Property by the national government.

When Commodore Perry and his Black Ships arrived in 1853, Yokohama was just a poor fishing village next to a rank swamp. Under the terms of a treaty negotiated in 1858 by the first U.S. envoy to Japan, Townsend Harris, the Port of Kanagawa, smack on the Tokaido – or the East Sea Road between

Left, Yokohama Port from Yamashita Park. Right, Yokohama Port.

Edo Tokyo and Kyoto – was to be opened to foreign settlement. But the shogunate reconsidered and built an artificial island on the mud flats of Yokohama instead.

That attempt to segregate the "red-haired barbarians" proved fortuitous for all concerned, since Yokohama's superb natural harbor helped international trade to flourish. The wild early days of the predominantly-male community centered around such recreational facilities as Dirty Village, the incomparable Gankiro Teahouse, and the local race track. Periodic attacks by sword-wielding, xenophobic samurai added to the lively atmosphere.

Eventually, foreign garrisons were brought in and the merchants could concentrate in a more sedate environment. **Honcho Dori** became the center of commercial activities. The wide street is still bracketed with banks and office buildings. There is, for example, the stately **Yokohama Banker's Club** and, on the right four blocks down, the lovely red-brick **Yokohama Port Opening Memorial Hall**, which miraculously survived the Great Kanto Earthquake of 1923 and the fire bombings of World War II. Also in this area are numerous prefectural offices, and near the waterfront, the **Yokohama Custom House**.

This district is sometimes called the Bund, and its oldest buildings have a distinctly European look, something shared with buildings along the Bund in Shanghai, built about the same time.

The **Yokohama Archives of History**, on the site of the former British consulate, houses a museum with various exhibits about Yokohama's fascinating history, and a library with related audio-visual materials.

Across from it is the **Yokohama Port Opening Square**, where the Japan-US Treaty of Peace and Amity was signed in 1854, and the **Silk Center**, with a delightful museum on the history of that mysterious fabric; at one time, Yokohama owed its prosperity primarily to silk, in which the local Indian community was intimately involved.

Steamship at dockside in the 1930s.

A little bit farther down the same road is the **New Grand Hotel**, which, although slightly down at the heel, is still a civic institution and the best spot for a break over coffee and cake. Next to it is the somewhat garish 106-meter (348-ft) **Marine Tower**, and a doll museum.

Yamashita Park is well worth a visit. Among the attractions at the park are the Girl with the Red Shoes, a statue dedicated to international friendship among children. If serendipity brings you here on a clear summer night, you are likely to hear a rock band wailing away on a temporary stage several hundred feet offshore. The former passenger liner and hospital ship, *Hikawa Maru*, is permanently moored here, and can be visited. Conveniently, there is a beer garden on deck, and boat tours of the harbor leave from next to the ship. Occasionally, distinguished visitors such as the *Queen Elizabeth II* are also to be found in port.

No visit to Yokohama would be complete without a meal in Chukagai, or **Chinatown**. This dozen or so blocks is the largest Chinatown in Japan, and is nearly as old as the port. The area within its five gates accounts for 90 percent of the former foreign settlement.

Chinatown also takes pride in the historical role it had in providing staunch support to Sun Yatsen when he was here in exile, trying to rally support for revolution on the Chinese mainland.

On days when a baseball game is on at nearby **Yokohama Stadium**, the area is visited by more than 200,000 people, the majority intent on dining at one of the approximately 150 local restaurants. Most also sneak in at least a peak at the exotic shops selling imported Chinese sweets and sundries from elsewhere in Asia. There are also many herbal medicine and tea shops. Although in most Chinatowns, from San Francisco to London, restaurants prepare food for Chinese tastes, in Yokohama everything is adjusted to Japanese taste buds, with a tad of French influence. Top chefs recruited from Hong Kong and Taiwan have to be deprogramed to an extent.

Chinatown, and Victorian house on the Bluff.

Back in the old days, the waterfront Bund often stood in contrast with the **Bluff**, or Yamate Heights, where the leading foreign merchants lived in palatial homes. **Nanmon Dori** in Chinatown was the central street that ran through the international settlement and connected the two. It became a local tradition – known as **Zondag**, from the Dutch word for leisure – that on every Sunday, the flags of the many nations were flown and brass bands would strut down the road.

Virtually every guidebook ever written about Yokohama urges readers to visit the famed **foreign cemetery** *(gaijin bochi)*, where around 4,200 foreigners from 40 countries who somehow found their way to Japan are buried. The adjacent **Yamate Museum**, with quaint displays on the life of early foreign residents, sits near where Japan's first brewery was located.

And while here, let's also look up some of the city's lesser known attractions. An amble through the hilly Yamate residential district is one that is highly recommended. A cup of coffee in the Edwardian Yamate Jubankan should help prepare the visitor in the right mood to descend once again to the turbulent world below, specifically, the carnival-like atmosphere and excitement of **Motomachi**.

The name of this popular shopping street, just below the Bluff and slightly inland from the portside Yamashita Park, means "original town." This is somewhat of a misnomer, because the area was developed long after Yokohama itself was established; still, Motomachi, adjacent as it was to the foreign district – now Chinatown – has played an important role in the city's history, serving the needs of foreign vessels and their crews visiting the port.

Motomachi's legacy of "foreignness" led to its revival in the 1960s and 1970s as a center of trendy boutiques and a few flashy discotheques. However, the focus of fashion in Yokohama has shifted to **Isezakicho**, south of Kannai Station, and the big department stores around Yokohama Station.

Dancing in Yamashita Park, and visiting near Marine Tower.

KAMAKURA

Kamakura lies cradled in a spectacular natural amphitheater, surrounded on three sides by wooded mountains and on the fourth by the blue Pacific. For roughly 150 years, from 1192, when Minamoto no Yoritomo made it the headquarters of the first shogunate, until 1333, when imperial forces breached its seven "impregnable" passes and annihilated the defenders, Kamakura was the de facto political and cultural capital of Japan. During those years, the warrior administration based here built impressive temples and commissioned notable works of art, a great deal of it Zen-influenced. Despite the endemic violence of Japan's middle ages, most survived and can be viewed today.

It is a pity that the majority of visitors spend only a day or two in Kamakura, since it is best appreciated leisurely, with visits to famous historical sites – there are 65 Buddhist temples and 19 Shinto shrines – interspersed with walks through quiet surrounding hills.

Kamakura is only an hour from Tokyo Station, and 30 minutes from Yokohama, on the JR Yokosuka Line. For that reason much of it resembles an open-air madhouse on weekends. Visitors customarily begin their sightseeing from **Kamakura Station** or Kita-Kamakura, the station nearest the five great Zen temples. A different approach to the city is recommended, however.

Take the private Odakyu Line from Shinjuku and get off either at Fujisawa or Enoshima. This offers a chance to ride the delightful **Enoden** (Enoshima Dentetsu) electric trolley line and consequently slip gently into a Kamakura frame of mind. If starting early from Tokyo, the chronic congestion in front of the Great Buddha can be avoided.

The Enoden, which began operations in 1902, starts from **Fujisawa** and ends at Kamakura Station, with 13 stops in between. For about half its 10-kilometer (6-mi) length, the cars run along the ocean, and when they are not crowded, the conductors even allow surfers to bring their boards aboard. Unfortunately, the delightful old cars have been replaced with modern ones. When the tram stops for a red light along with the motor vehicles, it's obvious that the *shinkansen* is not all there is to transportation in Japan.

Hop off the Enoden at **Hase**, the station closest to Daibutsu, the Great Buddha. Either walk up the large road that runs towards the statue, or catch a taxi or bus. In the hills to the left on the way are: **Goryo-jinja** (next to the Enoden tracks), which holds a unique festival every September 18 with humorous characters sporting macabre masks; **Hase-dera**, the temple with a nine-meter (30-ft), 11-headed Hase Kannon statue, along with thousands of small *jiso* statues decked out in colorful bibs and bonnets, dedicated to lost babies (mostly due to abortion); and **Kosoku-ji**, a temple known for its collection associated with the priest Nichiren.

On a knoll to the right of the approach to the Buddha is the 1,200-year-old **Amanawa Myojin.** Dedicated to the Sun Goddess, Amaterasu Omikami, the shrine offers majestic views.

Detail at Kamakura shrine.

Even first-time visitors to Japan have no doubt seen photos of **Daibutsu**, the Great Buddha. But even if not, there's little chance of missing the colossus. At 11 meters (40 ft) in height – minus the pedestal – and weighing 93 tons, this representation of the compassionate Amida is unlikely to get lost in a crowd. Because the features of the statue were purposely cast out of proportion when it was built in 1252, stand four to five meters in front of the statue to get the full impact of the art work. For a fee, crawl around inside the statue.

Astonishingly, the Great Buddha has survived, almost intact, the onslaughts of earthquakes, typhoons and *tsunami* – like the one that in 1495 ripped away the wooden building that once enclosed it.

From the Great Buddha, the best bet is to catch a taxi to Kamakura Station, or else retrace steps to Hase Station and continue the Enoden odyssey to the end of the line, at Kamakura Station.

Central Kamakura: On the east side of the station is **Wakamiya Dori**, the broad boulevard that leads under three massive *torii* archways to the Tsurugaoka Hachiman-gu, to the north. Parallel to Wakamiya Dori is **Kamachi Dori**, Kamakura's modest answer to the Ginza. The area abounds with all kinds of trendy shops and eating places, and many of the Japanese-style restaurants here and elsewhere in the city have incorporated Zen principles of cooking. Quite crowded on weekends.

Folk-craft shops encourage serious browsing. But Kamakura is most famous for *Kamakura-bori* (lacquerware), which originated in the area in the thirteenth century for the production of utensils used in religious ceremonies. Unlike the traditional Chinese lacquerware, from which it drew its inspiration, with Kamakura-bori, the artist starts by carving the design and only then applies the lacquer. Like fine wine, Kamakura-bori improves with age, taking on richer and subtler hues and luster.

Learn more about this art at the **Kamakura-bori Kaikan,** on the right as you start up Wakamiya Dori towards Tsurugaoka Hachiman-gu.

Sagami Bay from Kamakura temple.

The approach into **Tsurugaoka Hachiman-gu** crosses a steep, red half-moon bridge that separates the Gempei Ponds. (The name Gempei refers to the Minamoto (Genji) and Taira (Heike) clans, which fought to the end in the samurai power struggle known as the Gempei War.)

The three islands on the right – the Genji side – signify the Chinese character for birth, that is, the victory of Yoritomo and his followers, while the four in the Heike pond stand for the death of the rival Taira. Yoritomo's indomitable wife, Masako, who ironically was of Taira blood, apparently built the pond to rub in her husband's absolute victory over the ill-fated heirs of Kiyomori.

Art and archery: Behind the Heike Pond is the **Kanagawa Prefectural Museum of Modern Art**, and a little past the Genji Pond is the **Kokuhokan** (National Treasure Hall). Each month, the latter teasingly changes the limited displays of the 2,000 treasures from the temples of Kamakura, which are in its possession. Still, whatever is being shown at any given moment should be stimulating for those interested in Buddhist art. Incidentally, the Kokuhokan building is a copy of the Shosoin repository in Nara.

Continuing up the avenue towards the main shrine, cross a 25-meter (82-ft) dirt track, along which every September 16 mounted archers gallop and unloosen their arrows at targets in the ancient samurai ritual of *yabusame*. Then there is an open area below the steps to the **Hongu**, or shrine hall. Here is the red stage upon which Shizuka, Yoritomo's paramour, danced defiantly at the order of his vengeful older half-brother, using the occasion to sing the praises of her lover. The pregnant girl's courage sent Yoritomo into a furious and vengeful rage, and although he spared her life, he later executed her son, whose father was Yoshitsune.

Just past the stage, on the left of the steps, is a huge gingko tree measuring eight meters (26 ft) around and is reputed to be 1,000 years old. It was

Main hall of Tsurugaoka Hachiman-gu.

beside this track, in 1219, that Yoritomo's second son, Sanetomo, at 26 years old already an accomplished poet, was assassinated by his own nephew. Thus came to an end Yoritomo's line; thereafter, the shogunate was controlled by Masako's family, the Hojo, through a regency.

Tsurugaoka Hachiman-gu's prominence on the top of Stork Mountain, and the shrine's dedication to Hachiman, the god of war and tutelary deity of the Minamoto, made it the central point of reference for the numerous offices of the "tent government" located below. Actually, the shrine was founded way back in 1063 by one of Yoritomo's ancestors. Yoritomo's very unpretentious tomb is to be found off to the right of the shrine near a hill. It is a grave befitting a samurai, unlike the monstrous art-deco mausoleums for the Tokugawa shoguns at Nikko, which look as if were built for *mafioso* dons.

Two isolated temples of great interest and few crowds are the **Kakuon-ji**, back in the hills behind Yoritomo's tomb, and the **Zuisen-ji**, considerably to the east. The former was founded in 1296. Its Buddha Hall, dating to 1354, houses a beautiful Yakushi Nyorai, flanked by guardians representing the sun and moon, as well as a shrine to the Black Jizo, whose indelible color results from its constantly being scorched by the flames of hell in its efforts to save souls. Access to this temple is strictly controlled. Zuisen-ji boasts a Zen rock and water garden designed by its founder, the monk Muso Kokushi.

Another spot to visit that is not so far off the beaten track, but nevertheless is largely missed by the tourist hordes, is **Harakiri Cave**, a 20-minute walk to the northeast of Kamakura Station, past the shallow, meandering Nameri-gawa. It was here, in July of 1333 in what was then a temple called Tosho-ji, that the last Kamakura regent, the weak Hojo Takatoki, who had been scorned for his patronage of dog-fights, died by his own hand, surrounded by over 800 of his cornered followers.

Nichiren: The area due east of Kamakura Station is largely the province of temples of the Nichiren sect. Although most foreigners have heard of Zen, few know much about Nichiren (1222–82) and his teachings, despite the fact that the iconoclast priest founded the only true Japanese Buddhist sect. Nichiren was an imposing personality who, in his lifetime, was nearly executed, exiled twice and set upon by mobs on more than one occasion, and who continues to generate feelings of both respect and disdain centuries after his death.

Nichiren's importance in political as opposed to religious history lies in his prediction of the Mongol invasion as divine punishment for the failure of the authorities to accept his arguments. The irascible Nichiren seems to have been quite put out that the Mongols did not actually conquer the country.

The temples of **Hongaku-ji**, **Myohon-ji**, **Chosho-ji**, **Myoho-ji**, and **Ankokuron-ji** are all Nichiren temples and are worth a visit. The Myohon-ji, for example, although only 10 minutes from the station, seems a world apart.

Jizo images in temple.

The wooded islet of **Enoshima** (Bay Island) is one of those charming spots that few Japanese these days would think of recommending to visitors for a day-trip. But it has many attractions in any weather and is easily reached either from Shinjuku in Tokyo on the private Odayku Line (a pleasant 75-minute ride), or from Kamakura on the quaint and rattling Enoden railway.

In the good old days before the popularity of off-road vehicles and windsurfing, Enoshima was one of *the* places to visit from Tokyo, at least until Disneyland and other theme parks took over. However, this is a point in its favor for travelers tired of endless queues and high prices, especially in summer when everywhere else seems impossibly packed and sweaty.

The island, about two kilometers in circumference, is basically a wooded hill surrounded by rocky beaches and cliffs. But these days it hardly deserves the name of island: the 600-meter-long **Benten Bridge**, which connects Enoshima to the bright lights of **Katase Beach** and the adjacent resort town, has gradually turned into a major causeway. The usually crowded beaches of **Shichirigahama** and **Miami** stretch far to east and west. Access on foot or by car is simple, and there is plenty of parking space at the foot of the hill. Just beyond where the causeway meets the island is the yacht harbor constructed for the Olympics in 1964.

The ascent of the hill begins at the end of Benten Bridge with a narrow street crammed with restaurants and souvenir shops. Genuine crafts nestle next to plastic octopi and real shellfish bubbling away ready for consumption.

The narrow street leads up to the start of a series of user-friendly, covered escalators, which make the upward progress very simple. First stop is the charming **Enoshima-jinja**, built in 1182 and dedicated to Benten, the goddess of fortune. Her naked statue used to reside in a cave on the far side, but fears for her safety led to a place in the shrine itself.

Akiya Beach at sunset, and Enoshima Beach.

And on up, the top is a fun place for adults and kids alike. It features tropical plants, greenhouses, a small zoo, game machines, miniature trains, a short go-kart track, and restaurants and patios providing views of the ocean – everything one needs for a less-than-quiet getaway. An observation tower, 50 meters high and accessible by elevator, gives more exposed views.

Beaches around the island are worth exploring, or else cross the causeway again to visit all the noisier attractions of life on the other side, including swimming pools with giant chutes and performing aquatic mammals at **Enoshima Marineland**. The more spiritually minded might like to visit the famous **Ryuko-ji**, a temple near the station that features a fine pagoda, albeit one of the twentieth century. The temple is dedicated to Nichiren, founder of the only genuinely Japanese sect of Buddhism. It was here that he was saved from execution by a timely stroke of lightning, which hit the uplifted blade of the executioner's sword.

Miura Peninsula: The woodblock artist Hiroshige Ando (1797–1858) stood on the beach at **Akiya**, on the west coast of **Miura Hanto**, and looked out across the sea. In the foreground were the impressive rocks of **Tateishi**, with black-eared kites soaring on the evening breeze, and on the horizon, **Fuji-san** outlined 80 kilometers away against a pollution-free sunset. He immortalized the view with his chisel. The beach at Akiya has hardly changed, save for more people on weekends.

There have been many changes on the peninsula itself, of course, especially during the 1980s, when the apartment blocks and weekend homes began to sprout, and when the newly-affluent youth of Tokyo and Yokohama discovered that a day-trip round the peninsula was a perfect way to indulge in *doraibigu,* or driving, especially bumper-to-bumper *doraibigu.*

Over on the east side of Miuri Hanto is the city of **Yokosuka**, anchored by the American naval base, home of the Seventh Fleet, responsible for one-third of the world's oceans. Like Yokohama, its history is bound up with Japan's less-than-voluntary opening to the world in the mid 1800s. Yokosuka has close associations with Will Adams (*Miura Anjin* in Japanese), the English pilot who was advisor to Tokugawa Ieyasu, the shogun of the book with the same name. Adams is buried in **Tsukayama Koen**. Just to the south is the port of **Uraga**, where Commodore Perry anchored in 1853, and **Kurihama**, where a monument commemorates Perry's delivery of the presidential letter. Yokosuka also features Admiral Togo's flagship in the Russo-Japanese War (from 1904 until 1905, won by Japan), the *Mikasa*, now a floating museum.

But the real attraction of the Miura Peninsula for the Tokyo visitor is that it has so much to offer to anyone interested in clean air, excellent water, fresh fish and vegetables, ocean activities or gentle hiking.

The gray, volcanic-sand beaches may not quite be Maui, but the many little inlets all down the west coast from **Zushi** – **Hayama** (site of a villa for the imperial family), **Chojagasaki**, **Kuruwa**, **Akiya** – provide safe swimming with refreshment stands and changing facilities throughout the summer. Most beaches have wind-surfing facilities, and there are several yachting harbors and marinas, including at Zushi, Hayama, Sajima, Seabornia and Aburatsubo.

The Japanese have a peculiar attitude regarding seasonal activities. Not only is there appropriate wear and tools for every activity, there are definite times when various sports can, and cannot, be undertaken. They regard September 1st as the start of autumn and the end of summer, and thus the end of swimming in the ocean, even if summer has lingered beyond its cutoff date.

Farther down the coast, there are rocky coasts with walking courses and a view towards **Oshima**, an island that's technically part of Metropolitan Tokyo and with an active volcano, and **Ito**, on **Izu Hanto**, where an underwater eruption in 1989 gave hope of extending Japan's land area – it didn't. Izu is also popular for its *onsen,* the hot springs found in volcanically-active Japan.

Daibutsu, the Great Buddha, Kamakura.

関茶店
アポロ
写真館

FUJI, HAKONE AND IZU

If time restricts travel around the archipelago in search of castles, temples, shrines, and for those quaint farming and fishing villages, consider the Fuji and Hakone region, reached in a few hours from Tokyo.

The region has been the inspiration for the works of many of Japan's most celebrated writers, poets and artists. It is also a "continental divide" for Japan, separating the west and south from the cooler north in a strip of volcanic-based topography, whose flora and fauna are both unique and wonderful.

It would be hard to find a mountain more highly praised for its beauty than Fuji-san, or a lake more often photographed than Hakone's Lake Ashi. Most of the region is designated a "national park," but due to Japan's rather weak laws protecting and restricting commercial exploitation of such assets, consider national parks to be "nature" amusement parks. Still, as evidenced by the millions who return year after year, the magic is rewarding.

The mountain: Sweeping up from the Pacific to form a nearly perfect symmetrical cone, 3,776 meters (12,388 ft) above sea level, the elegantly-shaped **Fuji-san** watches over Japan and her people. But the mountain loses its temper on occasion. Fuji's last eruption in 1707 covered Edo Tokyo, some 100 kilometers (60 mi) away, with ash.

Like many natural monuments held to be sacred and imbued with a living spirit, Fuji-san was off limits to women for many centuries. It was not until 1867, when an Englishwoman (figures) boldly scaled the mountain, that there is any record of a woman setting foot on its slopes. Today, about half of the 400,000 Fuji annual hikers are women.

The climb: Although expeditions are known to set out to challenge the mountain throughout the year, the "official" climbing season for Fuji-san begins on July 1 and ends on August 31. The mountain huts and services found along the trails to Fuji's peak are open only then, and casual hikers are advised to pick this period to make the journey to the top. Expect thick crowds, not only around the facilities, but along the entire trail to the top.

The five main trails – Kawaguchi, Subashiri, Fujinomiya, Fuji-Yoshida, and Gotemba – is each divided into ten stages known as *go*. The Kawaguchi trail is the most popular route up, and Subashiri seems to be the preferred way down, but Fujinomiya is more convenient if coming from the direction of Kansai, to the southwest. The ascent should take about 9 hours from the first *go* to the tip of the cone.

For those who wish to see the rising sun from Fuji's peak, a pleasant way of making the trek is to start in the afternoon, stay overnight (forget sleeping – it's noisy) at one of the cabins near the top, and make the remaining climb while the sky is still dark. The option is to climb through the night. The trails are well-traveled and are hard to miss for the most part, but you will be groping helplessly about at night without a light.

Preceding pages: rising sun atop Fuji-san. **Left**, Hakone and Fuji-san. **Right**, mountain shrine altar.

The mountain air can be quite cold and rain is not uncommon, so a warm sweater, thick gloves and a waterproof jacket are recommended.

The fifth stations along the Kawaguchi, Subashiri and Fujinomiya – all called *gogome* – are accessible by road, and if the nine-hour hike is too long, take a bus or car to one of those points. Buses to Kawaguchi's gogome are available from the bus terminal at Hamamatsucho or Shinjuku JR stations in Tokyo, and the trip will take about two hours.

Those who prefer the train can either catch the JR Chuo Line from Shinjuku Station or the Fuji Kyuko Line via Otsuki, to Kawagushi or Gotemba stations, from where buses run to the gogome of the respective trails.

To get to the Fujinomiya trail, take the Tokaido Main Line to Fuji, or the bullet train to Mishima. Buses should be running regularly during the official climbing season.

Fuji Five Lakes: The Five Lakes district skirts the northern base of Fuji-san and provides an ideal year-round resort, offering a range of outdoor recreational activities such as camping and water sports during the summer months, and skiing and skating in the winter. From east to west, the lakes are **Yamanaka**, **Kawaguchi**, **Sai**, **Shoji** and **Motosu**. (A *ko* added to the end of these names signifies "lake".)

Yamanaka-ko, which is the largest in the group, and the picturesque Kawaguchiko are the most frequented of the five, but some of the best spots are hidden near the smaller and more secluded Motosu-ko, Shoji-ko and Saiko. Some recommended visits include the **Narusawa Ice Cave** and **Fugaku Wind Cave**, both formed by the volcanic activities of one of Fuji's early eruptions; the delicate **Shiraito Falls**; and **Koyodai** (Maple Hill), which offers one of the best views of the surrounding area. The primeval forests of **Junkai** and **Aokigahara** are also worth noting.

All five lakes are connected by excellent roads and are regularly serviced by buses from Gotemba, Fuji-Yoshida and Kawaguchi-ko.

Hakone: Local history has it that when Toyotomi Hideyoshi, one of Japan's great warriors and the first to unite the country, seized Odawara Castle in 1590, he ordered a rock mineral bath to be built in the neighboring mountains, where his men could ease their travel-weary bodies. This area, known as Hakone, is set against the backdrop of Fuji-san, and has been a popular place for rest and recreation ever since.

The optimal tour starts at Odawara Station, where the **Hakone Tozan Densha** (mountain railway) begins its nine-kilometer (5-mi) zig-zag up to **Gora**. This amazing single-track train, built in 1919, climbs and clangs its 40-minute journey up the steep slope. And it's not just for tourists; in the early morning and late afternoon hours, the small train is packed with children.

Hakone-Yumoto, the first stop on the line and the gateway to Hakone's 16 hot springs, nestles in a shallow ravine where the Hayakawa and Sukumo rivers flow together. An overnight stay at one of the inns here is recommended; all

Idyllic serenity atop Fuji-san

have natural mineral baths. If on a day-trip, the **Tenzan** public bath provides an exquisite hot spring treat for just a few hundred yen. The area is crowded on weekends and holidays, so plan ahead.

Twenty minutes up from Yumoto lies **Miyanoshita**, the oldest and the most thriving of the spa towns. The original *Taiko no Iwayu,* the rock bath attributed to Hideyoshi, can be found here, although it is no longer in use.

Miyanoshita is also the home of the famed **Fujiya Hotel** and **Naraya Ryokan**. Fujiya, dating from 1878, is the second-oldest existing hotel in Japan. Naraya has a fine reputation and is also used by the imperial family on special occasions. For many years, the two establishments competed fiercely for guests to the area. However, in true Japanese fashion, they decided on a compromise: Fujiya would cater to Western styles and Naraya would remain Japanese-style. It was also agreed that Fujiya, which seemed to have the better deal, would pay a fee to cover Naraya's losses.

Outdoor art: The Tozan Tetsudo also makes a stop at **Chokoku-no-Mori**, an outdoor sculpture garden where the works of Picasso, Rodin, Leger and Takamura Kotaro and many others are on permanent display.

At the Gora terminal, change over to the cable car to Sounzan and then transfer to the Hakone Ropeway headed for Togendai. On the way is **Owakudani** – Valley of the Greater Boiling – in the old crater of Kami. It is an interesting place but the yellow, sulphurous fumes can be rather overwhelming.

Togendai lies on the shore of **Ashino-ko** (Lake Ashi), a beautiful caldera lake crisscrossed by regular pleasure boats. There are many attractions around this lake. The **Hakone-jinja**, said to have been founded during the eighth century, is the reason behind the flourishing of the town of **Moto-Hakone**, a samurai religious center in its heyday.

Of course, the building which stands today was constructed at a much later date, but interesting relics can be found about the area.

Ashino-ko and Fuji-san.

The **Suginamiki**, or Ancient Cedar Avenue, makes for a wonderful stroll. This was part of the **Tokaido Highway**, down which the grand processions of the shogun lords and hundreds of their retainers made their way to the capital. Near here stood the Hakone Sekisho, a barrier originally built in 1618 to defend Edo and keep an eye on the comings and goings on the highway. The **Hakone Shiryokan Museum** nearby offers a glimpse of life as it lived was during the reign of the Tokugawa shogunate.

From **Hakonen**, the Komagatake Ropeway reaches the summit of **Komaga-dake**, one of the last of the Hakone volcanos to erupt. The much-talked-about view from the top takes in Ashi-ko and the Amagi range.

Izu Peninsula: Extending into the Pacific between the Sagami and Sugura bays is Izu Hanto, where countless bays, beaches and onsen, together with a very inviting climate, give Izu its reputation as a resort for all seasons. in 1853.

Eastern Izu begins at **Atami**, a hot spring dating back over a thousand years. During the Edo Period, the shogun had its waters brought to the palace so he could enjoy a relaxing bath. Today, Atami is a lively town, albeit somewhat bawdy, offering reasonably sophisticated night life and numerous recreational facilities. The MOA Art Museum boasts a fine collection of *ukiyo-e*, ceramics and lacquer works, many of which have been designated as National Treasures and Important Cultural Properties by the national government.

Those travelers who have read James Clavell's *Shogun* may recognize **Ito** as the temporary abode of the shipwrecked Englishman who – so serendipitously, at least in Clavell's version – ingratiated himself into Japanese affairs. The **Ikeda Art Museum** offers some 600 paintings and sculptures by Matisse, Picasso, Chagall, Dali and other masters.

Shimoda is a somewhat sleepy resort town. A fine view of **Iro-misaki** to the south can be had from the top of **Nesugata**, three minutes by ropeway from Shimoda Station. The view includes volcanically-active Oshima.

Izu rice farming...

It should also be mentioned that the fresh seafood – particularly the prawns – served in hotels, *ryokan* and restaurants in eastern Izu can be heavenly.

Central Izu is the cultural heart of Izu. The **Taisha-jinja** in **Mishima** is revered as Izu's first shrine, and its treasure hall keeps documents of the first Kamakura shogun as well as swords and other artifacts. The Egawa Old House in Nirama is the oldest private dwelling in Japan. **Shuzen-ji**, along the Katsura-gawa, sprang up around a temple founded by the monk Kobo Daishi; this quiet hot-spring town became a favorite hideaway for Japan's great literary talents, such as Natsume Soseki, Nobel prizewinner Kawabata Yasunari and Kido Okamoto.

The west coast is less visited by tourists, for unlike the east, it has no train service. Still, resort towns such as **Toi** and others here are interesting, and some have, reputedly, the best hot springs anywhere in the region.

In the middle of May, Shimoda celebrates the Kurofune Matsuri (Black Ship Festival), in commemoration of Commodore Perry's landing. Various ceremonies, parades and a fireworks display take place.

Ito holds its Tarainori Kyoso on the first Sunday in July, with a race of wooden washtubs equipped with sails, followed by fireworks. Then August sees the Ito Anji Sai, dedicated to William Adams, as Ito townspeople float paper lanterns on the river in his memory. The Annual Festival of the Mishima Taisha, at Mishima, falls between August 15 and 17, allowing onlookers an idea of what the procession of Minamoto no Yoritomo, the first Kamakura shogun, may have looked like. There is also a archery performance, from horseback, on the last day.

The main gateways to Izu are Atami (a stop on the *shinkansen*) and Mishima, on the Tokaido Main Line. The JR limited express "Odoriko" also makes direct trips to Ito and Shimoda from Tokyo (the name of the train is the title of Kawabata's famous short story, known in English as *The Izu Dancer*).

... and fish farms.

NIKKO

After learning that the main attraction at Nikko, **Tosho-gu**, comprises 42 structures, and that 29 of these are embellished with some sort of carving – 5,147 in all, according to a six-year-long survey concluded in 1991 by shrine officials – more than a few tourists begin to realize that they've alloted either too little or too much time for Nikko.

The small city of **Nikko** itself is of little interest, serving merely as a commercial anchor to the splendors that decorate the hillsides and plateau, across the river to the west from the main railway stations. The Tobu train arrives in exactly (and a watch can be set by it) 101 minutes after departing Tokyo's Ueno Station, something of which the railway's advertising department has made a catch-phrase for years.

How this region, once a several-day trek from the shogunate's capital in Edo (now Tokyo), was chosen as the site of Tokugawa Ieyasu's mausolea is a story in itself. True, Nikko forms a sort of cap or crown at the northern perimeter of the great Kanto Plain, of which Edo was the center. However, Ieyasu was from Kansai, not Kanto, and he had established his capital in Kanto primarily to distance himself from the imperial forces in Kansai's Kyoto, forces he had vanquished to seize power in the first place.

Still, Ieyasu's grandson, Iemitsu (1604–51) set in motion the process that turned this once out-of-the-way region into Tokugawa territory about 20 years after Ieyasu's death, and who himself, followed by his successor Ietsuna – and, indeed by Tokugawa shoguns and princes for the next 250 years – made at least three annual pilgrimages to the site to pay tribute to the founder of the dynasty that kept Japan and its people isolated from the outside world.

Ironically, however, given the Tokugawa adversion to things from outside Japan, many of the 5,000-odd carvings at Tosho-gu depict things foreign. The facade of the main shrine, for example, features carvings of three Chinese men, said to represent important figures of that country who, having turned down their chances to be kings or emperors, became folk heroes. Perhaps the carvings are meant to convey the fallacy that Ieyasu had come to power only after the Toyotomi emperor had voluntarily abdicated in his favor.

Most ironic of all – and most hypocritical, considering its importance in the annals of Japanese art – is the famous, not to say fabulous, **Yomei-mon**, the gate beyond which only the highest ranking samurai could pass into the inner sanctum of the shrine, and then only after laying aside their swords.

This gate is, indeed, a masterpiece. Technically, it is a 12-column, two-story structure, with hip-gable ends on right and left, and cusped gables on four sides. This description, while accurate, is somewhat misleading, however. The gate, even though its *keyaki*-wood columns are painted white to make it appear larger, is quite small.

Nearly every surface of the gate is adorned with delicate carvings of every

Preceding pages: autumn smile. Left, Nikko's fall foliage. Right, Tosho-gu's five-story pagoda.

sort – children at play, clouds, tree peonies, pines, bamboo, Japanese apricots, phoenixes, pheasants, cranes, wild ducks and other waterfowl, turtles, elephants, rabbits, a couple of furry tigers, Chinese lions, and the traditional symbols of regal power, dragons.

A large white dragon (one of 92 in and around the shrine) is the main feature of the central beam in front of the second story of this fanciful structure, and two drawings of dragons appear on the ceiling of the porticos; the drawing nearer the entrance is known as *nobori-ryu* or ascending dragon; the other, *kudari-ryu* or descending dragon.

Keep in mind that, although it is designated a National Treasure and is considered an example of the heights of Japanese art, the nameless artisans who created Yomei-mon (and many of the other treasures at Nikko) were of Korean, not Japanese, origin. This is no small matter, given the sense of racial and cultural superiority that the Japanese tend to have over Koreans.

What lies beyond this gate? Another gate, of course: **Kara-mon** (Chinese Gate), also a National Treasure. It is even smaller than the Yomei-mon (about three by two meters overall) and is also laden with carvings – dragons (ascending and descending, and just laying around), apricots, bamboo, tree peonies and more.

The ceiling has a carved figure of a fairy playing a harp, while on the ridge of the front gable is a bronze figure of a *tsutsuga*, which, like quite a few other carvings and castings in the shrine precincts, is not quite a real animal, but rather one created from hearsay and myth, and mixed with a healthy (Korean, perhaps) imagination.

To help one get bearings, the Kara-mon is the last barrier to pass through before reaching the entrance to the *haiden* (oratory) and the *honden* (main hall), which is the place most visitors remember as they are requested to remove shoes.

An official guidebook describes haiden and honden as the "chief edifices of the shrine." Chief they are, but inter-

One of 42 structures at Tosho-gu.

esting they are not – at least not to the casual visitor who, not knowing what to look for, tends to shuffle along with the crowd and then returning back to the shoe-lockers without a pause. Unfortunately, many of the key elements inside are partially or entirely hidden from the view of this method.

The Sleeping Cat: Confused (and no doubt somewhat bored) after their shuffle through the "chief edifices," most visitors exit, redon their shoes and spend the next 10 minutes or so looking for the famous **Nemuri-neko**, or carving of the Sleeping Cat. Some never find it at all, and make their way back down the hillside feeling somewhat cheated.

To make sure this doesn't happen to you, do *not* follow the logical path back toward the Yomei-mon. Instead, turn left (right if facing the Haiden/Honden complex) until you are back on the terrace between the Yomei-mon and the Kara-mon. Next, advance straight ahead (paying the small fee charged at a makeshift entrance to the **Oku-no-In**, or Inner Precincts) and into the open-sided, red-lacquered corridor that skirts the foot of the steep hillside, atop which is the actual Tokugawa tomb. Nemuri-neko, a painted relief carving, is over the gateway.

This small and gray cat, well-enough executed and rather cute but otherwise unremarkable, is said to symbolize tranquility. The fact that it is asleep is taken to mean that all "harmful mice" have been sent packing and the shrine is, therefore, safe. The carved sparrows seen behind the dozing cat are not, presumably, a threat.

While here, climb the 200-odd stone steps to the top of the hill and the Tokugawa tomb, called **Hoto**, wherein, it is said, lie the remains of Ieyasu. Some spectacular views of rooftops and the surrounding terrain are had from here.

On the way back down, past the Yomei-mon to the main entrance and beyond, be sure to stop by the **Yakushido**, one of the few places in these sacred Shinto surroundings with a Buddhist atmosphere. It's off to the right. Here, too, remove shoes, but it'll

Inner courtyard of Tosho-gu.

be worth it. The attraction of this building (it is not exactly a Buddhist temple) is the huge *naku-ryu* drawing on the ceiling. The word means Crying Dragon, and, of course, the dragon is not crying.

It seems that when people stood under the original – drawn in India ink by Kano Yasunobu (1613–85) – and clapped their hands (as in prayer), the dragon was heard to utter a long, agonized groan. What this was meant to signify is not recorded, and perhaps we will never know, because in 1961, a fire destroyed the building – and the drawing along with it.

Among the other sights to take note of as one leaves the shrine are the **sutra library**, which boasts nearly 7,000 volumes of the Buddhist sutras in a large, revolving bookcase that was invented by the Chinese.

Its other treasures include numerous stone, bronze and iron lanterns presented by the *daimyo* paying their respects to the shogunate, and a pair of stone *tobikoe-no-shishi* (leaping lions) as the main pillars of the stone balustrade, in the middle court and bell presented by a king of Korea.

The bronze candelabrum, and a bronze lantern and large revolving lantern, were presented by the government of the Netherlands to Japan in 1636. The revolving lantern, in front of the drum tower, is adorned with the three-leaf crests of the Tokugawa clan, but they are placed upside down, perhaps, as an official guidebook to the sutra library explains, "by mistake."

Here, also, are the sacred storehouses on the sides of the middle court. The upper one shows two (imaginary) elephants carved in relief, as well as the *mikoshi-gura* (sacred palanquin house), the repository for the sacred portable shrines used in the annual festival, and the *kagura-den* (sacred dance stage). The flower basket in the gilded panel at the right corner probably was inspired by a basket used by early Dutch traders, and is the only carving in the precincts that shows Western artistic influences.

Monkey trio: Beyond the 40-meter-high (130-ft) **five-story pagoda**, its first

One of Nikko's many bridges.

story decorated with the 12 signs of the Chinese zodiac, and just before reaching the nine-meter-tall (30-ft) **Omotemon** (Front Gate) with its large images of the two deva kings, there is what may be the most famous carvings of all – not just in Nikko, but in all the world. There, just under the eaves of the royal stables building (which happens to be the only unlacquered structure in the shrine precincts) are the **three famous monkeys**: Hear no evil, speak no evil, see no evil. Small carvings they are, despite their fame, but so are all the other 5,000-plus carvings at Tosho-gu.

Just a short stroll down the broad avenue leading from the Thousand Steps (there are only 10) entrance to Tosho-gu is the **Treasure House** – a small museum housing various articles (including carvings) from Tosho-gu and other places around Nikko; during peak tourist seasons, there probably will be a number of kiosks set up in the small adjoining park, **Koyoen**, selling beverages and food. Continue along the wide avenue for a few minutes to reach the **Futarasan-jinja**, on the right side and away from Tosho-gu. Futarasan-jinja enshrines the three primary Shinto deities: Okuninushi no Mikoto, his consort Tagorihime no Mikoto, and their son Ajisukitakahikone no Mikoto. All three are revered for having helped to create – and then make prosperous – the numerous Japanese Islands.

Within the grounds is a large bronze lantern, called Bake-Doro (Goblin Lantern), which is once supposed to have taken on the shape of a goblin so frightening that a samurai attacked it one night, leaving "sword scratches" that are still visible to this day.

Further afield but still within the general area of Tosho-gu are several other places of interest. One is the **Hon-gu** (more popularly called Futaarasan-Hongu), one of the oldest shrines in Nikko and established in 767 by the priest Shodo; the present buildings date back only to the end of the seventeenth century, when the shrine was rebuilt after being destroyed by fire. Just behind it is **Shihonryu-ji,** although also founded in

Stone images of the shogun's samurai.

766 by Shodo, is not a Shinto shrine, but rather a Buddhist temple. It also was destroyed by fire, and the present three-story pagoda was erected in its place at the end of the seventeenth century. The pagoda, and the image of the thousand-hand Kannon inside, are the temple's main attractions.

Then there is **Rinno-ji**, a temple of the Tendai sect of Buddhism. Its main claim to fame is the fact that General Ulysses S. Grant, the eighteenth president of the United States and a hero of the American Civil War, stayed here during his eight-day sojourn to Japan and Nikko in 1879. It was one of Grant's few trips outside of North America.

Actually, the temple has more than Grant-slept-here going for it. In its spirit hall are the tablets of its long line of abbots, all drawn from the imperial family, and in another building – built in 1648 and still the largest in Nikko – are three quite amazing Buddhist statues, all measuring eight meters (26 ft) in height, and worked in gilded wood. The Bato Kannon, on the left, has the figure of a horse's head on its forehead, and is worshiped as the deity for the protection of animals.

In the forests: The lush forests of Nikko and how pleasant they are, even in the rain, has already been mentioned.

Seeing these ancient trees – the majority are *suji*, or Japanese cedar – one would think they have stood here since the beginning of time, or at the very least are part of a primeval virgin forest. They don't go back quite that far, but they are nevertheless very old – especially those trees in the Tosho-gu precincts proper, and also those along the many, many kilometers of avenues and roads within and leading to Nikko. They were all planted as seedlings, one by one, from year to year, under the direction of a man named Matsudaira Masatsuna (1576–1648).

Matsudaira, so the story goes, was the *daimyo* of Kawagoe, and one of the two persons honored by edict of the shogun to supervise the construction of Tosho-gu. The extent of the man's personal wealth is not recorded, nor how much of

Fishing on Chuzenji-ko, and autumn skyline.

it was spent, in addition to the budget he was given by the Tokugawa shogun, for carrying out this worthy task.

However, it can be assumed that either he wasn't very well off to begin with, or that he overspent more than he ought to have, because when his turn to present a grand offering to the shrine came – as all the other daimyo were obliged to do – Matsudaira was broke.

What could he do? he wondered. Around 1631, several years before the shrine itself was finished, he began to transplant cedar seedlings – plentiful in the surrounding mountains (which he owned) – into strategic positions around the shrine grounds and along those endless roads. It took him 20 years and an estimated 25,000 seedlings, but it was done and the tale completed. Today, these trees are what, in part, define Nikko and its surroundings for travelers.

The beneficence continues: the trees – and the banks along the avenues – are now specially protected as Natural Treasures and Places of Historical Importance under Japanese law.

Excursions: Thanks to the numbers of tourists who flock to Nikko, and to the region's fine scenery, the area abounds with other diversions. Unfortunately, getting around without a vehicle is a problem. If money permits, rent a car. (Not cheap.) If time permits, take a taxi (not bus) up the famed *I-Ro-Ha* switchback road to **Chuzenji-ko**, a large and quite picturesque lake due west of Nikko, and whose heavily-wooded shores are lined with hotels, inns, camping grounds and other tourist wonders.

If choosing not to stay overnight at the lake, try one of the several *onsen* on the picturesque **Kinu-gawa**, closer to Nikko itself.

Also in the area of the Kinu-gawa is **Nikko Edo-mura**, a theme park; the not-so-cheap entrance fee entitles one to stroll around the extensive grounds on streets that look like a movie set of the old Edo days. There is a "real" *ninja* show, a "poetry maze," and other attractions. It's great fun, and a good way to spend a few hours to learn about the old days of pre-Meiji Japan.

Chuzenji-ko.

THE KANSAI

The old Tokaido (Eastern Sea Road) that connected the ancient capital at Kyoto with the seat of the feudal shogunate at Kamakura (and later, with Edo Tokyo) has all but disappeared. But it was along that much-traveled highway, at a point where it passed through the Hakone hills, that the Kamakura *bakufu* set up a heavily-armed outpost in the thirteenth century to stifle threats by the western warlords and imperial loyalists. It is from this post that the regions to the west got their name: *Kansai,* or Western Barrier.

In the Kamakura days, virtually all lands west and south of those barriers – including the Nagoya and Gifu regions – were considered to be in the Kansai. Later, around or just before the beginning of the Edo era, the definition narrowed to include only the Kyoto, Nara, Osaka and Kobe areas. For this book, we've retained Nagoya and Gifu in the Kansai section.

Naturally, persons native to the Kansai feel an intense rivalry with other parts of the country, particularly the Kanto region, home of Tokyo. Although much of the Kansai region is still agricultural, declaring that one is from Kansai doesn't evoke a backwater image. In fact, despite their snickers at the Osaka dialect and at the rather sophomoric sense of humor to be found in Kansai, those in Tokyo must yield to the renown and respect of the entrepreneurial skills of people from Osaka and Kobe. Indeed, the great commercial and industrial complexes of Osaka and Kobe are the centers of Japan's international commerce. Moreover, there is the unquestionable urban sophistication of ancient Kyoto, which, after all, was the nation's powerful premier city for well over 1,000 years.

Osaka is a street-smart city, a place where the successful person has read the signals and kept an eye out for both opportunities and problems. For what it's worth, Osaka is the center of the *yakuza*, the organized crime activity in Japan. But it is also the base of Japan's most innovative electronics manufacturer, Matsushita, and is a leader – together with Nagoya – in the development of robotic production techniques.

Whether the traveler chooses the hills of Kobe, the hustle of Osaka, the antiquities of Kyoto, or the industry of Nagoya, the Kansai region probably offers more to the first-time visitor than does that megalopolis 500 kilometers (300 mi) to the north, Tokyo.

Preceding pages: mountain commercial onsen. Left, traditional performer.

NAGOYA AND GIFU

Nagoya may be the biggest small town one might chance to visit. Although it ranks as the fourth-largest city in Japan, and is the capital of crab-shaped Aichi Prefecture, Nagoya has a mood more like a *furusato*, a hometown, that has gotten way too big for its britches.

Known for its flat, white *kishimen* noodles, its pickles known as *moriguchi-zuke*, and its confection, *uiro*, Nagoya is better recognized as a center of industry, producing construction materials and automobiles. Another of Nagoya's claims to industrial fame is the pinball game, *pachinko*, invented (actually adapted from a Western game) here just after World War II. Most of Japan's millions of addictive pachinko machines are made in this region.

Nagoya is located almost precisely in the center of Japan, along the old Tokaido Highway, and is a major hub for transportation to and from other cities, including Tokyo and Osaka.

In the center: Behind **Meieki**, the neighborhood where **Nagoya Station** is located and the station's unofficial name, lies Eska, a sparkling-clean underground shopping mall, and Apita, a pricey department store, which stands out among a number of business hotels, fading love hotels and tiny art cinemas.

The *shinkansen* tracks are near the back of the station, to the west, but in the front, to the east, is an entirely different scene. There are several major department stores in the immediate vicinity, along with numerous cinema complexes, and a wedge of a building called Lejac, in which much of Nagoya's affluent youths seems to experience its nightlife.

Nearby is the venerable **Dai Nagoya Building**, with the odd orange globe on its roof. That globe is one of the original commercial symbols of modern Japan, and it belongs to Morinaga, a caramel company in the late 1800s that has since become one of Japan's food-processing giants. Morinaga maintains one of its restaurants in the building, which at night is illuminated by a violet light.

Left, temple fortune. Right, castle artist.

A statue of Serve, Nagoya's celebrated seeing-eye dog, guards one of the east entrances to the large station complex, which includes several underground subway lines, the Meitetsu and Kintetsu train lines, the Tokaido shinkansen line, and a network of underground shopping complexes. Indeed, the underground shopping complex spills over nearly to the next subway stop. The glass-walled Kokusai Center houses an information center, two lending libraries, comfortable reading rooms and businesses.

Theoretically, one could spend the day at Meieki without leaving the station. It's not advised, however. Above ground, a walk from Meieki to the Kokusai Center passes one of Nagoya's many *karakuri* dolls – automated wooden puppets – devised during the Edo period and which emerge from clock towers to announce the time.

Nagoya was originally planned by the shogun Tokugawa Ieyasu to be a castle town; he built **Nagoya-jo** in 1612 for his ninth son, Yoshinao. But the town didn't quite develop that way; at

any rate, Nagoya had to be redesigned and reconstructed after suffering extensive air-raid damage in 1945. The castle, rebuilt in 1959 and now functioning as a cultural and historical museum, is considered Nagoya's primary attraction. The golden dolphins on the roof of its restored *donjon* are the adopted symbols of Nagoya. The rebuilt Nagoya-jo, in **Meijo Koen** (Park) near the center of government offices, is a short taxi or subway trip from Nagoya Station.

One kilometer to the south is the 180-meter-high (590 ft) television broadcasting tower, on Hisaya Dori and with one of the best views of Nagoya. Below the tower and extending every which way is yet another underground arcade. This area is known as **Sakae**, and is the center of Nagoya's legal nightlife, and a shopping paradise for non-bargain hunters. Its two main east–west streets, which begin at Meieki and parallel the Higashiyama subway line, are Hirokoji Dori, and Nishiki Dori. On the second weekend of every October, these avenues are thronged with Nagoyans celebrating the Nagoya Festival, which features a parade of men in armor and a streetside theatrical display arranged by Atsuta-jingu.

Both Hisaya Odori and the Meijo subway line run north–south straight down from Nagoya-jo through Sakae to Yabacho, about two kilometers south of the castle. From there, one can walk west on Wakamiya Odori to **Shirakawa Koen**, with a science museum that offers a "Theater of the Stars." One more stop on the Meijo line – or a walk down Hisaya Odori, which later becomes Maezu Dori – is Kamimaezu, where cramped secondhand bookstores mark nearly every corner. From Kamimaezu, venture east until **Tsurumai Koen**, a calm 24-hectare (60-acre) collection of gardens in Asian and Western styles.

Or walk northwest a few blocks and enter yet another shopping arcade, this one above-ground but roofed. Ameyoko is an electronics haven, and the **Komeihyo** area is a combination of pawnshops and five-and-dime stalls. In between these are shops.

Nagoya-jo and sakura.

The arcade ends at the bright-orange **Ozu Kannon-ji**, perched high atop its white stairway and specializing in blessings for automobiles. (Aichi Prefecture, by the way, is infamous as the home of Japan's worst drivers.) On the 18th and 28th of every month, antique dealers spread their wares along the temple grounds for a flea market of grand proportions; every weekend, Komeihyo has a giant used-kimono sale. During the last week of July and the first week of August, the arcade whirls with the Street Performances Festival.

The subway goes south to the **Port of Nagoya**, where the **Nagoya City Exhibition Hall** and the **Nagoya Port Building** are located. The latter houses an observatory, a restaurant and the **Nagoya Maritime Museum**, whose principal attraction is the retired Antarctic icebreaker, *Fuji Maru*. It is in this area where the Port Festival, in July, attracts thousands of people with fireworks, a brass-band parade and a *matsuri*, complete with *omikoshi*.

Atsuta-jingu, at Jingu-mae, is second only to the Ise Jingu, in Mie Prefecture, in its importance to the emperor of Japan and Shintoism. One of the family's three sacred treasures, the Kusanagi sword, is kept here. Hundreds of ancient trees thrive amidst equally-ancient artifacts, including the 600-year-old **Nijugocho Bashi**, made of 25 blocks of stone. The shrine's festival is in June.

There are museums all over Nagoya, ranging from the treasure-laden **Tokugawa Art Museum**, including heirlooms of the Owari-Tokugawa family, to the **Aichi Bijutsukan** (Fine Arts Museum), near the TV tower and which often displays the works of Japan's up-and-coming artists. (Visitors may participate in a quiet tea ceremony at the Tokugawa Art Museum.)

Nagoya is packed with universities and junior colleges. Its two most prestigious, Nagoya University, or Meidai, and Nanzan University, are set within shouting distance of each other along Yotsuya Dori, a high-tech, high-fashion boulevard. The **Meidai/Nanzan** area is in such a hurry to develop itself that

Pachinko parlor.

even its newer buildings, less than a decade old, are often torn down to make way for edifices and structures a bit more state-of-the-art.

A trek between subway lines leads from cafe to boutique, from below street level to well above it. An airy, post-modern, experimental architecture now characterizes the district. Glass-and-chrome columns are illuminated in ice-cream colors, while atria and loft-like cafes look out upon the hill. It's the closest one will ever come to true glitz in Nagoya.

Further up the Higashiyama line is the Higashiyama Zoo, with 3,200 captive animals, and the botanical gardens. The zoo's **Sky Tower** provides another splendid view of Nagoya.

Outside of Nagoya: The Nagoya environs hold much to be explored. There is, for example, nearby **Kasugai** to the northeast, with its peach orchards and paper factories. Or a town called **Toyota**, due east towards the hills and whose main industry has become an automotive name around the world. **Seto**, a kiln town north of Toyota, has lent its name as the generic term for all pottery in Japan, *setomono*. Every September, the potters of this sleepy hamlet bring their wares out to be sold at discount rates along both sides of the Seto-gawa. This *setomono-ichi* (market) is brief, lasting only three days.

Southwest along the coast of Ise Bay, **Suzuka** – locale of a circuit used to test vehicles built by a hometown boy named Honda – is also the site of world-class Formula One racing. Gamagori has motorboat-racing, and Tokoname, also with a motorboat race course, has a number of kilns whose ceramic output has notable style. **Arimatsu** is the home of a dyeing technique called *shibori*, which is used in making kimono, and is also known for the unique methods of fireproofing its houses.

Like most urban train stations in Japan, Nagoya Station is the best starting point for out-of-city ventures. The Meitetsu Inuyama line goes to **Inuyama-jo**, directly north of the city and just 10 minutes away, perched on a cliff above

Gifu in winter.

the Kiso-gawa. It claims to be Japan's oldest castle tower, and is one of the few privately-owned castles left in Japan. Also in the Inuyama area are **Little World**, an outdoor ethnic museum of dwellings from all over the world; **Japan Monkey Park**, where visitors can mingle with some of the approximately 1,000 simian residents; and **Meiji-mura**, where Meiji-era trains chug through a "village" full of Meiji and post-Meiji buildings (including a section of Frank Lloyd Wright's original Imperial Hotel) collected from all over Japan. Other attractions include a riverboat ride and cormorant fishing on the Kiso-gawa.

Every March, one of Japan's strangest festivals occurs not far from Inuyama, at a little shrine – **Tagata-jingu** – dedicated to phalluses. A huge and anatomically-correct phallus is carried through the streets, and crowds of men and especially women try to touch it, hoping to enhance their fertility. Sake flows freely and amiable mass confusion reigns. The shrine is open year-round, and its gift shop is stocked with appropriately-shaped sweets, toys and reminders.

Gifu: This quiet town, northwest of Nagoya, has a modern-apparel industry, which attracts international buyers (especially from underdeveloped nations). But for Japanese tourists, Gifu is undoubtedly better-known for its 200-year history of cormorant fishing – *uaki* – on its three rivers, the Kiso, Ibi and Nagara, which cut through the city. In the sixteenth century, Oda Nobunaga legitimized the fishing of *ayu,* or trout, with cormorants.

Later, shogun Tokugawa Ieyasu, who liked sashimi cut from ayu and often presented this delicacy at court, popularized the dish in Edo.

Today, uaki is a lucrative tourist attraction, with the collared birds doing their thing at night, illuminated by small fires suspended in iron baskets from the front of the boats.

Gifu-jo commands an impressive view from the top of **Kinka-zan** (Golden Flower Mountain) in the city; it was built about seven centuries ago, has suffered numerous razings, and was rebuilt in 1956. A three-minute gondola ride to the foot of the mountain arrives at **Gifu Koen**, and the **Museum of History** and the **Museum of Insects**. The latter contains various bugs, butterflies and spiders – some of which are uncomfortably large – from around the world.

Mountainous Gifu Prefecture has much to offer in the way of natural beauty. High in the mountains north of Nagano, the resort towns of **Gero** and **Takayama** lure with their *onsen* and ubiquitous hikes, tennis courts and other vacation activities. From Gifu and Nagoya, the buses to Gero are often crowded with aged citizens, making their way to the baths (or the Gero Onsen Hospital), where the natural hot springs are said to ease the effects of numerous ailments.

On the other hand, the JR trains bound for Takayama (from Nagoya Station via Gifu City) are more often crammed with more youthful travelers, especially in mid April, when the town's Hachiman-jinja holds its annual festival of two dozen colorfully-decorated floats.

Takayama is packed with museums and other points of interest; the quiet beauty of the town, its *shunkei-nuri* lacquerware and its sake make it a good off-the-beaten-track place to visit.

Finally, no summary of the sights in the Nagoya region would be complete without mention of **Seki**, a blade-forging village a bit east of Gifu and the site of the Battle of Sekigahara, waged in the early seventeenth century between the forces of Tokugawa Ieyasu and Toyotomi Hideyori. The battle was a significant turning point in Japanese history, a catalyst for a complete shift in the archipelago's power structure.

Though Tokugawa was outnumbered nearly two to one, his warriors slaughtered more than a third of the enemy troops to put their leader in the shogun's throne, which he and his descendants held for the next 250-odd years.

It is considered sad by some that, today, only an unassuming stone marks the spot of Tokugawa's heroic triumph. In lieu of a memorial to him or an appropriate museum, Sekigahara offers only an amusement park and an ice-skating rink.

GRAND SHRINES OF ISE

Whether perceived as that which is simple, good and lasting in the Japanese aesthetic, or the focus of an anachronistic and ultra-nationalistic religion, do visit these magnificent Shinto shrines, just a short detour from Nagoya.

No one can say exactly how long the two main shrines of what are collectively called the Grand Shrines of Ise have existed. Historical evidence suggests that **Naiku**, or the Inner Shrine, has been in place since around the fourth century, and **Geku**, or the Outer Shrine, since the late fifth century. It's likely that some sort of shrine has been here much longer.

At Ise, the venerable cypress-wood shrine buildings stand today in perfect condition – almost new and mocking the ravages of time. The secret of the fine condition of these most sacred of Shinto shrines is in *sengu*, or shrine removal, performed every 20 years over the last 13 centuries, the latest and 61st sengu taking place in 1993.

Sengu consists of the razing of the two main buildings (**Toyouke-Daijingu**, of the Outer Shrine, and **Kotaijingu**, of the Inner Shrine), along with 14 smaller auxiliary structures, *betsugu*.

In the sengu, before the existing structures are destroyed, new shrine buildings of identical scale and materials are erected on adjacent foundations set aside for that purpose. When all is ready, Japan's largest and most important festival, Jingu Shikinen Sengu, begins – the deities of the respective shrines are invited to pass from the old into the new structures. Later, the old structures are torn down and sections of the timbers sent to Shinto shrines throughout Japan.

Not only are the buildings reborn, but too a long list of divine apparel and treasures – clothing, decorations and accouterments for the gods.

The prefabrication of the new shrine buildings from *hinoki*, or Japanese cypress, began early with the timber harvested from a special state forest to the north in Nagano and blessed there in a 1985 ceremony.

Why this work? First, the 20-year period can be viewed as a transition point. In human life, it is a line of demarcation between generations. Thus, sengu perpetuates an appreciation and an awareness of the cultural and religious significance of the shrines from age to age. Two decades is also perhaps the most logical period in terms of passing on, from generation to generation, the technological expertise needed for the reconstruction.

Geku, the Outer Shrine: The proper practice when visiting the shrines is to stop at Geku first. This shrine, located a few blocks from Ise Station in a magnificent grove of old Japanese cedars, is dedicated to Toyouke no Omikami, the goddess of agriculture, worshipped in the Ise region for some 2,000 years. During that period, prayers have been offered at Ise for the continuity and safety of the imperial house, the security of the nation, and the peaceful lives of the people.

The grounds of Geku cover about 90 hectares (220 acres), 23 hectares larger than the Inner Shrine. After crossing the bridge in front of the first *torii*, the **Kiyomori-no-Kusu** is to the right.

A tale is attached to this large camphor tree, about six meters in circumference but otherwise unremarkable. It seems that when the famous general Taira no Kiyomori visited the shrine as an imperial messenger in the twelfth century, his ornamental coronet got caught in a branch of the tree. He became so angry that he ordered the branch cut off. Is that scar on the trunk proof? Further on is the **Shoden**, or **Main Hall**. A

Ceremonial stalks of rice.

thatched gateway stands at the outermost of the three formidable fences, which is as far as anyone except imperial personages, envoys and shrine officials get to Shoden.

Shoden is six meters (20 ft) high, with a base of 10 by six meters (33 by 19 ft), and is made of unpainted hinoki, and with a thatched roof. The clean, simple lines of the building are the very essence of Japanese architecture, showing nary a trace of the often bolder Chinese and Korean influences that dominate shrines elsewhere in Japan. The barest minimum of metal ornamentation on its roof and uprights, and the pristine, raked-gravel grounds surrounding it, add to the impression of purity.

(Tradition is to remove hats and overcoats in front of fences here, and in the Inner Shrine. Before the Meiji Restoration of 1868, no nonbeliever, particularly any Buddhist priest or nun, was permitted to enter either of these sacred precincts.)

Naiku, Inner Shrine: A taxi or bus (or very strong legs) is necessary to get to the precincts of the Naiku, a few kilometers from Geku. Cross the Isuzu-gawa via the Ujibashi, a long and arched footbridge entirely rebuilt (as part of the removal) in 1989. Proper form requires walking on the left side.

Here, as in the Outer Shrine, the object of attention is enclosed in a series of fences, and can be viewed only from the front of a thatched-roof gate in the outermost fence. Here, too, the view is limited (and, again, no photos permitted) but worthwhile: Kotaijingu, while a little larger than the Main Hall of the Outer Shrine, seems even more pristine – the same clean, simple shape of a rice storehouse, the same natural glow of the unpainted wood, the same lines of the massive thatched roof.

Kotaijingu is said to contain the **Yata no Kagami** (sacred mirror), which, along with a sword and a jewel, constitute the Three Sacred Treasures of the Japanese imperial throne. Mythology says that the mirror was handed by Amaterasu Omikami to her grandson when the latter came down from heaven to reign on earth. She gave him the gift of rice agriculture, together with a blessing that the land and people of Japan should continue to prosper forever.

The mirror was to be kept at the palace of Emperor Sujin. Then in about the third century, for fear that too close of contact might possibly desecrate it, the mirror was moved to Kasanui, in Yamato Province near Nara, where it was placed in a shrine. Some 88 years later it was moved to Ise. ■

Entrance to Outer Shrine.

NARA

Nara belongs to an era before Zen gardens and tea ceremony, before Japan became Japan. Buddhist thought from India and arts from as far as Greece and Turkey flowed east along the Silk Road, and Nara was the last stop. Preserved here, long after extinction in their home countries, are the finest examples of Tang-dynasty architecture from China, early Korean religious sculpture, and treasures from Iran. To explore Nara is to look beyond Japan.

Japan had its capital at Nara from AD 710 to 784, after which the government moved to Kyoto and the area lost political importance. This was Nara's great blessing. As a result, it avoided the wars that destroyed other ancient capitals of China, Korea and Japan.

Nara Buddhism represented an early exuberant form of Buddhist thought, rich in symbolism. Everywhere in Nara are *mandala*, the diagrams or arrangements representing cosmic truth. Represented at the center is the essence of the main god. Expanding outward in circles or squares are other gods exerting their powers to help the center. Mandalas can be represented in the arrangement of statues on an altar to the layout of temple buildings.

Every placement and gesture has meaning. For example, two guardian figures flank the gates to large temples. One has his mouth open, the other closed. These symbolize the sounds *a* and *om*, the first and last letters of the Sanskrit alphabet. Being first and last, they encompass all, and hence have magical power to protect against evil.

Hand gestures, clothing and implements are significant. Most ornate are the *mandorla*, or halos, in which can be seen the intercultural impact of the Silk Road. The halos originated in Indian Buddhism, and traveled east to Japan, and west to Europe, where they were adopted by Christianity. The flames in the halos signify divine light.

Statues with great power were hidden from the public, and these became the so-called secret Buddhas, shown only on rare occasions. For instance, the Kuze Kannon of Horyu-ji was hidden from the public for a thousand years before seeing the light of day, in the late nineteenth century. Many statues are still only shown in the spring or fall, or on religious holidays.

Many Nara masterpieces owe their beauty to the technique of dry lacquer, in which the contours of the figure are molded out of a paste of lacquer applied over a central core. The use of a soft plastic material, rather than carving, allows for great subtlety of expression.

Nara Park: Old Nara, much larger than the city today, followed the model of Chinese imperial cities: a sacred square, with streets radiating from the central palace in a grid pattern. During the centuries of neglect after 784, the palaces disappeared, but the temples and shrines on the northeastern edge of the city survived. This corner of the city is now a public park, **Nara Koen**. Tame deer, sacred to the shrine of **Kasuga Taisha**, are its symbol.

Preceding pages: rock garden detail. Left, lanterns at Kasuga Taisha. Right, temple in hills outside of Nara.

The best place to begin exploring the park is **Kofuku-ji**, a temple on the west side and near the Kintetsu Railway station. The patrons of Kofuku-ji were the Fujiwara clan, who gained power in the mid seventh century and succeeded in dominating the government for the next 500 years. Even after the capital moved to Kyoto, the Fujiwara continued to support Kofuku-ji as the family temple. Kofuku-ji is known for its two pagodas. The five-story pagoda, built in 1426, is a copy of an original dating from 730; the three-story pagoda dates from 1114.

The attached **Kokuhokan Museum** – a dreary, concrete building – offers the best introduction to Japanese sculpture available. Most famous is the set of guardians (734) with sweet, child-like faces molded out of dry lacquer. Of these, the six-armed Ashura is one of the best loved statues in Japan. In addition, the museum displays a cast bronze head of Yakushi Nyorai, practically Egyptian in its abstract simplicity, and massive heads of temple guardians, originally from statues that must have been 15 to 20 meters (50 to 65 ft) high. (Nara developed in an age before Japan became the land of the miniature. The buildings and statues aimed to exceed even the grandeur of Imperial China.)

From Kofuku-ji, walk east across the street to the **National Museum**. The most interesting part of the museum is the East Gallery.

The museum borders on Nara Park's central avenue. Walk north to the **Nandai-mon**, a gate dating from 1199. With its 18 pillars and elaborate roof construction, it is one of the outstanding monuments of the Kamakura period. Inside the gate stand great wooden statues, called *nio*, who guard the entrance to Todai-ji. They were carved by the sculptors Unkei and Kaikei, around the thirteenth century.

Straight ahead is **Todai-ji**, the temple also known as the Hall of the Great Buddha. Founded in 743, it is the most important temple in Nara. Enshrining a monumental bronze image of Vairocana, the Cosmic Buddha, the hall was meant to proclaim the power of the

Tame deer in Nara Koen.

imperial state. It was destroyed numerous times by fire, and the present building dates from 1706. The Buddha has been greatly altered in later restorations, but the petals of the lotus upon which the Buddha sits retain original engravings, in fine lines showing Shaka (the historical Buddha) as one of 110 billion avatars of Vairocana.

Although only two-thirds of its original size, Todai-ji is said to be the largest wooden structure in the world. The present building is not entirely a first-rate piece of architecture (note the pillars made of bound timbers, rather than single beams such as those of Nandaimon). Still, the interior retains a sense of the medieval grandeur that was Nara.

The bronze statue, by the way, is 16 meters (55 ft) tall and weighs 500 tons. Like the statuary found in the Sangatsu Hall and the Kaidan Monastery, it shows off Tempyo period (729–764) art and craftsmanship.

The road behind Todai-ji, lined with picturesque clay walls, leads east up the hill to two temples. **Sangatsu-do**, built in 746, contains a large central statue of Fukukenjaku Kannon (god of compassion), radiating light beams, and surrounded by a mandala arrangement of attendants and guardian beings.

Next door is **Nigatsu-do**, the perfect place for a final view of the park. Raised high over the city, this pyramidal building was frequently burned and rebuilt, most recently in 1669. Every March 13 since its founding in 752, the emperor sends an emissary at midnight with water symbolizing the coming of spring. The arrival of the water is the occasion for a fire festival, where monks with burning pine brands run around the verandah spinning sparks into the night.

The city of Nara contains numerous other temples of historical importance. The most interesting temple outside Nara Koen, to the southeast, is **Shin Yakushi-ji**, built in 747. This, along with Sangatsu-do, is one of the few original Nara buildings. The central figure of Yakushi Nyorai (Healer) grants aid to those suffering from ailments of

Below, Todai-ji, Hall of the Great Buddha. Right, the Buddha himself.

the eyes and ears. Most unusual is the set of 12 clay guardian images still standing intact. Shin Yakushi-ji, tucked away among crowded streets in a forgotten part of town, is a favorite.

Northwest: The best place to begin here is **Hannya-ji**, the Temple of Wisdom. Surrounded by a garden of wildflowers, it has great charm. In the garden is a Kamakura-era gate with elegant upturned gables, and a 13-story Heian stone pagoda. The temple houses a Kamakura statue of Monju, the god of wisdom. Monju rides on his sacred lion, carrying in his hand the sword to cut through ignorance.

From Hannya-ji, the road turns west. Here, about two kilometers from Nara Koen, was the center of the ancient city. Of the palace, nothing survives but a large field, with circular clipped hedges showing where the pillars used to stand. Near the palace field, just east, is **Hokke-ji**, a nunnery known for its eighth-century statue of Kannon. The statue is of unpainted wood, with features said to be copied from the face of Empress Komyo and surrounded by a halo of sprouting lotus leaves. The statue is one of the secret Buddhas, only on view from March 30 to April 7, June 6 to 8, and October 25 to November 8.

North of Hokke-ji are imperial tomb mounds surrounded by moats, and beyond them to the northwest is **Akishino-dera**, patron temple of the arts. The original temple was founded in 775, but the present hall dates from the Kamakura period.

Inside is Gigeiten, god of the arts, a favorite of Nara cognoscenti. The head is original Nara, with the delicacy of expression typical of dry lacquer. The body, a recreation from the Kamakura period, has taken on the S-curve of Chinese sculpture, creating a graceful sense of motion.

Southwest: The southwestern temples are a major destination for travelers. The first temple from Nara Koen is **Toshodai-ji**, founded by a Chinese monk, Ganjin, in 751. The roof of the *kondo* (main hall) is the finest surviving example of Tang-dynasty architecture.

Procession of Buddhas in Nara.

Note the inward curving fish tails on the roof, unique to Nara.

Yakushi-ji is a 10-minute walk due south from Toshodai-ji. All of the original buildings have been destroyed by fires except the Eastern Pagoda (698, rebuilt 718). This is constructed of a harmonious arrangement of three roofs, with smaller roofs underneath creating the illusion of six stories. Unfortunately, the complex as a whole lacks the Nara charm, due to modern reconstructions of the Western Pagoda (1981) and the main hall (1976). The main hall houses an original triad (considerably restored) of Yakushi flanked by Nikko, Light of the Sun, and Gakko, Light of the Moon.

The goal of most travelers in this area is **Horyu-ji**, which boasts the oldest wooden buildings in the world. Horyu-ji was founded in 607 by Prince Shotoku, the pivotal figure who established Chinese culture in Japan. It is another time capsule, preserving hundreds of art works from the seventh and eighth centuries.

Horyu-ji is divided into two wings. Most visitors start from the western cloister. The main gate, dating from 1438, leads to an avenue lined by earthen walls characteristic of Horyu-ji. Note the wood-grain patterns created by pressing the walls with boards, thought to make the walls earthquake resistant. At the end of the avenue is **Chu-mon** (Middle Gate). The pillars of the gate (607, rebuilt circa 670) are famous for their entasis (outward curvature), a feature of Greek architecture that traveled to Japan via the Silk Road.

Inside the western cloister are the pagoda and kondo (main hall), circa 670. The kondo houses a rare group of bronzes (620) in Wei style. They are distinguished by elongated faces, the "archaic smile," and the abstract, almost art-deco lines of the falling drapery and the flames of the mandorla. In the center is the Shaka Triad (Sakyamuni, the historical Buddha, with attendants). To the right is Yakushi and to the left is Amida, the Buddha of Paradise. The wooden guardians, stand-

Entrance to tea shop, and bamboo shelter for bicycle.

ing on demons, are Japan's oldest "Four Heavenly Kings."

One of the pleasures of Horyu-ji is the walk out through the cloister, an old example of a Chinese form that influenced temples and palaces across East Asia. Outside the cloister, walk east to the two concrete buildings of the museum, Daihozoden. These buildings are even uglier than the museum of Kofuku-ji, but the treasures inside are important. Among the displays in the museum: the Kudara Kannon from Korea, the portable shrine of Lady Tachibana, and the Hyakuman pagodas, which contain strips of paper printed with short prayers. Published in 764 in an edition of one million, they are the world's oldest printed material.

From the museum, there is a walk bordered by temples and earthen walls to the eastern cloister. In the center is an octagonal building of Chinese inspiration, surmounted by a flaming jewel and known as the Yumedono, Hall of Dreams. Built around 740, it commemorates a dream of Prince Shotoku, in which an angel appeared to him while he was copying the sutras. The Yumedono contains a secret Buddha, the Kuze Kannon, only on view in the spring and fall.

Behind the eastern cloister is **Chugu-ji**, a nunnery housing a wooden statue of Miroku, god of the future, the supreme statue of Nara. Possibly of Korean workmanship, it dates from the early seventh century. With one leg hanging down in the posture known as "princely ease," Miroku sits with his head tilted slightly and a hand raised to his cheek in a thinking gesture. Although Miroku is enshrined in a drab concrete building, this is an ideal place to stop, rest, and meditate for a while. Slightly removed from the Horyu-ji complex are the two temples of **Hokki-ji** and **Horin-ji**. Hokki-ji contains a three-story pagoda built in 706. Horin-ji was rebuilt only in 1975, but is enjoyable to visit, around one kilometer north of Chugu-ji.

South Yamato and Asuka: Taima-dera and **Shakko-ji** are known for their thousands of varieties of peonies. Taima-

Temple roofs, Taima-dera.

dera contains two Nara-period pagodas, and a "secret" mandala painting (an Edo-period copy is on view). On May 14, parishioners don masks of the Buddhas and parade through the grounds, in a unique display of walking sculpture.

Asuka, the capital before Nara from 552 to 645, was the first city to have avenues on the Chinese grid pattern and large Buddhist temples. It was here that Prince Shotoku introduced Chinese law and philosophy. And it was here that the poems of the *Manyoshu*, Japan's first anthology of poetry, was written. Today, there is only a village of farmhouses and rice paddies, but the ruins conjure up a scent of the past.

In Asuka, two burial mounds are open to the public, containing Japan's only known tomb murals. Excavated in 1972, they are displayed in a modern building often crowded with visitors. More evocative is the inner chamber of a seventh-century tumulus. The earthen covering has disappeared, leaving the 75-ton boulders exposed.

Tachibana-dera stands at the site of Prince Shotoku's birthplace. Most of the temple's buildings date from the Edo period, but the pleasant country surroundings exude something of old Asuka. Most important of the area's temples is **Asuka-dera**, enshrining the Great Buddha of Asuka, a bronze image of Shaka and which is Japan's oldest large-scale Buddhist statue. Although frequently burned and restored, the ambiance of the original still remains.

The year 643 was a pivotal point in Japanese history. The powerful Soga clan plotted against the emperor, but was defeated with the help of Nakatomi Kamatari, founder of the Fujiwara clan. This led to the Taika Reformation of 645, establishing the victory of continental civilization. Pillar bases of the Asuka Itabuki no miya, the palace where these events took place, are visible in a field near Tachibana-dera.

Northern hills: The northern and eastern hills are convenient for relaxing afternoon drives out of Nara, notably the Nara Okuyama road, starting from behind Todai-ji. The roads up in the hills wind through beautiful valleys, and past old temples, stone carvings, and waterfalls.

The jewel of the northern hills is **Joruri-ji**, one of the few surviving Heian temples. Joruri-ji, establish in 1179, is a miniature Buddhist paradise. In the center is a pond, symbolizing the lake of heaven.

To the right is the Western Paradise and the temple of Nine Amida. During the year, the rays of the sun sweep across the temple, lighting each Buddha image in turn. In a direct line across the pond is a pagoda with a statue of Yakushi, lord of the Eastern Paradise. Joruri-ji contains other great sculptures, including Kisshoten, an image of an Indian goddess displayed only on January 1 to 15, March 21 to May 20, and October 1 to November 30.

About one kilometer's walk into the hills are the **Tono-o Sekibutsu**, stone carvings dating from the Kamakura period. Buddhas cut into the rock – in an abstract, even crude style, and covered with lichens – these *magaibutsu* have a magical aura about them. The hills of Nara contain hundreds of such carvings. One kilometer further is **Gansen-ji**, boasting another group of stone carvings, and also a fine view from the hilltop behind the temple.

Eastern mountains: For nature lovers, the Eastern Mountains are most enjoyable. Soon after leaving Sakurai, at the southeastern end of the Yamato Plain, the road begins to climb into verdant hills. The first stop is **Hase-dera**, the Flower Temple, known for its peony festival held in the last week of April. A covered stairway of 399 steps hung with lanterns leads up to the main hall, which enshrines Japan's largest wooden statue, an eleven-headed Kannon carved in 1538. From the temple platform there is a good view of the picturesque town of Hase-dera and the surrounding hills.

A half hour's drive to the east leads to the village of Ono. Turn south on the winding road along the Muro-gawa. Across the river is the **Miroku Magaibutsu** cut into the cliff face. This is the largest hillside carving in Japan, dating from 1207.

an
進出
KIRIN
PLAZA OSAKA
HIROTA
シュークリーム

OSAKA

Osaka shakes and hustles. You can see it in the restless crowds on the streets and packed in the subways. It's an entrepreneurial city where lost time is a vacuum of lost opportunities and lost profits. Osaka thrives, as it has for centuries, on the manipulation of the *soroban* (abacus), which many here claim has a language all its own – and that only Osakans understand.

Many Japanese look askance at Osaka, as if it belonged to another, somewhat unrelated, part of the planet. Its humor is different and a bit more rollicking than Tokyo, and greetings are to the point: *Mokarimakka?* Making money? Even the language and intonation has a distinct, earthy flavor, raising eyebrows of disdain in sophisticated Tokyo.

Osaka goes by all sorts of nicknames, so many that they would put even a civic promoter to sleep, among them the City of Water for its numerous rivers and one-time canals, and City of a Thousand Bridges for the nearly 1,000 *bashi* that span the waterways. But all the waterways and bridges have only served one purpose, moving goods and material in and out of Osaka, Japan's commercial outlet to the world.

Osaka's business connection is documented as far back as the fourth century, when Emperor Nintoku made Naniwa (Osaka) his capital. He astutely decided to rebate all taxes to local businesses for three years, after he was informed of an impending recession. His ploy worked rather well, and the Osaka business ethic was conceived, as was its unique language of the merchants, *akinai kotoba*.

The city's stellar port and river connection to the capital in Kyoto played a central role in its economic and cultural development. Merchants from around the country – and from China and Korea – flooded the city. Osaka grew in strength and economic power, culminating with the shogunate of legendary Toyotomi Hideyoshi (1536–98), who chose Osaka as his seat of government, built himself a fine castle, and then turned the city into Japan's foremost commercial and industrial center. For the next 270 years, Osaka was the kitchen of Japan, with raw materials pouring in and high-quality finished products flowing out. Kyoto and fledgling Edo (Tokyo) were consumers, Osaka the provider.

And even when the capital and commercial center moved to Tokyo, Osaka was – and remains – where the coin-of-the-realm is minted.

There were notable cultural contributions from Osaka through the centuries as well, such as the poet Matsuo Basho (1644–94) and the country's foremost playwright, Chikamatsu Monzaemon (1653–1724). *Bunraku*, with its large, two-thirds of life-size puppets, was another Osaka cultural contribution that still thrives today.

Tokyo, of course, is Japan's economic and political engine, but Osaka remains an industrial and business dynamo, with a gross product greater than that of Canada. While Tokyo looks toward New York and London, Osaka casts its gaze towards the Asian mainland. Centuries of commerce and entrepreneurialism has given Osakans an ingenuity, enthusiasm and friendliness that outshines those people up in Tokyo.

Downtown: Osaka has an extensive, user-friendly subway and train system that makes exploring the city a pleasure. Their are two sides of the Osakan coin: one side centers on Umeda, in Kita-ku around Osaka Station, and the other on Namba, in Chuo-ku around Namba Station. While only 10 minutes apart by subway, they are worlds apart in mind and manner. Osaka's newer face, Umeda is where most of the new skyscrapers, office blocks, hotels and shopping centers are sprouting. Namba is the unpretentious side of the city, where residents say is the real Osaka. Most Osakans will say that Umeda is where one works, but Namba is where the good times are. It's where the friendly, funny *Osaka-ben* (Osaka dialect) is spoken with pride, and where Osakans feel most at home.

Umeda: Since most trains (except the *shinkansen*) arrive at the Osaka Station complex in Umeda, it is from here that a tour of the city should start. Explore

Preceding pages: Osaka-jo against modern skyline. **Left,** Kirin Plaza Building.

the vast subterranean shopping network that connects the three clustered train stations with Osaka's three main north–south subway lines; it's the largest in Japan and one of the largest in the world. Corridors connect department stores with hotels and hundreds of shops and boutiques, and uncountable eateries. The main underground shopping areas are the massive Whity Umeda and D'Amore Mall, together over a three-hectare (7.4 acre) shopping experience. One good example of Umeda's underground architecture is Bangai, located directly under the Hankyu Umeda part of the station, with the creative use of water and lights.

Up on the street from the station complex is Midosuji, Osaka's main north–south boulevard. South on the other side of the river is **Nakanoshima**, one of the most important pieces of real estate in the city. This narrow island is the center of city government, and the home to many major Osaka companies. A footpath runs most of the way around Nakanoshima, offering splendid views of the river and city. An hour or two here is well worth the time.

From Midosuji, follow the path east along the river, passing in front of Osaka city hall, library, and the quaint, red-brick central public hall. Across from the public hall is the superb **Museum of Oriental Ceramics**, housing the famous Ataka collection of Chinese and Korean porcelain. Beyond the museum is **Nakanoshima Koen**, with a rose garden and willow-draped paths. The footpath also continues along the river to the west. The lovely building on the west side of Midosuji is the Bank of Japan building. And farther west on Nakanoshima is a science museum, near the Royal Hotel.

Back on Midosuji, continue south under the *ginkgo* trees. Japan's thriving pharmaceutical industry started in Osaka with the import of Chinese herbal remedies. Most of Japan's drug companies still have their headquarters here along Doshomachi, just off Midosuji. Tucked away in a corner sits the pharmaceutical **shrine of Sukuna-Hikona**. It's a tiny little place that blossoms in importance all out of proportion to its size once a year in November, when the Shinno Festival is held. The festival memorializes the discovery by Osaka drug companies that a medicine containing ground tiger bones, among other things, combated malaria.

Continuing south on Midosuji is the district of Honmachi, where Midosuji and Honmachi boulevards cross. Just north of the crossing is **Semba**, the apparel wholesale area of Osaka. Most large wholesalers have outgrown their Semba homes, but some 800 small wholesalers still operate in the Semba Center Building, a two-story structure entirely under a 930-meter-long expanse of elevated highway. Many of Osaka's most venerated businesses got their start in Semba, and many Japanese say that there is no one quite as astute in business as a Semba-trained businessman, who can manipulate a soroban faster than a calculator.

Follow Midosuji south until the next major crossing, Nagahori. The first landmark to look for is the **Sony Tower**, at

Rooftop tables.

the mouth of Osaka's premier covered-shopping street, **Shinsaibashi**, which extends south toward Takashimaya department store and Namba Station. Here are ancient little shops sitting in apparent ignorance of the outrageously fancy boutique plazas towering on either side. The Shinsaibashi Daimaru, flagship of the prestigious chain of department stores, is worth a few minutes, if for nothing else than to admire its lovely art-deco interior. (Be sure to seek out the elevators.)

South on Shinsaibashi is one of the most fascinating stretches in Osaka, the **Dotonbori** amusement quarter. At the Dotonbori Canal, Shinsaibashi ends and Ebisusuji begins. At this point, the *son et lumire* **Kirin Plaza Building**, architecturally akin to something out of Blade Runner, stands on the left.

Venture about halfway across the bridge, squeeze in along the stone railing, and then sit tight for one of the best nonstop parades in the country – Osakans from every walk of life out for a walk. There is more to Dotonbori than just the passing crowds, however. For hundreds of years, this was the theatrical heart of Japan, with six *kabuki* theaters, five *bunraku* playhouses, and a myriad of other halls at one point, where the great storytellers and comics of Osaka performed. Today, most of the old theaters have been replaced by cinemas, among which the elegant old **Shochiku-za** is an architectural link to the golden age of black-and-white films. The venerable **Naka-za**, with its kabuki and geisha dances, and the vaudevillian **Kado-za** are still active, but they are the last of the legitimate theaters left in Dotonbori. Several years ago, the Bunraku Puppet Theater moved from its old Asahi-za home to the **National Theater**, a few blocks to the east.

Just south of Naka-za, the alley named Hozenji Yokocho is lined with scores of traditional Osaka eating and drinking establishments. (Some can be quite expensive, so confirm prices before ordering.) Continue down the alley to **Hozen-ji**, one of the most visited and venerated temples in Osaka. Local businessmen

Dotonbori Canal.

come to pray for good business, young couples ask for happy futures, and older people pray for good health. A very serviceable temple, indeed, with something for everyone.

South is the wide boulevard of Sennichimae-dori. Cross it and walk east a block to Printemps department store, which Japanese pronounce *plantum*. Turn right and enter the Sennichimae shopping arcade, a typical blue-collar area full of *pachinko* parlors, movie theaters and cheap restaurants. The arcade leads to one of Osaka's most famous wholesale areas, **Doguyasuji**, an entire market devoted to kitchen and restaurant supplies. As is the case in most Japanese cities, certain streets and neighborhoods in Osaka are noted for a particular commodity: Matchamachi, or Toy Town; Nipponbashi, or Den-Den Town, for computers and electric appliances; Tachibana-dori for furniture; Hakimonodonya-gai for Japanese-style footwear and umbrellas; Itachibori for tools and machinery.

From Doguyasuji, it's just two blocks to **Namba Station**, where there is nothing too remarkable, save the vast underground shopping arcade of Namba City and Rainbow Town. Three main subway lines connect at Namba Station, also the terminus for both the Kintetsu and Nankai railways serving Nara, Wakayama and points south. Namba is also one of the best connecting points to the **Kansai International Airport**. Both JR West and Nankai Railroads serve the airport from here.

Osaka Castle: The hard-to-miss Osaka-jo is reached by following the footpath to the eastern end of Nakanoshima, then up the spiral ramp onto Tenjin-bashi. Walk north across the bridge, then right at the police box. A short jaunt ends at the entrance of **Sakuranomiya Koen**. A few blocks north of this point sits funky **Tenmangu Jingu**, dedicated to the god of learning. As its name implies, Sakuranomiya (Cherry Garden) Koen has nearly 20 kilometers of trails lined with cherry trees. If lucky enough to be there on the second week in April, you'll

Osaka-style fun.

get a good look at Japan's national flower, the cherry blossom, along with uncountable numbers of Osakans at their merriest while drinking and singing under the trees.

Follow the footpath along the river to the **Osaka mint** (about a kilometer) and the mint museum. Then take the foot bridge (Kawasaki Bashi) over the river to Osaka-jo, the castle, straight ahead. Up and then down through an underpass, and then up onto an overpass eventually leads to it. (One might also have taken a taxi and relaxed.)

Osaka-jo is one of the most visited sites in the city. It is an ode to everything that was great in the past and a symbol of the possibilities of Osaka in the future. The main *donjon*, towering above the vast expanse of gardens and stone walls, is a replica of the original built by Toyotomi Hideyoshi, in 1585. With the conscripted help of all the feudal lords of the nation and the labor of tens of thousands, the massive castle was completed in three years. Much of the original grounds, moats and walls still stand.

Adjacent to the castle is the **Osaka Business Park**, worth a visit to see what the future of Osaka may be like. Planners aim to make this one of Osaka's main centers. Already it sports a slew of state-of-the-art skyscrapers, theaters, shopping centers, eateries, and the New Otani Hotel. It is a pleasant place to spend time.

Female troupes: Theater lovers might want to make the trek (about 30 minutes by Hankyu Railway from Umeda) out to **Takarazuka**. Here, troupes of high-steeping women have been putting on musical extravaganzas for over eighty years. Back in 1910, Takarazuka was a small town at the end of the then newly-opened Hankyu line. In order to attract passengers, the train company built a hot spring and put together an all-female performing company. Today, it is a booming business and a popular form of entertainment. There are 400 performers divided into four casts, two performing simultaneously here and in the Takarazuka Theater of Tokyo, while the other two troupes rehearse.

Osaka is known for its yakuza daring.

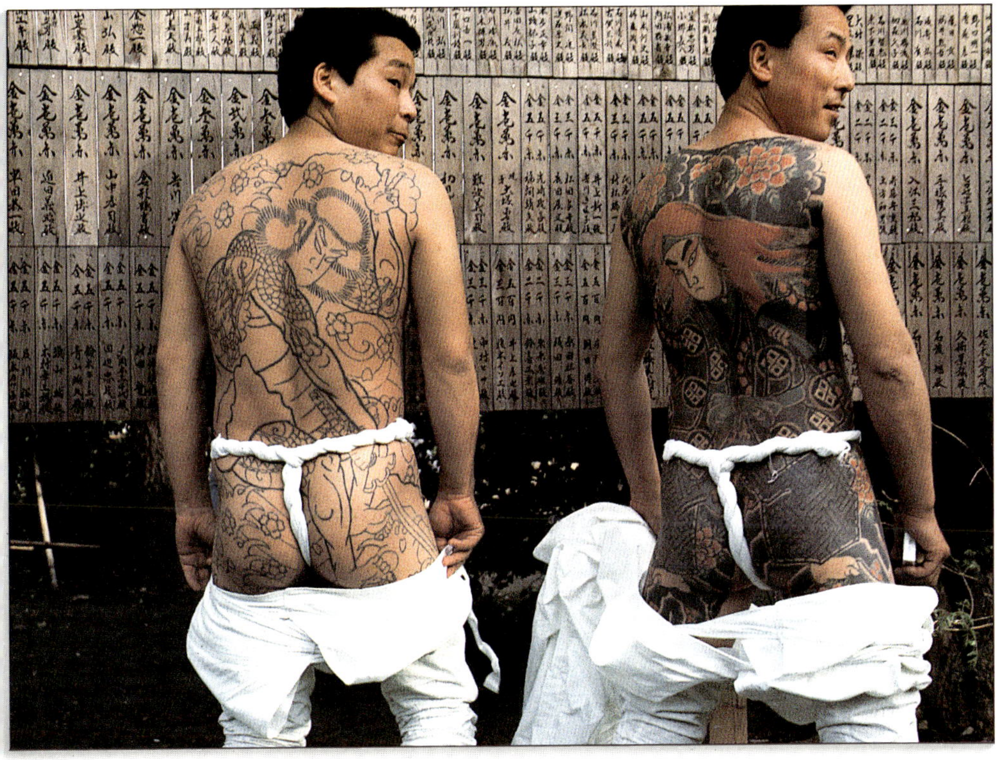

KOBE

The *kanji* characters for Kobe translate as god's door. But Kobe, 30 kilometers (20 mi) east of Osaka, is more like a doorsill – a long and narrow ledge squeezed between the mountains and Osaka Bay. Kobe is best known for its port, pearl and fashion industries, and, of course, for its beef. It boasts no world-class attractions and is consequently bypassed by most tourists, despite its long history of trade and foreign contact, and a Hong Kong-like topography.

In 1995, Kobe was jolted by a massive earthquake that killed 6,000 people in the Kansai region. Entire neighborhoods, especially in the western sections of the city, were flattened when Japanese-style homes – wooden post-and-beam frames with heavy tiled roofs – collapsed and burned in the resulting gas fires. Buildings and elevated roads, mostly of contemporary concrete construction, collapsed. All transportation and port facilities were also damaged, especially Kobe's port facilities, built on reclaimed land.

Although the earthquake was destructive beyond belief, and the government's inept emergency response equally beyond belief, the dire predictions that Kobe would take several years to rebuild have not proven true.

By 1997, Kobe had, for the most part, returned to normal. Yes, damage from the earthquake can still be seen in empty blocks and boarded buildings, but the trains are running, and the port is busy, and shops, restaurants and hotels are open. Travelers are welcome.

The cardinal point on the Kobe compass is **Sannomiya**, a popular shopping and entertainment district. North from **Hankyu Station**, look for Kitanozaka Dori, which leads uphill past the India Social Club to **Kitanocho**. Here, on the high ground, rich foreign traders once staked out impressive residences at the turn of the twentieth century, their growing influence freeing them from the foreign ghetto originally allocated near

Kobe Port.

the wharfs. Presenting a fanciful potpourri of European and American architectural styles, several of these *ijinkan* – now sharing the hill with trendy boutiques and restaurants – are open to the public. Westerners tend to find the interiors unexceptional (and full of cheap souvenirs for domestic tourists), but standouts include the impeccably-restored **Kazamidori**, and the **Choueke House**, which offers an intimate glimpse into the life-style of one long-time resident family.

While in the neighborhood, try to locate the mosque and synagogue, and the Catholic, Baptist and Russian Orthodox churches, all within a few blocks of one another – a unique assemblage for an Asian city this size.

Extending west from Sannomiya, parallel shopping arcades extend to **Motomachi Station** and beyond. The one directly under the tracks – the remnants of a black-market that surfaced amid the post-war rubble – is a mecca for bargain-hunters seeking second-hand and imitation goods.

South of Motomachi Station and just west of the elegant Daimaru department store, look for the dragon gate announcing Kobe's two-block-long **Chinatown**. This small but vibrant enclave, like Kitanocho, surpasses in its aura of foreignness anything that can be seen in the historic ports of Yokohama and Nagasaki, thus cementing Kobe's reputation as the most non-Japanese corner of the country.

From Chinatown, it's a short walk south to **Meriken Koen** and the waterfront. The park was named for the American consulate that once stood nearby. The surrounding redeveloped wharf frontage is the site of the strikingly-designed **Maritime Museum**. It is an informative, user-friendly resource with audio explanations in English. A visit here should also include a ride to the top of adjacent **Port Tower** and the 45-minute harbor cruise. The Kobe Meriken Park Oriental Hotel towers over the entire reclaimed area.

In a feat of near science fiction, and with a biblical dimension, Kobe has

Kobe sends ships into the Seto Naikai.

"recycled" its surplus mountains to build up from the sea floor two of the world's largest artificial islands. This massive undertaking was to assure Kobe as a prime trading port – it already has sea links with 150 countries – and its position as a world leader in efficient handling of containerized cargo.

For an intriguing look at the cultural side of foreign trade, drop in at the nearby **Kobe City Museum**, housed in a doric-columned former bank. This small, admirable museum focuses on Japan's early encounters with the West and features a rare collection of *namban* (southern barbarian) art, works inspired by contacts with the first Portuguese and Spanish traders arriving here in the sixteenth and seventeenth centuries.

For those who do not relish tramping about, a bus shuttle for tourists retraces a similar route and offers a day-pass. Taxis, alas, are not recommended, due to the short-distance trips – and possibly because many of the drivers are seasonal workers in the local sake distilleries. In fact, Kobe cabbies are undoubtedly the surliest in the nation, a rude awakening if expecting otherwise.

The Portliner monorail from Sannomiya provides a convenient elevated loop ride around **Port Island**. Here – and on neighboring **Rokko Island**, also reachable by a monorail from JR Sumiyoshi Station – visitors can get a first-hand look at the future of container vessels. Moreover, the center of the island has been zoned to accommodate a hotel, sports and convention facilities, plus an amusement park and spacious sea-view apartments for 20,000 residents. Port Island is also where the jet-boat shuttle from **Kobe City Air Terminal** (KCAT) departs for the 30-minute ride to the Kansai International Airport, in Osaka Bay.

Port Island, incidentally, offers a good vantage point from which to gaze back nostalgically at the "old" Kobe, especially at night when it becomes a flickering tiara augmented by two insignia on the mountainside. One symbol is an anchor and the other a pair of interlocking fans that represent the marriage of Hyogo and Kobe. It was due to the fan-shaped perfection of the harbors of these villages that the trading port flourished as early as 700.

Hot springs: Scalding hot springs await weary hikers on the backside of Rokko Mountain, in the *onsen* town of **Arima**. Reached by bus, cable car and ropeway from Hankyu Rokko Station, this ancient spa boasts all the usual hot springs amenities, plus nationally-recognized basket-makers.

One bargain in town is the public bath, **Arima Onsen Kaikan**, where, for a few hundred yen, one can bathe in the same curative waters as offered at the much costlier inns. Arima's waters are said to be capable of soothing all human ailments except love – itself an irony since, over the centuries, the town has done much to increase and nurture that particular affliction.

Finally, 15 minutes on the train down the coast from Sannomiya drops one at one of the largest beaches in western Japan, **Suma**, where there is Aqualife Park, with its large aquarium and a dolphin show.

Left, swim fun. Right, Kobe damage, 1995.

EARTHQUAKES

Japan is highly prone to earthquakes. There are minor shakes recorded on seismological instruments almost every day, and bigger ones that startle people from their sleep, rattle dishes, and knock objects off shelves several times a year. From time to time over the centuries, a major quake has hit the Tokyo area, causing heavy damage to property and leading to huge loss of life.

The reason for the earthquakes is that the Japanese archipelago is at a place where three moving segments of the earth's crust – the Pacific Plate, the Philippine Plate, and the Eurasian Plate – come into violent contact. (This also explains why there is so much volcanic activity, and so many hot springs, in Japan.)

The Philippine Plate is the prime culprit, sliding in under the Kanto Plain in a northeast direction at about 3 centimeters a year. The movement, in turn, puts stress on the primary fault that affects Tokyo and other earthquake-prone regions. And add to this a nest of faults spread widely under the Kanto Plain, sometimes as deep as 100 kilometers.

In Tokyo, the danger from earthquakes is made worse because much of the city is on unconsolidated alluvial soil and on land-fill. This is a very poor foundation, which makes buildings tremble and oscillate more than they would on solid ground.

A major tremor whiplashes the Tokyo area every 60 or 70 years on the average, and the last one, the Great Kanto Earthquake – a 7.9 magnitude jolt on the Richter scale – took place in 1923. Let's see... 23 plus 70... It's about that time.

In the 1923 earthquake, most of the central part of the city was leveled and totally destroyed by fire, and over 100,000 people were killed. There is a haunting memorial to this disaster near the sumo stadium, close to Ryogoku Station. Called Cenotaph Hall, it is on the spot where 40,000 people were incinerated to death when a fire tornado swept across the open area where they had sought safety.

When it does happen, what will it be like? Some experts say that Tokyo is now much safer than it was in 1923. Buildings, bridges, and elevated highways are reinforced and built according to the latest techniques. In addition, much of the city is made to be fireproof. There are also shelters and other emergency facilities, and elaborate plans to provide food, water, and medical help should the worst happen. But the 1995 Kobe earthquake has shattered just about every one of those assurances. In Kobe, earthquake-proof structures collapsed like jelly; rescue and relief plans proved unworkable, and government response, both on the local and national levels, was inept and embarrassingly inadequate. Nearly 6,000 people died.

Is Japan – and the world's largest metropolitan area, Tokyo – prepared? Every year, on the anniversary of the 1923 earthquake, the city goes through a series of earthquake drills and rescue demonstrations to reassure city residents. Given the experience in the 1995 Kobe quake, the entire system of preparations and assumptions for a Tokyo-area earthquake of similar proportions has had to be reassessed.

Tokyo is the world's most-populated city, with extensive underground networks of subways and gas lines, and above ground, glass-covered buildings and flimsily-constructed residences. Tens of thousands of people will die in a Kobe-strength quake. And many private experts, Japanese and foreign, doubt that government plans for disaster relief will be sufficient. Still, Kanto's population just gets larger and larger. ■

恵美

KYOTO

Kyoto defines traditional Japan. Tokyo might have the national government and Osaka might have the entrepreneurial savvy, but Kyoto's got the class. As Japan's artistic and cultural depository, Kyoto ranks with Athens and Beijing as a living museum. The city sits on a flat plain enclosed by a horseshoe of mountains on three sides. Open to the south, between the rivers **Katsura-gawa** to the west and **Kamo-gawa** to the east, Kyoto is Japan's seventh largest city, with a population of 1.4 million. With several colleges and universities, it is the educational center of western Japan.

The best time to visit is the early spring, in April, when the cherry blossoms bloom, or else May, when everything else blossoms in ritual radiance. The rains of June offer a misty contrast to venerable temples and shrines, and they also thin the crowds.

The heat of summer is cooled by breezes off the surrounding mountains, making July and August evenings some of the longest and best. September and October deliver near-perfect temperature for trekking Kyoto's temple paths. The autumn colors break out in earthy reds and oranges in November, making it one of the most popular times to visit. The festive air of December and January is contagious all over town, and the light dusting of snow in February and March casts Kyoto in a near Zen-like state, and should not be missed. Be aware that, at all the best times to visit Kyoto, all of Japan is doing likewise.

Beginnings: For nearly 1,100 years, from 794 until 1868, Kyoto was home of the emperor and thus capital of the nation. Japan's first permanent capital was established in Nara in 710, but by 784, the intrigues of power-hungry Buddhist priests forced the Emperor Kammu to move the capital to Nagaoka, between Nara and present-day Kyoto.

Ten years later, in 794, Emperor Kammu moved the capital again to the village of Uda, northeast of Nagaoka, and renamed it Heiankyo, the Capital of Peace. It wasn't until 988 that the use of *kyoto* (capital) began to appear in official records; a century later, Kyoto was the city's proper name.

The arrival of Buddhist thought in Japan, in the sixth century, introduced Chinese influence to the archipelago, which reached its peak during the Heian period (794–1185).

Kyoto (then Heiankyo) was built to a scale model of the Tang dynasty's (618–906) capital of Chang'an (now Xi'an), in China. The city extended in a regular grid pattern, still in evidence today, for 5.2 kilometers (3.2 mi) from north to south, and 4.4 kilometers (2.7 mi) east to west. Walls with 18 gates and a double moat surrounded the city. And because of the persistent trouble with priests in Nara, temples were forbidden inside Heiankyo, explaining why many of Kyoto's most venerated temples are in the hills surrounding the city, not in the city's center.

Frequently leveled by earthquakes, floods, fires and wars over the centuries, the buildings of Kyoto have been

Preceding pages: Kiyomizu-dera. Left, maiko off to work. Right, maiko in kimono.

moved, rebuilt and enlarged, and now represent a mosaic of historical periods. As a result, few buildings in Kyoto predate 1600, though most of them faithfully reproduce the earlier structures. Fortunately, a decision by the Americans not to bomb Kyoto during World War II – its historical heritage was considered too important – assured that these ancient structures stand today.

Most people encounter Kyoto first from **Kyoto Station**, most likely having taken the *shinkansen* from Tokyo, less than three hours away.

Unfortunately, it's not the loveliest of views as one exits the station – Kyoto shows the same cluttered urban sprawl as all Japanese cities. Its treasure of sights lie hidden in the surrounding hills, behind yellowing imperial walls, and down narrow lanes. Despite rapid modernization, thousands of old traditional houses still line Kyoto's narrow back streets. Their facades are a never-ending dance of rectilinear patterns: sliding paper doors, window slats in clay walls, lattices, trellises, benches, and hanging blinds of reeds and bamboo. Most distinctive of these are the *inuyarai*, or dog barriers, which are curved bamboo fences protruding about one foot out from the walls of the houses as a protection against street traffic.

Kyoto has some 1,500 Buddhist temples, 300 Shinto shrines, 100 museums, two imperial villas, one palace and castle, plus 5,000 arts and crafts shops.

Don't even think of taking them all in on one visit, or even ten. Concentrate, instead, on absorbing what's encountered: A garden leads to an eloquent tea house; an ancient pagoda wings towards the sky; a flower arrangement adorns a room. But visitors often miss the significance of the view. The tea garden sits between the outside world and the tea room to instill solitude and detachment. The pagoda carries thoughts skyward to reveal the five unifying elements of the universe. The flower arrangement plants humanity in a natural relationship between heaven and earth. Like the Zen master intones, everything exists in relation to other things.

Archers.

Temple trek: Kyoto's eastern hills are peppered with temples, shrines, shops and eateries, and thus a good place to start one's temple trek.

(**Note**: Shrines are always Shinto, and temples are always Buddhist. The suffixes *-jinja*, *-jingu* and *-gu* normally denote a shrine, while *-tera*, *-dera* and *-ji* normally denote a temple.)

Just east of Kyoto Station and across the Kamo-gawa, **Sanjusangen-do** has served as the backdrop for countless pictures of Japanese archery. Its archery festival, on January 15th, is famous across Japan.

The temple, last rebuilt in 1266, houses 33 alcoves, between 33 pillars under a 60-meter-long (200 ft) roof. Inside is a thousand-handed Kannon, the bodhisattva of mercy and compassion, and her 1,000 disciples. Each of their faces are different, causing Japanese to look for the face that resembles their own – or that of a relative – to whom to make an offering.

North on the other side of Shichijo Dori is the **Kyoto National Museum**, founded in 1897 and exhibiting artifacts of history, art and crafts. Several other temples are in the vicinity of the museum, including Toyokuni, Myoho, Chishaku, and Yogen.

East up the slope (*zaka*), on the east side Higashioji Dori, leads to **Kiyomizu-dera**. The temple's main hall (*hondo*) sits perched out over the mountain side on massive wooden pilings. The veranda, or *butai* (dancing stage), juts out over the valley floor. To Japanese, taking any big chance in life is like jumping off the stage at Kiyomizu.

Founded in 788, Kiyomizu-dera predates even Kyoto. Dedicated to the eleven-faced Kannon, the temple stands as a treasure-trove. The two 3.6-meter-tall (12-ft) deva kings (*nio*) guarding the front gate speak the whole of Buddhist wisdom: the right one has lips pursed in the first letter of the Sanskrit alphabet, *a*, while the one on the left mouths *om*, the last letter. Behind the main hall, with its dancing stage, is **Jishu**, one of the most popular Shinto shrines in the country, where the god of love and good

Sanjusangen.

marriage resides. (Most Buddhist temples in Japan house some sort of Shinto shrine.) Don't trip over the blind stones (*mekura-ishi*), or the girls walking between them with their eyes closed. The belief is that if they can negotiate the 20 meters (60 ft) between the stones with their eyes closed, silently repeating the name of their loved one, love and marriage are assured.

Steps lead down from Kiyomizu's main hall to **Otowa-no-taki**, a waterfall where visitors sip water from the spring, said to have many health benefits, if not sheer divine power for the true believer. A short walk leads up the other side of the valley to a small pagoda, with a view encompassing the entire hillside.

Exiting Kiyomizu, take the first right, followed by another down a flight of stone steps to Sannen-zaka, a street whose name means three-year slope. It is said that pilgrims who trip along this slope will have three years of bad luck. Today, the cobbled lane is less superstitiously known as Teapot Lane, for all the pottery shops lining its path. The restaurants along here are also a good place to sample a classic bowl of *soba* or *udon* noodles.

Back across Higashioji Dori sits **Rokuharamitsu-ji**, one of Kyoto's gems. At the rear of the main hall, built in 1363, is a museum with two fine Kamakura-period (1185–1333) sculptures: Taira-no Kiyomori, of the Heike clan, and Kuya, founder of the temple. The eyes of Kiyomori, presaging the tragic destruction of his clan, sum up the anguish often seen in Kamakura-period art. Kuya, who popularized the chanting of the lotus sutra, is shown reciting magic syllables, each of which becomes Amida, the savior.

North are the brilliant-orange buildings of **Yasaka-jinja**, affectionately called Gion-san after the adjoining Gion pleasure quarter. One of the tallest granite *torii* in Japan, at nine meters (30 ft) in height, marks the portal to the shrine. The unusual main hall is built in the residential Gion-style. From the shrine's back gate, one enters adjoining **Maruyama Koen**. The park is known

Heian-jingu.

for its beautiful garden and magnificent cherry blossoms in early April. Two interesting temples sit just beyond: Chion-in and Shoren-in.

Crossover Sanjo Dori and continue north through **Okazaki Koen**. This park holds museums, halls, a library and zoo. An arching 24-meter-high (80 ft) torii leads from Okazaki Koen to the vermilion-colored gate of **Heian-jingu**, more of an architectural study than a Shinto center. The shrine, dedicated to Kyoto's first and last emperors, is a replica of the original Imperial Palace, built in 794 and last destroyed by fire in 1227. The shrine was erected in 1895 to commemorate Kyoto's 1,100th anniversary. The shrine displays the architecture of the Heian period, when Chinese influence was at its zenith. Shinto shrines took on Buddhist temple features during this period, when the plain wooden structures were first painted.

Passing through the shrine's massive gate, it's hard to imagine that the shrine is but a two-thirds scale version of the original Imperial Palace. The expansive, white-stone courtyard carries the eye to the Daigoku-den, or main hall, where government business was conducted. The Blue Dragon and White Tiger pagodas dominate the view to the east and west. Other distinctive features of Heian architecture include the long corridors extending from each side of the gate to the east and west halls.

To the left of the main hall is the entrance to the garden, designed in the spirit of the Heian period for the pleasures of walking and boating. Mirror ponds, dragon stepping-stones, and a Chinese-style bridge are some of the beguiling features.

From Heian-jingu, walk east a bit to **Nanzen-ji**, which simply means South Zen Temple and which was originally the residence of 26-year-old Emperor Kameyama (1249–1305), after his abdication in 1274. Impressed by the powers of *zazen* (seated meditation), he deeded part of his palace to the establishment of the temple, in 1290.

Nanzen-ji sits nestled in a pine grove at the foot of Daimonji-yama, part of the

Purification, Heian-jingu.

Rinzai school of Zen Buddhism, Zen's largest and best-known school. It's also one of Kyoto's most important Zen temples. The complex consists of the main temple and 12 sub-temples, of which only four are regularly open to the public.

Nanzen-ji provides an example of the Zen's belief in the relationship between all things. The pine grove influences the architecture, art influences the garden, and it all influences the observer. The temple reflects the Chinese style (*kara-yo*) that arrived in Japan along with Zen. This style, evolving through the Ashikaga period (1338–1573), achieved a near-perfect balance between the lordly Chinese style and the lightness of the native Japanese style.

Exploring the two buildings of the abbots' quarters – Daihojo and Shohojo – reveals how garden architecture and landscape painting interrelate. The quarters are full of famous paintings, like *Tiger in the Bamboo Grove*, and the surrounding gardens are renowned as some of the best in Japan. Here, the gardens are for sitting contemplating, not for strolling.

From Nanzen-ji, follow **Tetsugaku no Michi**, or the Philosopher's Walk, north past the temple of Zenrin and the Nomura Museum. The walk, named for the strolling path of Japanese philosopher Kitaro Nishida (1870–1945), snakes about two kilometers along the bank of a narrow canal to Ginkaku-ji. The quiet path – save for the crowds of tourists at times – is noted for its spring cherry blossoms and fall foliage. Along the path are interesting homes, shops, tea rooms and small restaurants – try a bowl of Kyoto's famous tofu and vegetable stew (*kyo-yudofu*) – and intriguing Honen-in on the hillside.

Philosopher's Walk ends at the Silver Pavilion, or **Ginkaku-ji**. The Ashikaga-era shogun who erected it in 1489 died before its completion, and it remains sans silver. However, its exquisite pavilion and Zen garden are not disappointing. The first floor of the pavilion was a residence and displays the Japanese *shinden* style. The second floor

Ginkaku-ji.

served as the alter room and shows a Chinese Buddhist style. The mound of white stones (Kogetsudai) in the garden was designed to reflect moonlight onto the garden. The quaint tea room in the northeastern section of the pavilion is touted as the oldest in Japan.

Imperial ways: Due west and back across Kamo-gawa, the **Kyoto Imperial Palace** remains the emperor's residence and thus under the control of the Imperial Household Agency, which dictates every nuance and moment of the imperial family's life.

Originally built as a second palace for the emperor, the Kyoto Imperial Palace was used as a primary residence from 1331 until 1868, when Tokyo became the new residence with the fall of the shogunate, and with the Meiji restoration of the imperial system. The palace has gone through many restorations over the centuries; the current buildings and structures were built in the mid 1800s, and as such, are frowned upon by Kyoto purists. However, Shishinden (Enthronement Hall), standing with its sweeping cedar roof before a silent stone courtyard, is an impressive emblem of imperial rule. It was constructed in the shinden style, where all buildings are connected by covered walkways or galleries. The court town that once surrounded the hall is now **Kyoto Gyoen**, the public Kyoto Imperial Park.

From the palace, a few blocks west is **Nishijin**, the weaver's quarter. The Nishijin Textile Center has excellent displays of working looms and woven goods. Here, try on a kimono. After browsing the center, walk through the narrow side streets – the ancient crafts of weaving and dying are still practiced in the old wooden buildings.

South is **Nijo-jo**, a castle begun in 1569 by the warlord Oda Nobunaga, and finished by Tokugawa Ieyasu, ally to Oda Nobunaga, to demonstrate his military dominance over the city. In 1867, it served as the seat of government from where Emperor Meiji abolished the shogunate. Rectangular in dimensions, the castle's magnificent stone walls and gorgeous gold-leafed audi-

Games in Kyoto Gyoen.

ence halls reflect the power of the Edo-period shoguns. The linking corridors of the castle's Ninomaru Palace feature "nightingale" (creaking) floors to warn of intruders. The garden is a grand example of a lord's strolling garden.

Just south of the castle is **Nijo Jinya**, originally the home of a wealthy merchant and later used as an inn by visiting *daimyo*. The old manor house is full of trap doors, secret passageways and hidden rooms – the stuff from which are made samurai dramas.

Further south and back near Kyoto Station are two notable temples, Nishi (West) Hongan-ji and Higashi (East) Hongan-ji. As was the case with many of Kyoto's historical treasures, Japan's great unifier, Toyotomi Hideyoshi (1536–98), was responsible for establishing **Nishi Hongan-ji**. In 1591, Toyotomi brought the Jodo-shinshu Buddhist sect to the temple's current location. Its Chinese influences are many, and historians sometimes consider it the best example of Buddhist architecture still around. The *hondo*, or main hall, was rebuilt in 1760 after fire destroyed it. The founder's hall – *daishido* – contains a self-carved effigy of the sect's founder. Cremated after his death, his ashes were mixed with lacquer and then applied to the effigy. The study hall (*shoin*) contains a number of rooms named for their decorations: Wild Geese Chamber, Sparrow Chamber, and Chrysanthemum Chamber.

To the east, **Higashi Hongan-ji** was established in 1603 when the first Tokugawa shogun, wary of the Jodo-shinshu sect's power at Nishi Hongan-ji, attempted to thwart their influence by establishing an offshoot of the sect. Only the main hall and founder's hall are open to the public. The present buildings were erected in 1895, after fire destroyed the predecessors. When these current structures were being built, female devotees cut and donated their hair, which was woven into 50 ropes used during construction.

Zen paths: To the north and west of the city center, skirting the foothills, are three renowned Zen temples that should

Kinkaku-ji in the early 1900s.

not be missed. Established as a small monastery in 1315, **Daitoku-ji**'s present buildings were built after 1468, when one of the several fires in its history burned down the temple. It is the holy of holies, where Zen married art. The great Zen calligrapher Ikkyu (d. 1481), painter Soga Dasoku (d. 1483), and founders of the tea ceremony, Murata Juko (d. 1502) and Sen-no Rikyu (d. 1591) all came from Daitoku-ji.

The great warlord Oda Nobunaga is buried here. Although a brutal warrior, Nobunaga was fundamental to the sixteenth-century unification of Japan, and was a leading patron of the arts.

Some eight of Daitoku-ji's 22 subsidiary temples are open to the public. The three best-known are Daisen, Zuiho and Koto. In **Daisen-in** is Kyoto's second most famous, maybe the best, Zen garden. Unlike the abstractions of other gardens, the Daisen garden more closely resembles the ink-wash paintings of Zen art. Look for the mountains, rivers and islands in the water, which appears to flow under the veranda.

The Daitoku complex has been criticized for its commercialism, but it is still worth the visit. This is also one of the best places to sample authentic Zen temple food, just like the monks eat. The Izusen, in the Daiiji-in sub-temple, offers traditional high-protein, low-calorie vegetarian meals of soybean, wheat gluten and tofu, served in a delightful garden setting. The meal is delivered in red lacquer begging bowls, which are nestled into each other when finished.

Walk west along Kitaoji Dori, past Funaokayama Koen, to the best-known temple in Kyoto, if not all Japan: **Kinkaku-ji**, or the Golden Pavilion. It's a replica built in 1955 of a fifteenth-century structure, and last recovered in gold-leaf in 1987. Each of the pavilion's three stories reflect a different architectural style. The first floor is of the palace-style, the second floor of the samurai-house style, while the third floor reveals the Zen-temple style. The large reflecting pond in front of the pavilion and the surrounding grounds make it a perfect setting.

Kinkaku-ji.

It is probably the youngest temple in Kyoto. The original was burned down in 1950 by a man who entered the Buddhist priesthood after being seduced by the pavilion's beauty. Thinking that his sense of aesthetics might approach perfect if he burned down the very object that had enchanted him in the first place, he did exactly that. The author and right-wing nationalist Mishima Yukio fictionalized the burning episode in his 1956 book, *Kinkakuji.*

Further west, visit **Ryoan-ji**, or Temple of the Peaceful Dragon, early in the day, before the peace is shattered by the bus-loads of tourists. Here is the most famous Zen rock garden (*karesansui*, or dry landscape) in the world, and one of Kyoto's main tourist attractions. The sixteenth-century garden is an abstract of an ink-wash painting executed in rock and stone. No one knows the exact meaning of its fifteen rocks (one is always out of sight) and raked gravel, but speculations abound. Take a seat on the veranda and let the mind empty. The barren area of the raked stones and the contours of the rocks convey a sense of infinite space, said to lift the mind into a Zen state.

A little past Ryoan-ji, **Ninna-ji**'s formidable gate, with its fierce-looking nio guardians, is one of the best in Japan. Walking back east, tenth-century **Kitano Tenman-gu** is one of Kyoto's most earthy shrines. Its restrained wooden architecture enshrines Sugawara Michizane, a ninth-century scholar and statesman. Small wood votives, or *ema* – with a picture of a horse on one side (cheaper than a real horse donation) and a wish or prayer (most for success in school exams) written on the other side – hang in the courtyard. The shrine also celebrates the first calligraphy of the year, when school children offer their writings to the shrine. The present shrine structure was built in 1607. Tenman-gu is widely known for its splendid plum trees that bloom in the snows of February, and for the geisha that serve tea under the flowering trees.

Westward: Out in the western hills, **Arashiyama** was once the playground

Students decipher zen in Ryoan-ji.

of Heian aristocrats, and is today punctuated by quaint temples. Visitors cross over the Hozu-gawa on picturesque Togetsu Bridge to the restaurant and shop-lined promenade along the river. Just beyond sits **Jikishian**, a refuge temple for women escaping messy relationships, many of whom wrote their sorted tales in some 2,000 books of sad reminiscences, or *omoide-gusa*.

One of the most famous strolling gardens in Japan lies inside Katsura Rikyo, or the **Katsura Imperial Villa**, due west of Kyoto Station on the west side of Katsura-gawa. Its garden features a number of splendid tea houses overlooking a large central pond. Katsura, with its severe refinement, has exercised more influence on contemporary architecture than perhaps any other building in Japan. The imperial villa at Shugakuin, in the northeast and with its three levels, seems pure fantasy compared to Katsura. (Visitors to Katsura, as to Shugakuin and the Imperial Palace, require permission from the Imperial Household Agency.)

Northward: In the northern foothills, the **Shugakuin Imperial Villa** was built in 1659 as an emperor's retreat. It consists of three large, separate gardens and villas. In Rakushiken (Middle Villa) stands a ceder door with carp painted on both sides. It's said that the carp would escape each night to swim in the villa's pond. Not until golden nets were painted over them, in the eighteenth century, did they stay put. (Like the Imperial Palace, Shugakuin requires permission from the Imperial Household Agency before visiting.)

Hiei-zan, an 850-meter-high (2,800 ft) mountain northeast of Shugakuin Imperial Villa, has long held historic and religious importance to Kyoto. Here, **Enryaku-ji** was founded to protect the new capitol from evil northeast spirits. Apparently this exalted mission gave the temple's monks an inflated sense of importance. Over the decades, they became aggressive friars of the martial arts and swept into Kyoto on destructive raids. Their not-so-monastic rumbles were quenched by warlord Oda

Temple tour leadership.

Nobunaga, who destroyed the temple in 1571. Today, there are three pagodas and 100 sub-temples, some offering accommodations, dispersed in an alpine setting that makes Hiei-zan one of the most accessible trekking areas in Japan.

Southward: Just a few blocks south of Kyoto Station, **To-ji** boasts one of the nation's enduring postcard images: the five-story Goju-no-to. This pagoda was rebuilt in 1644 and stands at 55 meters (180 ft) as Japan's tallest pagoda. The temple itself was established in 796, around the same time as Kyoto. Built next to the old city's main gate, which faced south, the temple became the main Buddhist temple in Japan. Its main hall, or *kondo*, reflects Buddhist traditions from India, China, and Japan.

To the east, up against the hills, **Tofuku-ji** rests as one of the best places for autumn foliage. It contains Japan's oldest, and perhaps most important, Zen-style gate, from the fifteenth century. Yet its 25 subsidiary temples are rarely visited, and the grounds are usually quiet. Be sure to walk through the abbot's quarters (*hojo*) to the platform over the ravine looking down on Tsuten bridge – it's one of the most delightful views in Kyoto. And if there during the last week of November, don't miss the festival of old brushes and pens. Writers and painters bring their used pens and brushes to be cast into a sacred fire.

A few block south of Tofuku-ji is one of Japan's icons. Almost everyone has seen pictures of tunnel-like paths of hundreds of bright-red torii. Actually, there are over 10,000 torii covering the paths of **Fushimi Inari Taisha** – the fox shrine founded in the ninth century in honor of the fox that farmers believe is the messenger of the harvest god. To experience Fushimi, walk the full four-kilometer (2.5 mi) course, which takes about two hours.

Old quarters: Along the Kamo-gawa in central Kyoto, **Gion** is Kyoto's famous pleasure-quarter, or *geisha* district. But in Kyoto, they're known as *maiko* and *geiko*, not geisha. The word geisha in old Kyoto referred to male entertainers dressed as women; in Tokyo and Osaka,

Left, manicured garden. Below, torii tunnel, Fushimi Inari Taisha.

however, it came to mean women. Maiko debut at about 16 years old and wear distinctive long trailing *obi*. At about 21, they advance to the ranks of geiko, with the highly-ornate kimono. Along Gion's narrow streets, one won't see geiko, but there's a good chance to catch sight of a maiko hurrying to entertain a guest, especially around Gion Shimbashi. The geisha houses in the quarter are in the style of Kyoto's old town houses, but with added delicate touches, such as the orange-pink plastered walls (*ichirikijaya*). The best place to see the houses is along the alleyways south of Shijo Dori.

The neighborhood of old wooden buildings near **Gion Shimbashi**, the bridge over Kamo-gawa, is a national preservation district. North a few blocks, **Minami-za** (Theater), built in the early 1600s, is the oldest theater in Japan and is still used for kabuki performances.

The thousands of bars of the area are another diversion, but check prices before sitting down. An hour or two in one of these clubs can easily run US$250 to $500. Other areas for night life include the zany **Ponto-cho** entertainment district, one of Kyoto's old red-light districts, along the west bank of Kamo-gawa and just across from Gion. The narrow street is lined with bars, restaurants and *tayu* (top-ranked courtesan) houses. Kawaramachi is another small but bustling shopping, eating and entertainment neighborhood also located on the Kamo's west bank. Shinkyogoku, or the Arcade and the main entertainment district established in the 1870s, also draws many at night with its lights.

An excellent spot to dine in summer are the restaurants along Kamo-gawa, between Shijo and Sanjo streets. The restaurants extend wooden platforms out over the river, where diners can sit in the cool evening breeze. The platforms remain out until mid September.

Shopping: If templed out, let the gods of shopping take over. Walk east along the north side of Shijo Dori, from Karasuma Dori (Daimaru department store) east to Yasaka-jinja. One of Kyoto's most unique and redeeming

Sayonara to ryokan guests.

features is the fertility of its arts and crafts, whether a comb made as it was for a Heian princess or a thousand-year-old tea cup. Prices are not cheap, but the quality is high.

Antique lovers should not miss Shinmonzen Dori, a few blocks north of Shijo Dori in the Gion. Dozens of shops sell screens, scrolls, Imari porcelain, lacquer, and bronzes from China, Korea and Japan. Other antique stores are sprinkled nearby: in Higashiyama north and south of Shijo Dori, along Sanjo Dori near the Miyako Hotel, and in the neighborhood of Chion-ji.

Drama: For the height of imperial drama, try a *noh* play, which developed in Kyoto in the fourteenth century. Rooted in *sarugaku*, or ballad operas, the lyrical and melodramatic form became known as *sarugaku-no-noh*, later shortened to noh. A classical presentation includes five plays with several humorous interludes, *kyogen*. Most presentations today show only two plays and two interludes. Noh greatly departs from Western ideas of drama, abandoning realism in favor of symbolism. Three performers, all men, enact the play on a bare stage, with a painted pine-tree backdrop. Musicians and chorus sit openly on the stage.

Noh developed in Kyoto as one of Japan's original art forms, along with *kabuki* and *bunraku* (puppet theater). Kabuki (*ka-bu-ki*, or singing-dancing-performing) was the last purely Japanese art form to develop, originating during the Edo period as a commoner's entertainment. Originating from dancing shows of women, which the shogun declared immoral and forbidden to women, kabuki turned to men. It has more variety and greater dynamic force than noh, and appeals to a wider audience. The best place to catch a kabuki performance in Kyoto is the vintage Minami-za, in the Gion.

For traditional dance and music performances, try Gion Corner, in the Gion, which also offers tea-ceremony presentations by skilled geiko. For a more classical tea ceremony, try Ura Senke, one of Japan's leading schools of the tea

Performance in Gion.

ceremony. The school was founded in the seventeenth century and has 150 chapters in Japan, and 70 in other countries. Ura Senke offers special programs for foreigners. (This is quite serious business – no cameras, no levity.)

Festivals: If nothing else, tradition drives Kyoto. Japanese, especially in Kyoto, define their year with festivals, rituals and ceremonies. The years pass infused with a natural rhythm; the 1,200th recorded cycle of the four seasons passed in Kyoto in 1994. Lucky, indeed, is any visitor who can experience any or all of Kyoto's festivals.

January: At the stroke of midnight, people dressed in their finest kimono head for the nearest temple or shrine to pay their New Year's respects.

February: Kyoto awakens with plum blossoms in February. The last day of lunar winter falls during the first week, with the celebration of *setsubun*. In the courtyard of Yasaka-jinja, butterfly-like maiko dancers swing to the lilting twang of ancient lutes (*biwa*). Throwing symbols of luck – red *adzuki* beans – into the gathered crowed, they chant, "Out with demons, in with good fortune."

March: Camellias fall like the heads of samurai worriers, which, years ago, didn't make samurai very happy. But for the tea masters, falling camellia symbolized spring. The best place to see falling camellias is at Seiryo-ji.

April: Spring arrives with geisha dancing under the blossoming cherry trees. Kyoto has a multitude of blossom-viewing (*hanami*) parties, the most famous being Daigo-ji. Nothing quiet and serene about hanami.

May: Spring is in full bloom. Azaleas, peaches and rhododendrons blossom, and temples air their sacred treasures in the fresh breeze. Jingo-ji displays its art collection, normally hidden from public view, in its Insect-Drying Festival, or Mushibarai.

June: The summer rains (*tsuyu*) blanket Kyoto from mid-June through mid-July, when rain falls constantly in a heavy drizzle. Kifune-jinja, dedicated to the god of water, celebrates the season in a vibrant water festival.

Aoi Matsuri, downtown.

July: With the end of tsuyu comes the heat of summer, and Tanabata. According to legend, two stars that are lovers cross the milky way to meet once a year on Tanabata. The biggest Tanabata festival is at Kitano Tenman-gu.

However, the biggest of any festival in Kyoto during July is the Gion Festival, dating from the tenth century and considered one of Japan's premier festivals. On 17 July, floats decorated in Chinese and old Dutch styles parade through town.

August: This is the month of *Obon*, when the spirits of the dead revisit the world of the living, to be entertained for a few days before returning back to the other shore. Lamps and fires are lit by families to guide their departed relatives along their way.

Around Kiyomizu-dera, once the site of an immense burial ground, thousands of paper lanterns are strung by the gravestones, and the grounds are open all night to visitors. On the five mountains around the city, *gosan okuribi* sends the spirits of the dead back to the other world with spectacular bonfires in the shape of Chinese characters, and which stretch hundreds of meters up the mountain sides.

September: This is the neutral month of Zen. Mid September is the time for moon-viewing, with numerous events across town. Osawa Pond, behind Daikaku-ji, has been known since Heian times as one of Japan's three great moon-viewing sites. As with any time or place or event that is "famous" in Japan, expect massive crowds.

October: This is the month of dress-up and strange happenings. The Bull Festival at Koryu-ji is known as one of the "weird festivals" of Kyoto. It features demon caricatures, a god riding atop a bull, and a long and slow announcement, punctuated by audience cries to speed up.

Jidai Matsuri (Festival of the Ages) climaxes the Weird Festivals and apexes October's round of fancy dress. Some 2,000 participants lead a colorful parade through town, representing all the famous people in Japanese history, dressed in their traditional styles.

November: People travel out of the city to see the fall foliage. North of town, the small village of Ohara, with its hillside villages, is spectacular.

December: Face-showing (*kaomise*) is Kyoto's gala kabuki performance at Minami-za, when the actors reveal their real faces. Senbon Shaka-do celebrates the day of Buddha's enlightenment with a radish-boiling ceremony, where the radishes are inscribed with magic Sanskrit letters.

And in December, temples and shrines all over town begin cleaning in preparation for the New Year. At Higashi Hongan-ji, the cleaning is herculean, with hundreds of volunteers pounding the tatami, wiping the pillars and steps, and brushing away the dust and memories of the old year.

And then, on the last day of December, the old year departs at midnight with 108 strikings of temple bells (*joya no kane*) all across town. It takes seventeen monks at Chion-ji to ring Japan's largest bell. In fact, anywhere in Kyoto at this time of year is enchanting.

Left, okay, sure. Right, contrasts in Ponto-cho.

THE SOUTHLANDS

Here we should mention that "southlands" is a bit of a misnomer, as the Japanese will refer to this area as western Japan. Still, this part of the Japanese archipelago extends south*ward.*

Chugoku, Shikoku and Kyushu – exceedingly different yet with one element in common: Seto Naikai, or the Inland Sea. All three regions also face the open ocean. And as a result, each area has widely varying climate and local qualities. In fact, beyond geography and the fact they are all Japanese, these regions sometimes bear little or no resemblance to each other.

That section of Honshu from, say, Okayama down the coast of the Inland Sea to Hiroshima is markedly different from the Sea of Japan side. Likewise, Shikoku, though the smallest of Japan's four main islands, could as well be in a different hemisphere from the one occupied by the islands in Okinawa. As for Kyushu – well, there are those who believe that this large island, particularly the southern part, is a nation unto itself, and who cite the long tradition of fierce independence stemming from the Satsuma clans as proof.

Even in the most populous and industrial cities of Kyushu, or even in large and well-developed cities like Honshu's Okayama and Hiroshima, the pace is mellow, if not downright placid, compared with Tokyo and Osaka.

Not all is idyllic down this way, however. The Southlands lie in the path of seasonal typhoons, and thus are regularly given good soakings by torrential rains riding up from the Philippines and Taiwan. Moreover, there are more active volcanoes on Kyushu than on any other Japanese island. Among the most notable are Sakurajima, near Kagoshima, Aso-san (with the world's largest-diameter crater), and Unzen-dake, which violently blew up in 1991.

Volcanoes have given the archipelago an unlimited amount and variety of ceramic-quality clays, along with natural chemicals for glazes. Kyushu, along with parts of Chugoku, is noted for its hearty pottery, an art with a considerable amount of Korean influence.

Shikoku, Chugoku and Kyushu are large enough to keep travelers occupied for quite some time. Smaller gems await even further south, however. Like pearls upon the ocean, islands drip away from Kyushu's southern tip and stretch down to within 200 kilometers of Taiwan. This string of islands, Nansai Shoto, is over 1,200 kilometers in length. Best-known by foreigners is Okinawa, for its historical importance in World War II, and also for its cultural uniqueness. There are numerous other islands, each significantly distinct from its neighbors, and worthy of exploration by the traveler.

Preceding pages: Within the walls of Himeji-jo. Left, the Inland Sea and the rocky coastline of Shikoku.

CHUGOKU

Most travelers would look at a map of Japan's main island of Honshu and consider Chugoku to be the southern part. The Japanese, however, consider it to be the western part. In fact, of course, it is southwest.

Nevertheless, compass directions aside, the Chugoku region (*chugoku chiho*) spreads over the bottom third of Honshu, bound by Seto Naikai (Inland Sea) to the south and the Sea of Japan to the north. Not many foreign travels get to Chugoku, other than to its main cities of Okayama and Hiroshima. The region includes the prefectures of Okayama, Hiroshima, Yamaguchi, Shimane and Tottori, and offers some splendid views of rustic Japan, especially along the Sea of Japan coast.

Seto Naikai, or the Inland Sea of Seto, is a 9,500-square-kilometer body of water surrounded by Kyushu, Shikoku and the western extent of Honshu. Over 1,000 small islands pepper the sea. Osaka, Kobe and Hiroshima are all on the sea's coast. Although often industrialized these days, the sea still retains some exquisite vistas, enough for the area to have been designated Japan's first national park, in 1934.

Himeji: At the upper end of Chugoku sits the castle town of Himeji. A 15-minute stroll from the *shinkansen* station, along a road lined with modern sculptures, leads to **Himeji-jo**. Resplendent, it is called the White Egret Castle, as it quite resembles a nesting crane, majestically resting on the banks of the Senba-gawa. It is the largest, and most elegant, of the dozen existing Japanese medieval castles in Japan. Although the city was extensively bombed during World War II, the castle itself emerged unscathed and has been maintained in pristine condition.

The site occupied by the castle has been fortified since 1333, and an actual castle was built here in 1580 by Toyotomi Hideyoshi. In 1681, Ikeda Terumasa, Tokugawa Ieyasu's son-in-law, rebuilt and expanded the castle to its present form. Castles in this period served both as military strongholds and as administrative centers. Terumasa's design, with financial help from the shogunate, elegantly merged martial necessity and artistic form on a scale previously unknown in Japan.

The castle's construction was a Herculean task, requiring 400 tons of wood, 75,000 tiles weighing 3,000 tons, and a huge number of large stones. These stones weren't easy to come by, and tales of their procurement live on in the ramparts. Ancient stone coffins, mined from nearby tombs, can be seen in one part of the precinct. The contribution of a millstone, from a woman living in the town below the castle, is still remembered today.

The castle's seemingly impregnable defences, never tested in battle, start with three concentric moats, surrounding high and curved stone ramparts punctuated with several gates and watchtowers. The walls and watchtowers feature small holes, from which arrows and bullets could be fired at attackers.

Left, tending to cherry trees. Right, barrels of sake at a temple.

Roads within the castle grounds twist and turn, the better to confuse hostile forces in the event the outer defences were to be breached.

Himeji-jo is a hillock (as distinct from a mountain or flatland) castle, atop a 45-meter-high (150-ft) hill. There are spectacular views from the main *donjon*, which rises 30 meters (100 ft) from the castle grounds. *Shachihoko*, huge ornamental fish that were strategically placed on the roof as charms to ward off fire, can be seen close up from the top floor. (Some now support lightning rods.)

The **Hyogo-Kenritsu Rekishi Hakubutsukan** (History Museum) nearby contains displays about Japanese castles, including the most magnificent of all, Himeji.

Okayama: The rapidly growing city of Okayama has once again asserted itself as the region's most dynamic metropolis, and, for this reason, finds itself often playing host to visiting foreigners, mostly on business, not for sightseeing.

Okayama's most notable attraction, the **Koraku-en**, was originally laid out in 1686 for the warlord Ikeda. This garden is generally regarded as one of the three or four most beautiful gardens in Japan.

Located on an island in the Asahi-gawa, across from **Okayama-jo** ("Crow Castle" because of its black color), Korakuen is unusual for its large grassy areas and cultivation of edible crops, including rice and wheat. Tea is also grown and harvested here, and there are tea houses scattered throughout the fine strolling garden.

Other sights in Okayama include the **Orient Museum**, with exhibits tracing the impact of Near Eastern civilization on Japan, the Okayama Prefectural Museum of Art, and the Yumeji Art Museum, with works by Yumeji Takehisa.

Bizen, about 45 minutes by train east along the coast from Okayama, is famous for its unglazed, coarse pottery that is frequently enhanced by kiln "accidents," such as a stray leaf or a bit of straw sticking to the side of a pot, which leave interesting patterns after firing.

Left, carp banners on Boys' Day. Below, Kurashiki architecture.

There are more than 100 kilns in **Imbe**, the 700-year-old pottery-making section of Bizen, along with several museums, including the Bizen Togei Bijutsukan (Ceramics Museum) and Fujiwara Kei Kinenkan gallery.

Kurashiki: West of Okayama, this small and rather unpretentious textile-producing town boasts the pearl of Japanese tourist attractions – an arts district that brings world-class Japanese and international art and traditional crafts together in an exquisite setting. Thirteen and a half hectares of 300-year-old rice warehouses, Meiji-era factories, and the homes of samurai and wealthy merchant families have been elegantly preserved and converted into museums, craft shops and art galleries.

Kurashiki is for walkers, with most of the attractions within a block or two of the canal. The streets and alleys bordering on Kurashiki's central canal look much as they did during the town's cultural and economic zenith in the eighteenth century. Automobiles are not allowed to disturb the elegant ambiance of its preserved quarter. The centrally-located tourist center provides maps, information, and a cheerful place to rest weary feet.

During the Edo Period, Kurashiki was a central collection and storage site for the shogun's taxes and tribute, paid in rice, from communities throughout western Honshu, Seto Naikai and Shikoku. Numerous stone rice warehouses, *kura*, are clustered around willow-lined canals, thus giving the town its name. Their striking designs employ dark-black tiles deeply set in bright-white mortar, capped by roofs of black tile. Stone bridges, arched so that barges piled high with sacks of rice from the hinterland could pass below them, span the waterways.

Kurashiki is about the only such city in Japan to escape the ravages of wrecking balls, World War II bombings, and urban development. As the town attracts millions of visitors annually, it is best to avoid weekends and holidays. Most of its many fine museums are closed all day on Mondays.

Canal through Kurashiki.

Kurashiki's preservation was largely the work of Ohara Magosaburo, the wealthy scion of Kurashiki's leading family. The Ohara family's textile mills were the principal source of employment in Kurashiki during the Meiji period, by which time rice levies had been replaced by cash taxes, making the city's huge rice warehouses redundant.

Ohara Magosaburo built the nation's first museum of Western art in 1930, the **Ohara Museum**, and stocked it with works by El Greco, Monet, Matisse, Renoir, Gauguin and Picasso. The neoclassical building remains the city's centerpiece, although new galleries have proliferated around it over the years. The restored kura next to the main gallery are likely to be of more interest to visitors already familiar with European art, as they contain Japanese folk art and a fine collection of ancient Chinese art. Semi-separate rooms are devoted to the works of the great *mingei* (Japanese folk art) potters, such as Hamada Shoji, Bernard Leach, Kawai Kanjiro and Tomimoto Kenkichi.

Many of Kurashiki's warehouses-turned-art-houses are devoted to preserving and revitalizing mingei. Among the most interesting is the **Japanese Rural Toy Museum**. The first floor is packed with traditional Japanese toys, dolls and kites, while a collection of toys from around the world can be seen on the second floor. The adjacent toy store is as interesting as the museum. The **Kurashiki Museum of Folk Craft** displays about 4,000 simple, handmade objects that are, or were, used in everyday life. The building that houses this museum, parenthetically, is itself of historical interest, remodeled from four two-story wooden rice granaries.

Visitors can learn about the daily life of one of Kurashiki's leading families at the **Ohashi House**, constructed in 1796 for a merchant family. Of samurai status, the house is much larger than typical merchant houses of that time. (Note the unusual roof tiles.) The curious can delve into the region's ancient history at the Kurashiki Archaeological Museum and the Kurashiki City Museum of Natural

Pearl farms.

History. **Ivy Square**, an arts complex created out of the red-brick textile factories that brought about the Ohara family its fortune, houses the Kurabo Memorial Hall, with displays on the textile industry, as well as scores of shops and restaurants.

Leaving the canal area, weary travelers might stop for a drink at the Kurashiki Kokusai Hotel, designed by Kurashiki native Shizutaro Urabe, before heading for the city's more distant attractions. These include the **Seto Ohashi Memorial Museum of Bridges** (the building is shaped like an arched *taiko* bridge), and **Washu-zan**, a hill with tremendous views of the great bridge itself, **Seto Ohashi**, as well as the Inland Sea, Seto Naikai. There is also Kurashiki's former city hall, designed by Japan's most famous architect, Tange Kenzo, which was transformed in 1983 into the Kurashiki City Art Museum.

Onomichi: This city at the northern center of the Inland Sea was an important commercial port 800 years ago. Wealthy merchants flocked to the city during the Edo Period, building 81 temples on the steep slopes overlooking the sea to celebrate their prosperity. With the coming of the railroad in the late nineteenth century, however, commerce literally passed the city by. Because of its relative lack of importance, American bombers also passed by Onomichi, and when the *shinkansen* route was mapped, Onomichi was passed over again, a station being placed in the up-and-coming Fukuyama instead. As a result of its slide into relative obscurity, the city has unselfconsciously retained much of its pre-Meiji heritage. Some 25 of the temples remain, the most interesting being **Senko-ji**, which is best reached via the rope-way tram.

Hiroshima: One moment – 8.15am, 6 August 1945 – irrevocably changed world history. An atomic flash signaled Hiroshima's instant destruction and the ultimate loss of over 200,000 lives. The immediate and lasting impact on Hiroshima gives concrete reality to the horrors of atomic and nuclear war.

Amazingly, Hiroshima's people

No shoes on the tour bus.

quickly rebuilt a vibrant city from the ashes, making it larger and more prosperous than the old one, leaving only a few carefully chosen scars to memorialize its abiding atomic legacy.

Unlike Nagasaki, the second city to have received such an attack but which doesn't dwell especially much on past history, there seem to be reminders of Hiroshima's atomic bombing around virtually every corner in the city.

The best way to see Hiroshima is through the window of a street car. As most other Japanese cities tore up their streetcar tracks after World War II, their cars were added to Hiroshima's collection, and so the city has acquired an eclectic collection of tram cars, many dating back to the 1940s.

Hiroshima was chosen for the first atomic bomb attack because of its military importance. The city was one of Japan's most vital military depots and industrial areas (not mentioned in the museum's exhibit).

But Hiroshima's military significance predates World War II by several hundred years. Troops were staged here in preparation for the invasion of Korea in 1582. A castle incorporating the latest construction and defensive techniques was built here seven years later by the Mori clan. It rested on pilings driven into reclaimed swampland, and the outer moats were built above the level of the surrounding land so that their walls could be breached, flooding the plain where siege troops would likely mass. The castle was an important bastion of the Tokugawa shogun's forces, a western outpost facing the often hostile Choshu and Satsuma clans. In the nineteenth century, **Hiroshima-jo** was occupied by the emperor during the occupation of Manchuria. The castle also served as an important Japanese Army headquarters during World War II, and was completely destroyed by the atomic bomb. Reconstructed in 1958, the castle contains an excellent museum, which is appropriately devoted to castles.

A few blocks east of the castle, Shukkei-en was built on the banks of the Kyobashi-gawa in 1620, in emulation

Genbaku Domu.

of a famous Chinese lake. Early spring brings cherry blossoms, azaleas bloom a little later, and multicolored carp inhabit the garden's central pond throughout the year.

Half an hour away and northwest of central Hiroshima, **Mitaki-ji** is set in a lush forest with three waterfalls. Buddhas adorn the hillsides, and a fierce, life-size baby-killing devil statue of wood hangs out on the temple's porch. A friendly dog often welcomes visitors to the tea house, which is decorated with a colorful collection of masks and kites. The walk from the central train station to the temple grounds passes a grouping of graves belonging to many unknown atomic-bomb victims.

Peace Park: The Heiwa Kinen Koen (Peace Memorial Park), wedged between the rivers of Motoyasu and Ota, is adjacent to the **Genbaku Domu** (Atomic Dome), which marks ground zero of Hiroshima's atomic explosion. At its maximum intensity, the temperature approached that on the sun's surface, and almost everything within sight was vaporized instantly. The building with the carefully maintained skeletal dome once housed the Industrial Promotion Hall, and was one of the few surviving vertical structures.

Tange Kenzo designed the heart of the park complex, which comprises the **Peace Memorial Museum**, Peace Memorial Hall, Cenotaph and Peace Flame. The museum contains graphic portrayals of the bombing. Although the museum is filled with powerful images of terrible suffering, it certainly is not the hall of horrors one might expect.

A visit to the museum is an emotional experience for most, even though the exhibit has been justly accused of failing to place the bombing in historical perspective, mostly a result of right-wing nationalist opposition. "It is as though the bomb fell on Hiroshima, figuratively as well as literally, out of the blue. Nowhere is there any suggestion that it might have been triggered by past actions. Nowhere is there the least sign that any other nation or race might have suffered comparable wartime tragedies," charges writer Alan Booth.

The **cenotaph**'s inverted U-shape reflects the design of the thatched-roof houses of Japanese antiquity. It contains a stone chest with the names of the victims of the atomic bombing, and bears the inscription, "Sleep in peace: the error will not be repeated." The Peace Flame and Atomic Dome can be seen through it.

The statue of the A-Bomb Children is dedicated to a child who died of leukemia caused by atomic radiation. She believed that if she could fold 1,000 origami cranes, the act would prevent her death. She died just after the 954th crane. School children come from around the country to place wreaths of folded cranes around the statue's neck.

Many visitors ring the Peace Bell before crossing the Motoyasu-gawa to the dome. Colorful rowboats can be rented by the hour near the Heiwa Ohashi (Peace Bridge), offering a more cheerful perspective on Hiroshima; cruises depart from the nearby pier.

Miyajima: Though it is formally called Itsukushima (Strict Island), this major

Paper cranes, Peace Park.

Hiroshima-area tourist attraction is more often, and more appropriately, called Miyajima, the Island of Shrines. To find the spirit and splendor of Miyajima, one of the country's holiest sites, visitors must wade through the litter and droppings of hordes of tourists and herds of tame deer. The large crimson *torii* (shrine gate), rising out of the sea in front of the **Itsukushima-jinga**, is probably the most familiar Japanese cultural icon. The familiar sight, plastered on nearly every travel poster and guide book that has anything to do with Japan, hasn't suffered from the exposure. It is especially breathtaking at sunset, even when the tide is out and one is able to filter the noise from fellow admirers.

Itsukushima-jinga itself rests on stilts and seems to float like a giant ship when the tide comes in. Costumes and masks used in the *bugaku*-dance festival (first week of January) and the *noh* plays, performed in mid April, are on display in the Asazaya (morning prayer room), which is reached via a vermillion-colored bridge.

Most of the island is covered with uninhabited virgin forest. A good way to see it is from the 1.6-kilometer-long cable car that runs over Momijidani Koen to the top of Misen.

The current gate was built in 1874, but a similar torii has lured visitors for seven centuries. The island's spiritual roots are much older, however. The first shrine, honoring Amaterasu's three daughters, goddesses of the sea, was built in the sixth century. To maintain the island's "purity," births and deaths have been prohibited on Miyajima from the earliest times.

The entire island of Miyajima was dedicated as a sanctuary by Taira no Kiyomori, who ordered the Itsukushima-jinga completely rebuilt in 1168. Kiyomori and his clan prospered, eventually attaining a brief rule over Japan, which ended tumultuously in 1185.

Next to Itsukushima, one of the oldest noh theaters in Japan, built in 1568, also seems to float a few inches above the sea. A nearby building contains hundreds of government-designated Na-

Torii at Miyajima.

tional Treasures and Important Cultural Objects, including illuminated sutras made by the Taira clan in the 1160s.

A five-story pagoda, built in 1407, and the hall of **Senjokaku** (A Thousand Mats) are at the top of a hill behind the shrine. Senjokaku, built in 1587, is the great warlord Toyotomi Hideyoshi's contribution to Miyajima.

Shimonoseki: At the western limit of Honshu, Shimonoseki is the gateway to Kyushu, and to Korea as well, with *shinkansen* service to Hakata Station in Fukuoka, and daily overnight ferries to Pusan, South Korea. There isn't much reason to linger here, but the largest aquarium in Asia, the **Shimonoseki Suizokukan**, and the shrine of Akamon may be of interest to those waiting for a boat. History and literature students will recall that the final scenes of *Tale of the Heike* took place here, as the exiled empress dowager hurled herself and the infant emperor into the swirling tides; several spots in the area claim to be the actual location, but, in fact, any would do, as the cliffs are high and the waters do swirl frighteningly as the Sea of Japan meets Seto Naikai.

Shimane: From Shimonoseki, the coastal road loops back around east along the northern coast of Honshu and the Sea of Japan. Still in Yamaguchi Prefecture, the small town of **Hagi** retains much of its nineteenth-century samurai ambiance in some neighborhoods, and its pottery is among the finest that Japan has to offer.

Shimane and its modest peninsula consists of three ancient districts: Izumo, Iwami and the islands of Oki Shoto. It is one of the most ancient areas of Japan and offers special insights into the cultural heritage of the nation.

Izumo covers the eastern part of the prefecture, and is known as the mythical province where the history of Japan began. Several shrines, temples and ancient buildings can be seen around the province.

Shinji-ko sits at the eastern end of the province. The lake's 45-kilometer-long coastline offers a host of beautiful sights throughout the year. Sunset over the

Coastal train, near Hagi.

lake is one of the finest evening scenes in Japan. At the eastern end of the lake sits **Matsue-jo**. Often called Plover Castle because of its shape, the castle was built in 1611 by Yoshiharu Horio, a samurai general. It is the only remaining castle in the Izumo area. Across the castle moat to the north lies Shiominawate, an area where ranking samurai once lived.

It was also the home of renowned writer and observer of Japan, Lafcadio Hearn (1850-1904). Greek-born Hearn was raised in America and came to Japan in 1891 as a *Harper's* magazine reporter. In his many years in Japan, he wrote numerous works, including *Kwaidan: Stories and Studies of Strange Things*, *Shadowings*, *Japan: An Attempt at Interpretation*, *Bushido: The Soul of Japan*, and *A Daughter of the Samurai*. They all make for as good reading today, although written over a century ago. In Matsue is the ancient Kamosu Shrine. Its unique architectural style, *taisha-zukuri*, is the oldest architectural style in Japan.

The islands of **Oki Shoto** sit between 40 and 80 kilometers off Shimane Hanto. The old province surrounds some 180 islands and islets in the Sea of Japan. The islands, once a dumping grounds for convicts, sit inside the Daisen-Oki National Park.

A unique sight in the islands are the bullfights, sans matador. Two bulls just lock horns and push away. Bullfighting was originally devised by the people of the islands, in the thirteenth century, to entertain Emperor Go-Daigo while he was in exile. Temples, shrines, rugged costs, white-sand beaches and great fishing mark the area as a good stop far off the beaten path.

Tottori: The prefecture of Tottori lays at the top end of Chugoku, along the north coast facing the venerable Sea of Japan. It is a rural area with small villages and towns dotting the countryside. Tottori is its largest city, with a population of just 135,000. The whole prefecture has a population of only 615,000, making it the least-populated prefecture in the nation.

The illustrious sand dunes of Tottori lie just east of the capital, beyond the Sendai-gawa. The dunes skirt the Sea of Japan and lie in the eastern reaches of Saninkaigan National Park. When the wind blows, which seems to be always, the patterns in the sands are continually changing. The shifting views of the dunes have been well-recorded in Japanese literature and art for hundreds of years. The middle section of the dunes is designated as a national monument, and thus filled with the essential paraphernalia of Japanese tourism: children's amusement park, planetarium, music hall, a marvelous bicycle path and other amusement facilities.

Hakuto Beach stretches along the shore west of Tottori. It marks the beginning of a score of beaches, including Hawaii Beach, that stretches all along the coast of Tottori. Hakuto Beach is known throughout Japan from an ancient legend about the wealth and harvest god Daikoku, one of the seven good-luck deities, and a rabbit. The beach is rather crowded throughout summer. Behind the beach lies a shrine.

Left, drying daikon. Right, cast-cement barriers are used to prevent coastal erosion.

SHIKOKU

The least-developed and rarely visited of Japan's four main islands, Shikoku's attractions (and drawbacks) are attendant on its relative isolation. The island can provide a more "Japanese" experience than either Honshu or Kyushu: its people are less familiar with foreigners and its ambiance has been less influenced by the homogenizing aspects of modern culture. It is also more diffused. Places likely to be of interest to travelers are relatively far apart and more difficult to get to than on more widely traveled pathways.

Shikoku's separate identity may not be long-lived. The smallest of Japan's main islands, it was the last to be linked by bridge with Honshu, the largest and most populated. Its physical separation ended in 1988, with the completion of the **Seto Ohashi**, a bridge that carries automobiles and trains from Kojima, on Honshu, to Sakaide, on Shikoku. There is considerable debate as to whether this will stimulate the island's economic development, increase the dissipation of its uniqueness, or speed the departure of young people to Osaka and Tokyo.

The Seto Ohashi is actually a series of six bridges using five small islands as stepping-stones across **Seto Naikai**, the Inland Sea. At 12.3 kilometers (7.6 mi) in length, it is one of the longer double-deck bridges in the world, carrying four lanes of automobiles above dual train tracks. First suggested by a prefectural assemblyman in 1889, officials were finally persuaded of its logic in the late 1960s. Construction was set to begin in 1973, but was postponed in the aftermath of the first oil shock of the 1970s. Construction began in 1978, and after nearly ten years of work and expenditures exceeding 211 trillion yen (some US$1 billion), the first cars and trains finally rolled across in 1988. It is a popular tourist attraction for Japanese tourists, but unless a bridge engineer or civil engineer, just use it to get to Shikoku, or take one of the ferries from Osaka or Kobe.

Preceding pages: planting igusa, used for making tatami mats. **Left**, Ashizuri-misaki. **Right**, Seto Ohashi under construction.

The most numerous and distinctive visitors to Shikoku today – arriving by plane as often as not – are *ohenrosan*, devout Buddhist pilgrims making the rounds of the 88 holy temples and shrines established by the priest Kobo Daishi some 1,200 years ago. In the feudal period, it was common for white-robed pilgrims carrying staffs to complete the circuit on foot, a feat requiring more than two months. Today's similarly-adorned pilgrims usually make the rounds in two weeks or less, via air-conditioned buses.

Shikoku is split into northern and southern sections by steep, rugged mountains. The relatively dry northern part, facing the Seto Naikai, is more industrialized. The south is wilder, warmer, and wetter. The weather is most favorable in early spring and at the beginning of the fall.

Takamatsu: This coastal city, the capital of Kagawa Prefecture, is the main railway terminal and ferry port in eastern Shikoku. **Ritsurin Koen** contains one of the finest traditional gardens in

Japan, 54 hectares (133 acres) of ponds, hills, pine forests and a botanical garden. One of the garden's best rewards is a cup of tea at the beautiful Kikugetsutei tea house. The **Sanuki Mingeikan** (Folk Art Museum), near the entrance of the park, displays comprehensive collections of crafts from Shikoku and throughout Japan. The local wood crafts are particularly valued. However, the region's most popular craft (not on display here) are the distinctive *sanuki-udon* noodles, presented daily at thousands of *udon* restaurants throughout Kagawa Prefecture.

About 20 minutes by train from the center of Takamatsu is **Yashima**. It was one of the seemingly countless battlefields of the Gempei War (1180–85), between the Minamoto and Taira clans. The architectural embodiments of Shikoku's past – an open-air *kabuki* theater, a vine suspension bridge, thatch-roofed farmhouses, and a variety of other traditional buildings – have been collected and preserved in **Shikoku-mura** (Village). The Yashima Plateau, served by bus, tram and cable car, was itself once an island; now a narrow strip connects it to the mainland. It juts out into Seto Naikai, providing extensive views, particularly from Yashima's lofty temple on the hill.

Kotohira: Southwest of Takamatsu, Kotohira is home to one of the most famous and popular shrines in Japan – **Kotohira-gu**, also called Konpira-san. It is dedicated to Okuninushi no Mikoto, the guardian of seafarers. Sailors and fishermen have come here seeking propitious sailing since the shrine's inception in the eleventh century. In recent years, their numbers have been swelled by the four million Japanese and foreign tourists arriving each year. The main shrine is at the end of a long, steep path lined with stone lanterns. A trip to the top of the 785 stairs and back takes at least an hour.

The **Kanamaruza**, restored to its original early nineteenth-century condition, is the oldest existing kabuki theater in Japan. Its stage, resonating with the echoes of thousands of performances,

Seto Naikai, near Takamatsu.

is exciting to visit even when empty. In the third week of April, the nation's best kabuki actors bring it alive. The revolving section is turned by strong men pushing the 150-year-old mechanism under the stage, and the audience is seated on cushions on *tatami*.

Tokushima: Tokushima Prefecture faces Osaka Bay and the Pacific Ocean along the western end of Shikoku. In ancient times, Tokushima was known as Awa no Kuni – millet country. Today, most of the prefecture's traditional arts still use the characters for millet country: *awa* indigo dye, awa puppet theater and the awa *odori* carnival.

The Awa Odori – summer "crazy dance" festival – is held in mid August. It is perhaps the most humorous of Japanese festivals, with residents and tourists joining in processional dances and contests for the "biggest fool of all." Another home-grown entertainment, puppet shows, featuring giant puppets accompanied by *samisen*, are performed by farmers between seasons.

The garden of the old castle of Tokushima, in the city, is set against the backdrop of forest-covered Shiro-yama. The garden consists of a traditional landscaped area with a fountain. Tokushima also has several old, fire-resistant *godown* (warehouses), used by merchants to store their goods in early times. The godown line both sides of the once-prosperous and busy main highway through town.

Otaki Hill is topped by the Peace Memorial Pagoda, built in 1958 and which can be reached by a cable car. Over a quarter of the 88 Kobo Daishi temples are in the immediate vicinity of Tokushima.

To the north and opposite the large island of Awaji, Naruto faces the **Naruto Straits**, where the O-Narutokyo (Great Naruto Bridge) connects Tokushima with **Awaji**. It is one of the longer suspension bridges in Asia. The attraction to travelers is not the bridge, however. It is, rather, the countless whirlpools, some as large as twenty meters in diameter, that swirl in the 1,300-meter-wide Naruto Straits under the bridge. The

Fishing boat, Uwajima.

whirlpools are largest in the spring and autumn, when tides reach a speed of 20 kilometers an hour.

The 100-kilometer-long coastline of Tokushima Prefecture holds some of the best beaches in Japan. Along the center of the coast, **Komoda-misaki** stretches out into the Pacific. The peninsula is noted for its luxuriant subtropical flora. The reefs, washed by the warm Japan Current, are the site of some of the best surf-fishing in Japan. The area is also noted as an egg-laying location for giant loggerhead turtles. In **Hiwasa**, to the south, is the **Sea Turtle Museum**, dedicated to these great sea reptiles. Also there is Yakuo-ji, a temple known to ward off evil. Men and women in their *yakudoshi* (unlucky years) visit here to ask for divine help. They place a one-yen coin on each step as they climb up to the temple.

Tsurugi-san dominates the interior of Tokushima. At 1,955 meters (6,400 ft), it is one of the main peaks of Shikoku. In contrast to its name – sword – the crest of the mountain slopes gently. A lift brings visitors up to Minokoshi; from there, it is a 40-minute hike to the peak. A lodging house, skiing area and several old shrines make Tsurugi a major recreation area in Tokushima.

South of Tsurugi-san, the gorge of **Konose** lies deep in the mountains at the source of the Naka-gawa. It is a site of magnificent natural beauty. In autumn, red and yellow foliage covers the surrounding mountains.

To the west of Tsurugi-san runs **Oboke Gorge**. The upper reaches of the Yoshino-gawa form the deep gorge. The site is noted for towering cliffs and giant rocks, polished like marble from the cascading waters. Spring and autumn are the best times to visit the gorge, filled with bus-loads of tourists.

The valley along **Yoshino-gawa**, north of Tsurugi-san and running east-west from Tokushima, holds most of the area's main attractions. The valley is full of ancient temples, shrines, museums and cultural sites. *Ai yashiki* (indigo-dyeing plants) are located all around Tokushima. Awa-style indigo

Drying vegetables, Kochi.

dyeing has flourished as the main industry of Tokushima for centuries.

About 30 kilometers up the Yoshinogawa from Tokushima is **Do-Chu** (Earthen Pillars). The strangely-shaped pillars were formed over millions of years as the result of soil erosion. Nearby are the historic streets of **Udatsu**, and the Awagami traditional paper factory. The entire valley is served by the JR Yoshinogawa rail line from Tokushima.

Ehime: Facing Seto Naikai along Shikoku's northeastern shore, Ehime Prefecture was described in the *Kojiki*, in 712, Japan's first chronicle of historical events and legends. Ehime has many cultural properties, historical places, hot springs and festivals.

Several castles dot the Ehime landscape. In **Imabari** can be found **Imabari-jo**. It is a rare coastal castle built in 1604, by Takatora Todo. The massive walls and moats, filled by water from the sea, let its masters fight on land or at sea.

Ancient temples and shrines are another attraction of Ehime prefecture. **Oyamazumi-jinja**, on Omi-shima at the center of the Geiyo Archipelago, has been worshipped since ancient times as the general headquarters of all village shrines in Japan. It is a shrine to the gods of the sea and of soldiers. There are many old camphor trees that give the shrine a solemn atmosphere. **Ishite-ji**, the 51st temple on Shikoku's 88-temple pilgrimage, was built by the decree of Emperor Shomu in 728. It was restored by the great priest Kobo in the early ninth century. Its treasure hall holds some 300 important historical articles.

Matsuyama-jo, in **Matsuyama**, stands as one of Japan's three large-scale multi-wing castles. Its 21 one buildings are built on a hill above the town. There are many myths and legends about nearby 3,000-year-old **Dogo Onsen**, just outside of Matsuyama. It's reputed to be Japan's oldest hot spring, first mentioned in Japan's oldest historical record, the *Kojiki*, and in the *Manyoshu*, Japan's first anthology, started in the fifth century and completed in 759.

One of Ehime's more interesting his-

Harvesting pearl oysters.

torical sites is the kabuki theater in **Uchiko**. This full-scale kabuki theater was built in 1916, in the Irimoya-zukuri style and with a tiled roof, a typical Japanese housing style of the 1800s. Its restoration in 1985 preserved the old-style drum tower on the top floor, a rotating stage, an elevated passageway, and box seats.

Uwajima-jo was built in 1595, by Takatora Todo. The castle's three-storied tower stands atop an 80-meter hill overlooking the city of **Uwajima**, noted throughout Japan for bull-fights.

In **Tsushima** is a strolling garden, Nanrakuen Koen, covering over fifteen hectares and the largest on Shikoku. Developed in 1985, the garden has four theme areas: mountains, villages, towns and the sea. Some 30,000 irises, which bloom in early May, cover most of the gardens. Nearby Nanrakuen Koen sits **Nametoko Gorge**, carved out by the Shimanto-gawa, reported to be the last clear river in Japan. The gorge runs through Ashizuri-Uwakai National Park.

Ehime is also note for its many and varied festivals. The Ikazaki Kite Festival in May displays Ehime's 300-year history of kite-making. The Saijo Festival in October features 80 movable shrines. Niihama Drum Festival in October features a competition between 33 massive drums. Other festivals include bullfights, samba competitions, a deer-mask dance, and the Matsuyama Spring Festival, at Dogo, in April.

Kochi: The prefecture of Kochi broadly encircles the wide Tosa Bay, with its capital of Kochi facing the south on a flat plain. Kochi is best known for the role its leading families played in forging the alliance between the Satsuma and Choshu clans, and the ensuing imperial Meiji Restoration. Its most renowned citizen from this period is Sakamoto Ryoma, who was assassinated in 1867, a year before the restoration. He is remembered in the museum at **Kochi-jo**, an elegant castle built in the seventeenth century and rebuilt in the eighteenth. A market is held every Sunday on the road leading to the Ote gate of Kochi-jo. It is a popular spot for local residents, with as many as 700 small stands selling vegetables, antiques, plants, and just about everything else imaginable. The market runs for about a kilometer along both sides of the road.

A statue of Ryoma graces the beach at **Katsurahama**, more famous as one of the few locations in Japan where dog-fighting is legal. This beautiful beach is a popular spot for admiring the moon. Katsurahama Koen is nearby, and there are many places of interest in the areas, such as the shell museum, the dog-fighting center, and the aquarium.

Ryuga-do, a limestone cave gradually molded over a period of 50 million years, boasts a mysterious natural beauty that supposedly enthralls everyone who visits. However, the scenic skyline road to the top of the mountain, where the cave is buried, offers the better vista. From the road, the Pacific Ocean spreads out below.

West of Kochi, in **Ino**, is a fabulous paper museum. Ino has a long history of paper-making, making Kochi paper famous throughout Japan. (For a place to be viable in Japan's domestic tourism industry, it must be "famous" for something, for anything.) In the museum, visitors can try their hand at paper-making and observe the paper-making process.

Near Kochi sits the Nishijima Fruit Farm. Its 11 huge hothouses, each measuring 70 meters (230 ft) in length and 45 meters (150 ft) in width, cover the spacious grounds. The temperature within each hothouse is maintained at 25°C (77°F). Sample delicious Kochi melons here year-round.

Two large capes frame Kochi prefecture. On the far eastern side of Kochi, **Muroto-zaki** points out into the vast Pacific Ocean. The cape is warm year-round, and at its tip the towering waves of the Pacific have eroded the rocks and reefs into strange shapes. The area is also noted for its connection with Kobo Daishi, founder of the Shingon sect of Buddhism. On the far western side of Kochi lies **Ashizuri-misaki**. This cape is noted for its towering marble cliffs and Japan's first underwater park. In early spring, camellia cover the cape in a dazzling red carpet of blossoms.

Mikan orchard, south coast of Shikoku.

YAMAHA

KYUSHU

Kyushu is far to the south and, it seems at times, almost forgotten by the rest of Japan. But Kyushu has always been in the vanguard of development and change. Kyushu is where the Yamoto tribe, and thus the Japanese people, first took root in what was to become their homeland. It was Kyushu that withstood the onslaught of the Mongols. It is also from where the Japanese first struck out on foreign conquest – the invasion of Korea, in 1594 – and into where ancient Chinese and Korean culture entered the archipelago as foundations for later Japanese art and philosophy. In later years, it was the place where Westerners gained a foothold in the then closed islands.

Any traveler coming from the north usually enters Kyushu at **Kitakyushu**, considered by some as a city in search of a soul – it is an amalgamation of five cities (Moji, Kokura, Yawata, Tobata and Wakamatsu) with a combined population of just over a million. The civic marriage was arranged by Tokyo bureaucrats in 1963, but has yet to consummated by a blending of culture or politics. It is a lackluster city with little of interest for travelers.

Kitakyushu is linked to Shimonoseki, on Honshu, by a bridge across the Kanmon Strait. Immense steel mills (now an endangered species) and factories were built here to take advantage of the region's rich coal deposits.

Fukuoka: During the Nara and Heian periods, the Fukuoka area was the principal Japanese port for trade with China and Korea. In 1274, a scouting party of some 30,000 Mongols landed near Fukuoka, having decimated garrisons on the islands of Tsushima and Iki, just to the north of Kyushu in the Korea Strait. The invaders were similarly successful on Kyushu, but the death of their commander, along with serious storms that threatened their ships, encouraged a hasty departure. Seven years later, in 1281, Kublai Khan sent a force of 150,000 soldiers, the largest amphibious assault in history prior to World War II. After 53 days of fighting, during which the Mongols, using catapults and cannons, overwhelmed fanatical Japanese resistance, a terrific typhoon – *kamikaze* (divine wind) – sent most of the invading fleet to the bottom of the sea. On the outskirts of Fukuoka, remnants of the wall built to repel the Mongols can be seen, though there's not much to see, actually, and finding it is difficult.

In 1601, Fukuoka-jo was built on the west side of the Naka-gawa, in what is today **Obori Koen**, and the town that grew up around the castle was also called Fukuoka. A town for merchants, Hakata, was built on the other side of the river. Hakata-ku has been a ward within Fukuoka since 1889, but the name remains, and **Hakata Station** – the southern terminus of the *shinkansen* – Hakata clay dolls, and the popular Hakata Yamagasa festival are all named after the merchant city.

Fukuoka is the capital of Fukuoka Prefecture and with a population of 1.2 million, competes with Kitakyushu as

Preceding pages: Kagoshima and Sakurajima. **Left**, Sata, Kyushu's southern cape. **Right**, waiting for the train.

the largest city on Kyushu. Fukuoka is the main port of entry to Kyushu, and is famous for its *fugu* (blowfish), particularly in winter.

Relics of Fukuoka's most famous visitors are preserved at the **Genko Kinekan** (Mongol Invasion Memorial Hall), along with a statue of Nichiren, who was among the mystics taking credit for the fortuitous kamikaze storm that sank the Mongol fleet.

In its role as the crossroads between Japan and China, Fukuoka was the place that Zen Buddhism first touched the archipelago's shores. Located just northwest of Hakata Station near Mikasagawa, **Shofuku-ji** is the oldest Zen temple in Japan, founded in 1195 by Eisai after years of study in China. Eisai is also credited with bringing the first tea seeds into the country; tea shrubs here are said to be their descendants.

The **Sumiyoshi-jinja**, the oldest extant Shinto shrine on Kyushu, was built in 1623. South of Shofuku-ji and due west of the train station, it sits atop a hill that provides an excellent city view.

Other points of interest in Fukuoka include Fukuoka-shi Bijutsukan, an art museum housing a collection of Japanese art; Ohori Koen, a park harboring the remains of **Fukuoka-jo** and reconstructions of its turret and gates; and the **Shiritsu Rekishu Shiryokan** (near Tenjin station), a museum dedicated to Fukuoka's history.

Forty minutes from Fukuoka and inland to the southeast, **Dazaifu** is home to the Dazaifu Temmangu Shrine, built in 1591 to commemorate the scholar Sugawara Michizane. Students clamber over its orange bridges to pray for success in examinations. (Sections of defensive walls built after the first Mongol invasion can still be seen on the road to Dazaifu.)

Karatsu, Imari and Arita: West of Fukuoka, the pottery towns of Karatsu, Imari, and Arita date back to the sixteenth century, when captive Korean artisans were brought to the area. Anyone with an interest in Japanese ceramics could easily spend a week investigating these villages.

Painted Buddha.

Karatsu is famous for its stoneware. Several galleries and workshops, including the Nakazato Taroemon and the Ryuta kilns, are open to visitors. The Hikiyama Tenijo museum exhibits nineteenth-century Karatsu Kun-chi Festival floats. A famous pine grove, Nijino-Matsubara, stretches five kilometers along Matsuuragate Beach.

Imari porcelain, which is actually produced in nearby Okawachiyama and Arita, is famous around the world. The first kilns in this region were created in the early 1600s by Ri Sanpei, a Korean prisoner of the Nabeshima *daimyo*. Sanpei and his countrymen were not allowed to leave the small villages that were established around their kilns; their graves are located in Okawachiyama's Nabeshima Honyo Koen, along with a replica of one of the original kilns.

Kyushu Toji Bunkakan (Kyushu Ceramic Museum) in Arita is the best place to view the full range of Kyushu pottery. Imaizumi Imaemon and Sakaida Kakiemon are famous workshops with galleries and shops open to the public.

Hirado-shima: Continuing west, the focus shifts to Japan's early Christians. The first foreign settlement in Japan was established on Hirado-shima in 1550, where the Dutch began trading activities. The Francis Xavier Memorial Chapel consecrates the saint's visit to Hirado. European activity ended when the Dutch were forced to move to Dejima, in Nagasaki Harbor, in 1641, but secretive Christians maintained a version of the faith here for centuries. This bit of historical lore has provided the basis for a thriving domestic tourist industry here, with "real" icons for sale.

Nagasaki: A city of nearly half a million, Nagasaki clings to steep hills wrapped around a very active deepwater harbor, competing with Kobe for designation as Japan's San Francisco. Like San Francisco, it has a lively Chinatown (Shinchimachi) and a spirit of receptiveness to novel ideas. One of the most interesting cities in Japan, travelers on a restricted time budget should allow for at least two days in Nagasaki.

Nagasaki's harbor has played a promi-

Visit to the onsen.

nent role in Japan's relations with the outside world. Dutch traders organized the first sustained European presence here, on an island in the harbor, through which most of the early Christian missionaries came. The port at Nagasaki was established in 1571 to serve Portuguese traders. A decade later, Omura Sumitada, a local daimyo who had grown rich on trade with the foreigners, turned over partial administration of the port to the Jesuit missionaries who came in the merchants' wake.

A generation later, fearing that the Christians and their converts would subvert his authority, the shogun Toyotomi Hideyoshi banned Christianity. He had six Spanish priests and 20 Japanese Christians rounded up in Kyoto and Osaka, then brought to Nagasaki, where they were crucified in 1597 as a warning to Japan's largest Christian community. A memorial, constructed in 1962, stands in **Nishizaka Koen** on the spot of the crucifixions, across from **Nagasaki Station**, at the north end of downtown.

Christianity was completely and brutally suppressed following the Christian-led Shimbara Rebellion of 40,000 peasants, south of Nagasaki in 1637. As a result, Japan's sole officially-sanctioned contact with Europeans for the next two centuries was through a settlement on **Dejima**, in Nagasaki Harbor. The artificial island – now part of the mainland – was built for Portuguese traders, but was occupied by Dutchmen after the Portuguese were banished in 1638. Its occupants were confined to a small, walled area, and contact with Japanese was limited to a small circle of officials, traders, prostitutes, and, in the later years, scholars. As no other Europeans were permitted in Japan until 1854, whatever news of European technology and culture that filtered into Japan came through this settlement. The **Dejima Museum**, near the site, preserves relics of the settlement.

Like the Dutch, Nagasaki's Chinese, mostly from Fujian along China's southern coast, were officially confined to a walled ghetto, but restrictions on their movements were not as strictly enforced.

Kyushu farmland.

The Chinese in Nagasaki left the only pure Chinese architecture to be found in Japan, along with one of the three Chinatowns remaining in Japan. (The others are in Yokohama and Kobe.) **Shinchimachi**'s narrow and winding streets are filled with Chinese restaurants catering to tourists, as there are very few Chinese remaining in Nagasaki.

Two popular "Chinese" dishes in Japan, *saraudon* and *champpon*, were invented in Shinchimachi. Like most of the foreign food served in Japan, they bear only a passing resemblance to the original, but they are quite delicious.

The Chinese community was granted permission to build its own temples. Teramachi (Temple Town) contains two of the oldest Chinese temples in Japan, as well as numerous Japanese Buddhist temples and graveyards. **Kokufu-ji**, founded in 1620, was built on the edge of the original Chinatown, in the northeast part of town and which burned down in 1698; the current Shinchimachi occupies land designated for Chinese merchants following the fire.

Centrally located, **Sofuku-ji** is a bright, elaborate Ming-style temple, and is in better condition than most Ming-era temples in China. A Zen priest from Fujian built Sofuku-ji in 1629. Shaka and 18 disciples inhabit the main hall; the Masodo (Hall of the Bodhisattva) contains an image of the goddess of the seas, flanked by fierce guardians reputed to have thousand-mile vision.

Spectacles Bridge, so named because of the resemblance of it and its reflection to eyeglasses when there's enough water in the river, is the oldest stone arch bridge in Japan, built in 1634 by the priest from Kofuku-ji.

True to its traditional receptiveness to new ideas, Nagasaki embarked on an aggressive modernization campaign in the later part of the nineteenth century. Thomas Glover, a Scotsman, was one of the first and most important of the European traders who arrived soon after Commodore Perry's Black Ships reopened the country. Glover helped Nagasaki achieve many Japanese firsts: the first railroad, the first mint and the

Sofuku-ji.

first printing press with movable type were all built in Nagasaki as a result of his efforts. He was also very active in supporting the rebels who defeated the shogun's forces, restoring the emperor's rule in 1868 in the Meiji Restoration. There is considerable controversy over whether Glover's marriage to a geisha did, as many guidebooks assert, inspire Puccini's opera, Madame Butterfly.

Glover also built the first western-style mansion in Japan. **Glover-en** (Gardens) contains this house, built in 1863, and several other early Meiji-era, western-style houses, which are elegant mixtures of Japanese and European architecture. The grounds provide excellent views of the harbor and the city. If not fortunate enough to visit during the annual Okunchi Festival in October, a trip to the Kunchi Shiryokan Museum, on the edge of the gardens, displays Chinese dragon dances, floats and energetic revelry. Nearby in the same neighborhood is **Oura Roman Catholic Church**, said to be the oldest gothic-style structure in Japan.

Atomic bombing: If construction of Glover's mansion marked the beginning of an era of infatuation with European institutions in Nagasaki, and in the country as a whole, the detonation of a plutonium bomb over Nagasaki 82 years later marked its realignment.

A simple stone obelisk stands at the epicenter ("hypocenter" in Japan) of the atomic blast that devastated much of Nagasaki, on the morning of 9 August 1945. The plutonium bomb, which was three times more powerful than the uranium bomb dropped two days before over Hiroshima, landed about three kilometers (2 mi) off target, over **Urakami**, a Christian village just to the north of downtown. (The Mitsubishi Shipyards, on the west side of the port and the first modern shipbuilding facility in Japan, was the intended target.)

Urakami Roman Catholic Church, the largest Christian church in Japan, stood a few hundred meters from the epicenter; it was rebuilt in 1958. Headless statues of saints, scorched in the blast, remain as silent witnesses.

Left, Peace Statue. Below, Glover House.

The **International Culture Hall** (housing the Atomic Bomb Museum) contains photos, relics, and poignant details of the blast and its 150,000 victims. Simple objects – a melted bottle, the charred remains of a kimono – as well as photos of victims, provide stark evidence of the bomb's destructiveness.

As important as its displays are, the museum, like the more elaborate one in Hiroshima, fails to provide any historical context or background to the bombing. Nothing is said about the reasons for the war, and there is no comparison with other mass killings of civilians, such as those committed by Japan in China and Korea. (In fact, the Japanese brutally killed more civilians in Nanjing than were killed by both of the atomic bombs; nevertheless, Japanese text books call the Rape of Nanjing a "minor incident".)

Heiwa Koen (Peace Park) is dominated by the Peace Statue, depicting a man with right hand pointing to the sky (signaling the threat from the atomic bomb) and left hand extended (symbolizing world peace). The Peace Fountain, on the south side of the park, was built in remembrance of the bomb victims who died crying for water.

The ropeway cable car to the top of **Inasa-yama** provides fantastic vistas of the harbor and surrounding hills, especially at night. If time permits, travelers might venture to other sights: Nagasaki Museum of History and Folklore, and Holland Village, just outside the city, which is presumably of more interest to Japanese than to foreign visitors. The chief attraction is a replica of a "typical" Dutch village, complete with windmills and numerous Dutch expats pretending to be Dutch.

Shimbara Peninsula: The most scenic route between Nagasaki and Kumamoto takes travelers through the Shimbara Hanto and the Amakusa Islands, on a combination of buses and ferries.

Down the peninsula, roughly midway between Nagasaki and Kumamoto, is **Unzen-dake**, whose *jigoku* (hell) pits of boiling mud and colored mineral waters are less dramatic, but less com-

New foreign influence.

mercialized, than those in Beppu, on the east coast of Kyushu. Christians who refused to renounce their faith were thrown into these jigoku in the seventeenth century. Unzen was a popular resort among colonial officials based in Shanghai during the glory days of the British Empire. The town is named after the 1,360-meter-high (4,460 ft) volcano Unzen-dake, which is in the center of the peninsula and is surrounded by Unzen-Amakusa National Park. Unzen violently erupted in 1991, causing considerable death and damage.

Shimabara-jo, which was destroyed in the 1637 Christian rebellion, was reconstructed in 1964. The castle houses a museum displaying the *fumi-e* Christian images, which suspected believers at the time were forced to walk upon.

The **Amakusa Islands**, about 70 islands in all, lie between Unzen and Kumamoto. The Kirishitankan, in Hondo, is a museum containing relics of the Amakusa Christians. Hondo is also home to the Amakusa Ocean Floor Natural Aquarium.

Kumamoto: Although it isn't a popular tourist destination, Kumamoto is an interesting and dynamic provincial capital. This city of half a million people is best known for its seventeenth-century castle, 350-year-old Suizenji Koen, and, believe it or not, its horse-meat *sashimi*. Eager to retain its vitality into the twenty-first century, Kumamoto also boasts the most successful technical research park (adjacent to the airport) in Japan. Kumamoto Prefecture has a sister state relationship with Montana, which is due more to the power and influence of the former American ambassador to Japan, Mike Mansfield, a Montanan, than to any similarity between the two places. The Texas swing music on one of the newer street cars is explained by Kumamoto's sister-city relationship with San Antonio, Texas.

Kumamoto-jo was built in 1607 by Kato Kiyomasa. Unfortunately, the castle's 49 towers were made of wood and most were incinerated in an 1877 siege. The restored *donjon*, housing a museum, as well as original turrets,

moats and stone palisades, evoke the grandeur of what was one of Japan's most impressive castles. **Honmyo-ji**, a Nichiren temple housing Kato's tomb, can be seen from the castle's towers.

A cup of tea can be enjoyed in the basement of the **Kumamoto Traditional Crafts Center**, across the street from the castle. The first floor features a colorful collection of toys, tools, jewelry and ceramics produced by Kumamoto craftsmen. The museum is part of the prefecture's efforts to sustain traditional crafts, which were largely abandoned after World War II. Most of the items are on sale in the museum.

Suizenji Koen, designed in 1632, contains landscaped models of Mount Fuji and the 53 stops on the Tokaido Highway, between Kyoto and Tokyo.

Aso-Kuju National Park, an hour's drive east from Kumamoto, contains the world's largest volcanic crater, an active volcano, and a volcano museum. Actually comprised of three minor craters, **Aso-san** (1,592 meters/5,223 ft) erupts every two or three years, but in a passive way. The drive from Kumamoto leads past Aspecta, which some say is largest outdoor theater in the world. (Spend enough time in Japan, and one recognizes the Japanese love of superlatives, whether true or not.)

Aso's main crater.

West of Kumamoto and on the other side of Aso, the shrine at **Takachiho** is where the *iwato kagura*, a sacred dance, is performed for tourists every night. The Takachiho Gorge, featuring 80-meter (262 ft) cliffs, is another one of the many spots where the sun goddess Amaterasu is said to have emerged from her cave to create the islands and people of the country. A cave near the shrine at Iwato is touted as the very one.

The recently-restored Edo-style **Yachiyo-za**, in **Yanaga** and 50 minutes by bus from Kumamoto, is one of 10 kabuki theaters in Japan, and well worth a visit. Built in 1910, it is a mixture of traditional Japanese construction and imported innovations, including a revolving stage and concealed trap doors. Patrons sat on *tatami*, warming themselves with a *hibachi* in winter. Around the corner, the Lantern Museum displays hundreds of handmade lantern headdresses, worn by young women in the local annual festival.

The bay of **Minamata**, in the southern part of Kumamoto Prefecture, is a monument to the excesses of industry, the results of laissez-faire government controls, and to sheer ignorance, greed and disregard for ethical conduct in general. The reason: a severely debilitating and often fatal ailment known as Minamata disease, (in Japanese, *itai-itai byoki*, or hurt-hurt disease). The affliction was traced to shellfish and other products taken from its waters, into which local industries had been discharging mercury and other heavy-metal wastes for decades. Legislation hurriedly passed by the Diet soon after the disease's discovery in the 1970s now constitutes the basis of Japan's still-weak pollution-control laws. Nevertheless, litigation regarding the responsibility for the mercury dumping was dragged out until the mid 1990s, with no one and no entity eventually taking responsibility. Minamata Bay itself is being reclaimed and turned into an ecological park.

Beppu: If seeking to go to hell and then come back, head for Beppu, on the northeastern coast of Kyushu. The resort town is famous for its jigoku, variously-colored ponds of water and mud that steam and boil, as well as its hot springs. A popular destination for Japanese tourists, Beppu is gaudy and commercial, rather tacky and a far cry from the serene elegance of Japanese travel posters. There are more hells than can be experienced in a lifetime, including: Blood Pond Hell (a vermillion-colored boiling pond); Sea Hell, a boiling mud pond 120 meters (400 ft) deep; Mountain Hell (a mud pond in the hills, complete with statues of gorillas); and Oniyama Hell (with mockups of crocodiles). All these are far too hot for bathing, but out on the beach and in the many *onsen* inns, comfortable hot-sand and hot-mud baths are available.

Beppu is also well-known for its *fugu* (blowfish). Takasakiya Hill, 15 minutes from Beppu, is covered with wild monkeys. Nearby is **Yufuin**, a rustic onsen resort providing a tranquil counterpoint to Beppu.

The **Usuki Sekibutsu**, a collection of more than 60 stone Buddhas, is all that remains of the Mangetsu-ji, once an important temple. They are some of the most exquisite and mysterious Buddhist images in Japan. Archaeologists have dated their carving to slightly over 1,000 years ago, but have not determined who created them or why.

The small city of **Miyazaki** is considered the hometown of Jimmu, the mythological progenitor of the Japanese imperial family. Jimmu is enshrined in Miyazaki Jingu, which also features an interesting museum containing relics from local ancient tombs.

Heiwadai Koen (Peace Park), built in 1940, has a 40-meter-high (130-ft) tower; if you clap your hands at the correct place, the tower resonates with a strange groaning sound. Reproductions of *haniwa*, clay figurines found in ancient burial mounds near the Miyazaki, are scattered throughout the park.

Blood Pond Hell, Beppu.

Saitobaru, near the town of **Saito** to north of Miyazaki, is one of the richest archaeological sites in Japan. About 300 burial mounds from the fifth and sixth centuries have been excavated here, and two of the larger ones can be visited. Artifacts, including original haniwa, are on display at the Saitobaru Shiryokan.

Kagoshima: This prefecture, in the far south of Kyushu, consists of two peninsulas, Satsuma and Osumi, that encircle **Kagoshima Wan** (Bay), and a chain of islands stretching south towards Okinawa. A distinct, rapid-fire dialect is spoken here. The speech of older people, lacking the homogenizing influences of national television and radio, is almost incomprehensible to other Japanese.

Kagoshima, on the interior side of **Satsuma Hanto** and the southernmost metropolis in Kyushu, is situated on large Kagoshima Bay. It is famous for being Japan's most polluted city: the pollution comes from **Sakura-jima**, the very active volcano across the bay and rising 1,120 meters (3,670 ft) above the water. The mountain has erupted over 5,000 times since 1955, sending clouds of ash, and often large boulders, raining down on Kagoshima. (Umbrellas are used as much for ash as for rain.) More than half a million people live within 10 kilometers of Sakura-jima's crater. No other major city is as precariously positioned; Naples, Kagoshima's sister city, is twice as far from Vesuvius.

Sakura-jima (Cherry Island) itself can be reached via a short ferry ride from Kagoshima, or by road around the periphery of the bay. As the name indicates, it was once an island, but an eruption in 1914 spilled some three billion tons of lava, joining the island to the peninsula. There are dramatic views from the Yogan Tenbodai, on the southeast side of Sakura-jima. Extra large *daikon* (radishes) grow in the rich volcanic soil, along with kumquats, summer oranges, and other fruits.

Aside from the gritty ash and often polluted air of Kagoshima, the city itself is delightful, and retains much of the spirit of the once-powerful Satsuma

Summit of Sakura-jima.

clans, from whom the area takes its name. The Satsumas were ruled by the Shimazu daimyo, who were among the most dynamic of the Japanese hereditary rulers, for seven centuries. The Shimazu's distance from Edo Tokyo bred a fierce independence.

The Shimazu were open to new ideas from abroad. They welcomed Francis Xavier to Kagoshima, the first Japanese city he visited, in 1549. Returning from Japan's ill-fated invasion of the Korean peninsula in the early seventeenth century, the Shimazu brought captive Korean potters to Kagoshima, the originators of *satsuma* ware.

Despite their receptiveness to outsiders, the Satsuma clans opposed the Edo shogunate's capitulation to European demands that Japan open its ports to trade. Demonstrating the resistance to the shogun's edicts, Shimazu retainers killed an Englishman near Edo, in 1862. The British retaliated the following year, sending a squadron of ships to bombard Kagoshima. To the British sailors' surprise, the lords of Satsuma reacted favorably to this demonstration of modern naval power. They welcomed her majesty's officers to the still-smoking city and purchased some of their ships, which later were incorporated into the Japanese navy. Close relations between the Japanese and British navies lasted until the 1920s, and Satsuma clansmen dominated the navy until World War II.

In 1866, the Satsumas joined with the rival Choshu clan in a successful military coup against the shogun, which restored imperial rule with the Meiji Restoration. Ironically, a decade later, the Satsumas led a bloody, and unsuccessful, rebellion against the new order.

Satsuma-ware, and the more rustic Kuro-Satsuma pottery, can be purchased in Naeshirogawa, a village that was settled by Korean potters in the 1600s. In addition to pottery, Kagoshima is known for *kiriko* cut-glass. Local artisans were compelled to cease kiriko production under the terms of peace imposed on the region in 1877. They resumed kiriko production in 1985, following a hiatus of 180 years.

Iso Koen, containing a garden laid out in 1661, provides excellent views of Sakura-jima. Just outside the park, the **Shokoshuseikan** houses one of the first Western-style factories in Japan. It contains exhibits on the factory and the Shimazu family. The Shimazu Yashiki (mansion) has also been preserved.

Nanshu Cemetery holds the remains of Takamori Saigo (1827–77), who led the forces that defeated the shogun. Saigo later perished after leading the 1877 rebellion against the regime he had created. Saigo made his last stand on Shiroyama Hill. With defeat inevitable, he had a loyal follower decapitate him. Saigo was buried at Jyokomyo-ji.

Ibusuki is a spa town southwest of Kagoshima, with hot-sand baths near **Kaimon-dake**, a 900-meter-high (3,000 ft) volcano looking much like Fuji.

Japan's ambitious space program, if small by American, Chinese, French and Russian standards, operates a launch pad at **Uchinoura**, on the Osumi Hanto; most launches, however, are now made from Tanega-shima, south of Kagoshima.

Left, Ibusuki. Right, preparation for shichi-go-san, Minamata.

SEU DE ARTE DE SÃO PAULO
xhibition in Japan 1982-83

OKINAWA

Extending for 1,200 kilometers (600 mi) from Kyushu to within sight of Taiwan, the 70-plus islands of the Ryukyus, or **Nansei-shoto**, stretch across the ocean to within 200 kilometers (125 mi) of Taiwan.

Ryukyu is the Japanese pronunciation of the Chinese name Liugiu, which is what the Chinese during the Ming dynasty called the islands. Taken over by Japan, which ignored the islands like a faraway province, Okinawa was the final beachhead for a planned Allied invasion of the Japanese archipelago in World War II. Under American control following the end of World War II, the islands reverted back to Japanese sovereignty in 1972. Now, all islands north of the main island of Okinawa are part of Kyushu, and the main island and islands to the south are in Okinawa Prefecture.

Okinawa sits in a subtropical belt, blessed with average temperatures of around 23°C (73°F). A short rainy season blankets the area in heavy rains during May and June. More enjoyable are spring and autumn, typhoons in September and October notwithstanding.

Is Okinawa a tropical paradise? There are exquisite white-sand beaches, azure waters and some unusual flora and fauna. Okinawa is, along with Guam, Japan's backyard resort escape. But Okinawa also has the highest unemployment rate of any prefecture in Japan and an average annual income that is less than half of Tokyo's average. Yet, the ever-ready smiles of its gentle, friendly people give no hint of Tokyo-envy, nor of the incredible suffering that Okinawans have known through times of war – and even during times of peace.

For centuries, the Okinawans minded their own business and accommodated themselves to outsiders. But during the age of imperialism in the late nineteenth century, their independence fell prey to the ambitions of powerful neighbors.

Okinawa was once known as Ryukyu, independent of Japanese control. Indeed, Okinawans are proud of their heritage, and will often remind travelers that they are not Japanese, nor do they especially appreciate Japan's historical treatment of the islands.

Naha: The center of tourist activity is the city of Naha, and its center of tourist activity is **Kokusai Dori** (International Road), which is a jangle of typical Japanese urban architecture – cluttered and without aesthetic appeal – and crowds of walkers and swarms of vehicles. Indeed, Kokusai Dori is nearly indistinguishable from any other urban center in Japan. Yet only a short distance away are typically Okinawan neighborhoods. **Naminou-gu**, a small Confucian shrine, and the **Gokoku-ji**, a temple that was once considered a national religious center, are along the waterfront, not far from the central post office and just north of an old pleasure quarter that, even today, retains its fair share of bars, cabarets and steak houses.

A fine, and relaxing, manner in which to gauge the differences between Okinawa and the rest of Japan is a visit to a local pub. No disco or the ubiqui-

Preceding pages: protective shisa. **Left**, Nakijin Castle. **Right**, resort on Miyako-jima.

tous karaoke that is de rigueur at big-city clubs elsewhere in Japan. Rather, listen to the frequently-plaintive sounds of the *sanshin*, the three-stringed, snake-skin-covered Okinawan banjo known elsewhere as the *samisen*.

Traditional Okinawan dance and theater, which differ considerably from their Japanese counterparts, are performed frequently at various locations in Naha; arrangements are easy.

Okinawans are quite proud of their exquisite textiles, which are typically handwoven from linen and silk, and feature beautiful designs created with painted-on dyes. The designs and details of craftsmanship traditionally differed by area, and the *bingata* stencil-dyed fabric, originally made exclusively for aristocrats, is the most highly prized, often using exotic tropical patterns.

Okinawan crafts are also a delight. Active since 1617, the **Tsuboya** pottery-making district, off Himeyuri Dori, southeast of Kokusai Dori, houses two dozen kilns, which make everything from the *kara-kara* flasks country gentlemen used to carry to the *shisa* figures that guard dwellings. A central pottery outlet sells items from all the kilns.

Tsuboya's pottery history began in the early 1600s, when a Korean potter was forced to settle here after being taken prisoner during Hideyoshi's invasion of the Korean peninsula, during the late 1500s. The pottery produced in Tsuboya bears strong seventeenth-century Korean characteristics, as is also the case in Kyushu and some parts of western Honshu.

Naha is the perfect spot for initial experiments with Okinawan cuisine. Now familiar with the *sashimi, unagi, yakisoba* and other delicacies of central Japan, travelers might now be ready to plunge into *mimiga* (sliced pig ears with vinegar), *ashite-bichi* (stewed pig legs), *rafutei* (pork simmered in *miso,* sugar, rice wine and soy sauce), *goya champuru* (stir-fried meat and bitter melon), or one of the many kinds of local *somen* noodles. *Awamori,* the local distilled rice brew that is served with ice and water, packs a wallop that puts anything

Naha Port.

else to shame. Some bottles of awamori come with a coiled *habu,* or snake, in the bottom for increased male virility.

Shuri Castle: The first castle on Shuri, due west of downtown on a lofty hill overlooking Naha and the vast oceans beyond, was established in 1237. Under the second Sho dynasty, which was established in 1469 by King Sho En, Shuri became a mighty palace and temple complex. Shuri remained the political and cultural center of the Ryukyus until 1879, when the last Okinawan king, Sho Tai, was forced to abdicate by the Meiji government in Tokyo.

During the 82-day battle of Okinawa in 1945, when the Japanese army chose Okinawa as the definitive last stand against the Allies before an anticipated invasion of the main Japanese islands, Shuri was the headquarters of the Japanese forces. It was destroyed during the fighting. Prewar accounts describe a marvel on a par in architectural and artistic interest with Kyoto, Nara, and Nikko. Much of the castle's stonework has been rebuilt. **Ryutan Koen** is an expansive park barely able to absorb the hordes of tour buses, nor the clusters of on-going group photographs posing with classically-attired Okinawan women in front of **Shuri no Mon**, the traditional gate to the castle grounds. The Tamaudon Mausoleum, minutes from the gate, contains the bodies of King Sho En and other members of his family.

Nearby, the **Okinawa Prefectural Museum** offers displays on Okinawan history and culture.

South of Naha: South along the western coast, past the international airport, leads to **Itoman**, claimed to be the home of some of the most fearless sailors in the world. Itoman's mid-August tug-of-war – with intertwined "male" and "female" ropes – draws crowds from afar. Several caverns – heavily promoted and developed – pepper the southern coastline, including **Hakugin-do**, a cavern with a shrine dedicated to the guardian deity of Itoman. To the east, **Gyokusen-do** is said to be Asia's largest cave. Only about one-fifth of it is open to the public; unfortunately, visitors have broken

Souvenir guard, Naha airport.

off most of the stalactites and stalagmites, and the cave's floor has been pockmarked with wayward shoes. Near the entrance to the caves is the **Habu Koen**, or Snake Park, where there are displays of fights between mongooses and habu snakes, whose venom is strong enough to fell a horse or water buffalo.

The most famous caves are the tunnel labyrinths at **Romogusuku**, near the Naha airport, which was the last headquarters of the Imperial Navy. The military commanders refused to surrender as the Allies pounded the island's south with naval bombardments; over 4,000 men committed suicide. Reminders of the bloodiest battle of the Pacific war, which cost the lives of 13,000 Americans, 110,000 Japanese and 140,000 Okinawan civilians (one-eighth of the population) are numerous throughout the south of the island.

Famous is the story of **Himeyuri no To** (Lily of the Valley Tower), a deep pit where a group of high school girls and their teachers committed suicide – rather than endure the possibility of capture – after singing their school song. **Mabuniga-oka**, on a promontory overlooking the ocean, is the site of the last resistance of the Japanese army.

A five-kilometer ferry ride from **Chinen Hanto**, on Okinawa's southeast coast, brings visitors to small and flat **Kudaka-jima**, the so-called island of the gods. This is where the great ancestress of the Ryukyuan people, Amamikiyo, is said to have descended from heaven and bestowed on them the five grains. Covered with sugar cane and *fukugi* trees, Kudaka-jima, which has a resident population of about 300 people, is usually somnolent. But in mid November, every 12th year, the five-day-long Izaiho Festival is held, in which local women between the ages of 30 and 41 serve collectively as *noro*, or priestesses, to perform rites and communicate with the gods.

Central Okinawa: The central portions of Okinawa are largely occupied by U.S. military bases, most important of which is the air base at **Kadena**, about a quarter of the way up this skinny island. In the mid 1990s, Okinawans vocally sent the message that they wanted some of their land returned; much of the bases' land is atop leased private land, which the Japanese government has mandated. Some of the American presence is being shifted away from Okinawa.

Outside Kadena, offerings are sleazy and garish, but there are good beaches in the area. The Nakamura home, at Nagasuku, offers an inspection of how an eighteenth-century gentry family lived. The ruins of the castle at **Nagasuku**, built in the mid-fifteenth century, are the largest in Okinawa.

Jutting out from the west coast, about two-thirds of the way to the northern tip of Okinawa, **Motobu Hanto** was the site of an ocean exposition in the 1970s. Most of the tourist-focused offerings are on the exposition's former site, **Exposition Memorial Park**, including several exhibitions about Okinawan culture and the ocean. The ruins of **Nakijin-jo**, on the peninsula's northern tip, are a fine place to watch a sunset over castle, ocean and sugar-cane fields. Offshore, tiny **Ie-jima** is where the fa-

Naha minimart.

mous American war correspondent, Ernie Pile, was killed in World War II.

Northern Okinawa: A visit to the far north of Okinawa Island, or *yanbaru*, will reward the adventurous with rugged hills, beaches and secluded fishing villages, along with some of the friendliest people anywhere. In the village of **Kijoka**, one can watch the various steps required to produce the plantain-fiber textile, *bashofu*. The view at **Hedo-misaki**, the cape at the northern tip of the island, is stunning. But don't go wandering off in the bush in yanbaru, as this is habu country.

One of the Ryukyu's sacred island is **Iheya-jima**, to the northeast of Okinawa. According to Okinawan legend, Emperor Jimmu Tenno began his conquest of Japan from here. Moreover, a huge cave on the island, referred to as the Hiding Place, is said to be the very cave where the sun goddess Amaterasu hid herself until the other deities could coax her out of the cave, thereby restoring light to the world. Priestesses governed that island until the nineteenth century.

Outer Islands: The best bet for experiencing the Ryukyuan way of life is to visit the outer islands, or *saki-shima*, reached by ferry or air from Naha.

Kerama, only 35 kilometers (20 mi) west of Naha, is an excellent scuba-diving haunt, embellished with numerous sea snakes among its gorgeous coral reefs. **Kume-jima**, three hours by ferry from Naha's Tomari Harbor, has preserved several fine traditional homes in Nakazato and elsewhere.

Further afield is the Miyako group of eight islands. **Miyako-jima**, the main island, is an hour by air or 10 hours by boat from Naha. At its port of **Hiraya** are the *o-honoyama* (tax stone). After the samurai of Satsuma (now Kagoshima) on Kyushu invaded the Ryukyu kingdom in 1609, it became in everything but name a tributary to that fief's lord, even though the country continued to pay tribute to the Ming dynasty, in China.

At the time, all children on Miyako-jima were paraded once a year before the *ninto-zeiseki*. Those taller than the

Miyako-jima resort.

stone had to pay the tax, or else were shipped off to work as forced labor. So burdensome were the taxes that, on some remote islands, islanders resorted to killing the weak and old because there was not enough food. This *nintozei* system was abolished in 1918.

Miyako-jima earned a place in Japanese school books when five local fishermen spotted the Czarist fleet steaming towards Japan, during the Russo-Japanese War (1904–05). The timely warning allowed the Imperial Navy, under Admiral Togo Shigenori, to surprise and annihilate the Russians in the Battle of Tsushima Straits.

Nearby **Irabu**, an island that can be reached by boat from Hiraya, offers attractive scenery and fine diving.

Yaeyama Shoto, best reached by air (the ferry from Naha only puts in about once a week), was long relatively isolated from the rest of the Ryukyus. It will appeal to those interested in folklore or the outdoor life.

The main island of **Ishigaki-jima** was, for years, embroiled in an ongoing controversy regarding whether an offshore airport would be built near Shiraho, one of the largest and most unique coral reefs in this part of the Pacific. Finally, in the mid 1990s, after over a decade of dispute, it was decided that the airport would not be built near the reefs, an unusual environmental victory in Japan, where the will of development typically runs rampant.

The municipal Yaeyama Museum, near the harbor, has a collection of local artifacts and folk crafts. Kabira Bay is an idyllic lagoon-like area with small islands and sandy beaches.

A short ferry or hovercraft ride from Ishigaki takes one to **Taketomi**, a flat island famed throughout Japan for the star-shaped sand at Kondoi. The island is beautiful and peaceful, but locals warn tourists to beware of not only the habu, but also of the undercurrents in the surf.

A ferry or jetfoil also goes to the large island of **Iriomote**, which is no doubt the most unusual and unique island in the Japanese archipelago, a touch of New Guinea in Japan.

Except for the towns of Ohara, in the southeast, and Funaura, in the north, the island is mostly tropical rain forest. Thankfully, development on the island has been limited, with only one resort, although others have been threatened. *Minshuku* – boarding houses – abound, and visitors can camp on the beach at Hosisuna no Hama, which provides free showers. A river boat heads up the Urauchi-gawa, to Mariudo and Kampira Falls, amidst spectacular jungle. If adventurous, there is the cross-island trail. This, too, is habu territory.

Iriomote is noted for several unique flora and fauna, especially the Iriomote cat, a quite wild feline that is found nowhere else, as is the case with a large moth over a foot in diameter.

Scuba divers – especially women, for some reason – come from all over Japan to the waters between Iriomote and the island of **Kohama**. Awesome giant manta rays can be seen here. The deep-sea fishing in the area off **Yonaguni** is also interesting, but the price of going on a trip is high. Taiwan is less than 200 kilometers to the southeast from here.

Left, off of Taketomi. Right, baseball practice, Naha little league.

HA
18

KEY DLOP

INSIGHT GUIDES
Travel Tips

FOR THOSE WITH MORE THAN A PASSING INTEREST IN TIME...

Before you put your name down for a Patek Philippe watch *fig. 1*, there are a few basic things you might like to know, without knowing exactly whom to ask. In addressing such issues as accuracy, reliability and value for money, we would like to demonstrate why the watch we will make for you will be quite unlike any other watch currently produced.

"Punctuality", Louis XVIII was fond of saying, "is the politeness of kings."

We believe that in the matter of punctuality, we can rise to the occasion by making you a mechanical timepiece that will keep its rendezvous with the Gregorian calendar at the end of every century, omitting the leap-years in 2100, 2200 and 2300 and recording them in 2000 and 2400 *fig. 2*. Nevertheless, such a watch does need the occasional adjustment. Every 3333 years and 122 days you should remember to set it forward one day to the true time of the celestial clock. We suspect, however, that you are simply content to observe the politeness of kings. Be assured, therefore, that when you order your watch, we will be exploring for you the physical—if not the metaphysical—limits of precision.

Does everything have to depend on how much?

Consider, if you will, the motives of collectors who set record prices at auction to acquire a Patek Philippe. They may be paying for rarity, for looks or for micromechanical ingenuity. But we believe that behind each $500,000-plus bid is the conviction that a Patek Philippe, even if 50 years old or older, can be expected to work perfectly for future generations.
In case your ambitions to own a Patek Philippe are somewhat discouraged by the scale of the sacrifice involved, may we hasten to point out that the watch we will make for you today will certainly be a technical improvement on the Pateks bought at auction? In keeping with our tradition of inventing new mechanical solutions for greater reliability and better time-keeping, we will bring to your watch innovations *fig. 3* inconceivable to our watchmakers who created the supreme wristwatches of 50 years ago *fig. 4*.
At the same time, we will of course do our utmost to avoid placing undue strain on your financial resources.

Can it really be mine?

May we turn your thoughts to the day you take delivery of your watch? Sealed within its case is your watchmaker's tribute to the mysterious process of time. He has decorated each wheel with a chamfer carved into its hub and polished into a shining circle. Delicate ribbing flows over the plates and bridges of gold and rare alloys. Millimetric surfaces are bevelled and burnished to exactitudes measured in microns. Rubies are transformed into jewels that triumph over friction. And after many months—or even years—of work, your watchmaker stamps a small badge into the mainbridge of your watch. The Geneva Seal—the highest possible attestation of fine watchmaking *fig. 5*.

Looks that speak of inner grace *fig. 6*.

When you order your watch, you will no doubt like its outward appearance to reflect the harmony and elegance of the movement within. You may therefore find it helpful to know that we are uniquely able to cater for any special decorative needs you might like to express. For example, our engravers will delight in conjuring a subtle play of light and shadow on the gold case-back of one of our rare pocket-watches *fig. 7*. If you bring us your favourite picture, our enamellers will reproduce it in a brilliant miniature of hair-breadth detail *fig. 8*. The perfect execution of a double hobnail pattern on the bezel of a wristwatch is the pride of our casemakers and the satisfaction of our designers, while our chainsmiths will weave for you a rich brocade in gold *figs. 9 & 10*. May we also recommend the artistry of our goldsmiths and the experience of our lapidaries in the selection and setting of the finest gemstones? *figs. 11 & 12*.

How to enjoy your watch before you own it.

As you will appreciate, the very nature of our watches imposes a limit on the number we can make available. (The four Calibre 89 time-pieces we are now making will take up to nine years to complete). We cannot therefore promise instant gratification, but while you look forward to the day on which you take delivery of your Patek Philippe *fig. 13*, you will have the pleasure of reflecting that time is a universal and everlasting commodity, freely available to be enjoyed by all.

Should you require information on any particular Patek Philippe watch, or even on watchmaking in general, we would be delighted to reply to your letter of enquiry. And if you send us

fig. 1: The classic face of Patek Philippe.

fig. 2: One of the 33 complications of the Calibre 89 astronomical clock-watch is a satellite wheel that completes one revolution every 400 years.

fig. 3: Recognized as the most advanced mechanical regulating device to date, Patek Philippe's Gyromax balance wheel demonstrates the equivalence of simplicity and precision.

fig. 4: Complicated wristwatches circa 1930 (left) and 1990. The golden age of watchmaking will always be with us.

fig. 5: The Geneva Seal is awarded only to watches which achieve the standards of horological purity laid down in the laws of Geneva. These rules define the supreme quality of watchmaking.

fig. 6: Your pleasure in owning a Patek Philippe is the purpose of those who made it for you.

fig. 7: Arabesques come to life on a gold case-back.

fig. 8: An artist working six hours a day takes about four months to complete a miniature in enamel on the case of a pocket-watch.

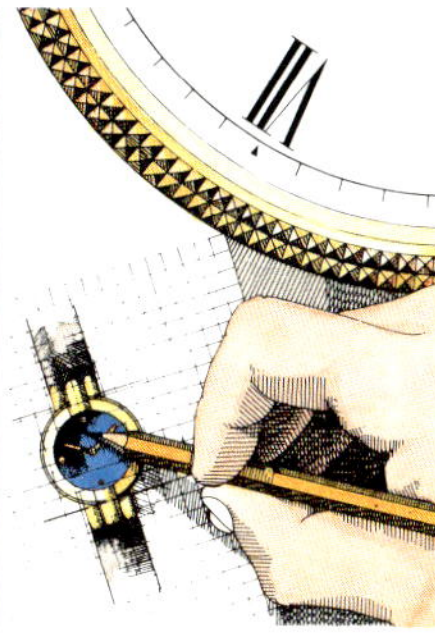

fig. 9: Harmony of design is executed in a work of simplicity and perfection in a lady's Calatrava wristwatch.

fig. 10: The chainsmith's hands impart strength and delicacy to a tracery of gold.

fig. 11: Circles in gold: symbols of perfection in the making.

fig. 12: The test of a master lapidary is his ability to express the splendour of precious gemstones.

PATEK PHILIPPE
GENEVE

fig. 13: The discreet sign of those who value their time.

your card marked "book catalogue" we shall post you a catalogue of our publications. Patek Philippe, 41 rue du Rhône, 1204 Geneva, Switzerland, Tel. +41 22/310 03 66.

You close your laptop and adjust your footrest. A taste of Brie. A sip of Bordeaux. You lean back and hope you won't be arriving too soon.
That depends on how far you're going.
The fact that Lufthansa flies to 220 global destinations comes as a surprise to some. Perhaps we've been too busy with our award-winning service to tell everybody that we are one of the world's largest airline networks. A network that can offer you fast and convenient connections to anywhere. A network that offers rewards with Miles and More, one of the world's leading frequent flyer programmes. And above all, a network that makes you feel at home, however far you're going. So call Lufthansa on 0345 252 252 and we'll tell you the full story.
Lufthansa

Getting Acquainted

Planning the Trip

Practical Tips

Getting Around

Where to Stay

Attractions

Festivals

Shopping

Sports and Leisure

Language

Further Reading

Getting Acquainted

The Place

Japan is made up of four main islands, Honshu, Hokkaido, Kyoshu and Shikoku, and several thousand smaller ones that stretch nearly 3,000 km (1,900 miles) in the temperate and sub-tropical zones, between 20° and 45° latitude. The total land area is 377,435 sq. km (145,728 sq. miles), 85 percent of which is mountainous. The country is divided into four different climatic and cultural zones by mountain ranges: the Japan Sea and Pacific Ocean on the northeast half, and the Japan Sea and Inland Sea on the southwest half. The famed Mount Fuji, seen on clear days from many places in and around Tokyo, is the country's highest mountain at 3,776 meters (2.3 miles). The population of Japan is about 125 million.

Climate

"Japan has four seasons" is a phrase you will hear often, though it is still not clear why the Japanese feel that it is a feature unique to their country. The climate in Tokyo can be a bit of everything, and in recent years, the manifestation of the "four seasons" has not been all that clear, but generally in spring most of Japan is pleasant until May. In June begins the rainy season which should last about a month, but often longer. The summers are hot and sticky through to September. The typhoons usually come through in August and September. Fall begins in late September and lasts through mid-November and is cool and pleasant. The winter lasts from mid-November to the end of February or beginning of March.

The People

Population density: 326 persons per square kilometer
Life expectancy at birth: 76 male; 82 female

Life expectancy has been steadily rising for the last three decades, and the "greying" of Japan is becoming a major social concern. In 1985, only 10.3 percent of the population was 65 or older; in the year 2000 it is expected to reach 16.2 percent.

Retirement age for salaried employees, stable at 55 during most of the post-war era, is now gradually being raised to 60 by many major companies. Private and national pension plans are provided, covering 99 percent of the country's working population.

Government

Form: Parliamentary Democracy
Head of State: Emperor Akihito (born December 23, 1933, took office January 7, 1989)

While it is generally felt that the emperor's actual power is less than that of, say, the queen of England, his social, cultural and political influence is much stronger than intended by the allied powers who, during the occupation of Japan following World War II, "guided" the drafting of Japan's present constitution.

Although Article 1 of that document states the the "Emperor shall be the symbol of the State," and that he derives his position from the will of the people, the exact powers of the emperor are not specifically defined.
Prime Minister: (President of majority party in Lower House, currently – and since 1955 except 1993–1996 – the LDP)

Education

Japan's public education system is tax-funded (although many private schools exists). Compulsory for all children are 6 years junior high school (enrolment 100 percent); high school (3 years) is elective (enrolment over 90 percent nationwide, nearly 100 percent in urban areas); higher education at college/university (4 years) or trade schools is also elective (over 30 percent of all high school graduates go on to higher educational studies).

The school year begins in April; vacations include about 40 days in summer and around 10 days each for spring and New Years.

The three-year high school program is compressed to two in many of the best high schools to allow students to prepare for college entrance exams.

There are about 95 national, 34 public and 31 private 4-year universities/colleges in Japan. The quasi-national radio/TV network NHK runs the University of the Air that combines radio and TV and correspondence.
Literacy: 99 percent
Juku: These "after-school schools" are estimated to number about 200,000, earn ¥500 billion annually, and attract as many as 1.5 million elementary and 2 million high school students. In the main, they focus on preparing students for entrance exams.

Customs and Culture

At work and in most formal situations, the Japanese may seem a very reticent and reserved people, lacking in spontaneity or personality. There are books and theories explaining this behavior, but it only provides one side of the picture. Japanese (especially men) can become extremely raucous when drinking, and often let out their real opinions and feelings after a few drinks.

On the crowded trains you will find yourself being pushed and bumped around. You do not need to be polite here; just push along with everyone else. It is often said that "the Japanese are only polite with their shoes off," which means that they are polite and courteous with people they know well and would be indoors with (where shoes are almost always removed).

The Japanese distinguish between inside and outside the home. Inside the entrance to all homes (and some restaurants) is an area for removing shoes. You then step up into the living area, wearing slippers or in your stockinged feet. (Slippers are never worn on *tatami* mats, however.) Taking shoes off keeps the house clean, besides being more relaxing, and it also increases the amount of usable space, since you can sit on the floor without worrying about getting dirty. The toilet, however, is one area of the house that is considered "dirty," so separate slippers are provided there.

The custom of bowing has, in many cases, become somewhat a conditioned reflex. Foreigners, in general, are not expected to bow, and this is especially evident if a Japanese person first reaches out to shake hands.

CAMEL
BAGS
YOUR TRAVEL PARTNER

FLY SMOOTH AS SILK TO EXOTIC THAILAND ON A ROYAL ORCHID HOLIDAY.

Watching exquisite cotton and silk umbrellas being hand-painted in Chiang Mai. Lazing in the shade in sun-drenched Phuket. This

Wherever you're going we'll be there.

From Alice Springs to Zimbabwe, you can be sure Hertz will be at your service.

With over 500,000 cars in more than 150 countries, and 5,000 rental locations with 2,000 at airports, you can always rely on Hertz to offer the car you want, when you want it, and at the right price.

And wherever you go you'll always find the same friendly quality service that is second to none.

It's not surprising then that our combination of unbelievable prices and unbeatable service has made us the world's #1 car rental company.

Simply call your local travel agent, or Hertz direct for further information.

Highest Quality. Low, Low Prices.

Hertz

Hertz rents and leases Fords and other fine cars.

As to punctuality and keeping appointments, the Japanese have a reputation for not being very punctual. At several of the famous "meeting places" you can observe people waiting, often for an hour or more, for someone. After several apologies and explanations, everything is usually forgotten and forgiven.

The way the Japanese usually speak and express themselves gives a very good picture of their culture. Direct statements of fact are most often avoided as this implies that the speaker has a superior knowledge, and this is considered impolite. Therefore, much "beating around the bush" is done which often leads to misunderstandings and seems like a waste of time to foreigners, but this must be taken into consideration when dealing with the Japanese.

When eating with Japanese, if you don't know what to do, just watch what the people around you are doing and do as they do. Below are a few helpful tips:

- Do not rest your chopsticks vertically in your rice, as this is associated with death.
- Do not pass food from chopstick to chopstick, as this is only done with the cremated bones of the dead at funeral services.
- When drinking beer or sake, one person will pour for the other, who will hold up his glass while it is being filled. Each person takes turns at pouring until enough is drunk and people will often begin to pour their own.

In any case, whatever happens, foreigners are usually forgiven for any breach of etiquette, so there's no need to spend time worrying about what is right and wrong. Japanese behavior in general is situational, and the Japanese themselves often do not know the right thing to do in any given situation. "It all depends on the situation," remarks the smart alec, but it's often fun for everyone involved when one of "us" makes a slip. Sometimes it actually does help to break the ice and put everyone in a more relaxed mood.

Planning The Trip

Getting There

The most practical way of entering Japan is by air and through one of its several international airports. **New Tokyo International Airport (Narita Airport)**, 60 km (37 mi) from Tokyo city center, is the busiest and one of the two main gateways to Japan. Flights on China Airlines are served by **Haneda Airport**, Tokyo's domestic airport located between Tokyo and Yokohama. Osaka's 24-hour, offshore **Kansai International Airport**, the other main gateway, serves routes plying the Americas, Europe and Asia. **Nagoya Airport** connects flights to and from various points in the Pacific and the Americas. Three airports on Kyushu – **Fukuoka**, **Kumamoto** and **Kagoshima** – serve those from cities in Europe, Korea and mainland Asia. Three major domestic airlines maintain air routes throughout Japan: Japan Air Lines (JAL), All Nippon Airways (ANA) and Japan Air Systems (JAS).

There is an airport tax for all passengers departing on international flights.

Entry Regulations

Visas and passports

A proper visa is necessary for foreigners living in Japan and engaged in business or study. Passengers with confirmed departure reservations can obtain a stopover pass for up to 72 hours.

Visitors from the following countries are not required to obtain a visa prior to arrival in Japan, provided they do not intend to stay for more than 90 days nor receive remuneration in Japan: Argentina, Bahamas, Bangladesh, Barbados, Belgium, Canada, Chile, Colombia, Costa Rica, Cyprus, Denmark, Dominican Republic, El Salvador, Finland, Greece, Guatemala, Holland, Honduras, Iceland, Israel, Italy, Lesotho, Luxembourg, Malaysia, Malta, Mauritius, Norway, Pakistan, Peru, Portugal, San Marino, Singapore, Spain, Surinam, Sweden, Tunisia, Turkey, Uruguay, USA.

Visitors from the following countries may reside in Japan for up to 6 months providing they are not earning an income: Austria, Germany, Ireland, Liechtenstein, Mexico, Switzerland and the United Kingdom.

Extension of Stay

Foreigners wishing to extend their stay in Japan must report, in person, to the Immigration Bureau within two weeks before their visa expiration. Present your passport, a statement with the reasons why you want an extension of stay, and documents certifying the reasons. The fee is ¥4,000.

Foreigners living in Japan must obtain a re-entry permit from the Immigration Bureau if they leave Japan and plan to return. Present, in person, your passport and certificate of alien registration (held by foreign residents in Japan) along with the appropriate re-entry form to the Immigration Office. The fee for a single re-entry is ¥3,000 and for a multiple re-entry ¥6,000.

Those wishing to transfer visas to new passports must report to the Immigration Bureau in Tokyo. Present both old and new passports and certificate of alien registration.

Immigration Information. Tel: (03) 3213-8523 or 3213-8527. Open Monday–Friday 9.30am–noon, 1–4pm. Answers to questions regarding immigration rules, regulations and restrictions. Languages: English, Chinese, Korean, Spanish, Portuguese, and Thai.

Tokyo Regional Immigration Bureau, 1st Otemachi Common Government Office 2nd Floor, 1-3-1 Otemachi, Chiyoda-ku, Tokyo. Tel: (03) 3213-8523–8527. Open 9am–noon, 1–4pm. Closed on Saturday and Sunday.

Shibuya Immigration Office, 1-3-5 Jinnan, Shibuya-ku (just beyond "In the Room" dept. Store). Tel: (03) 5458-0370 or (03) 3286-5241. Open Monday–Friday 9am–noon, 1–5pm.

Hakozaki Immigration Branch Office, Tokyo City Air Terminal, 42-1 Nihombashihakozaki, Chuo-ku. Tel: (03) 3664-3046. Open 9am–noon, 1–5pm. Closed on Saturday and Sunday.

Yokohama Regional Immigration Bureau. Tel: (045) 681-6801.

Osaka Immigration Information, Tel:

(06) 774-3409. Visa/Immigration Information in Osaka. Language: English, Chinese, Portuguese, Spanish. Open Monday–Friday 9.30am–12 noon, 1pm–4.30pm.

Automated Immigration Information, Tel: (03) 3213-8141. Usage: with a touch-tone phone, enter 1 for Japanese, 2 for English. Dial the code number for the information you want (about 800 available). The code list is available at immigration/ward offices.

Alien Registration

Foreigners planning to stay in Japan for more than three months are required to register at the ward office in their residing area. The application must be made in person within 90 days. The applicant must have his/her passport containing the proper visa and two photographs (3 cm x 4 cm).

If the alien registration card is lost or defaced, report to the ward office within 14 days. Take your passport and two new photographs and you will be issued a new one.

For visitors under 16 years of age, applications may be made by a parent or legal guardian by producing the applicant's passport. No photograph is necessary.

Ward office hours are from 8.45am–5pm. Monday through Friday, and 8.45am–12.30pm on Saturdays.

Tokyo Metropolitan Government, Tokyo Daisan Chosha, 3-5-1 Marunouchi, Chiyoda-ku, Tokyo, tel: (03) 3211-4433. English service is available on Monday and Thursday from 1–4pm.

Information regarding alien status and visas presented above is general and subject to change. For further information contact your appropriate embassy, consulate or the Japan Immigration Bureau.

Customs

Japan strictly bans the import and use of narcotic drugs, firearms and ammunition. If caught in possession of any of these, the offender will not face the death penalty, but can expect no leniency. Many a foreigner is still sitting in a Japanese prison, long forgotten by everyone but himself. Pornographic magazines and videos showing any pubic hair are technically forbidden in Japan.

This issue of films and magazines displaying pubic hair is a curious one. Photographs in *Playboy* magazine, for example, are literally sanded to obliterate pubic hair, but maybe only every other photo. Yet at convenience stores like 7-Eleven, teenage boys can buy magazines with very, very explicit photographs or *manga* illustrations. Likewise, films sometimes will have fuzzy flesh-colored spots or electronic mosaics floating over offending parts. Other films are shown untouched.

You can bring in any currency, personal ornaments and other valuables into Japan, but there is an official limit of ¥5 million that can be taken out.

You are also allowed to bring with you into Japan, free of tax, three 760 ml (25 fl oz) bottles of spirits, 400 cigarettes and 100 cigars or a total of 500 g of tobacco, and 2 fl oz (50 g) of perfume.

Health

In general, levels of hygiene are very high, and it is very unlikely that you will become ill as a result of eating or drinking something. The tap water, though heavily chlorinated, is potable. Most food is of a high standard. However, because the Japanese place so much emphasis on presentation and how food looks, there is wide use of chemical fertilizers in Japan, and therefore it is not recommended to eat the peels of fruits and some vegetables.

Toilets: Apart from major hotels and some train stations, most toilets in Japan are of the Asian squatting type, which takes some getting used to, but are supposed to be the most hygienic (no part of your body actually touches them) and physiologically best. In Tokyo and other major cities, they are slowly being replaced with Western-style toilets in many establishments. By law, every coffee shop and restaurant etc. must have its own toilet, or access to one in the same building.

Electricity

The power supply is 100 volts AC. Eastern cities in Japan, including Tokyo, run on 50 cycles, while those in the west such as Kyoto, Osaka and Nagoya, use 60 cycles. Most hotels have adaptors for shavers and hair dryers.

Currency

The unit of currency is the yen (indicated as ¥), and the coins are ¥1, ¥5, ¥10, ¥50, ¥100 and ¥500. Bills are ¥1,000, ¥5,000 and ¥10,000. Foreign currencies are accepted at a very limited number of hotels, restaurants and souvenir shops. You can buy yen at foreign exchange banks and other authorized money changers on presentation of your passport. At the international airport at Narita, the bank is open 24 hours.

Traveler's checks are useful only at banks and major hotels. Elsewhere, they are virtually worthless. Many banks in Japan will issue international traveler's checks.

Major credit cards, such as American Express, Diner's Club, MasterCard and Visa, are accepted at establishments in and around Tokyo and Osaka/Kyoto, and there is no surcharge for their use. Unfortunately, acceptance is sporadic. It is often quite difficult for a merchant to get approval for a purchase with a foreign-issued credit card. If they refuse your card, don't get testy. Carry lots of cash instead, just in case.

Banks

Despite the wide use of computers and on-line systems, Japanese banks are often slow and inefficient in many fields. Especially when transferring money in or out of the country, you can expect the process to take a long time and to be costly. Also, small neighborhood branches are often not able to process any international transactions. In order to send money out of the country, or cash foreign checks, you will find it much easier to go to a major branch, where someone will be able to speak English and usually understand what you want to do. The bank charges for remitting money out of the country are expensive.

Banks are open Monday to Friday between 9am and 3pm for normal banking. Cash dispensers are open from 9am to 6pm on weekdays, and 9am to 2pm on Saturdays. Most cash dispensers, however, cannot be used for cash advances on credit cards *not* issued by a Japanese bank. Even if there is a logo for Visa or MasterCard, almost always it is for a Japanese bank-issued card only.

HOLIDAY
MAKER
18
CAPSULES
FAST AND EFFECTIVE
ARRET™
THERE'S NO QUICKER WAY
TO STOP DIARRHOEA
If diarrhoea disrupts your holiday, remember Arret can relieve the symptoms within one hour.
So you lose as little holiday time as possible.
To make the most of your holiday, make sure you pack Arret.
ARRET. HOLIDAY INSURANCE
FROM YOUR PHARMACIST.
Always read the label. Contains loperamide.

PRIMA SUPER 135 38-135 MM

PRIMA SUPER 115 38-115 MM

PRIMA SUPER 28V 28-70 MM

PRIMA ZOOM 70F 35-70 MM

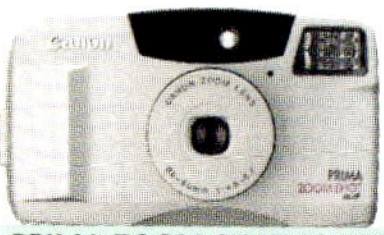

PRIMA ZOOM SHOT 38-60 MM

Public Holidays

January 1 – Ganjitsu (New Year's Day)
January 15 – Seijin no Hi (Coming-of-Age Day)
February 11 – Kenkoku Kinen no Hi (National Foundation Day)
March 21 – Shumbun no Hi (Vernal Equinox Day)
April 29 – Midori no Hi (Greenery Day)
May 3 – Kempo Kinembi (Constitution Memorial Day)
May 4 – Kokumin no Kyujitsu (National Holiday)
May 5 – Kodomo no Hi (Children's Day)
September 15 – Keiro no Hi (Respect-for-the-Aged Day)
September 23 – Shubun no Hi (Autumnal Equinox Day)
October 10 – Taiiku no Hi (Sports Day)
November 3 – Bunka no Hi (Culture Day)
November 23 – Kinro Kansha no Hi (Labor Thanksgiving Day)
December 23 – Tenno Tanjobi (Emperor's Birthday)

If a holiday falls upon Sunday, the following Monday will be a 'substitute holiday'.

Special Facilities

Disabled

In general, Japan is not user-friendly for the disabled. Doors, elevators, toilets and just about everything else have not been designed for wheelchairs, nor are there any regulations regarding access for the disabled. It is a struggle for the disabled to get around Japan, but it can be done.

Forget about using a wheelchair in train or subway stations, much less trains, during rush hour, 7–9am and 5–7pm. The crowds are just too thick, and too rude.

To arrange assistance – in advance – at **Tokyo Station**, call the JR English InfoLine at (03) 3423-0111. They will make arrangements at Tokyo Station for you.

It is possible to reserve a special seat for wheelchairs on the *shinkansen*, or bullet train. Reservations can be made from one month to two days before departure. You must also reserve ahead to use the elevators for the shinkansen platforms.

In many stations, staff will help with escalators and elevators, although a wait of half an hour to an hour may be involved.

Useful Addresses

Tourist Offices

Tourists may write or contact any of the following offices of the Japan National Travel Organization for assistance:

JNTO Overseas Offices

Australia: Level 33, The Chifley Tower, 2 Chifley Square, Sydney, NSW 2000. Tel: (02) 232-4522, fax: (02) 232-1494.
Brazil: Av. Paulista, 509-S/405, 01311-000 Sao Paulo, S.P. Tel: (011) 289-2931, fax: (011) 288-5738.
Canada: 165 University Ave, Toronto, Ont. M5H 3B8. Tel: (416) 366-7140, fax: (416) 366-4530, e-mail: jnto@inforamp.net
France: 4-8, rue Sainte-Anne, 75001 Paris. Tel: (01) 42-96-20-29, fax: (01) 40-20-92-79.
Germany: Kaiserstrasse 11, 60311 Frankfurt /M. Tel: (069) 20353, fax: (069) 284281, e-mail: info@jntofra.rhein-main.com
Hong Kong: Suite 3704-05, 37/F, Dorset House, Taikoo place, Quarry Bay. Tel: 2968-5688, fax: 2968-1722.
Korea: 10th fl., Press Center Bldg, 25 Taepyongno1-ga, Chung-gu, Seoul. Tel: (02) 732-7525, fax: (02) 732-7527.
Switzerland: 13 rue de Berne, 1201 Geneva. Tel: (022) 731-81-40, fax: (022) 738-13-14.
Thailand: 3/61, 13th fl., Wall Street Tower Bldg, Suriwong Road, Bangkok 10500. Tel: (02) 233-5108, fax: (02) 236-8356.
United Kingdom: Heathcoat House, 20 Savile Row, London W1X 1AE. Tel: (0171) 734-9638, fax: (0171) 734-4290, e-mail: jntolon@dircon.co.uk
United States
New York: One Rockefeller Plaza, Suite 1250, New York, NY 10111. Tel: (212) 757-5640, fax: (212) 307-6754, e-mail: jntonyc@interport.net.
Chicago: 401 North Michigan Ave., Suite 770, Chicago, IL 60611. Tel: (312) 222-0874, fax: (312) 222-0876, e-mail: jntochi@aol.com
San Francisco: 360 Post St, Suite 601, San Francisco,CA 94108. Tel: (415) 989-7140, fax: (415) 398-5461, e-mail: sfjnto@aol.com
Los Angeles: 624 South Grand Ave, Suite 1611, Los Angeles, CA 90017. Tel: (213) 623-1952, fax: (213) 623-6301, e-mail: hideki.tomioka@sit.com

Domestic Offices of JNTO

Head office: 10-1, Yurakucho 2-chome, Chiyoda-ku, Tokyo 100. If you have message or questions, please send e-mail to JNTO. Mail to: jnto@jnto.go.jp. It may take some time until you get the answer from JNTO.

Tourist Information Centers (TICs):
Tokyo TIC, Kotani Bldg, 6-6 Yurakucho 1-chome, Chiyoda-ku, Tokyo 100. Tel: (03) 3502-1461. Open from 9am to 5pm on weekdays, 9am to 12 noon Saturday, closed Sundays and national holidays.
Narita TIC, Airport Terminal Bldg, Narita, Chiba Pref. 282. tel: (0475) 32-8711.
Kyoto Office (TICs): 1st fl., Kyoto Tower Bldg, Higashi-Shiokojicho, Shimogyo-ku, Kyoto 600. Tel: (075) 371-5649. Open from 9am to 5pm weekdays, 9am to 12 noon Saturday, closed on Sunday and national holidays.

Japan Travel-Phone is a nationwide toll-free service offering travel-related information and language assistance. It is operated by JNTO.

If within Tokyo or Kyoto, call the respective TIC offices. You will be connected to an English-speaking travel officer. Service is available daily between 9am and 5pm. All numbers are toll-free.
Eastern Japan: (0088) 22-2800 or (0120) 222-800.
Western Japan: (0088) 22-4800 or (0120) 444-800.

Embassies and Consulates

All embassies and consulates are open from Monday to Friday.

Australia, 2-1-14 Mita, Minato-ku. Tel: (03) 5232-4111.
Austria, 1-1-20 Moto Azabu, Minato-ku. Tel: (03) 3451-8281.
Belgium, 5-4 Nibancho, Chiyoda-ku. Tel: (03) 3262-0191.
Canada, 7-3-38 Akasaka, Minato-ku. Tel: (03) 3408-2101.
China, 3-4-33 Moto Azabu, Minato-ku. Tel: (03) 3403-3380.
Denmark, 29-6 Sarugakucho, Shibuya-

ku. Tel: (03) 3496-3001.
Finland, 3-5-39 Minami Azabu, Minato-ku. Tel: (03) 3442-2231.
France, 4-11-44 Minami Azabu, Minato-ku. Tel: (03) 5420-8800.
Germany, 4-5-10 Minami Azabu, Minato-ku. Tel: (03) 3473-0151.
Indonesia, 5-2-9 Higashi Gotanda, Shinagawa-ku. Tel: (03) 3441-4201.
Ireland, No. 25 Kowa Bldg, 8-7 Sanbancho, Chiyoda-ku. Tel: (03) 3263-0695.
Israel, 3 Nibancho, Chiyoda-ku. Tel: (03) 3264-0911.
Korea, 1-2-5 Minami Azabu, Minato-ku. Tel: (03) 3452-7611.
Laos, 3-3-21 Nishi Azabu, Minato-ku. Tel: (03) 5411-2291.
Malaysia, 20-16 Nanpeidaicho, Shibuya-ku. Tel: (03) 3476-3840.
Myanmar, 4-8-26 Kita Shinagawa, Shinagawa-ku. Tel: (03) 3441-9291.
Netherlands, 3-6 Shibakoen, Minato-ku. Tel: (03) 5401-0411.
New Zealand, 20-40 Kamiyamacho, Shibuya-ku. Tel: (03) 3467-2271.
Norway, 5-12-2 Minami Azabu, Minato-ku. Tel: (03) 3440-2611.
Philippines, 11-24 Nanpeidaicho, Shibuya-ku. Tel: (03) 3496-2731.
Singapore, 5-12-3 Roppongi, Minato-ku. Tel: (03) 3586-9111.
Sri Lanka, 1-14-1 Akasaka, Minato-ku. Tel: (03) 3585-7431.
Sweden, 1-3-10 Roppongi, Minato-ku. Tel: (03) 5562-5050.
Switzerland, 5-9-12 Minami Azabu, Minato-ku. Tel: (03) 3473-0121.
Taiwan (Visitor's Association), Imperial Tower, A-9 5th Floor, Imperial Hotel, 1-1-1 Uchisaiwaicho, Chiyoda-ku. Tel: (03) 3501-3591.
Thailand, 3-14-6 Kami Osaki, Shinagawa-ku. Tel: (03) 3441-7352.
United Kingdom, 1 Ichibancho, Chiyoda-ku. Tel: (03) 3265-5511.
United States, 1-10-5 Akasaka, Minato-ku. Tel: (03) 3224-5000.
Vietnam, 50-11 Motoyoyogicho, Shibuya-ku. Tel: (03) 3466-3311.

Airline Offices

Air Canada, New Akasaka Bldg, 6th Floor, 3-2-3 Akasaka, Minato-ku. Tel: (03) 3586-3891.
Air France, Shin Aoyama Bldg, Nishi-kan, 15th Floor, 1-1-1 Minami Aoyama, Minato-ku. Tel: (03) 3475-1511.
Air New Zealand, Shin Kokusai Bldg, 3-4-1 Marunouchi, Chiyoda-ku. Tel: (03) 3287-1641.
Alitalia, Tokyo Club Bldg, 3-2-6 Kasumigaseki, Chiyoda-ku. Tel: (03) 3580-2242.
ANA, Yammer Tokyo Bldg, 2-1-1 Yaesu, Chuo-ku. Tel: International (03) 5489-1212. Domestic (03) 5489-8800.
American Airlines, Kokusai Bldg, 3-1-1 Marunouchi, Chiyoda-ku. Tel: (03) 3248-2011.
British Airways, 1-16-4 Toranomon, Minato-ku. Tel: (03) 3593-8811.
Canadian Airlines, Hibiya Park Bldg, 1-8-1 Yurakucho, Chiyoda-ku. Tel: (03) 3281-7426.
Cathay Pacific Airways, Toho Twin Towers Bldg, 1-5-2 Yurakucho, Chiyoda-ku. Tel: (03) 3504-1531.
China Airlines, Matsuoka Bldg, 5-22-10 Shimbashi, Minato-ku. Tel: (03) 3436-1661.
Continental Airlines, Sanno Grand Bldg, 5th Floor, 2-14-2 Nagatacho, Chiyoda-ku. Tel: (03) 3508-6411.
Delta Airlines, Kokusai Bldg. #254, 3-1-1 Marunouchi, Chiyoda-ku. Tel: (03) 5275-7000.
Garuda Indonesian Airways, Kasumigaseki Bldg, 3-2-5 Kasumigaseki, Chiyoda-ku. Tel: (03) 3593-1181.
Iberia Airlines, 3-1-13 Shibakoen, Minato-ku. Tel: (03) 3578-3555.
Japan Air Lines, Daini Tekko Bldg, 1-8-2 Marunouchi, Chiyoda-ku. Tel: Tokyo (03) 5489-1111, Narita (0476) 32-3125.
KLM Royal Dutch Airlines, Yurakucho Denki Bldg, 1-7-1 Yurakucho, Chiyoda-ku. Tel: (03) 3216-0771.
Korean Air, Shin Kokusai Bldg, 3-4-1 Marunouchi, Chiyoda-ku. Tel: (03) 5443-3311.
Lufthansa Airlines, 3-1-13 Shibakoen, Minato-ku. Tel: (03) 3578-6777.
Malaysian Airlines, Hankyu Kotsusha Bldg, 3-3-9 Shimbashi, Minato-ku. Tel: (03) 3503-5961.
Northwest Airlines, 1-1 Uchisaiwaicho, Chiyoda-ku. Tel: (03) 3533-6000 (Imperial Hotel).
Qantas Airways, Urban Toranomon Bldg, 4th Floor, 1-16-4 Toranomon, Minato-ku. Tel: (03) 3593-7000.
SAS, Toho Twin Tower Bldg, 1-5-2 Yurakucho, Chiyoda-ku. Tel: (03) 3503-8101.
Singapore Airlines, Yurakucho Bldg, 1-10-1 Yurakucho, Chiyoda-ku. Tel: (03) 3213-3431.
Swissair, Hibiya Park Bldg, 1-8-1 Yurakucho, Chiyoda-ku. Tel: (03) 3212-1011.
Thai Airways, Asahi Seimei Hibiya Bldg, 1-5-1 Yurakucho, Chiyoda-ku. Tel: (03) 3503-3311.
United Airlines, Kokusai Bldg, 3-1-1 Marunouchi, Chiyoda-ku. Tel: (03) 3817-4411.
Virgin Atlantic Airways, Alliance Bldg, 4th Floor, 5-2-1 Minami Aoyamd, Minato-ku. Tel: (03) 3499-8811.

Foreign Banks

Bank of America, 1-12-32 Akasaka, Minato-ku. Tel: (03) 3587-3111.
Bank of Korea, Hibiya Park Bldg, 1-8-1 Yurakucho, Chiyoda-ku. Tel: (03) 3213-6961.
Banque Indosuez, 3-29-16 Kanda Jimbocho, Chiyoda-ku. Tel: (03) 3261-3001.
Barclays Bank, 2-2-2 Otemachi, Chiyoda-ku. Tel: (03) 5255-0011.
Chase Manhattan Bank, 1-2-1 Marunouchi, Chiyoda-ku. Tel: (03) 3287-4000.
Citibank, Chiyoda-ku. Tel: (0120) 223-773 (toll-free).
Commerzbank A.G., Nippon Press Center Bldg, 2-2-1 Uchisaiwaicho, Chiyoda-ku. Tel: (03) 3502-4371.
Commonwealth Bank of Australia, 1-1-3 Marunouchi, Chiyoda-ku. Tel: (03) 3213-7311.
Credit Lyonnais, Hibiya Park Bldg, 1-8-1 Yurakucho, Chiyoda-ku. Tel: (03) 3217-1111.
Credit Suisse, 1-11-30 Akasaka, Minato-ku. Tel: (03) 3589-3636.
Standard Chartered Bank, 3-2-3 Marunouchi, Chiyoda-ku. Tel: (03) 3213-6541.
Union Bank of Switzerland, Yurakucho Bldg, 1-10-1 Yurakucho, Chiyoda-ku. Tel: (03) 3214-7471.

Credit Card Companies

American Express, Toranomon Mitsui Bldg, 3-8-1 Kasumigaseki, Chiyoda-ku. Tel: (03) 3504-3348.
Cardmember services: (0120) 020-222 (toll-free)
Lost/stolen card: (0120) 376-100 (toll-free)
Diner's Club, Senshu Bldg, 1-13-7 Shibuya, Shibuya-ku. Tel: (03) 3499-1311.
MasterCard. Tel: (03) 5350-8051.
Visa Card. Tel: (0031) 65-3624 (toll-free).

Courier Services

DHL, 1-37-8 Higashi Shinagawa, Shinagawa-ku. Tel: (03) 5479-2580.

Federal Express, Kyodo Bldg, 1st Floor, 16 Ichibancho, Chiyoda-ku. Tel: (0120) 003-200 (toll-free).

OCS (Overseas Courier Service), 2-9 Shibaura, Minato-ku. Tel: (03) 5476-8111.

Organizations

America-Japan Society, Marunouchi Bldg, 3rd Floor, 2-4-1 Marunouchi, Chiyoda-ku. Tel: (03) 3201-0780.

American Center, ABC Kaikan, 2-6-3 Shibakoen, Minato-ku. Tel: (03) 3436-0901.

ACCJ (American Chamber of Commerce in Japan), Bridgestone Toranomon Bldg, 3-25-2 Toranomon, Minato-ku. Tel: (03) 3433-5381.

Asia Center of Japan, 8-10-32 Akasaka, Minato-ku. Tel: (03) 3402-6111.

British Council, 1-2 Kagurazaka, Shinjuku-ku. Tel: (03) 3235-8031.

Foreign Correspondents' Club, Yurakucho Denki Bldg, 20th Floor, 1-7-1 Yurakucho, Chiyoda-ku. Tel: (03) 3211-3161.

Institute Franco-Japonais, 15 Funagawaracho, Ichigaya, Shinjuku-ku. Tel: (03) 5261-3930.

Italian Institute of Culture, 2-1-30 Kudan Minami, Chiyoda-ku. Tel: (03) 3264-6011.

Tokyo German Culture Center, 7-5-56 Akasaka, Minato-ku. Tel: (03) 3583-7280.

Japan Chamber of Commerce, Tokyo Kaijo Bldg, #311, 3-2-2 Marunouchi, Chiyoda-ku. Tel: (03) 3283-7696.

JETRO (Japan External Trade Organization), 2-2-5 Toranomon, Minato-ku. Tel: (03) 3582-5511.

AA (Alcoholics Anonymous). Tel: (03) 3971-1471.

Amnesty International, Dai San Yamatake Bldg, 3rd Floor, 2-3-22 Nishi Waseda, Shinjuku-ku. Tel: (03) 3203-1050.

Practical Tips

Emergencies

Security and Crime

About 13 million crimes are reported a year, about one-eighth the number reported in the United States in the same year. Murders and violent assaults each average about 1.5 per 100,000 population. Although the crime rate has risen by 20 percent in Japan over the past decade, its growth is far lower, and the arrest/conviction rate remarkably higher, than in other industrialized nations.

Emergency Numbers

Police (crime and accidents): 110
Fire and ambulance: 119
Police, info in English: (03) 3501-0110

Japan Hotline, information and help about everything, in English, 10am–4pm weekdays, tel: (03) 3586-0110.

For **hospital information**, call (03) 5285-8181 in Tokyo (English, Chinese, Korean, Thai and Spanish spoken).

Loss of Belongings

Fortunately, the Japanese are quite honest about turning in found items. If you've lost a wallet packed with cash or a camera, or simply an overnight bag with dirty socks, chances are you will recover it.

JR trains: Items left on trains will usually be kept for a couple of days at the nearest station. After that, they are taken to one of the major stations to be stored for five more days. Inquiries can be made in Japanese to lost-and-found centers at Tokyo Station (03) 3231-1880, or Ueno Station (03) 3841-8069. In English, inquiries can be made with the JR East Infoline (03) 3423-0111 from 10am to 6pm weekdays.

Subways: Things left on Tokyo's Eidan trains are stored for three or four days at the station nearest to where the item was found, then taken to a lost-and-found center. In Japanese, call the center at (03) 3834-5577, 9.30am–7pm weekdays, 9.30am–4pm Saturday. On the Toei trains, or on Tokyo city-operated buses inquire about lost property at terminals the same day, or call the lost-and-found center, in Japanese, at (03) 3815-7229, from 9am–6pm weekdays.

Taxis: All taxi companies in Tokyo report unclaimed items to a single center, the Tokyo Taxi Kindaika Center. Call (03) 3648-0300, In Japanese.

Police: At last resort, contact the police. The Tokyo Metropolitan Police Department maintains an immense – a *very* immense – lost-and-found center in Iidabashi, with everything from forgotten umbrellas (zillions of them) to bags full of cash. Call (03) 3814-4151, 8.30am–5.15pm weekdays. English sometimes, Japanese mostly.

Medical Services

Try to remember that you are in Japan, and must be prepared to adapt to the Japanese system. Although some doctors may speak English, the receptionist and nursing staff will not, so it is advisable to bring along a Japanese friend or someone else who can speak both languages. Most hospitals and clinics do not have appointment systems, so you have to be prepared to wait your turn, however frustrating that may be. Here is a list of hospitals and clinics in Tokyo where you would have no problem in being understood or treated. They all have different hours and systems.

Hospitals in Tokyo

International Catholic Hospital (Seibo Byoin), 2-5-1 Nakaochiai, Shinjuku-ku. Tel: (03) 3951-1111. Open Monday–Saturday 8–11am. Closed Sunday and 3rd Saturday.

Red Cross Medical Center (Nisseki), 4-1-22 Hiroo, Shibuya-ku. Tel: (03) 3400-1311. Open Monday–Friday 8.30–11am; Saturday 8.30–10.30am. Closed Sunday.

St Luke's International Hospital (Seiroka Byoin), 10-1 Akashicho, Chuo-ku. Tel: (03) 3541-5151. Open Monday–Saturday 8.30–11am. Closed Sunday.

International Clinic, 1-5-9 Azabudai, Minato-ku. Tel: (03) 3582-2646. Open Monday–Friday 9am–noon, 2.30–5pm; Saturday 9am–noon. Closed Sunday.

Toho Fujin Women's Clinic, 5-3-10

Kiba, Koto-ku. Tel: (03) 3630-0303. Open Monday–Saturday 1–5pm. Closed Sunday.

Left Luggage

If possible, carry as little luggage as possible when traveling in Japan. Trains and stations, especially, are not designed for travelers with more than a small overnight bag. If you think you can make all your Tokyo train and subway connections while hauling several large bags, forget it. The train/subway map looks neat and tidy. But station connections are serious hikes with no carts or porters available, and lots of steep stairs.

Hotels, of course, will usually store luggage for guests heading off on adventures.

International Airports. For security reasons, bombs in particular, the international airports have no coin lockers. There are checkrooms, however, at Narita airport:

ABC Skypartners: between the South Wing and the Central Building. ¥400 or ¥800/day per bag, with no time limit for storage. 7am–10pm.

GPA (Green Port Agency): South Wing, 1F and 4F. ¥400/day per bag, 30 day limit. 7am–10pm.

Train and subway stations. Most train and subway stations have coin lockers of varying sizes for ¥200 to ¥500 per day, depending on station and size of the locker. Time limit is 3 days. After that, contents are removed.

Checkrooms for large bags are located at several main JR stations. Luggage can be stored for up to two weeks, ¥400/day per bag for the first five days, ¥800/day per bag for each additional day.

Tokyo Station, outside Yaesu south exit, 8.30am–6pm.

Ueno Station, in front of central exit, 8am–8pm.

Shin Osaka Station, outside the central exit, 5am–10pm.

Kyoto Station, Karasuma central exit and Hachijo central exit, 8am–8pm.

Business Hours

Officially, business is done on a 9am to 5pm basis, but this is in theory only. The Japanese will often do overtime till 8 or 9pm. In general, **government** offices are open from 8.30 or 9am to 4 or 5pm Monday to Friday, and from 9am to noon on the 1st and 3rd Saturday of the month. **Main post offices** are open 9am to 7pm Monday to Friday, 9am to 5pm on Saturday, and 9am to noon on Sunday and holidays. **Branch post offices** are open 9am to 5pm Monday to Friday. **Department stores** are open daily from 10am to 7.30 or 8pm, except that they tend to close the store only twice or three times a month, which varies with each store. **Restaurants** are open for lunch from 11.30am to 2pm and for dinner from 5 to 9 or 10pm. **Major companies and offices** are open from 9am to 5pm Monday to Friday. Some are also open on Saturday mornings. **Most shops** open between 9 and 11am and close between 6 and 8pm.

Tipping

No tipping remains the rule in Japan, except for unusual or exceptional services. Porters at large stations and airports charge around ¥300 per piece of luggage.

Telecoms

To use the public telephones, which are colored either green, red, pink, or yellow, just insert a ¥10 coin and dial the number desired. ¥10 for three minutes. Yellow and green phones accept ¥100 coins, which make them more convenient for long-distance calls, but no change is returned for unused portions thereof.

Most common are the green phones, all taking prepaid telephone cards, and some taking only prepaid cards, no coins. Telephone cards can be obtained at any Nippon Telegraph and Telephone (NTT) office, KDD office, other stores, or through special vending machines near phones.

International calls can be made only from specially-marked – in English and Japanese – green telephones. Increasingly, dark gray card phones are appearing in hotels and at airports. They have computer connections, both analog and digital.

Japan's country code: 81
Domestic area codes start with zero:
Fukuoka: 092
Hiroshima: 082
Kagoshima: 099
Kyoto: 075
Nagasaki: 0958
Nagoya: 052
Naha: 098
Narita: 0476
Osaka: 06
Sapporo: 011
Sendai: 022
Tokyo: 03
Yokohama: 045

KDD Information, international telephone information, in English: 0057 (toll free).

NTT Information, domestic telephone directory information, in English. 9am–5pm weekdays.
Tokyo, tel: (03) 5295-1010.
Narita, tel: (0476) 28-1010.
Yokohama, tel: (045) 322-1010.
Hiroshima, tel: (082) 262–1010
English telephone directory from NTT. Tel: (03) 5256-3141, fax: (03) 5256-3148.

City Source, free English telephone directory from NTT. Tel: (03) 5256-3141, fax: (03) 5256-3148.
Osaka, tel: (06) 571-7866, fax: (06) 571-4185.

Japan Hotline (NTT/KDD), broad-based, hard-to-find phone numbers. Tel: (03) 3586-0110. Monday–Friday, 10am–4pm.

International

While there are several international carriers, person-to-person, collect and credit card calls can be made only through KDD: 0051

Toll-Free Numbers

Domestic telephone numbers that begin with "0120" or "0088" are toll-free, or "free-dial", calls

Telegrams

Domestic: 115
Overseas: (03) 3344-5151
Central Post Office
Domestic: (03) 3284-9539 (Japanese)
International: (03) 3284-9540 (Japanese)
For telegram inquiries, call: Tokyo, (03) 3346-2521; Yokohama, (045) 671-4347.

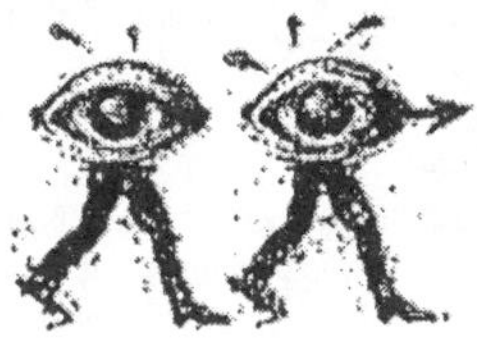

Getting Around

On Arrival

From Narita Airport

A taxi to downtown Tokyo from Narita costs between ¥20,000 and ¥30,000, depending on destination and traffic. Most people prefer either the bus or train, a tenth of the price of a taxi. Either way, it's 2–3 hours by road.

Bus: A regular limousine bus service runs between Narita and TCAT (Tokyo City Air Terminal) in downtown Tokyo, to Tokyo and Shinjuku Stations, and to most major hotels in Tokyo. Tickets (just under ¥3,000) are bought at the airport after clearing immigration and customs. There are several routes depending on destination. Buses are boarded outside the terminal at the curb, and will accept any amount of luggage at no extra charge. The buses leave every 20 minutes or so, taking two to three hours to arrive at the hotel. There are also buses to Yokohama and Haneda, the domestic airport.

Trains: There are two train alternatives into Tokyo: the Keisei Skyliner and the JR Narita Express. Both are twice as fast as by taxi or bus, but not as convenient.

In terms of connections, the Narita Express is more convenient, stopping at JR Stations in Chiba, Tokyo (Station), Shinjuku, Ikebukuro, Yokohama and Ofuna. The Skyliner stops just at Ueno Station and nearby Nippori. Both take about the same time to reach Tokyo, an hour, and both have no restrictions on luggage. (Be warned, however, that carrying luggage through train and subway stations in Japan, especially in Tokyo, is a feat of considerable effort with long hikes and Fuji-like climbs. If carrying more than one piece of luggage, and if not taking the limousine bus directly to a hotel, consider a baggage delivery service.)

The Narita Express costs about ¥3,000 for regular class, and tickets must be bought in advance. The Skyliner costs ¥1,740 and tickets can be bought in advance or at the Ueno Keisei Station for the next available train.

The Skyliner is far more comfortable than the Narita Express (unless traveling in first class, which is a delight). Narita Express's regular seats are small with almost no leg room: usually you sit facing another seat, knee to knee, in groups of four. When traveling with families, the Japanese prefer this style. But for the arriving traveler trying to shake jet lag, or exhausted from last-minute sightseeing before leaving Japan, this arrangement leaves a lot to be desired, especially for the price and especially when the train is overcrowded. (JR permits standing passengers when trains are full, making them even fuller.)

The Keisei Skyliner, on the other hand, is never overbooked or crowded, and the seats are quite comfortable with lots of leg room. Considering the difference in price, the Skyliner is far and away the better deal, both in price and in comfort. If one isn't carrying a lot of luggage, a connection can be made at Ueno Station to JR trains or the subway.

Note: If making a domestic airline connection, you must take the taxi, bus or train into Tokyo and make the connection at Haneda Airport. No domestic flights are made out of Narita. The limousine bus will take you directly from Narita to Haneda, as will a very expensive taxi.

Baggage delivery: Most residents of Japan take advantage of Japan's fast and reliable delivery network. After clearing immigration and customs, take your luggage to the ABC counter in the main terminal (there are several). Often a line indicates the counter. For about ¥1,500 per bag, ABC will deliver the bag by the following day wherever you are. If carrying more than a couple of bags, seriously consider this alternative.

From Kansai Int'l Airport

The new Kansai International Airport (KIX) has replaced Osaka Airport (Itami) as the international air terminus for the Kansai region. However, some domestic flights still fly from Itami. The second largest and the first 24-hour-operation airport in Japan, Kansai International Airport, opened on September 4, 1994. It is located southeast Osaka Bay, 5 km off the coast and about 60 km from JR Shin-Osaka Station for shinkansen train connections. KIX, constructed on an artificial island in Osaka Bay, and one of the world's most expensive – ¥2,600 departure tax – is architecturally impressive and extremely functional. All international and domestic connections at KIX are made at the same terminal in a matter of minutes. (Note: Make sure to confirm that domestic flight connections are from KIX and not Itami-Osaka Airport.) Despite being on an island, getting to and from KIX is relatively easy: two railways, two expressways, some 10 limousine bus lines, and four high-speed ferries connect the island to every point in the Kansai.

For your travel information, the **Kansai Tourist Information Center** is located in the arrival lobby (1st Fl.) and is open daily from 9am to 9pm. For handling currency exchange, there are 10 banks at the airport, with one or more open from 6am to 11pm. Your Japan Rail Pass can be exchanged either at the JR West Information Counter in the International Arrivals Lobby (1st Fl, open daily, 8am to 9pm), at the TiS-Travel Service Center (open daily, 10am to 6pm), or at the green-colored Midori-no-madoguchi Reservations Ticket Office (open daily, 5.30am to 12 midnight) of JR Kansai Airport Station.

To/From Osaka

Train: JR (Japan Railway) Haruka Express, reserved seating, runs between KIX and Osaka's Tennoji Station (29 min), and Shin Osaka Station (45 min), where you catch the *shinkansen*, or bullet train. The JR Kuko-Kaisoku connects KIX with Osaka's Tennoji Station (45 min) and Namba Station's Osaka City Air Terminal (O-CAT), which offers express baggage check-in (60 min).

For JR train information tel: (0724) 56-6242.

Nankai Railroad also connects KIX with Osaka's Namba Station. Three trains make the run. For Nankai train information tel: (0724) 56-6203.

Bus: There are a number of deluxe buses between KIX and various Osaka hotels and rail stations. These take about an hour, on a good day, and are a bit cheaper than the train. For bus information call Keihan Bus Co. tel: (07240 55-2500.

Ferry: Two high-speed ferries connect KIX with Osaka's Tenpozan port (40 min). For ferry information tel: (06) 575-1321.

To/From Kyoto

Train: JR Haruka Express, reserved seats, connects Kyoto Station with KIX (75 min). For JR train information tel: (075) 351-4004.

Bus: A Keihan bus leaves from Uji, south of Kyoto, for KIX and takes about 2 hours. For bus Keihan bus information call tel: (0724) 55-2500.

To/From Kobe

Bus: You can connect by bus from KIX to Kobe's Sannomiya Station (90 min). For bus information call Keihan Bus Co. Tel: (0724) 55-2500.

Ferry: The Kobe Jet Shuttle is the best and fastest way to get to or from Kobe. The Jet Shuttle runs between KIX and the Kobe City Air Terminal (K-CAT) on Port Island (30 min), where free bus service is provided to Kobe's Sannomiya Station. For Jet Shuttle information tel: (078) 306-2411.

To/From Southern Islands

Ferries: Two high-speed ferries connect KIX with Awaji and Shikoku Islands: To Tsuna and Sumoto on Awaji Island (40 min), for information tel: (0799) 24-3333. To Tokushima on Shikoku Island (82 min), for information tel: (06) 575-2101.

To/From Nara

Bus: A bus runs from KIX to Nara JR Station (95 min). For bus information call Keihan Bus Co. tel: 0724-55-2500.

From Haneda Airport

If you are coming into Haneda Airport, then a taxi to the town center will cost about ¥5,000 to ¥6,000 and takes about 30–40 minutes. Provided your luggage is light, you can take the Monorail to Hamamatsucho Station on the JR Yamanote Line. The trip takes about 17 minutes.

From Fukuoka

20 minutes from Fukuoka/Hakata and linked by regular bus services. Domestic flights connect to most cities (Tokyo 1 hour 40 minutes and Osaka 1 hour). International flights connect to Australia, China, Guam, Hong Kong, Honolulu, Indonesia, Korea, Malaysia, New Zealand, Philippines, Singapore, Taiwan, and Thailand.

From Hiroshima

40 minutes from town and linked by regular bus services. Domestic flights connect to most cities (Tokyo 1 hour 20 minutes and Osaka 45 minutes). International flights connect to China, Hong Kong, Korea, and Singapore.

From Nagasaki

1 hour or more from town and linked by regular bus services. Domestic flights connect to most cities (Tokyo 2 hours and Osaka 1 hour). International flights connect to China and Korea.

From Okinawa

15 minutes from Naha and linked by regular bus services. Domestic flights connect to most cities (Tokyo 3 hours and Osaka 2 hour). International flights connect to Guam, Hong Kong, Korea, and Taiwan.

From Sapporo

30 minutes from town and linked by regular bus services. Domestic flights connect to most cities (Tokyo 2 hours and Osaka 3 hours). International flights connect to Australia, Guam, Hong Kong, Honolulu, and Korea.

From Sendai

25 minutes from town and linked by regular bus services. Domestic flights connect to most cities (Tokyo 45 minutes and Osaka 1 hour 30 minutes). International flights connect to China, Guam, Hong Kong, Honolulu, Korea, and Singapore.

Public Transport

Rail

JR Train Information, in English, information only, no reservations, 10am–6pm weekdays, tel: (03) 3423-0111.

Japan has one of the most efficient and extensive rail networks in the world. Rail service is provided by **Japan Railways (JR)** and several regional private lines. The trains on important routes run every few minutes. Trains – such as JR's **shinkansen**, sometimes called the bullet train, which travels at speeds of up to 170 mph (275 kph) – offer alternatives to air and long-distance bus travel. Between Tokyo and Kyoto, travel times are the same for both air and shinkansen. The train, however, is from city center to city center; air, from airport to airport.

The **subway** systems in Japan are clean, safe, and convenient. It is faster than congested road transportation. However, Japanese trains are notorious for being crowded, especially during morning and evening rush hours. Trains and subways are sometimes packed to more than three times their specified capacity, though it actually feels like a lot more.

All subway stations post a timetable. Regular service is Monday through Saturday. The Sunday and holiday schedule has slightly fewer runs. Trains run until around after midnight, so be sure to check the time of the last train. All subway and train stations have a route map with fares for each stop near the ticket machines. However, it is not always in English. Your present location is indicated with a red mark. The fares are regulated on a station-to-station basis, so if you cannot determine the fare required, just purchase the cheapest ticket available. You can pay the difference, if needed, upon arrival at your destination. The ticket machine will dispense the ticket and give the correct change. A child's ticket is half fare.

Most ticket machines accept coins only, although some will take ¥1,000 notes or prepaid cards. There is usually a machine that gives change or sells prepaid cards nearby.

Transportation cost savings can be made by buying a ***teiki*** (train pass), valid for one, three or six months. Major subway and train stations issue passes. Another way to save on train fares is to buy a ***kaisuken***, a series of 11 tickets between two destinations for the price of 10. Lastly, one-day tickets good on either subway lines or JR trains are available.

Station arrivals are announced in Japanese inside the trains but are often difficult to understand. There is usually a map of the stops on the line and connecting lines above the train doors. The names of the stations are most often written in both Japanese and English.

Timetables and subway maps in Japanese can be obtained at most stations. Subway maps in English are available in various English-language publications and at some major train and subway stations.

Taxis

Taxis are the most convenient way of getting around, but unfortunately, also the most expensive. The basic fare in Tokyo is ¥650 for the flag drop. A short trip can easily run ¥3,000 to ¥5,000. Once again, no tipping is expected or required. Taxis are readily available on almost every street corner, and can certainly be found at every major hotel and railway station. There is a red light on in the front window if the taxi is free and available.

Don't touch the door when getting in or out of a taxi. The doors on taxis are opened and closed by the driver, who has a lever in the front, so when you've hailed a taxi and it stops, just wait for the door to open, and after arriving at your destination and paying, again the door will open by itself. You can get out and just walk away without trying to close the door.

Most taxi drivers do not speak any language other than Japanese, so it can be helpful to have your destination written in Japanese.

Private Transport

You will need an international driving license or a Japanese one. However, be warned that driving in Japan can be a headache and tedious. The major cities seem to be in a perpetual stage of renovation; there is always construction work going on somewhere, and road divisions are often not easy to see. The streets are narrow, crowded and often confusing. Most street signs are in Japanese.

Remember that in Japan, driving is on the left-hand side of the road. Renting a car will cost from about ¥6,000 for 6 hours, or from ¥10,000 for 24 hours.

You can obtain the *Driver's Map of Japan* issued by the JAF Publishing Co. 9-3, Shiba Sakaecho, Minato-ku, Tokyo. Tel. (03) 3433-8731.

Where To Stay

Hotels

There are hotels everywhere, but unfortunately few of them are up to international standards. Those that are reflect it in their price. However, convenience is a very dear commodity here, so often you are paying for the location more than the service or luxury. Below is a brief listing of major hotels in alphabetical order. Please note that the rankings are according to prices of single or twin rooms. In most hotels and all *ryokan,* you are provided with a *yukata* robe, toothbrush, razor, shower cap, etc.

Many hotels offer only twin beds, which are the most popular arrangement in Japan. Smoking rooms may have a thick stench of stale smoke.

Finally, hotel rooms are quite compact. Even a ¥20,000 room in a deluxe hotel can be snug. So-called business hotels, generally found in the moderate and budget categories (and a few in the expensive category), have rooms that are not just snug, but cramped. Expect submarine-style spaciousness.

Western-style hotels offer rooms whose rates may vary from ¥8,000 to ¥30,000. There are hotels which also provide Japanese-style guest rooms and landscaped gardens. Others have restaurants serving Continental food as well as local *sukiyaki, sushi, tempura.*

Ryokan (Japanese-style inns) exude an atmosphere of traditional Japanese living. They charge an average of ¥9,000 per person, depending on the type of bath facilities offered.

There are about 80,000 ryokan in Japan, of which 2,000 are members of the Japan Ryokan Association (JRA), who ensure that a high standard of service is maintained. Guests sleep in rooms covered with *tatami* (straw) mats, on *futon.* The baths are communal, though there are usually separate baths for men and women. Morning and evening meals are served in the guest's room.

Minshuku are bed-and-breakfast lodgings without the frills (toiletries and *yukata* gowns etc). Rates are from ¥5,000 up. The Japan National Tourist Organization (JNTO) lists some 230 minshuku for overseas visitors.

Japan Minshuku Center Booking office, B1, Tokyo Kotsu Kaikan Bldg, 2-10-1, Yurakucho, Tokyo. Tel: (03) 3216-6556 (English spoken). 10am–6pm, Monday–Saturday, closed Sunday & national holidays. Average fee: ¥6,000–¥13,000 per person with 2 meals. Guarantee ¥1,000 (per person per night). Commission ¥500 (per MInshuku). Reservation by phone is basically not accepted. Reservation for high tourist season (July–August, April 29–May 5, December 25–January 4, weekends) can only be accepted for more than 2 persons per room. Rooms are mostly Japanese-style.

Tokyo

Expensive

Akasaka Prince Hotel, 1-2 Kioicho, Chiyoda-ku. Tel: (03) 3234-1111. One of the Prince chain. Very modern and efficient, and great views from every room.

Akasaka Tokyu Hotel, 2-14-3 Nagatacho, Chiyoda-ku. Tel: (03) 3580-2311. One of the most conveniently located hotels in Akasaka; it is just minutes away from all the action.

ANA Hotel Tokyo, 1-12-33 Akasaka, Minato-ku. Tel: (03) 3505-1111. An exquisite hotel in the heart of Ark Hills, a popular office and shopping complex. Down the hill from Roppongi. Convenient for business and fun.

Capitol Tokyu Hotel, 2-10-3 Nagatacho, Chiyoda-ku. Tel: (03) 3581-4511. Formerly the Tokyo Hilton. A very comfortable and relaxing setting, blending Japanese and Western design. Excellent restaurants and pool (summer only).

Century Hyatt Tokyo, 2-7-2 Nishi Shinjuku, Shinjuku-ku. Tel: (03) 3349-0111. One of the buildings amidst all the skyscrapers of Shinjuku. Japanese-style Hyatt service and accommodation. Health facilities and disco.

Crowne Plaza Metropolitan, 1-6-1 Nishi-Ikebukuro, Toshima-ku. Tel: (03) 3980-1111. Three minutes from Ikebukuro Station's west exit, Ikebukuro's finest hotel.

Hotel Okura, 2-10-4 Toranomon, Minato-ku. Tel: (03) 3582-0111. Officially rated the 2nd-best hotel in the world. Health facilities, excellent restaurants and executive salon.

Hotel New Otani, 4-1 Kioicho, Chiyoda-ku. Tel: (03) 3265-1111. The largest hotel in Asia. Health facilities, a 400-year-old Japanese garden, and very good location.

Imperial Hotel, 1-1-1 Uchisaiwaicho, Chiyoda-ku. Tel: (03) 3504-1111. First built in 1890, with a new tower completed in 1983. Pool, shopping arcade, several excellent restaurants. Convenient to government offices and Ginza.

Keio Plaza Hotel, 2-2-1 Nishi Shinjuku, Shinjuku-ku. Tel: (03) 3344-0111. A 45-story skyscraper on the west side of Shinjuku. Near the Tokyo Metropolitan Government Office towers. Health facilities and executive salon.

Miyako Hotel, 1-1-50 Shiroganedai, Minato-ku. Tel: (03) 3447-3111. Affiliated with the famous Miyako Hotel in Kyoto. Health facilities and quiet, though not too convenient.

New Takanawa Prince Hotel, 3-13-1 Takanawa, Minato-ku. Tel: (03) 3442-1111. Addition to the Takanawa Prince. All of the rooms have private balconies. Pool (summer only).

Roppongi Prince Hotel, 3-2-7 Roppongi, Minato-ku. Tel: (03) 3587-1111. A few minutes from Roppongi Station. Outdoor heated pool.

Palace Hotel, 1-1-1 Marunouchi, Chiyoda-ku. Tel: (03) 3211-5211. Old but quiet and peaceful surroundings overlooking the Imperial Palace moats and gardens.

Royal Park Hotel, 2-1-1 Nihombashi, Kakigaracho, Chuo-ku. Tel: (03) 3667-1111. Next door to the Tokyo City Air Terminal. Indoor swimming pool, fitness club, Japanese garden and executive floors. Convenient to many different locations.

Takanawa Prince Hotel, 3-13-1 Takanawa, Minato-ku. Tel: (03) 3447-1111. Convenient to Shinagawa and the southwest part of Tokyo. Traditional Japanese garden. Pool (summer only).

Tokyo Hilton International, 6-6-2 Nishi Shinjuku, Shinjuku-ku. Tel: (03) 3344-5111. Completed in 1984 and follows in the tradition of the former Hilton. Health facilities and executive salon.

Tokyo Prince Hotel, 3-3-1 Shibakoen, Minato-ku. Tel: (03) 3432-1111. Another of the Prince chain. Located next to Zojo-ji temple. Pleasant outdoor garden restaurant, which is very popular in summer. Pool (summer only).

MODERATE

Asakusa View Hotel, 3-17-1 Nishiasakusa, Taito-ku. Tel: (03) 3842-2111. Good location for sightseeing and shopping in downtown Asakusa. There is always something happening in the area.

Diamond Hotel, 25 Ichibancho, Chiyoda-ku. Tel: (03) 3263-2211. Just a few minutes from Hanzomon Station. Nice quiet area.

Fairmont Hotel, 2-1-17 Kudan Minami, Chiyoda-ku. Tel: (03) 3262-1151. Old British style. About six minutes from Kudanshita Station, right in front of the Imperial Palace moat.

Ginza Dai-Ichi Hotel, 8-13-1 Ginza, Chuo-ku. Tel: (03) 3542-5311. Conveniently located, less than five minutes from Shimbashi Station.

Ginza Nikko Hotel, 8-4-21 Ginza, Chuo-ku. Tel: (03) 3571-4911. About four minutes from Shimbashi Station.

Ginza Tokyu Hotel, 5-15-9 Ginza, Chuo-ku. Tel: (03) 3541-2411. Reasonably priced hotel located close to the Kabuki-za Theater in Ginza.

Haneda Tokyu Hotel, 2-8-6 Haneda Kuko, Ota-ku. Tel: (03) 3747-0311. Right next to Haneda Airport. Shuttle service between the hotel and the airport.

Hillport Hotel, 23-19 Sakuragaokacho, Shibuya-ku. Tel: (03) 3462-5171. A three-minute walk from Shibuya Station. Excellent access to restaurants, department stores and theaters.

Hilltop Hotel, 1-1 Surugadai, Kanda, Chiyoda-ku. Tel: (03) 3293-2311. Five minutes from Ochanomizu Station. An and very pleasant hotel. This is an old favorite of writers and artists. Excellent food and service.

Hotel Atamiso, 4-14-3 Ginza, Chuo-ku. Tel: (03) 3541-3621. Convenient to the Kabuki-za (*Kabuki* Theater) and to all Ginza shopping. Two minutes from Higashi Ginza on the Hibiya line. Formerly a *ryokan,* it opened as a Western-style hotel in 1984.

Hotel Grand Palace, 1-1-1 Iidabashi, Chiyoda-ku. Tel: (03) 3264-1111. Downtown location. Ten minutes by car to Tokyo Station and Tokyo City Terminal.

Hotel Ibis, 7-14-4 Roppongi, Minato-ku. Tel: (03) 3403-4411. Trendy decor with 200 rooms located where a lot of the action can be found.

Hotel New Kanda, 2-10 Kanda, Awajicho, Chiyoda-ku. Tel: (03) 3258-3911. Quiet and yet only a 5-minute walk to noisy Akihabara electronic quarter.

Hotel Park Side, 2-11-18 Ueno, Taito-ku. Tel: (03) 3836-5711. Overlooking Ueno Park. Very delightful atmosphere. Easy access to public transport.

Mitsui Urban Hotel, 8-6-15 Ginza, Chuo-ku. Tel: (03) 3572-4131. Great location.

President Hotel, 2-2-3 Minami Aoyama, Minato-ku. Tel: (03) 3497-0111. Located near the Crown Prince's residence and the Roppongi and Aoyama areas.

Shiba Park Hotel, 1-5-10 Shibakoen, Minato-ku. Tel: (03) 3433-4141. Quiet and cozy, away from all the noise and bustle.

Shibuya Tokyu Inn, 1-24-10 Shibuya, Shibuya-ku. Tel: (03) 3498-0109. Good location.

Shimbashi Dai-Ichi Hotel, 1-2-6 Shimbashi, Minato-ku. Tel: (03) 3501-4411. Very central location. Convenient for business, shopping and sightseeing.

Shinagawa Prince Hotel, 4-10-30 Takanawa, Minato-ku. Tel: (03) 3440-1111. Good year-round sports facilities.

Shinjuku Prince Hotel, 1-30-1 Kabukicho, Shinjuku-ku. Tel: (03) 3205-1111. Right in the heart of exciting Shinjuku.

Sunshine City Prince Hotel, 3-1-5 Higashi-Ikebukuro, Toshima-ku. Tel: (03) 3988-1111. A modern hotel located in the Sunshine City complex.

Washington Hotel, 3-2-9 Nishi Shinjuku, Shinjuku-ku. Tel: (03) 3343-3111. Very modern, very reasonable and very convenient, though the rooms are rather small.

Yaesu Fujiya Hotel, 2-9-1 Yaesu, Chuo-ku. Tel: (03) 3273-2111. One minute from Tokyo Station.

BUDGET

Taisho Central Hotel, 1-27-7 Takadanobaba, Shinjuku-ku. Tel: (03) 3232-0101. Just one minute from Takadanobaba Station on the JR Yamanote Line.

Dai-ichi Inn Ikebukuro, 1-42-8 Higashi Ikebukuro, Toshima-ku. Tel: (03) 3986-1221. Good for shopping and business.

Hotel Sunroute Ikebukuro, 1-39-4 Higashi-Ikebukuro, Toshima-ku. Tel: (03) 3980-1911. Convenient location.

Minutes away from Ikebukuro Station on the JR Yamanote line.
Ryogoku River Hotel, 2-13-8 Ryogoku, Sumida-ku. Tel: (03) 3634-1711. One-minute from Ryogoku Station. Good for *sumo* watching if a tournament is on.
Tourist Hotel, 3-18-11 Higashi Ueno, Taito-ku. Tel: (03) 3831-0237. Minutes away from Ueno Station.

The Northlands

Tokohu

SENDAI (022)

Dai-Ichi Tokyo Hotel Sendai, 2-3-18 Chuo. Tel: 262-1355, fax: 265-2890.
Sendai Hotel, 1-10-25 Chuo, Aoba-Ku. Tel: 225-5171, fax: 268-9325.
Hotel Sendai Plaza, 2-20-1 Honcho, Aoba-Ku. Tel: 262-7111, fax: 262-8169.
Sendai Tokyu Hotel, 9-25 Ichibancho 2-chome, Aoba-Ku. Tel: 262-2411.
Hotel Zuiho, 26-1 Akiu-cho, Yumoto, Tel:397-1111, Fax:397-1131

AOMORI (0177)

Hotel Aomori, 1-1-23 Tsutsumi-Machi. Tel: 75-4141.
Aomori Grand Hotel, 1-1-23 Shin-machi. Tel: 23-1011, fax: 34-0505.
Hotel Sunroute Aomori, 1-9-10 Shin-machi. Tel: 0176-75-2321, fax: 0176-75-2329.

LAKE TOWADA (0176)

Towada Prince Hotel, Okawatai, Towadako, Kosaka-machi. Tel: 75-3111, fax: 75-3110.

YAMAGATA (0236)

Hotel Castle, 2-7 Toka Machi 4-chome. Tel: 31-3311, fax: 31-3373.
Onuma Hotel, 2-1-10 Kojirakawa-machi. Tel: 32-1111.
Hotel Yamagata, 1-1 Saiwai-cho. Tel: 42-2111, fax: 42-2119.
Yamagata Grand Hotel, 1-7-42 Honcho. Tel: 41-2611, fax: 41-2621.
Yamagata Tokyu Inn, 1-10-1 Kasumi cho. Tel: 33-0109.

MORIOKA (0196)

Morioka Grand Hotel, 1-10 Atago-shita. Tel: 25-2111, fax: 22-4804.
Morioka Terminal Hotel, 1-44 Morioka Ekimaedori. Tel: 25-1211.
Hotel Rich Morioka, Morioka ekimae-dori. Tel: 25-2611, fax: 25-2673.
Hotel Royal Morioka, 1-11-11 Saien. Tel: 53-1331, fax: 53-3330.
Star Hotel Morioka, 2-7-16 Chuodori. Tel: 52-3730.

Hokkaido

SAPPORO (011)

Hotel Alpha Sapporo, S1, W5, Chuo-Ku. Tel: 221-2333, fax: 221-0819.
ANA Hotel Sapporo, 2-9 Kita-Sanjo-Nishi 1-chome. Tel: 221-4411, fax: 222-7624.
Keio Plaza Hotel Sapporo, 7-2 Nishi Kita 5 Chuou. Tel: 271-0111, fax: 221-5450.
Hotel New Otani Sapporo, 1-1 Nishi 2-W, Chuo-Ku. Tel: 222-1111, fax: 222-1111.
Sapporo Grand Hotel, 4-2 Nishi, Kita-1, Chuo-Ku. Tel: 261-3311, fax: 222-5164.
Sapporo Park Hotel, 3-1-1 Nishi, Minami-10, Chuo-Ku. Tel: 511-3131, fax: 511-3451
Sapporo Prince Hotel, Nishi 11-chome, Minami 2-jo. Tel: 241-1111, fax: 231-5994.
Sapporo Renaissance, 1-1 Toyohira 4-Jo 1-chome. Tel: 821-1111, fax: 842-6191.
Sapporo Royal Hotel, Higashi 1, Minami 7, Chuo-Ku. Tel: 511-2121, fax: 511-2133.
Sapporo Tokyu Hotel, Nishi 4-chome, Kita 4-Jo, Chuo-Ku. Tel: 231-5611.

HAKODATE (0138)

Hakodate Harborview Hotel, 14-10 Wakamatsu-cho. Tel: 22-0111, fax: 23-0154.
Hakodate Kokusai Hotel, 5-10 Otemachi. Tel: 23-8751, fax: 23-0239.
Hotel Hakodate Royal, 16-9 Omoricho. Tel: 26-8181, fax: 27-4397.
Hotel Ocean, 19-13 Ohtemachi. Tel: 23-2200.
Hotel Rich Hakodate, 16-18 Matsu-kaze-cho. Tel: 26-2561.

KUSHIRO CITY (0154)

Kushiro Pacific Hotel, 2-6 Sakaecho. Tel: 24-8811, fax: 23-9192.
Hotel Sun Route Kushiro, 13-26 Kurogane. Tel: 24-2171, fax: 24-2180.

Kansai

ISE (0596)

Asakichi (Ryokan). Tel: 22-4101, fax: 22-4102.
Ise City Hotel & Annex. Tel: 22-5100, fax: 22-5101.
Ise City Hotel. Tel: 28-2111, fax: 28-1058.
Ise International Hotel. Tel: 23-0102, fax: 23-0109.
Todaya (Ryokan). Tel: 28-4855, fax: 28-2025.

ISE-SHIMA NAT'L PARK (0599)

Shima Kanko Hotel. Tel: 43-1211, fax: 43-3538.
Thalassa Shima. Tel: tel: 32-1111, fax: 32-1109.
Toba Hotel International. Tel: 25-3121, fax: 25-3129.
Toba Kowaki-en. Tel: 25-3261, fax: 25-3260.

KOBE (078)

Gaufres Ritz. Tel: 303-5555, fax: 303-5560.
Kobe Bay Sheraton Hotel & Towers. Tel: 857-7000, fax: 857-7001.
Kobe Meriken Park Oriental Hotel. Tel: 325-8111, fax: 332-3900.
New Otani Kobe Harborland. Tel: 360-1111, fax: 360-7799.
Okura. Tel: 333-0111, fax: 333-6673.
Portopia Hotel. Tel: 302-1111, fax: 302-6877.
Seishin Oriental Hotel. Tel: 992-8111, fax: 992-8108.
Shinkobe Oriental Hotel. Tel: 291-1121, fax: 291-1154.

KYOTO (075)

Alpha Kyoto. Tel: 241-2000, fax: 211-0533.
ANA Hotel Kyoto. Tel: 231-1155, fax: 231-5333.
Fujita Hotel Kyoto. Tel: 222-1511, fax: 256-4561.
Hiiragiya (Ryokan). Tel: 221-1136, fax: 221-1139.
Holiday Inn Kyoto. Tel: 721-3131, fax: 781-6178.
Kyoto Brighton Hotel. Tel: 441-4411, fax: 431-2360.
Kyoto Century Hotel. Tel: 351-0111, fax: 343-3721.
Kyoto Grand Hotel. Tel: 341-2311, fax: 341-3073.
Kyoto Hotel. Tel: 211-5111, fax: 221-7770.
Kyoto Royal Hotel. Tel: 223-1234, fax: 223-1702.
Kyoto Takaragaike Prince Hotel. Tel: 712-1111, fax: 712-7677.
Kyoto Tokyu Hotel. Tel: 341-2411, fax: 593-6520.
Miyako Hotel. Tel: 771-7111, fax:

751-2490.
New Hankyu Kyoto. Tel: 343-5300, fax: 343-5324.
Nikko Princess. Tel: 342-2111, fax: 342-2295.
Tawaraya. Tel: 211-5566, fax: 211-2204.

NAGOYA (052)

Castle Plaza. Tel: 582-2121, fax: 582-8666.
Century Hyatt. Tel: 571-0111, fax: 569-1717.
International Hotel Nagoya. Tel: 961-3111, fax: 962-5937.
Nagoya Castle. Tel: 521-2121, fax: 531-3313.
Nagoya Dai-Ichi Hotel. Tel: 581-4411, fax: 581-4427.
Nagoya Hilton. Tel: 212-1111, fax: 212-1225.
Nagoya Kanko Hotel. Tel: 231-7711, fax: 231-7719.
Nagoya Miyako Hotel. Tel: 571-3211, fax: 571-3242.
Nagoya Tokyu Hotel. Tel: 251-2411, fax: 251-2422.

NARA (0742)

Fujita Nara. Tel: 23-8111.
Kasuga Hotel. Tel: 22-4031.
Kikusuiro (Ryokan). Tel: 23-2001.
Nara Hotel & Annex. Tel: 26-3300, fax: 23-5252.
Nara International Hotel. Tel: 26-6001, fax: 23-1552.
Pacific Nara. Tel: 27-5808
Shikitei (Ryokan). Tel 22-5531, fax: 26-3289.

OSAKA (06)

ANA Hotel Osaka. Tel: 347-1112, fax: 348-9208.
Grandvia Osaka. Tel: 344-1235, fax: 344-1130.
Hankyu International. Tel: 377-2100, fax: 377-3628.
Holiday Inn Nankai Osaka. Tel: 213-8281, fax: 213-8640.
Hyatt Regency Osaka (near INTEX). Tel: 612-1234, fax: 614-7800.
Imperial Hotel Osaka. Tel: 881-1111, fax: 881-4111.
Mitsui Urban Hotel Osaka Bay Tower. Tel: 577-1111, fax: 576-5155.
Miyako Osaka Hotel. Tel: 773-1111, fax: 773-3322.
Nankai South Tower Hotel. Tel: 646-1111, fax: 648-0331.
New Hankyu & Annex. Tel: 372-6600, fax: 374-6885.
New Otani. Tel: 941-1111, fax: 941-9769.
Nikko Osaka. Tel: 244-1111, fax: 245-2432.
Osaka Dai-Ichi Hotel. Tel: 341-4411, fax: 341-4930.
Osaka Grand Hotel. Tel: 202-1212, fax: 227-5054.
Osaka Hilton. Tel: 347-7111, fax: 347-7001.
Osaka Tokyu Hotel. Tel: 373-2411, fax: 376-0343.
Osaka Toyo Hotel. Tel: 372-8181, fax: 372-8101.
Plaza. Tel: 453-1111, fax: 454-0169.
Royal Hotel. Tel: 448-1121, fax: 448-4414.
Westin Osaka. Tel: 440-1111, fax: 440-1100.

NEAR KANSAI INT'L AIRPORT – KIX (0724)

Holiday Inn Kansai International Airport. Tel: 69-1112, fax: 69-5660.
Hyatt Regency Osaka (near INTEX). Tel: 612-1234, fax: 614-7800.
Kansai Airport. Tel: 55-1111, fax: 55-1154.
Rihiga Royal Hotel Sakai. Tel: 24-1121, fax: 24-1120.

The Southlands

Chugoku

OKAYAMA (086)

Granvia Okayam, 1-5 Ekimotomachi. Tel: 234-7000, fax: 234-7099.
Hotel New Okayama, 1-1-25 Ekimaecho. Tel: 223-8211, fax: 223-1172.
Okayama Castle Hotel, 7-1 Saiwaicho. Tel: 233-3111.
Okayama Grand Hotel, 2-10 Funabashicho. Tel: 233-7777, fax: 225-1692.
Okayama Kokusai Hotel, 4-1-16 Kadota Honmachi. Tel: 273-7311, fax: 271-0292.
Okayama Plaza Hotel, 2-3-12 Hama. Tel: 272-1201, fax: 273-1557.
Okayama Royal Hotel, 2-4 Ezucho. Tel: 254-1155, fax: 254-0777.
Okayama Tokyu Hotel, 3-2-18 Daiku. Tel: 233-2411, fax: 223-8763.

HIMEJI (0792)

Himeji Castle Hotel. Tel: 84-3311, fax: 84-3729.
Hotel Himeji Plaza, 158 Toyosawacho. Tel: 81-9000.
Hotel Sunroute Himeji, 195-9 Ekimaecho. Tel: 85-0811, fax: 84-1025.

KURASHIKI (086)

Hotel Kurashiki, 1-1-1 Acchi. Tel: 422-0730, fax: 422-0990.
Kurashiki Ivy Square, 7-2 Honcho. Tel: 422-0011.
Kurashiki Kokusai Hotel, 1-1-44 Chuo. Tel: 422-5141, fax: 422-5192.
Mizushima Kokusai Hotel, 4-20 Mizushima-Aobacho. Tel: 444-4321, fax: 444-4320.

HIROSHIMA (082)

ANA Hotel Hiroshima, 7-20, Nakamachi, Naka-Ku. Tel: 241-1111, fax: 241-9123.
Granvia Hiroshima, 1-5, Matsubaracho, Minami-Ku. Tel: 262-1111, fax: 262-4050.
Hiroshima City Hotel, 1-4, Kyobashicho, Minami-Ku. Tel: 263-5111, fax: 262-2403.
Mitsui Garden Hotel, 9-12, Nakamachi, Naka-Ku. Tel: 240-1131, fax: 242-3001.
Rihga Royal Hotel, 4-4, Kami-hatchobori, Naka-Ku. Tel: 502-1121, fax: 228-5415.

TOTTORI (0857)

Hotel New Otani Tottori, 2-153 Imamachi. Tel: 23-1111, fax: 23-0979.

MATSUE (0852)

Matsue Washington Hotel, 2-22 Higashi-Homnachi. Tel: 22-4111.

HAGI (0838)

Hagi Grand Hotel, 25 Furuhagicho. Tel: 25-1211, fax: 25-4422.

SHIMONOSEKI (0832)

Sanyo Hotel, 2-9 Mimosusogawacho. Tel: 32-8666, fax: 22-7219.
Shimonoseki Grand Hotel, 31-2 Nabecho. Tel: 31-5000, fax: 35-0039.
Shimonoseki Station Hotel, 2-8-11 Takezakicho. Tel: 32-3511.
Shimonoseki Tokyu Inn, 4-4-1 Takezaki-cho. Tel: 33-0109.

Shikoku

TAKAMATSU (0878)

Keio Plaza Hotel Takamatsu, 11-5 Chuocho. Tel: 34-5511, fax: 34-0800.
Okura Hotel Takamatsu, 1-9-5 Joto. Tel: 21-2222
Rihga Hotel Zest Takamatsu, 9-1 Furujin-machi. Tel: 22-3555, fax: 22-7516.
Takamatsu Grand Hotel, 5-10

Kotobuki-Cho 1-chome. Tel: 51-5757, fax: 21-9422.
Takamasu Kokusai Hotel, 2191-1 Kiacho. Tel: 31-1511, fax: 61-0293.

MATSUYAMA (0899)

ANA Hotel Matsuyama, 3-2-1 Ichibancho. Tel: 33-5511, fax: 21-6053.
Hotel Nisshin, 8-11-2 Sanbancho. Tel: 46-3111.
Hotel Okudogo, 267 Suemachi. Tel: 77-1111, fax: 77-5331.

TOKUSHIMA (0886)

Awa Kanyo Hotel, 3-16-3 Ichiban-cho. Tel: 22-5161.
Hotel Sunroute Tokushima, 1-12 Tomitahama. Tel: 26-0311, fax: 54-7765.
Tokushima Park Hotel, 2-32-1 Tokushimacho. Tel: 25-3311, fax: 25-3319.

KOCHI (0888)

Dai-Ichi Kochi Hotel, 2-2-12 Kitahonmachi. Tel: 83-1441, fax: 84-3692.
Kochi Washington Hotel, 1-8-25 Outesuuji. Tel: 23-6111.
Hotel Sunroute Kochi, 1-1-28 Kita Moto-cho. Tel: 23-1311, fax: 23-1383.

Kyushu

FUKUOKA (092)

ANA Hotel Hakata, 3-3-3 Hakata-Ekimae. Tel: 471-7111, fax: 472-7707.
Central Hotel Fukuoka, 4-1-2 Watanabedori, Chuo-Ku. Tel: 712-1212, fax: 761-8980.
Dai-Ichi Tokyo Hotel Fukuoka, 5-2-18 Nakasu. Tel: 281-3311, fax: 281-3948.
Fukuoka Oriental Hotel, 12-17 Nishi Nakasu, Chuo-Ku. Tel: 781-2481.
Hakata Miyako Hotel, 2-1-1 Hakata-eki Higashi. Tel: 441-3111, fax: 481-1306.
Hakata Park Hotel, Hakata Ekimae 4-chome, Hakata-Ku. Tel: 451-1151, fax: 441-5614.
Hakata Tokyu Hotel, 1-16 Tenjin 1-chome, Chuo-Ku. Tel: 781-7111.
New Otani Hakata, 1-1-2 Watanabe-Dori, Chuo-Ku. Tel: 714-1111, fax: 715-5658.
Nishitetsu Grand Hotel, 6-60 Daimyo, Chuou-Ku. Tel: 771-7171, fax: 751-8224.
Hotel Station Plaza, 2-1-1 Hakata Ekimae, Hakata-Ku. Tel: 431-1211, fax: 431-8015.

NAGASAKI (0958)

Hotel Majestic, 2-28 Minami-Yamatemachi. Tel: 27-7777, fax: 27-6112.
Nagasaki Grand Hotel, 5-3 Manzaimachi. Tel: 23-1234, fax: 22-1793.
Nagasaki Tokyu Hotel, 1-18 Minami-Yamate-cho. Tel: 25-1501.
Nagasaki Washington Hotel, 1 Shinchimachi 9-chome. Tel: 28-1211, fax: 25-8023.

UNZEN-AMAKUSA NATIONAL PARK

Kyushu Hotel, 320 Unzen, Obamamachi. Tel: 73-3234, fax: 73-3733.
Unzen Kanko Hotel, 320 Unzen, Obamacho. Tel: 73-3263, fax: 73-3419.

KUMAMOTO (096)

Hotel Hokke Club, 20-1 Tori-cho. Tel: 322-5001.
Kumamoto Hotel Castle, 4-2 Jotomachi. Tel: 326-3311, fax: 326-3324.
Kumamoto Station Hotel, 1-3-6 Nihongi. Tel: 325-2001.
New Sky Hotel, 2 Higashi Amidaji Cho. Tel: 354-2111, fax: 354-8973.
Hotel Sunroute Kumamoto, 1-7-18 Shimotori. Tel: 322-2211, fax: 322-6987.

ASO NATIONAL PARK

Aso Kanko Hotel, Yunotani, Choyomura. Tel: 767-0311, fax: 767-1889.

BEPPU SPA (0977)

Hotel Hakuunsanso, 2473-1 Minami-Tateishi. Tel: 23-1151, fax: 23-1163.
Kamenoi Hotel, 5-17 Chuo-machi. Tel: 22-3301, fax: 21-1232.
Kijma Kogen Grand Hotel, Kijma Kogen. Tel: 22-1161.
Nippaku Hotel, 3-12-26 Kitahama. Tel: 23-2291, fax: 23-2293.
Suginoi Hotel, 2272 Minami-Tateishi. Tel: 24-1141, fax: 21-0010.

MIYAZAKI (0985)

Miyazaki Daiichi Hotel, 4-14 Higashi 5-chome. Tel: 24-8501.
Miyazaki Kanko Hotel, 1-1-1 Matsuyama. Tel: 27-1212, fax: 25-8748.
Miyazaki Washington Hotel, 3-11 Tachibanadori-Nishi. Tel: 28-9111.
Hotel Phoenix, 2-1-1 Matsuyama. Tel: 23-6111, fax: 26-4535.
Hotel Plaza Miyazaki, 1-1 Kawaharacho. Tel: 27-1111, fax: 27-2729.
Seaside Hotel Phoenix, 30-83 Hamayama, Shioji. Tel: 39-1111, fax: 39-1639.
Sun Hotel Phoenix, 30-83 Hamayama, Shioji. Tel: 39-3131, fax: 39-6496.

KAGOSHIMA (0992)

Kagoshima Hayashida Hotel, 12-22 Higashi-Sengokucho. Tel: 24-4111, fax: 24-4553.
Kagoshima Hokke Club, 3-22 Yamanokuchicho. Tel: 26-0011.
Kagoshima Sun Royal Hotel, 1-8-10 Yojiro. Tel: 53-2020, fax: 55-0186.
Kagoshima Tokyu Hotel, 22-1 Kamoike-Shinmachi. Tel: 57-2411.
Shiroyama Kanko Hotel, 41-1 Shinshoincho. Tel: 24-2211, fax: 24-2222.

Okinawa

NAHA (098)

Naha Tokyu Hotel, 1002 Ame-Ku. Tel: 868-2151, fax: 868-7895.
Okinawa Fuji Hotel, 1-6-1 Nishi. Tel: 868-1118, fax: 868-2189.
Okinawa Grand Castle Hotel, 1-132-1 Yamakawa-cho. Tel: 886-5454, fax: 887-0070.
Okinawa Harbor View Hotel, 2-46 Izumizaki. Tel: 853-2111, fax: 834-6043.
Okinawa Hotel, 35 Daido. Tel: 884-3191, fax: 885-2102.
Okinawa Miyako Hotel, 40 Matsukawa. Tel: 887-1111.
Okinawa Oceanview Hotel, 1-5 Kume 2-chome. Tel: 853-2112, fax: 862-6112.
Pacific Hotel Okinawa, 3-6-1 Nishi. Tel: 868-5162, fax: 868-8876.
Palace On The Hill, 165 Uenoya. Tel: 864-1111, fax: 863-3275.
Hotel Seibu Orion, 1-2-21 Asato. Tel: 866-5533, fax: 862-9039.
Sunroute Okinawa Hotel, 1-7-3 Asato. Tel: 862-8200.

Attractions

Culture

The following lists museums, galleries and theaters in Tokyo.

Museums and Art Galleries

In Japan, there are more than 1,400 museums and art galleries and their numbers are increasing year by year.

Listed are art galleries, folk history museums, treasure houses and folk art museums. Major science museums and those of a unique nature are also included.

These institutions are arranged geographically from north to south and are classified roughly by district and city according to their location.

SAPPORO (HOKKAIDO)

Historical Museum of Hokkaido, 53-2 Konopporo, Atsubetsucho, Atsubetsu-ku, Sapporo 061-004. Tel: (011) 898-0456. 40 minutes by bus from Sapporo Station, 5 minutes by bus from Shinrinkoen Station or 10 minutes by taxi from Shin-Sapporo Station. Palaeontological and biological specimens, archeological remains, implements and utensils used by the Ainu and immigrants, progress of colonization and industries of Hokkaido. Open 9.30am–4.30pm, closed Mondays and national holidays.

The Natural History Museum of Agriculture, Hokkaido University, 8-chome, Nishi, Kita-Sanjo, Chuo-ku, Sapporro 060 (in the botanical garden). Tel: (011) 251-8010. 10-minutes walk from Sapporro Station. Specimens of fauna and flora peculiar to Hokkaido, implements and utensils of the old Ainus and Gilyaks are on display. Open 29 April –3 November 9am–4pm, closed Mondays and 4 November–28 April.

NORTHEASTERN HONSHU

Munakata Shiko Memorial Museum of Art, 2-1-2, Matsubara, Aomori, Aomori Pref. 030. Tel: (0177) 77-4567. 15 minutes by bus from Aomori Station. Prints and paintings by Munakata Shiko (1903–75), Aomori's best-known artist. Open April–September 9.30am–4.30pm; October–March 9.30am–4pm, closed Mondays, national holidays and end of every month.

Chusonji Treasury, Chusonji, Hiraizumicho, Nishiiwaigun, Iwate Pref. 029-41. Tel: (0191) 46-2211. 5 minutes by bus from Hiraizumi Station to Chusonji bus stop, then a 20-minute walk. A fine collection of the art of the late Heian period, some 800 years ago. The collection includes Buddhist images, paintings and other cultural and historical relics of that period. Open April–October 8am–5pm; November–March 8.30am–4.30pm.

Homma Museum of Art, 7-7, Onaricho, Sakata, Yamagata Pref. 998. Tel: (0234) 24-4311. 5-minute walk from Sakata Station. Japanese paintings, calligraphy, prints, swords and various articles associated with the local culture and the folk arts. Many were the property of the Homma family, wealthy merchants in Sakata. Open April–October 9am–5pm; November–March 9am–4.30pm, closed Mondays of December–March.

Chido Museum, 10-18, Kachu-Shinmachi, Tsuruoka, Yamagata Pref. 997. Tel: (0235) 22-1199. 10 minutes by bus from Tsuruoka Station. Art objects, archaeological relics and folk items related to the rural customs of the area, and some of the possessions of the Sakai family, a feudal lord of the region. They are housed in a group of buildings among which are the former police station, government office and an old farm house. Open 9am–5pm, closed 28 December–1 January.

Sendai City Museum, Sannomaruato, Kawauchi, Sendai, Miyagi Pref. 980. Tel: (022) 225-2557. 10 minutes by bus from Sendai Station. *Samurai* armors, swords, old costumes and other art objects, many of which were possessed by the Date family, the well-known feudal lord of Sendai. Also on display are Japanese paintings, ukiyo-e, and pottery. Open 9am–4.45pm, closed Mondays and the day following national holidays.

Kurita Museum, 1542, Komabacho, Ashikaga, Tochigi Pref. 329-42. Tel: (0284) 91-1026. 10-minute walk from Tomita Station. A large collection of Imari and Nabeshima porcelains. There is a branch of this museum in Tokyo. (See Tokyo section.) Open 9.30am–5pm, closed 29-31 December.

Mashiko Reference Collection Museum, 3388, Mashiko, Mashiko-machi, Haga-gun, Tochigi Pref. 321-42. Tel: (0285) 72-5300. One hour by bus from Utsunomiya Station. Works of late Shoji Hamada and his collection. (Eastern and Western ceramics, fabrics, furniture, paintings etc.) Open 9.30am–4.30pm, closed Mondays, 28 December–4 January and all February.

TOKYO

Bridgestone Museum of Art, 1-10-1, Kyobashi, Chou-ku, Tokyo 104. Tel: (03) 3563-0241. 5-minute walk from Tokyo Station (Yaesuguchi side). Western paintings, prints, sculpture, pottery and metal items, and paintings by contemporary Japanese artists. Open 10am–5.30pm, closed Mondays.

Communications Museum, 2-3-1, Otemachi, Chiyoda-ku, Tokyo 100. Tel: (03) 3244-6821. 1-minute walk from Otemachi subway station. A large collection of postage stamps and various data on communications. Open 9am–4.30pm; Fridays 9am–6.30pm, closed Mondays.

Furniture Museum, JIC Building, 3-10, Harumi, Chuo-ku, Tokyo 104. Tel: (03) 3533-0098. 15 minutes by bus from Ginza. Old Japanese furniture. Open 10am–4.30pm, closed Wednesdays.

The Gotoh Museum, 3-9-25, Kaminoge, Setagaya-ku, Tokyo 158. Tel: (03) 3703-0661. 4-minute walk from Kaminoge Station on the Tokyu Oimachi Line. Fine arts and crafts of ancient Japan, China and other Oriental nations. Open 9.30am–4.30pm, closed Mondays and the day following a national holiday.

Hatakeyama Collection, 2-20-12, Shiroganedai, Minato-ku, Tokyo 108. Tel: (03) 3447-5787. 6-minute walk from Takanawadai subway station. Fine arts and crafts of ancient Japan, Korea and China. Many objects are relating to the tea ceremony. A tea ceremony room on the upper floor. Open April–September 10am–5pm; October–March 10am–4.30pm, closed Mondays.

Idemitsu Museum of Arts, 9th floor of Kokusai Building, 3-1-1, Marunouchi, Chiyoda-ku, Tokyo 100. Tel: (03) 3213-9402. 3-minute walk from Yurakucho Station. Zenga by Zen priest Sengai, Japanese ceramics, crafts & paintings, hand-painted Ukiyo-e and Chinese ceramics, crafts & bronzes. Open 10am–5pm, closed Mondays.

The Japan Folk Crafts Museum, 4-3-33, Komaba, Meguro-ku, Tokyo 153. Tel: (03) 3467-4527. 5-minute walk from Komaba-Todaimae Station on the Keio-Inokashira Line. Folk art of various parts of Japan and Korea, and other countries of the world, mostly assembled by Yanagi Soetsu. Open 10am–5pm, closed Mondays.

Japanese Sword Museum, 4-25-10,

Yoyogi, Shibuya-ku, Tokyo 151. Tel: (03) 3379-1386. 10-minute walk from Sangubashi Station on the Odakyu Line. Works of noted swordsmiths, both ancient and modern. Open 9am–4pm, closed Mondays.

Kite Museum, 5th floor of Taimeiken Building, 1-12-10, Nihombashi, Chuo-ku, Tokyo 103. Tel: (03) 3271-2465. 2-minute walk from Nihombashi subway station. Kites collected from throughout Japan and other countries. Open 11am–5pm, closed Sundays and national holidays.

Museum of Maritime Science, 3-1, Higashi-Yashio, Shinagawa-ku, Tokyo 135 (in the reclaimed land area). Tel: (03) 3528-1111. 20 minutes by bus from Shinagawa Station. Various nautical exhibits housed in a ferro-concrete replica of a 60,000-ton liner in the seaside park. Open 10am–5pm daily.

Matsuoka Museum of Art, 8th floor of Matsuoka Tamuracho Building, 5-22-10, Shimbashi, Minato-ku, Tokyo 105. Tel: (03) 3437-2787. 3-minute walk from Onarimon subway station. Oriental ceramics and Japanese paintings, and Egyptian, Greek, Roman and Indian sculptures. Open 10am–5pm, closed Mondays.

Meiji Jingu Treasure Museum, 1-1, Kamizonocho, Yoyogi, Shibuya-ku, Tokyo 151. Tel: (03) 3379-5511. 13-minute walk from JR Yoyogi Station or 5 minutes walk from Sangubashi Station on the Odakyu Line. Objects used by the Emperor Meiji (1852–1912). Open March–October 9am–4.30pm; November–February 9am–4pm, closed 3rd Friday.

Meiji Memorial Picture Gallery, Meiji Jingu Gaien, Meiji-jingu Gaien, 9, Kasumigaoka, Shinjuku-ku, Tokyo 160. Tel: (03) 3401-5179. 3-minute walk from Shinanomachi Station. Pictures showing the main events in the reign of the Emperor Meiji. Open 9am–4.30pm daily.

National Museum of Modern Art, Tokyo, 3, Kitanomaru-koen, Chiyoda-ku, Tokyo 102 (in Kitanomaru Park). Tel: (03) 3214-2561. 5-minute walk from Takebashi subway station. Japanese paintings, sculptures, prints, and calligraphy. Open 10am–5pm, closed Mondays.

Crafts Gallery, National Museum of Modern Art, Tokyo, 1, Kitanomaru-koen, Chiyoda-ku, Tokyo 102 (in Kitanomaru Park). Tel: (03) 3211-7781. 7-minute walk from Takebashi subway station. Contemporary Japanese handicrafts. Open 10am–5pm, closed Mondays.

National Science Museum, 7-20, Ueno-koen, Taito-ku, Tokyo 110 (in Ueno Park). Tel: (03) 3822-0111. 5-minute walk from Ueno Station. Exhibits in the field of natural history and physical sciences and technology. Open 9am–4.30pm, closed Mondays.

National Museum of Western Art, 7-7, Ueno-koen, Taito-ku, Tokyo 110 (in Ueno Park). Tel: (03) 3828-5131. 3-minute walk from Ueno Station. Works of famous Western painters and sculptors, mostly French artists from the 19th century to the recent past. Open 9.30am–5pm, closed Mondays.

Nezu Institute of Fine Arts, 6-5-1, Minami-Aoyama, Minato-ku, Tokyo 107. Tel: (03) 3400-2536. 10-minute walk from Omotesando subway station. Japanese paintings, calligraphy, sculpture, ceramics, lacquer and Chinese bronzes, Korean ceramics; a Japanese garden in which there are several tea houses. Open 9.30am–4.30pm, closed Mondays.

NHK Broadcast Museum, 2-1-1, Atago, Minato-ku, Tokyo 105. Tel: (03) 5400-6900. 6-minute walk from Kamiyacho subway station. Materials showing the history of the development of radio and TV broadcasting in Japan. Open 9.30am–4.30pm, closed Mondays (when Monday falls on a holiday, it is open) 26 December–4 January.

Sumo Museum, 1-3-28, Yokoami, Sumida-ku, Tokyo 130. Tel: (03) 3622-0366. 1-minute walk from Ryogoku Station. Records and documents concerning the history of sumo (Japanese wrestling) since the 18th century. Open 9.30am–4.30pm, closed Saturdays, Sundays and national holidays.

Ukiyo-e, Ota Memorial Museum of Art, 1-10-10, Jingumae, Shibuya-ku, Tokyo 150. Tel: (03) 3403-0880. 3-minute walk from Meiji-Jingumae subway station and Harajuku Station. A large collection of ukiyo-e woodblock prints collected by Mr. Seizo Ota. Open 10.30am–5.30pm, closed Mondays and 25th–end of each month.

The Okura Shukokan, 2-10-3, Toranomon, Minato-ku, Tokyo 105. Tel: (03) 3583-0781. 8-minute walk from Kamiyacho subway station or 10 minutes walk from Toranomon subway station. Fine arts and crafts of ancient Japan and other Asian countries. Adjacent to Okura Hotel. Open 10am–4pm, closed Mondays.

Paper Museum, 1-1-8, Horifune, Kita-ku, Tokyo 114. Tel: (03) 3911-3545. 1-minute walk from JR Oji Station. Various kinds of Japanese paper. Products and utensils for the making of handmade paper. Open 9.30am–4.30pm, closed Mondays and national holidays.

Pentax Gallery, Kasumicho Corporation, 3-21-20, Nishi-Azabu, Minato-ku, Tokyo 106. Tel: (03) 3401-2186. 8-minute walk from Roppongi subway station. Cameras. Open 10am–5pm, closed Sundays and national holidays.

Hiraki Ukiyo-e Museum, 6th floor, Yokohama Sogo Department Store, 2-18-1, Takashima, Nishi-ku, Yokohama, Kanagawa Pref. 220. Tel: (045) 465-2233. Adjacent to Yokohama Station. Hikaki collection of ukiyo-e prints. Open 10am–7pm, closed Tuesdays.

Science Museum, 2-1, Kitanomaru-koen, Chiyoda-ku, Tokyo 102 (in Kitanomaru Park). Tel: (03) 3212-8471. 5-minute walk from Takebashi subway station. Machinery of the latest type. Open 9.30am–4.50pm.

Suntory Museum of Art, 11th floor of Suntory Building, 1-2-3, Moto-Akasaka, Minato-ku, Tokyo 107. Tel: (03) 3470-1073. 3-minute walk from Akasakamitsuke subway station. Japanese lacquer, ceramics, glass, costumes, masks and other fine arts. A tea ceremony room is in the museum. Open 10am–5pm; Fridays 10am–7pm, closed Mondays.

Tobacco and Salt Museum, 1-16-8, Jinnan, Shibuya-ku, Tokyo 150. Tel: (03) 3476-2041. 8-minute walk from Shibuya Station or 10 minutes walk from Harajuku Station. Items and documents relating to smoking and salt. Special exhibits: – "Ukiyo-e prints depicting smoking custom" and others – on the 4th floor. Open 10am–6pm, closed Mondays, 1st Tuesday of June and 29 December–3 Janurary.

Tokyo Central Museum, 5th floor of Ginza Boeki Building, 2-7-18, Ginza, Chuo-ku, Tokyo 104. Tel: (03) 3564-4600. 3-minute walk from Ginza subway station. Contemporary paintings, sculptures, prints, calligraphy and handicrafts. Open 10am–6pm, closed Mondays.

Hara Museum of Contemporary Art, 4-

7-25, Kita-Shinagawa, Shinagawa-ku, Tokyo 140. Tel: (03) 3445-0651. 15-minute walk from Shinagawa Station. Collection of paintings and sculptures, after 1950 up to now, by leading artists of America, Europe and Japan. Open 11am–5pm; Wednesdays 11am–8pm, closed Mondays.

Tokyo Metropolitan Art Museum, 8-36, Ueno-koen, Taito-ku, Tokyo 110 (in Ueno Park). Tel: (03) 3823-6921. 7-minute walk from Ueno Station. Works of contemporary Japanese artists. Open 9am–5pm, closed 3rd Monday. (Gallery for Museum is closed on every Monday.)

Tokyo National Museum, 13-9, Ueno-koen, Taito-ku, Tokyo 110 (in Ueno Park). Tel: (03) 3822-1111. 10-minute walk from Ueno Station. The largest museum in Japan. Fine arts and archaeology of Japan including many that are designated as National Treasures or Important Cultural Properties. Also collections of Chinese, Korean and Indian art and archaeology. Open 9am–4.30pm, closed Mondays.

Transportation Museum, 1-25, Kanda Sudacho, Chiyoda-ku, Tokyo 101. Tel: (03) 3251-8481. 4-minute walk from Awajicho subway station or 5 minutes walk from Akihabara Station. Various items showing the progress of railways and other means of transportation in Japan. Open 9.30am–5pm, closed Mondays. (Open daily in August, 26 March–6 April.)

Tsubouchi Memorial Theater Museum, Waseda University, Waseda University, 1-6-1, Nishi-Waseda, Shinjuku-ku, Tokyo 169. Tel: (03) 3203-4141, ext. 5214. 6-minute walk from Waseda subway station. Items and documents connected with the Oriental and Occidental theaters. Open 9am–5pm, Sundays 10am–5pm, closed national holidays.

Yamatane Museum of Art, 8th and 9th floors of Yamatane Building, 7-12, Nihombashi-Kabutocho, Chou-ku, Tokyo 103. Tel: (03) 3669-7643. 1-minute walk from Kayabacho subway station. Japanese paintings of the Meiji period to the present. Tea ceremony rooms adjoin the museum. Open 10am–5pm, closed Mondays.

Vicinity of Tokyo

Japan Open-air Folkhouse Museum, 7-1-1, Masugata, Tama-ku, Kawasaki, Kanagawa Pref. 214. Tel: (044) 922-2181. 15-minute walk from Mukogaoka-yuen Station on the Odakyu Line. Outdoor museum featuring old and rare Japanese farmhouses. Open 9.30am–4pm, closed Mondays.

Toshiba Science Institute, 1, Komukai-Toshibacho, Saiwai-ku, Kawasaki, Kanagawa Pref. 210. Tel: (044) 511-2300. 10 minutes by bus from Kawasaki Station to Komukai-koban bus stop and then 3-minute walk to the institute. The newest technologies, concepts and visitor-operated displays on electricity along with electronic products. Open 9am–5pm, closed Saturdays, Sundays and national holidays.

Silk Museum, 2nd floor of Silk Center Building, 1, Yamashitacho, Naka-ku, Yokohama, Kanagawa Pref. 231. Tel: (045) 641-0841. 10-minute walk from Kannai Station or 15 minutes walk from Sakuragicho Station. Silk goods of various kinds and educational materials relating to silk. Open 9am–4.30pm, closed Mondays. (When Monday falls on a holiday, it is closed on Tuesday.)

Kanagawa Prefectural Kanazawa-Bunko Museum, 142, Kanazawacho, Kanazawa-ku, Yokohama, Kanagawa Pref. 236. Tel: (045) 701-9069. 10-minute walk from Kanazawa-Bunko Station on the Keihin-Kyuko Line. Sculpture, paintings, calligraphy, historical documents and a large library of the Chinese and Japanese classics. This Kanazawa Bunko was founded about 1260 by the Hojo family. Open 9am–4.30pm, closed Mondays, last two days of every 2 months and the day following national holidays.

Kamakura Museum, 2-1-1, Yukinoshita, Kamakura, Kanagawa Pref. 248 (in the precincts of the Tsurugaoka Hachiman-gu). Tel: (0467) 22-0753. 15-minute walk from Kamakura Station. Paintings, sculpture and other art objects of the 12th–16th centuries. Open 9am–4pm, closed Mondays.

Museum of Modern Art, Kanagawa, Annex; 2-1-53, Yukinoshita, Kamakura, Kanagawa Pref. 248 (in the precincts of the Tsurugaoka Hachiman-gu). Tel: (0467) 22-5000, 7718. 10-minute walk from Kamakura Station. Japanese and foreign art: paintings, sculpture, prints, from the 19th century to the present. Open 10am–5pm, closed Mondays and the day following national holidays.

Hakone

Hakone Open-Air Museum, Ninotaira, Hakonemachi, Ashigara-shimo-gun, Kanagawa Pref. 250-04. Tel: (0460) 2-1161. 2-minute walk from Chokoku-no-mori Station on the Hakone-Tozan Railway. A collection of late 19th and 20th century sculpture by Western and Japanese artists. Open March–October 9am–5pm, November–February 9am–4pm.

Hakone Art Museum, 1300, Gora, Hakonemachi, Ashigara-shimo-gun, Kanagawa Pref. 250-04. Tel: (0460) 2-2623. 1-minute walk from Koen-kami cable car stop. Cable car leaves from Gora Station on the Hakone-Tozan Railway. A collection of pottery and porcelain from Japan. bamboo and moss garden in the museum grounds. Open April–November 9.30am–4.30pm, December–March 9am–4pm, closed Thursdays.

Atami

MOA Museum of Art (MOA), 26-2, Momoyama-cho, Atami, Shizuoka Pref. 413. Tel: (0557) 84-2511. 20-minute walk or 5 minutes by taxi from Atami Station. A collection of Japanese and Chinese art objects which belong to the Church of World Messianity. Open 9.30am–5pm, closed Thursdays. (Open when Thursday falls on a holiday.)

Central Honshu

Utsukushigahara Open-Air Museum, Utsukushigahara-daijo, Takeshi-mura, Chiisagata-gun, Nagano Pref. 386-05. Tel: (0268) 86-2331. 1.5 hours by bus from Matsumoto Station or 1 hour 40 minutes by bus from Ueda Station. Collection of contemporary sculptures. Open 9am–5pm, closed mid-November–24 April.

Tokugawa Art Museum, 1017, Tokugawacho, Higashi-ku, Nagoya 461. Tel: (052) 935-6262. 20 minutes by bus from Nagoya Station. Japanese paintings, screens, swords and noh costumes belonging to the feudal lords, and Chinese paintings and ceramics. Open 10am–5pm, closed Mondays.

Museum Meiji-mura, 1, Uchiyama, Inuyama, Aichi Pref. 484. Tel: (0568) 67-0314, 3263-5566 (Tokyo Office). 20 minutes by bus from Inuyama Station on the Meitetsu Line. 60 buildings of the Meiji and Taisho periods (1868–

1926) in a large landscaped park. Open March–October 10am–5pm, November–February 9.30am–4pm.

Hida Folklore Village, 1-590, Kamiokamotocho, Yakayama, Gifu Pref. 506. Tel: (0577) 33-4714. 10 minutes by bus from Takayama Station. The Village is composed of several Japanese old farmhouses in "gassho-zukuri" style moved from the villages in the Hida district. Many folklore articles are preserved in each house. Open 8.30am–5pm.

Edo Village, A-36, Kitabukuromachi, Kanazawa, Ishikawa Pref. 920. Tel: (0762) 35-1336. 50 minutes by bus from Kanazawa Station. Restored Edo period (1603–1867) buildings: thatched farmhouses, merchants' houses, gates, etc, in a large open space. Open 8am–5pm.

Ishikawa Prefectural Museum of Art, 2-1, Dewamachi, Kanazawa, Ishikawa Pref. 920 (beside Kenrokuen Park). Tel: (0762) 31-7580. 20 minutes by bus from Kanazawa Station. Old Japanese paintings, lacquer, textiles and Kutani ware. Oil paintings, sculptures, Japanese-style paintings and art by modern and contemporary artists who are connected with Ishikawa prefecture. Open 9.30am–5pm, closed 29 December–3 January.

Seisonkaku, 1-2 Kenrokumachi, Kanazawa, Ishikawa Pref. 920 (in Kenrokuen Park, near the Ishikikawa Prefectural Museum of Art). Tel: (0762) 21-0580. 15 minutes by bus from Kanazawa Station. A collection of objects belonging to the Maeda family, the feudal lord of the region, displayed in a large Japanese-style house erected in 1863. Open 8.30am–4.30pm, closed Wednesdays and 29 December–2 January.

Kyoto

Chishaku-in Temple Storehouse, Higashiyama-Shichijo, Higashiyama-ku, Kyoto 605 (in the grounds of the Chishaku-in Temple). Tel: (075) 541-5361. Near Higashiyama-Shichijo bus stop. Japanese paintings on walls and screens of the Momoyama period (1573–1615). The Japanese garden is one of the best gardens in Kyoto. Open 9am–4pm.

Costume Museum, 5th floor of Izutsu Building, Shin-Hanayacho-Horikawakado, Shimogyo-ku, Kyoto 600. Tel: (075) 361-8388. 10-minute walk from Kyoto Station (near NishiHongan-ji). Japanese costumes, from ancient to modern times, displayed on life-sized dolls. Open 9am–5pm, closed Sundays and national holidays.

Domoto Art Museum, 26, Kamiyanagicho, Hirano, Kita-ku, Kyoto 603. Tel: (075) 463-1348. Near Ritsumeikan Daigaku-mae bus stop. Japanese paintings, prints, ceramics by the famous artist, Domoto Insho (1891–1975). Open 9.30am–5pm, closed Mondays.

Taiga, Ike Art Museum, 57, Matsuomangokucho, Nishikyo-ku, Kyoto 615. Tel: (075) 381-2832. In front of Kokedera bus stop operated by the Kyoto Bus. *Sumi-e* (black and white paintings) and calligraphy by Ike Taiga (1723–1776). Open 10am–5pm, closed Wednesdays.

Kawai Kanjiro's House, Kaneicho, Gojozaka, Higashiyama-ku, Kyoto 605. Tel: (075) 561-3585. 2-minute walk from Umamachi bus stop. Works of the famous potter, Kawai Kanjiro (1890–1966), the folkcraft objects used in his traditionally-styled Japanese house. His workroom and 2 kilns are preserved. Open 10am–5pm, closed Mondays, 24 December–7 January and 10–20 August.

Koryuji Reihoden Treasury, 36, Uzumasa Hachigaokacho, Ukyo-ku, Kyoto 616 (in the grounds of the Koryuji Temple). Tel: (075) 861-1461. Near Uzumasa Station on the Keifuku Line. Japanese sculpture, calligraphy, documents, and costumes, owned by the temple. The wooden image of Miroku Bosatsu is especially famous nationwide. Open March–November 9am–5pm; December–February 9am–4.30pm.

Kyoto Municipal Museum of Art, 124, Enshojicho, Okazaki, Sakyo-ku, Kyoto 606 (in Okazaki Park). Tel: (075) 771-4107. In front of Kyoto Kaikan Bijutsukan-mae bus stop. Works of modern Japanese artists. Japanese paintings of the Kyoto School are predominant. Open 9am–5pm, closed Mondays. (Open when Monday falls on a holiday.)

Kyoto Yuzen Dyeing Hall, 6, Mamedacho, Nishikyogoku, Ukyo-ku, Kyoto 615. Tel: (075) 311-0025. 5-minute walk from Nishikyogoku Station on the Hankyu Line. Demonstration of the process of Yuzen dyeing and display and sale of Yuzen products. Open 9am–5pm, closed Mondays.

Kyoto National Museum, 527, Chayamachi, Higashiyama-ku, Kyoto 605 (near the Sanjusangendo Hall). Tel: (075) 541-1151. 13 minutes by bus from Kyoto Station. Fine arts and archaeology of Japan, mainly from the Museum Collection. Many of exhibits include the art treasures principally from the shrines and temples in and around Kyoto. Open 9am–4.30pm, closed Mondays.

National Museum of Modern Art, Kyoto, Enshojicho, Okazaki, Sako-ku, Kyoto 606 (in Okazaki Park). Tel: (075) 761-4111. In front of Kyoto Kaikan Bijutsukan-mae bus stop. Contemporary arts of Japan and other countries. Open 9.30am–5pm, closed Mondays.

The Raku Museum, Aburanokoji, Nakadachiuri Agaru, Kamigyo-ku, Kyoto 602. Tel: (075) 414-0304. 5-minute walk from Horikawa Nakadachiuri bus stop. Open 10am–4.30pm, closed Mondays.

Sen'oku Hakkokan (Sumitomo Collection), 24, Shimo-Miyanomaecho, Shishigadani, Sakyo-ku, Kyoto 606. Tel: (075) 771-6411. Near Higashi Tennocho bus stop. Open March–June and September–November 10am–4pm, closed Mondays and national holidays. (Open when Monday falls on a holiday.)

Toji Treasure House, 1, Kujocho, Minami-ku, Kyoto 601 (in the grounds of the Toji Temple). Tel: (075) 691-3325. 15-minute walk from the southwest exit of Kyoto Station (Hachijoguchi exit). Buddhist statues, paintings, sutras and other objects owned by the temple. Open 9am–4.30pm.

Nara and Vicinity

Horyuji Daihozoden Treasure Museum, 1-1, Horyuji-sannai, Ikarugacho, Ikoma-gun, Nara Pref. 636-01 (in the grounds of the Horyuji temple). Tel: (0745) 75-2555. 20-minute walk from Horyuji Station. Buddhist statues, shrines and other works of Buddhist art belonging to the Horyuji temple. Open 11 March–19 November 8am–4.30pm, 20 November–10 March 8am–4pm.

Kofukuji National Treasure House, 48, Noboriojicho, Nara 630 (in the grounds of the Kofukuji Temple). Tel: (0742) 22-5370. 7-minute walk from Kintetsu Nara Station. Buddhist statues of national treasure merit and sculpture of the Nara period (710–784) & the Kamakura period (1192–1333). Open 9am–5pm.

Nara National Museum, 50, Noboriojicho, Nara 630. Tel: (0742) 22-7771. 15-minute walk from Kintetsu Nara Station. The best Buddhist art in Japan, belonging to temples in the Nara area. Open 9am–4.30pm, closed Mondays.

Nara Prefectural Museum of Art, 10-6, Noboriojicho, Nara 630. Tel: (0742) 23-3968. 10-minute walk from Kintetsu Nara Station. Contemporary arts of Japan and other countries. Old Japanese paintings, textiles, and contemporary arts of Japan and other countries. Open 9am–4.30pm, closed Mondays.

Neiraku Museum, 74, Suimoncho, Nara 630. Tel: (0742) 22-2173. 15-minute walk from Kintetsu Nara Station. Ancient Chinese bronze, old Korean celadon, and some quantity of famous Japanese art objects. The Isuien Japanese landscape garden is opposite the museum. Open 10am–4.30pm, closed Tuesdays. (Open when Tuesday falls on a holiday, but closed on the following day.)

Shosoin Treasure Repository, 129, Zoshicho, Nara 630. Tel: (0742) 26-2811. Located in the northwestern part of the Daibutsuden Hall. 15-minute walk from Kintetsu Nara Station. Precious art works of the late Nara period (710-784). Many of these objects formerly belonged to the Emperor Shomu. Some of the items are shown to the public annually at the Nara National Museum for a short period between late October and early November.

Toshodaiji Treasure House, Toshodaiji, Gojocho, Nara 630 (in the grounds of the Toshodaiji Temple). Tel: (0742) 33-7900. 10-minute walk from Nishinokyo Station on the Kintetsu Kashihara Line. Buddhist statues, paintings and art objects of national treasure merit of the Nara period (600-784). The statue of Ganjin, normally housed in a separate building, is shown only at the time of the temple festival, from 5–7 June usually. Open 21 March–19 May and 15 September–3 November 9am–4pm.

Museum Yamato Bunkakan, 1-11-6, Gakuen-Minami, Nara 631. Tel: (0742) 45-0544. 7-minute walk from Gakuenmae Station on the Kintetsu Nara Line. Art objects – paintings, sculpture, ceramics, lacquer, prints, textiles – of Japan, China, Korea and other Asian countries. Open 10am–5pm, closed Mondays.

OSAKA AND VICINITY

Fujita Museum of Art, 10-32, Amijimacho, Miyakojima-ku, Osaka 534. Tel: (06) 351-0582. 7-minute walk from Katamachi Station. Japanese and Chinese fine arts and crafts. Many objects are related to the tea ceremony. Open mid-March–mid-June and mid-September–early December 10am–4pm, closed Mondays.

Open Air Museum of Old Japanese Farm Houses, 1-2, Hattori-Ryokuchi, Toyonaka, Osaka Pref. 560. Tel: (06) 862-3137. 13-minute walk from Ryokuchi-koen Station on the Kita-Osaka Kyuko Line. Old Japanese farmhouses are reassembled and put on display in a village setting. Open April–October 9.30am–5pm, November–March 9.30am–4pm, closed Mondays.

Mint Museum, 1-1-7, Temma, Kita-ku, Osaka 530 (in the grounds of the Osaka Mint Bureau). Tel: (06) 351-8509. 15-minute walk from Minami-Morimachi subway station. Japanese coins from the feudal days to the present times. Open 9am–4pm, closed Saturdays, Sundays and national holidays.

National Museum of Art, Osaka, 10-4, Senri-Banpaku-Koen, Suita, Osaka Pref. 565 (in Expo Park). Tel: (06) 876-2481. Get off at JR Ibaraki Station, Hankyu Railways Ibarakishi Station, then take the bus to Nihon Teien-mae bus stop and then a 10-minute walk. Contemporary paintings and other works of art relating to the interchange of fine arts between the East and the West. Open 10am–5pm, closed Wednesdays. (Open when Wednesday falls on a holiday, but closed on the following day.)

National Museum of Ethnology, 10-1, Senri-Banpaku-Koen, Suita, Osaka Pref. 565 (in Expo Park). Tel: (06) 876-2151. 15-minute walk from Nihon Teien-mae bus stop. Display of artifacts from Japan and other countries and booths for individual viewing of films relating to the exhibits. Open 10am–5pm, closed Wednesdays.

Osaka Japan Folk Crafts Museum, 10-5, Senri-Banpaku-Koen, Suita, Osaka Pref. 565 (in Expo Park). Tel: (06) 877-1971. 10-minute walk from Nihon Teien-mae bus stop. Japanese folk craft objects which have been chosen with great care. Open 9.30am–5pm (last admittance at 4pm), closed Wednesdays. (Open when Wednesday falls on a holiday, but closed on the following day.)

Osaka City Museum, 1-1, Osakajo, Chou-ku, Osaka 540 (in the grounds of the Osaka Castle). Tel: (06) 941-7177. 15-minute walk from Morinomiya Station. Materials and records connected with the history, economy, and culture of Osaka. Open 9.15am–4.45pm, closed every 2nd and 4th Monday of the month. (Open when the 4th Monday falls on a holiday, but closed on the following day.)

Osaka Municipal Museum of Art, 1-82, Chausuyamacho, Tennoji-ku, Osaka 543 (in Tennoji Park). Tel: (06) 771-4874. 8-minute walk from Tennoji Station (Subway or JR). Japanese, Chinese, and Korean art objects, both ancient and modern. Open 9.30am–5pm, closed Mondays.

Osaka Museum of Natural History, 1-23, Nagai-koen, Higashi-Sumiyoshi-ku, Osaka 546 (in Nagai Park). Tel: (06) 697-6221. 10-minute walk from Nagai subway station. Material for study of natural science. Open 9.30am–4.30pm, closed Mondays.

Modern Transportation Museum, 3-11-10, Namiyoke, Minato-ku, Osaka 552. Tel: (06) 581-5771. Near JR Bentencho Station. Various items relating to air, land, and sea transportation and more specifically the modernizing of the Japanese National Railways. Open 9.30am–5pm, closed Mondays. (Open daily during spring holiday season and summer holiday season.)

KOBE AND VICINITY

Hakutsuru Art Museum, 6-1-1, Sumiyoshi-Yamate, Higashi-Nada-ku, Kobe 658. Tel: (078) 851-6001. 15-minute walk from Mikage Station on the Hankyu Line. Chinese bronzes, ceramics, lacquer ware, and ancient Japanese art objects. Open mid-March–end May and mid-September–end November 10am–4.30pm, closed Mondays and the day following national holidays.

Hyogo-ken Togei-kan, 5th floor of Zentan Kaikan Building, 4-5-1, Shimo-Yamatedori, Chou-ku, Kobe 650. Tel:

(078) 321-0769. 3-minute walk from JR Motomachi Station. A large collection of Japanese ceramics. Among the pieces, Tamba ware are predominant. Open 10am–5pm, closed Mondays.

Hyogo Prefectural Museum of Modern Art, Kobe, 3-8-30, Harada-dori, Nada-ku, Kobe 657. Tel: (078) 801-1591. 5-minute walk from Hankyu Ojikoen Station on the Hankyu Kobe Line. Contemporary arts of Japan and other countries. Open 10am–5pm, closed Mondays.

Kobe City Museum, 24 Kyomachi, Chou-ku, Kobe 650. Tel: (078) 391-0035. 10-minute walk from JR Sannomiya Station. A newly-opened museum of archaeology and history of Kobe. It also houses a fine collection of Japanese paintings and art objects of the 16th to 17th centuries produced under the influence of Portugal and Spain (Namban Art), Kohmoh Art (the 17th to 19th centuries, influenced by Holland) and old maps. Open 10am–5pm, closed Mondays and the day following national holidays.

Tekisui Art Museum, 13-3, Yama-Ashiyacho, Ashiya, Hyogo Pref. 659. Tel: (0797) 22-2228. 8-minute walk from Ashiyagawa Station on the Hankyu Line. Japanese art objects, collection of toys and games, Kyoto wares. Open 10am–5pm, closed Mondays, mid-July–mid-September and mid-December–mid-January.

CHUGOKU

Bizen Pottery Traditional and Contemporary Art Museum, 1659-6, Imbe, Bizen, Okayama Pref. 705. Tel: (0869) 64-1400. 2-minute walk from Imbe Station. A large collection of Bizen ware by contemporary potters. Open 9.30am–5pm, closed Mondays.

Japanese Rural Toy Museum, 1-4-16, Chou, Kurashiki, Okayama Pref. 710. Tel: (0864) 22-8058. 10-minute walk from Kurashiki Station. Old Japanese folk toys collected from all parts of the country. Open 8am–5pm, closed 1 January.

The Kej Fujiwara Art Museum, Honami, Bizen, Okayama Pref. 705. Tel: (0869) 67-0638. 10-minute taxi from JR Bizen-Katakami Station. Bizen Pottery made by Kei Fujiwara and old Bizen pottery. Open 10am–4.30pm, closed Mondays.

Kurashiki Archaeological Museum, 1-3-13, Chuo, Kurashiki, Okayama Pref. 710. Tel: (0864) 22-1542. 14-minute walk from Kurashiki Station. Archaeological relics unearthed in the Inland Sea districts. Open December–February 9am–4.30pm, March–November 9am–5pm, closed Mondays.

Kurashiki Museum of Folkcraft, 1-4-11, Chuo, Kurashiki, Okayama Pref. 710. Tel: (0864) 22-1637. 15-minute walk from Kurashiki Station. Folkcraft objects of Japan and other countries. Open December–February 9am–4.15pm, March–November 9am–5pm, closed Mondays (when Monday falls on a holiday, it is open), 29 December–1 January.

Ohara Museum of Art, 1-1-15, Chuo, Kurashiki, Okayama Pref. 710. Tel: (0864) 22-0005. 13-minute walk from Kurashiki Station. The art museum exhibits Western paintings and sculpture of the 17th to the 20th centuries while the craft museum displays contemporary Japanese ceramics, textiles, wood-block prints, etc. Open 9am–5pm, closed Mondays.

Hiroshima Museum of Art, 3-2, Motomachi, Naka-ku, Hiroshima 730 (in Chuo Park). Tel: (082) 223-2530. 15 minutes by bus or streetcar from Hiroshima Station. Works of Impressionists' and other European artists since the 19th century and also modern Japanese artists' works. Open 9am–5pm, closed Mondays.

Hiroshima Peace Memorial Museum, 1-3, Nakajimacho, Naka-ku, Hiroshima 730. Tel: (082) 241-4004. 20 minutes by bus from Hiroshima Station. Records on the 1945 atomic bomb explosion. Open 1 May–30 November 9am–6pm, 1 December–30 April 9am–5pm, closed 29 December–2 January.

Seto Inland Sea Folk History Museum, 1412-2, Tarumicho, Takamatsu, Kagawa Pref. 761. Tel: (0878) 81-4707. 35 minutes by bus from Takamatsu Station to Ogoshi, then a 25-minute walk. Wooden fishing boats and all kinds of fishing gear, farm tools and archaeological items that have been excavated in and around the Inland Sea. The museum is located atop one of the hills in the Goshikidai region with a magnificent view over the Inland Sea. Open 9am–5pm.

KYUSHU AND OKINAWA

Fukuoka Art Museum, 1-6, Ohorikoen, Chuo-ku, Fukuoka 810 (in Ohori Park). Tel: (092) 714-6051. 30 minutes by bus from Hakata Station. Objects once owned by the Kuroda family, the local feudal lord, the Matsunaga collection, which is noted for tea ceremony utensils, and oil paintings from both the West and Japan. Open 9.30am–5.30pm, closed Mondays.

Nagasaki Municipal Museum, Heiwa Kaikan, 7-8 Hirano-machi, Nagasaki 852. Tel: (0958) 45-8188. 5-minute walk from Hamaguchi-machi bus and streetcar stops. Art objects and materials associated with Christianity and trade which were brought in by Holland and China, allowed to trade at Nagasaki, the only open port during the isolation. Open 9am–5pm, closed Mondays.

Okinawa Prefectural Museum, 1-1, Onakacho, Shuri, Naha, Okinawa Pref. 903. Tel: (0988) 84-2243. 2-minute walk from Shurijo Koen Iriguchi bus stop. Art objects of the Okinawa islands including paintings, sculpture, pottery vessels, clothing and lacquer ware. Open 9am–5pm, closed Mondays and national holidays.

Ceramic Art and Crafts

Japan is a country of earthenware, a ceramic-loving nation and a storehouse of ceramic art and crafts. The origin of Japanese ceramic art is generally regarded to date back to the beginning of the 13th century, when Chinese ceramic techniques were introduced.

The development of the art was stimulated in the 16th century because of the popularity of the tea ceremony, and new kilns were opened in various parts of the country. The one in Arita, constructed in 1598 by a Korean potter who came from Korea that year, deserves special mention.

During the years of the Edo Period (1603–1867), many daimyo (feudal lords) encouraged the efforts of their potters and ordered them to make certain ceramic articles of exquisite shapes and designs.

Afterwards, because of the Meiji Restoration, some potters who were engaged in their work under the patronage of the daimyo, had to stop their work. On the other hand, there had been very many potters, protected by tradesmen, who kept firing their kilns and continued to create Japanese ceramic works of art.

The characteristics of Japanese ceramics are: (1) their expression is gentle and suave; (2) they are noted for their irregularity and freedom, simplicity and homeliness; and (3) they are free from artificiality and monotony. The decorations on Japanese wares are quiet and not piquant. Gentleness of expression, which is the chief feature of Japanese ceramics, has been influenced by Japanese taste, fostered by the unique climatic conditions and geographical features of the country.

There are a large number of kilns in Japan, each with a long history.

SHIBUKUSA-YAKI, KOITO-YAKI AND YAMADA-YAKI (0577)

Takayama City, Gifu Pref. Tel: 32-3333.

Hokokusha Pottery Works. Shibukusa-yaki. Located in Kami-nino machi, Takayama City. Tel: 34-0504. Open all year round.

Koito-yaki Kamamoto. Located in Kami-Okamotocho, Takayama City. Tel: 32-1981. Open 9am–5pm. Closed Sunday.

Kobayashi Tosha Pottery Works. Yamada-yaki. Located in Yamadacho, Takayama City. Tel: 32-4077. Open 8am–5pm. Closed Sunday.

MINO-YAKI (OR TAJIMI-YAKI) (0572)

Tajimi City and Toki City, Gifu Pref.

Mino-yaki Center. Tel: 27-7111. Located in Higashi-machi, Tajimi City. Display of Mino ware by contemporary potters. Open 8.30am–5pm. Closed Sunday.

Gifu Prefectural Ceramic Museum. Tel: 23-1191. Open 9.30am–4.30pm. Old Mino ware and the tools and instruments used for making Seto ware in olden times.

KIYOMIZU-YAKI (OR KYO-YAKI) (075)

Kyoto City, Kyoto Pref.

Kyoto Tojiki Kaikan (Pottery Center). Tel: 541-1102. Located in Gojozaka Higashi-iru, Higashiyama-ku. Display and sale of Kyo-yaki ware. Open 9.30am–5pm.

Kawai Kanjiro's House. 569 Kanei-machi, Gojozaka, Higashiyama-ku. Tel: 561-3585. Works of the famous potter, Kanjiro Kawai (1890–1966) and folkcraft objects used in his daily life are displayed in his traditionally styled Japanese house. Open 10am–5pm. Closed Monday.

Kyoto National Museum. Tel: 541-1151. Located in Higashi-oji, Higashiyama-ku (near the Sanjusangendo Hall). Open 9am–4.30pm. Closed Monday.

The Raku Museum. Tel: 414-0304. Located in Aburanokoji, Nakadachiuri-agaru, Kamigyo-ku. Open 10am–4.30pm. Closed Monday.

BIZEN-YAKI (0869)

Imbe, Bizen City, Okayama Pref. Tel: 64-3301.

Bizen Ceramics Hall, 1659-6 Imbe, Bizen City. Tel: 64-1400. Bizen ware by well-known contemporary potters. Open 9.30am–4.30pm. Closed Monday.

Kei Fujiwara Art Museum. Tel: 67-0638. Located in Honami, Bizen City. Bizen pottery made by Kai Fujiwara and old Bizen pottery. Open 10am–4.30pm. Closed Monday.

HAGI-YAKI (0869)

Hagi City, Yamaguchi Pref.

Kumaya Art Museum, 47 Imauono-tanacho, Hagi City. Tel 2-7547. Old Hagi ware and various art objects owned by the Kumaya family. Open 9am–5pm (December–February), 8.30–5.30pm (March–November).

TOBE-YAKI (0899)

Tobe-machi, Iyo-gun, Ehime Pref. Shikoku Island.

Tobe Ceramic Hall. Tel: 62-3900. Display and sale of Tobe-yaki ware created by 30 kilns.

Ehime Prefectural Products Association. Tel: 41-7584. Located in Ichibancho, Matsuyama City. Display and sale of Tobe-yaki ware, Iyo-Kasuri fabric, lacquer ware and other products of the prefecture. Open 8.30am–5pm. Closed Saturday afternoon, Sunday and national holidays.

Umeno Seitojo Workshop. Tel: 62-2311. You can try your hand in the workshop and observe Tobe-yaki ware on display. Open 8am–5pm. Closed Monday and second Sunday.

KOISHIWARA-YAKI AND TAKATORI-YAKI (0946)

Koishiwara-mura, Asakura-gun, Fukuoku Pref. Tel: 74-2311. 40 kilns are in the village. Almost all of them can be observed.

Koishiwara Potteries Hall. Tel: 74-2138. Display of Koshiwara ware. Open 9am–5pm. Closed Monday.

Takatori Seizan Kiln. Tel: 74-2045. Located in Kamatoko, Oaza-Tsuzumi. Open 8am–5pm. Open all year.

Takatori Hassen Kiln. Tel: 74-2211. Located in Sarayama, Koishiwara-mura. Open 8am–5pm.

ONTA-YAKI (ONDA-YAKI) (0973)

Motoecho, Hita City, Oita Pref. Kyushu.

Onda Potteries Hall. Display of Onda-yaki ware. Open 9am–5pm. Closed on 15th every month.

Sakamoto Haruzo Kiln. tel: 29-2405.

Sakamoto Shigeki Kiln. tel: 29-2404.

KARATSU-YAKI (0955)

Karatsu City, Saga Pref. Kyushu. Tel: 72-9111.

Karatsu Castle Donjon, 8-1 Higashi-Jonai, Karatsu City. Tel: 72-5697. Old Karatsu ware and local archaeological material are on display. Open 9am–5pm.

Nakazato Taroemon Kiln. Tel: 72-8171. Only the exhibition hall can be observed. Located in Choda, Karatsu City. Open 8.30am–5.30pm.

Ochanomizu Kiln. Tel: 72-6513. Located in Kami-Koda, Karatsu City. Visitors can make hand-molded earthenware. Open 9.30am–5.30pm. Closed Monday.

IMARI-YAKI (0955)

Okawauchiyama, Imari City, Saga Pref., Kyushu. Tel: 23-2111.

Imari Arita Ceramics Hall. Tel: 22-6333. Display of Imari and Arita wares. Open 9am–5pm. Closed Monday.

Imari Ceramics Hall. Tel: 23-7293. Located where the Imari Arita Ceramics Hall is. Display and sale of Imari ware. Open 9am–5pm.

ARITA-YAKI (0955)

Arita-machi, Nishi-Matsuura-gun, Saga Pref., Kyushu. Tel: 43-2101. 150 kilns in the town.

Arita Ceramics Museum. Tel: 42-3372. Display of local ceramics and documents and a large number of shards excavated at the kiln sites in the region. Open 9am–4.30pm. Closed Monday and National holidays.

Arita Folk History Museum. Tel: 43-2678. Located in Arita-machi, Nishi-Matsuura-gun. Display of old Imari, other ceramics and their documents of the region. Open 9am–4.30pm. Closed Monday.

Imaemon Kiln. Tel: 43-2267. Visitors

can only observe Imaemon Gallery, across from the Imaemon Kiln, which displays Nabeshima and Imari wares. Open 8am–5pm. Closed on 1st Sunday.
Kakiemon Kiln. Tel: 43-2267. Only the exhibition hall can be observed. Open 9am–5pm.

HASAMI-YAKI (0956)

Hasami-machi, Higashi-Sonoki-gun, Nagasaki Pref., Kyushu
Hasami Ceramics Hall. Tel: 85-2214. Located in Ishigo, Hasami-machi, **Higashi-Sonoki-gun**. Display and sale of Hasami ware. Open 9am–4.30pm. Closed Tuesday and national holidays.

KODA-YAKI & SHODAI-YAKI

Yatsushiro, Kumamoto & Arao Cities, Kuamoto Pref. Kilns are scattered in the Arao City.
Koda-yaki: There are four kilns. (0965)
Mr Saisuke Agano's Kiln. Tel: 38-0416. Located in Hinagu Higashi-machi, Yatsushiro City. Open 8am–6pm.
Mr Masae Sakai's Kiln. Tel: 33-2859. Kamikata-cho, Yatsushiro City. OPen 9am–5pm. Closed Sunday.
Shodai-yaki: There are seven kilns. (0968)
Shirohei Kiln. Tel: 62-0538. Located in Oshima, Arao City. Open 9am–5pm.
Sueyasu Kiln. Tel: 68-0058. Located in Fumoto-Kami, Arao City. Open 9am–5pm.
Kumamoto Prefectural Traditional Crafts Hall. Tel: 324-4930. Located in Chibajo-mcahi, Kumamoto City. Display of Koda and Shodai wares, bamboo wares and cutleries. Open 9am–5pm. Closed Monday.

TSUBOYA-YAKI (0988)

Tsuboyacho, Naha City, Okinawa Pref. Kobashigawa Seitojo Workshop. 1-28027, Tsuboya, Naha City. Tel: 53-4617.
Aragaki Seitojo Workshop, 1-21-23 Tsuboyacho, Naha City. Tel: 63-1107. Tsuboya Pottery Cooperative Union. Tel: 66-3284. To visit the workshops listed above, please contact the union first. Information on kilns can be obtained here.
Tsuboya Pottery Hall, 1-21-14 Tsuboya, Naha City. Tel: 66-3284. Display and sale of Tsuboya ware. Open 9am–6pm.
Okinawa Prefectural Museum. Tsuboya ware, Bingata dyed goods, paintings, etc are exhibited. Open 9am–4.30pm. Closed Monday and national holidays.

Galleries

There are art galleries all over the Ginza area and other parts of Tokyo, but below are four well-known ones that almost always hold interesting shows.
Kaneko Art Gallery, Mitsunari Building, 3-7-13 Kyobashi, Chuo-ku, tel: (03) 3564-0455. 11am–6.30pm. Closed Sundays and public holidays.
Maruzen Gallery, 2-3-10 Nihombashi, Chuo-ku, tel: (03) 3272-7211. 10am–6.30pm. Closed Sundays.
NichidoGallery, 7-4-12 Ginza, Chuo-ku, tel: (03) 3571-2553. 10am–7.30pm daily.
Parco Gallery, Parco Part 1, Udagawacho, Shibuya-ku, tel: (03) 3477-5781. 10am–8.30pm daily.

Theaters and Concerts

Bunkamura, 2-24-1 Dogenzaka, Shibuya-ku 150. Tel: Info: (03) 3477 3244, tickets: (03) 3477 9999.
Hibiya Kokaido (public hall), 1-3 Hibiya-koen, Chiyoda-ku. Tel: (03) 3591-6388.
Kabuki-za (kabuki), 4-12-15 Ginza, Chuo-ku. Tel: (03) 3541-3131.
Kanze Nogakudo (noh), 1-16-4 Shoto, Shibuya-ku. Tel: (03) 3469-5241.
Kinokuniya Hall (Japanese drama), 3-17-7 Shinjuku, Shinjuku-ku. Tel: (03) 3354-0141.
Kokuritsu Gekijo (contemporary Japanese drama), 4-1 Hayatocho, Chiyoda-ku. Tel: (03) 3265-7411.
Kosei Nenkin Hall, 5-3-1 Shinjuku, Shinjuku-ku. Tel: (03) 3356-1111.
Meijiza (historical Japanese drama), 2-31-1 Hamacho, Nihombashi, Chuo-ku. Tel: (03) 3660-3939.
National Theater Nogakudo (noh), 4-18-1 Sendagaya, Shibuya-ku. Tel: (03) 3423-1331.
NHK Hall (classical), 2-1 Jinan, Shibuya-ku. Tel: (03) 3465-1111.
Nihon Budokan, 2-3 Kitanomaru Koen, Chiyoda-ku. Tel: (03) 3216-0781.
Nissei Gekijo, 1-1-1 Yurakucho, Chiyoda-ku. Tel: (03) 3503-3111.
Shibuya Kokaido, 1-1 Udagawacho, Shibuya-ku. Tel: (03) 3463-5001.
Suehirotei (rakugo), 3-6-12 Shinjuku, Shinjuku-ku. Tel: (03) 3351-2974.
Sunshine Gekijo (Japanese versions of Broadway hits), Sunshine City Bunka Kaikan, 3-1-4 Higashi-Ikebukuro, Toshima-ku. Tel: (03) 3987-5281.
Suntory Hall (classical), 1-13-1 Akasaka, Minato-ku. Tel: (03) 3505-1001.
Teikoku Gekijo (Imperial Theater), 3-1-1 Marunouchi, Chiyoda-ku. Tel: (03) 3213-7221.
The Tokyo Globe (Shakespeare/opera), 3-1-2 Hyakunincho, Shinjuku-ku. Tel: (03) 3360-1151.
Tokyo Bunka Kaikan (classical/opera), 5-45 Ueno Park, Taito-ku. Tel: (03) 3828-2111.
Tokyo Dome (Big Egg), 1-3 Koraku, Bunkyo-ku. Tel: (03) 3811-2111.
Tokyo Takarazuka Gekijo (female revue), 1-1-3 Yurakucho, Chiyoda-ku. Tel: (03) 3591-1711.

Tea Ceremony (in English)

Imperial Hotel (Toko-an), 1-1-1 Uchisaiwai-cho, Chiyoda-ku, Tokyo. (4F the Main Wing). Tel: (03) 3504-1111. Near Hibiya Station on Hibiya, Chiyoda, or Toei Mita Line. Open 10am–4pm. Closed on Sunday and holidays. Fee, 20-min. participation periods. Advanced reservation is required.
Hotel Okura (Chosho-an), 2-10-4 Toranomon, Minato-ku, Tokyo. (7F of the Main Bldg.). Tel: (03) 3582-0111. Near Toranomon Station on Ginza Line or Kamiyacho Station on Hibiya Line. Open daily 11am–5pm. Fee, 20–30-min. participation periods. Advanced reservation is required.
Hotel New Otani, 4-1 Kioi-cho, Chiyoda-ku, Tokyo. (7F of Tower Bldg.). Tel: (03) 3265-1111, ext. 2443. Near Akasaka-mitsuke Station on Ginza or Marunouchi Line. Open Thursday, Friday and Saturday 11am–noon, 1–4pm. Fee, 15–20-min. participation periods. No reservation is needed if guests total less than 5 or 6.
Chado Kaikan, 3-39-17 Takadanobaba, Shinjuku-ku, Tokyo. Tel: (03) 3361-2446. 15-minute walk from Takadanobaba Station or take a bus for Otakibashi-Shako to Takadanobaba 4-chome stop. Open Monday–Thursday 10.30am–2.30pm. Closed on holidays. Fee, 1-hour participation periods. Advanced reservation is required.
Kenkyusha Nihongo Center, 1-2 Kagurazaka, Shinjuku-ku, Tokyo. Tel: (03) 5261-8940. 5-min. walk from the west exit of Iidabashi Station on JR Sobu Line, or the B-3 exit of Iidabashi Station on Yurakucho or Tozai Line.

Open Monday 6–8pm; Friday 2–4pm or 6–8pm. Fee, 2-hour participation periods. Advanced reservation is required. **Happoen** (Muan), 1-1-6 Shiroganedai, Minato-ku, Tokyo. Tel: (03) 3443-3111. 15-min. walk from Meguro Station on JR Yamanote Line. Open daily, when tour groups participate in the tea ceremony 10am–6pm. Only up to 1 or 2 persons can join the tea ceremony with them. Tea is served to the guests seated on chairs and not on tatami. Fee, 30-min. participation periods. Private tea ceremony is available (¥20,000 + ¥800 X the number of persons).

Imperial Palace Visits

Any visit to the Imperial residence is an honor and a privilege. Only the grounds of Tokyo's Imperial Palace are opened to the public on January 2 and December 23, Emperor Akihito's birthday, a national holiday (Tenno Tanjobi). The Imperial Palace and villas in Kyoto are open by appointment only, through the Imperial Household Agency.

To see the **Kyoto Imperial Palace, Shugakuin Imperial Villa**, or **Katsura Imperial Villa**, apply for permission at the Imperial Household Agency office on the Palace grounds in Kyoto. Admission to the Palace and villas is free. For palace tours, you must apply – with passport – 30 minutes before tour times: 10am and 2pm weekdays and Saturday morning. (The palace is closed on Sundays and national holidays.) While the palace is open on Saturday mornings, the agency office is closed, so you need to apply on weekdays. Only overseas visitors can apply and visit on the same day. Japanese must apply months in advance or wait for the week in April and October when the palace is open to the general public – a good time to avoid visiting. Palace tours begin at Seisho gate in the middle of the western wall and take about an hour; most, but not all, are conducted in English, but an English-language pamphlet is provided. You must also apply to the same office for visits to either of the imperial villas; this can normally be done a few days before your intended visit. Some restrictions do apply on children, so check with the Imperial Household Agency office before your visit. Your hotel can be helpful in pre-planning any visit. It might seem like a lot of work, but then, how many imperial residences have you ever visited?

Imperial Household Agency, Kyoto Palace – Kyoto Gosho, 3 Kyoto Gyoen, Kamigyo-Ku, Kyoto 602. Tel: (075) 211-1215. Office hours are 9am to 4.30pm weekdays only.

Festivals

General

Festivals, or matsuri seem to be happening at any given time somewhere in Tokyo, and indeed have been an important part of Japanese life for hundreds of years. Many of the festivals have their roots in the long history of Japan's agricultural society. In today's ever modernizing Japan, they are one of the few occasions when the Japanese can dress up and live a nostalgic past. Below is a short list of the main national holidays and the most important festivals. For information on upcoming events going on during any particular week or month, please consult TIC or any of the tourist publications.

January

The first ***sumo*** tournament of the year, ***Hatsubasho***, is held for fifteen days at the **Kokugikan** in mid January.

February

On the 3rd is ***Setsubun***, the traditional bean throwing ceremony that is meant to purify the home of evil. Roasted beans are scattered from the inside of the house to the outside while people shout, *"Oni wa soto"* (Devils, go out!), and from the outside of the home to the inside while *"Fuku wa uchi"* (good luck, come in) is shouted. The same ceremony is also held at temples and shrines.

March

On the 3rd of the month is ***Hina Matsuri*** (Girl's Day), a festival for little girls. Small *Hina* dolls, representing imperial court figures, are displayed at home and in several public places.

April

From early to mid April is ***Ohanami*** (Cherry Blossom viewing), one of the important spring rites. People love to turn out and picnic, drink *sake* and sing songs under the pink blossoms.

On the 8th is ***Hana Matsuri*** (Birthday of Buddha), when commemorative services are held at various temples such as **Gokokuji Temple, Sensoji Temple, Zojoji Temple and Hommonji Temple**.

May

In mid May, the ***Natsubasho*** (summer ***sumo*** tournament) is held for fifteen days at the **Kokugikan**.

On the 3rd Sat. and Sun. the ***Sanja Matsuri*** is held. This is one of the big *Edo* festivals honoring the three fishermen who found the image of *Kannon* in the river. The **Asakusa Shrine** is a great place to go at this time to see the dancing, music and many portable shrines.

June

On the second Sunday is ***Torigoe Jinja Taisai***, a night time festival, when the biggest and heaviest portable shrine in Tokyo is carried through the streets by lantern light. It all happens at the **Torigoe Shrine**.

From the 10th to the 16th is ***Sanno Sai***, another big *Edo* festival featuring a *gyoretsu* (people parading in traditional costumes) on Saturday at the **Hie Shrine**.

July

From the 6th to the 8th is the ***Asagao Ichi*** (Morning Glory Fair), when over one hundred merchants set up stalls selling the morning flower at **Iriya Kishibojin**.

On the 7th is the ***Tanabata Matsuri***, a festival celebrating the only day of the year when, according to the legend, the Weaver Princess (Vega) and her lover the Cowherder (Altair) can cross the Milky Way to meet. People write their wishes on pieces of colored paper, hang them on bamboo branches, and then float them down a river the next day.

On the 9th and 10th is the ***Hozuki Ichi*** (Ground Cherry Fair) at **Sensoji**

Temple from early morning to midnight. A visit to this temple on the 10th is meant to be equal to 46,000 visits at other times.

On the last Saturday of July, the ***Sumidagawa Hanabi Taikai*** (Sumida River Fireworks) is held. This is the biggest fireworks display in Tokyo, and the best places to watch the display is between the **Kototoi** and **Shirahige bridges**, or at the **Komagata Bridge**.

August

Between the 13th and the 16th is the ***Obon*** festival, when people return to their hometowns to clean up the graves and offer prayers to the souls of departed ancestors. The traditional ***Bon Odori*** folk dances are held all over around this time.

October

From mid to late October is Chrysanthemum viewing time. There are flower displays dotted around the cities.

November

The 15th is ***Shichi-Go-San*** (Three-Five-Seven), a ceremony for 5-year-old boys and 3- and 7-year-old girls. The children usually dress up in *kimono* and are taken to visit a shrine.

December

The 14th is ***Gishi Sai***, a memorial service for the famous *47 Ronin* who, on this day in 1702, avenged the death of their master and later committed ritual suicide. They are buried at the **Sengakuji Temple** where the service is held.

On the 31st at the stroke of midnight, every temple bell throughout the country begins to toll. The bells toll 108 times representing the 108 evil human passions. This is called ***Joya no Kane***, and the general public is allowed to strike the bells at various temples.

Shopping

Shopping Areas

Japan is a very expensive place to shop, but there are still bargains to be had if you look them up. The quality of Japanese products is well known, and there are some items which can only be bought in Japan. Certain areas promote only certain kinds of merchandise, which means that some domestic travel is involved for the serious shopper.

Following is a guide to the main shopping attractions in the cities and other areas throughout Japan.

In and Around Tokyo

Akihabara: The electronic jungle of the world featuring hundreds of discount stores.

Aoyama: High-class fashion boutiques.

Asakusa: Traditional Japanese toys, souvenirs, workmen's clothes, etc.

Ginza: The most expensive shopping center. Several major department stores are located here, such as **Hankyu**, **Matsuya**, **Matsuzakaya**, **Mitsukoshi**, **Printemps**, **Seibu** and **Wako**, and exclusive boutiques. Also some traditional Japanese goods stores.

Harajuku: Another fashion area, though mostly geared to the young, which makes shopping relatively cheap. Several antique shops, and **Kiddyland** for the kids.

Hibiya: Mostly antique shops, jewelry shops, and art galleries.

Kanda and **Jimbocho:** Many second-hand bookstores.

Nihombashi: A good place to pick up traditional craft work. Two of Japan's oldest department stores, **Mitsukoshi** and **Takashi-maya** are located here.

Roppongi: Several antique shops in the area, the **Axis** design building which features interior design as its main theme, and Seibu's **Wave** building which specializes in audio-visual equipment.

Shibuya: A good place to start with, Shibuya has a little bit of everything. **Tokyu Hands** is a must to visit; probably the most complete do-it-yourself department store in the world. Also here are the **Seibu**, **Tokyu** and **Marui** departments stores, the **Parco** "fashion buildings" besides the hundreds of small boutiques geared to young shoppers.

Shinjuku: Several big camera and electronic discount stores such as **Yodobashi** and **Sakuraya**. Also, **Isetan** and **Marui** department stores.

Ueno: Ameyoko is good for cheap food, cosmetics, clothing and toys. One of the few open markets in Tokyo. The shops in the back streets sell traditional Japanese goods.

ANTIQUES

In most of the shops listed here, the staff speak English and are helpful. Watch out for badly restored pieces that have been given a quick coat of glossy lacquer and sold like new at steep prices.

Antique Gallery Kikori, Hanae Mori Building, B1, 3-6-1 Kita Aoyama, Minato-ku. Tel: (03) 3407-9363. Small but interesting selection of *tansu* and other items.

Antique Gallery Meguro, Stork Building, 2nd Fl, 2-24-18 Kamiosaki, Shinagawa-ku. Tel: (03) 3493-1971. Antique market of sorts covering 740 sq. meters (885 sq. yards) that houses several small antique shops.

Edo Antiques, 2-21-12 Akasaka, Minato-ku. Tel: (03) 3584-5280. Large selection of *tansu* and *hibachi*.

Hasabe-ya Antiques, 1-5-24 Azabu Juban, Minato-ku, tel: (03) 3401-9998

Harumi Antiques, 9-6-14 Akasaka, Minato-ku. Tel: (03) 3403-1043. Mostly *tansu* that have been restored, but some unrestored pieces can be purchased.

Japan Old Folkcraft and Antique Center (Tokyo Komingu Kotto-kan), 3-9-5 Minami Ikebukuro, Toshima-ku. Tel: (03) 3980-8228. 35 dealers covering 600 sq. meters (718 sq. yards) and displaying various antique items.

Oriental Bazaar, 5-9-13 Jingæmae,

Shibuya-ku. Tel: (03) 3400-3933. Apart from antiques, it is also a nice place to browse and pick up traditional Japanese toys, paper (*washi*), *kimono*, etc.

Ceramics

Besides workshops, department stores are the best places for Japanese ceramics offered at reasonable prices. On back streets, small shops also sell ceramics but prices are higher.

Iseryu Shoten, 3-8-2 Ningyocho, Nihombashi, Chuo-ku, tel: (03) 3661-4820. Closed Sundays and holidays.

Saga Toen, 2-13-13 Nishi Azabu, Minato-ku, tel: (03) 3400-3682.

Tachikichi & Co. Ltd, 6-13 Ginza, Chuo-ku, tel: (03) 3571-2924.

Department Stores

Daimaru, 1-9-1 Marunouchi, Chiyoda-ku, tel: (03) 3212-8011. Closed Thursdays.

Isetan, 3-14-1 Shinjuku, Shinjuku-ku, tel: (03) 3352-1111. Closed Wednesdays.

Marui, 3-30-16 Shinjuku, Shinjuku-ku, tel: (03) 3354-0101. 10.30am–7.30pm. Closed 2nd or 3rd Wednesday.

Matsuya, 1-4-1 Hanakawado, Taito-ku, tel: (03) 3842-1111. Closed Thursdays.

Matsuzakaya, 3-29-5 Ueno, Taito-ku, tel: (03) 3832-1111.

Mitsukoshi, 1-7-4 Muromachi, Nihombashi, Chuo-ku, tel: (03) 3241-3311. Closed Mondays.

Printemps, 3-2-1 Ginza, Chuo-ku, tel: (03) 3567-0077. 10am–7pm. Closed Wednesdays.

Seibu (Main Store), 1-28-1 Minami Ikebukuro, Toshima-ku, tel: (03) 3981-0111. Closed Thursdays.

Sogo, 1-11-1 Yurakucho, Chiyoda-ku, tel: (03) 3284-6711. Closed Tuesdays.

Takashimaya, 2-4-1 Nihombashi, Chuo-ku, tel: (03) 3211-4111. Closed Wednesdays.

Tokyu, 2-24-1 Dogenzaka, Shibuya-ku, tel: (03) 3477-3111. Closed Thursdays.

Japanese Paper (*Washi*)

Haibara, 2-7-6 Nihombashi, Chuo-ku, tel: (03) 3272-3801. Closed Sundays and holidays.

Isetasu, 2-18-9 Yanaka, Taito-ku, tel: (03) 3823-1453.

Kurodaya, 1-2-11 Asakusa, Taito-ku, tel: (03) 3845-3830. Closed Mondays.

Kyækyodo, 5-7-4 Ginza, Chuo-ku, tel: (03) 3571-4429.

Ozu Shoten, 2-6-3 Nihombashi Honcho, Chuo-ku, tel: (03) 3663-8788. Closed on Sundays

Washikobo, 1-8-10 Nishi Azabu, Minato-ku, tel: (03) 3405-1841. Closed Sundays and public holidays.

Kimonos (Antique)

These shops specialize in antique *kimono, obi,* traditional blue and white textiles, *furoshiki, hanten,* etc. Prices from ¥1,000 up.

Flea markets (see list under *Flea Markets*) also sell them, and you can usually pick up very beautiful old *kimono* and *obi* in good condition.

Ayahata, 2-21-2 Akasaka, Minato-ku, tel: (03) 3582-9969. Closed Sundays and public holidays.

Hayashi Kimono, International Arcade, 1-7 Uchisaiwaicho, Chiyoda-ku, tel: (03) 3581-9826.

Ikeda, 5-22-11 Shiroganedai, Minato-ku, tel: (03) 3445-1269. Closed Sundays.

Konjaku Nishimura, Hanae Mori Building, B1, 3-6-1 Kita Aoyama, Minato-ku, tel: (03) 3498-1759. Closed Thursdays.

Lacquerware (*Shikki*)

Bushi, Axis Building, B1 5-17-1 Roppongi, Minato-ku, tel: (03) 3587-0317. Closed Mondays.

Heiando, 3-10-11 Nihombashi, Chuo-ku, tel: (03) 3272-2871. Closed Sundays and public holidays.

Inachu Japan, 1-5-2 Akasaka, Minato-ku, tel: (03) 3582-4451.

Kuroeya, Kuroeya Kokubu Building, 2nd Floor, 1-2-6 Nihombashi, Chuo-ku, tel: (03) 3271-3356. Closed Saturdays, Sundays and public holidays.

Musical Instruments

Bachi Ei Gakkiten *(Shamisen)*, 2-10-11 Ningyocho, Nihombashi, Chuo-ku, tel: (03) 3666-7263. Closed Sundays and holidays.

Kikuya Shamisen Ten *(Shamisen)*, 3-45-11 Yushima, Bunkyo-ku, tel: (03) 3831-4733. Closed Sundays and holidays.

Tsurukawa Gakki Honten *(Koto)*, 1-12-11 Kyobashi, Chuo-ku, tel: (03) 3561-1872. Closed Sundays and holidays.

Ishida Biwa Ten *(Biwa)*, 3-8-4 Toranomon, Minato-ku, tel: (03) 3431-6548. Closed Sundays and holidays.

Chikuyusha *(Shakuhachi)*, 3 Saneicho, Shinjuku-ku, tel: (03) 3351-1270. Closed Sundays and public holidays.

Miyamoto Unosuke Shoten (drums), 6-1-15 Asakusa, Taito-ku, tel: (03) 3874-4131. Closed Sundays and public holidays.

Paper Lanterns

Hanato, 2-25-6 Asakusa, Taito-ku, tel: (03) 3841-6411. 10am–9pm. Closed 2nd and 4th Tuesdays.

Kashiwaya, 2-3-13 Shintomi, Chuo-ku, tel: (03) 3551-1362. Closed Sundays.

Umbrellas (*Kasa*)

Hasegawa Hakimonoten, 2-4-4 Ueno, Taito-ku, tel: (03) 3831-3933. Closed Sundays.

Iidaya, 1-31-1 Asakusa, Taito-ku, tel: (03) 3841-3644.

Woodblock Print (*Ukiyoe*)

Asakusa Okuramae Shobo, 3-10-12 Kuramae, Taito-ku, tel: (03) 3866-5894. Closed on Sundays, but will stay open for appointments. Specialist on books and prints on *Edo* and *sumo*.

Hara Shobo, 2-3 Jimbocho, Kanda, Chiyoda-ku, tel: (03) 3261-7444. All types of prints old and new, from the highest quality to a "bargain drawer." English is spoken here.

Matsushita Associates, Inc., 6-3-12 Minami Aoyama, Shibuya-ku, tel: (03) 3407-4966. Closed Sundays and public holidays.

Oya Shobo, 1-1 Kanda, Jimbocho, Chiyoda-ku, tel: (03) 3291-0062. Closed Sundays.

Sakai Kokodo Gallery, 1-2-14 Yurakucho, Chiyoda-ku, tel: (03) 3591-4678.

Bookstores

There are bookstores all over Tokyo, and it is quite acceptable to browse through the books and magazines in the shop without having to buy them, so don't feel guilty. In spite of the large number of bookstores, there are relatively few that specialize in English books. Below is a list of the major stores that stock foreign books and books on Japan. They are usually helpful when phoning about information on books in stock. Besides these places, you can also get foreign newspapers and magazines in most hotels.

Aoyama Book Center. Tel: (03) 3479-0479. Open daily 10–5.30am; Sunday and holidays 10am–10pm. 1 minute from Roppongi Station (Hibiya Line).
Kinokuniya, 3-17-7 Shinjuku, Shinjuku-ku. Tel: (03) 3354-0131. Open 10am–7pm. Closed 3rd Wednesday of each month. Foreign books on the 6th floor.
Libro (Ikebukuro Branch), 1-28-1 Minami Ikebukuro, Toshima-ku (Seibu Dept. SMA BIF, B2F). Tel: (03) 5992-8800. Open daily 10am–8pm, except Tuesday.
Maruzen, 2-3-10 Nihombashi, Chuo-ku. Tel: (03) 3272-7211. Open 10am–6pm. Closed Sunday. Foreign books on the 3rd floor.
Jena (pronounced "yena"), 5-6-1 Ginza, Chuo-ku. Tel: (03) 3571-2980. Weekdays 10.30am–7.50pm; Sunday 12.30–6.45pm. Closed holidays. Foreign books on the 3rd floor.
Sanseido, 1-1 Kanda Jimbocho, Chiyoda-ku. Tel: (03) 3233-3312. Open 10am–7.30pm. Closed Tuesday. Foreign books on 5th floor.
Kitazawa Shoten, 2-5-3 Kanda Jimbocho, Chiyoda-ku. Tel: (03) 3263-0011. Open 10am–6pm. Closed Sunday. Second-hand books on the 2nd floor, and English and American literature on the 1st floor.
Biblos, F1 Bldg, 4th Floor, 1-26-5 Takadanobaba, Shinjuku-ku. Tel: (03) 3200-4531. Open daily 10.30am–7.30pm; Sunday and holidays 11am–6.30pm. Closed 3rd Sunday of each month.
National Book Store, National Azabu Supermarket 2nd Floor, 4-5-2 Minami Azabu, Minato-ku. Tel: (03) 3442-3181. Open daily 9.30am–6.30pm.

Outside Tokyo

Within Tohoku

- **Matsushima**

Shiogama Suisan Nakaoroshi Ichiban; morning market.
Owariya, in front of Suigen-ji; wind bells.

- **Aomori**

Murata Kogei-sha, Shinmachi Dori; local crafts.

- **Morioka**

Kyabatake, near Minami Ohashi on the Kitagami River, daily from 5am; morning market.
Zaimoku-cho, every Saturday, April to November, 3–9pm; night market offering colorful array of items for sale.
Iwachu, Nanbu Tekki; local iron crafts.

- **Iizaka Spa**

Kodai Gangu, Nihonmatsu; local crafts.

On Hokkaido

- **Hakodate**

Chiaki-kan, in Horai-cho; handmade Japanese confections.

- **Noboribetsu**

Kagetsu Do, Hyotan Ame; Japanese candy, gifts and souvenirs.

- **Akan National Park**

Rakan, on Route 240; local crafts.
Akan Kohan Visitor Center; local crafts.

Within Kansai

- **Ise**

Akafuku Honten, near Ise Naiguu; Japanese confections, souvenirs.

- **Nara**

Ikeda Gankohdo; Nara fans.
Somekawa Hakurokuen; Nara dolls.

- **Kyoto**

Kawaramachi, main north-south street: **Matsuya,** Kawaramachi Dori, Kyoto dolls.
Kiyamachi (parallels the Takase River, north-south): **Murakami Ju-honten,** at the end of 4-jo Dori, Japanese pickles; **Tachibana Syokai,** antiques.
Teramachi (downtown arcade): **Ippodo,** tea and accessories; **Kyukyodo,** high-class Japanese stationery; **Miyawaki Baisen-an,** fans.
Shijyo, main east-west street: **Erizen,** kimono and accessories; **Ichihara Heibei Shoten,** chopsticks; **Morita Wash,** paper crafts.
Arashiyama: Ishikawa Taki no Mise, bamboo crafts.

- **Kobe**

Hon Takasagoya, Motomachi Dori 3-2-11; colorful gift items, souvenirs and Japanese confections.

In Southern Honshu

- **Himeji**

Azumadou, Kawahara Shoutengai; Japanese confections.

- **Hagi**

Ochadokoro, near Kikuya Yokocho; Japanese tea and confections.

On Shikoku

- **Tokushima**

Fujiya; Japanese confections.
Aigura, Nishishinmachi Arcade; local crafts.

- **Kochi**

Kitaura,Konyacho; dyed goods.
Tosa Mingei Ten; folk handicrafts.

On Kyushu

- **Nagasaki**

Art Hata, in Kajiya-cho; original Nagasaki dolls.

- **Beppu Spa**

Kishima; bamboo crafts.

- **Kagoshima**

Satsuma Glass Kogei, near Shuseikan; local glass crafts.

On Okinawa

- **Naha**

Hirugi, Keizairen Mingei Center 2F, Kokusai Dori; Ryukyuan dishes, dances; crafts for sale; in other words, a place to shop and eat.
Morita Sango no Mise, Kokusai Dori; Okinawan coral jewelry.

- **Okinawa City**

Chuo Park Avenue, more than 100 shops and restaurants.

- **Ishigaki**

Mineya; fabrics.

- **Taketomi**

Tomokura; local crafts.

- **Iriomote**

Shoutokuan; accessories.

Sports and Leisure

Spectator Sports

Sumo Tournaments

Six tournaments annually, each lasting for 15 days, are held in January, May and September in Tokyo, in March in Osaka, in July in Nagoya, and in November in Fukuoka. During the tournament, matches are televised daily from 4–6pm. Matches by junior wrestlers begin at about 10am; by senior wrestlers at 3pm on the first and the last days, and at 3.30pm on other days.

Tokyo

January, May and September: Kokugikan Sumo Hall, 1-3-28 Yokoami, Sumida-ku, Tokyo. Tel: (03) 3623-5111. Near JR Ryogoku Station.

Osaka

March: Osaka Furitsu Taiikukaikan (Osaka Prefectural Gymnasium), 3-4-36 Namba Naka, Naniwa-ku, Osaka. Tel: (06) 631-0121. Near Namba subway station.

Nagoya

July: Aichi Ken Taiikukan (Aichi Prefectural Gymnasium), 1-1 Ninomaru, Naka-ku, Nagoya. Tel: (052) 971-2516. 15 minute by car from Nagoya Station. Tickets are sold from 9am. Competition starts from 9.20am.

Fukuoka

November: Fukuoka Kokusai Center Sogo Hall, 2-2 Chikuko-Honcho, Hakata-ku, Fukuoka. Tel: (092) 272-1111.

Admission for Tokyo: Chair Seat A ¥7,500; Chair Seat B ¥5,500; Chair Seat C ¥3,000; Unreserved Seat Y1,500.

Tickets for the Tokyo tournaments are sold at the office of the Nihon Sumo Kyokai at Kokugikan Sumo Hall in Ryogoku as well as at ticketing bureaus in downtown Tokyo. *Very difficult to obtain tickets.*

Ticketing Bureaus

Ginza

Kyukyodo. Tel: (03) 3571-0401. Open daily.

Matsuya Dept. Store. Tel: (03) 3567-8888. Closed on Tuesday.

Shinjuku

Isetan Dept. Store. Tel: (03) 3352-1111. Closed on Wednesday.

Keio Dept. Store. Tel: (03) 3343-1801. Open daily except New Year holidays.

Shibuya

Seibu Dept. Store. Tel: (03) 3462-0111. Closed on Wednesday.

Ikebukuro

Seibu Dept. Store. Tel: (03) 3981-0052. Closed on Tuesday.

Tobu Dept. Store. Tel: (03) 3981-2211. Closed on Wednesday.

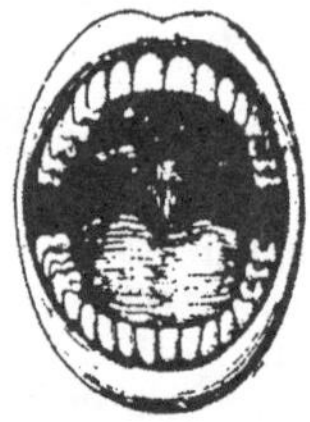

Language

General

Although more and more foreigners are making the effort to learn Japanese, and learn it to a high degree of fluency, few Japanese expect foreigners to be able to speak their language. Unfortunately, this lack of confidence in the ability of others to speak their language is not matched by a high level of proficiency in foreign languages on the part of the Japanese themselves. The number who can communicate effectively in any foreign language is very small, in spite of the fact that the majority of them have studied English for at least six years.

However, it is rare for the foreign visitor to Japan to be in a situation where absolutely nobody can be found to help out. Indeed, some Japanese will go to extraordinary lengths to help the bewildered tourist, using a curious blend of smiles, gestures and Japanese together with the odd recognizable word of English as a fairly effective means of communication. Simply looking helpless will often be enough to attract assistance.

The visitor will have few language problems within the confines of airports and the major Western-style hotels, but outside these the going can get tough for those who are unescorted. Quite apart from being unable to communicate verbally, the hapless visitor will also have the disconcerting experience of being almost totally illiterate.

The written language is made up of three different sets of characters: two simple homegrown syllabaries, *hiragana* and *katakana,* consisting of forty-six characters each; and the much more formidable Chinese ideograms, *kanji.* Knowledge of just under two thousand of these is necessary to read a daily newspaper. While the expenditure of the enormous effort required to memorize this number of kanji (it takes the Japanese most of their school career to do so) is clearly unjustifiable for those with only a passing interest in the language, a few hours spent learning the two syllabaries (on the plane trip to Japan, for example) would not be time completely wasted for those who can afford it. Hiragana can be useful for identifying which station your train has stopped at; the platforms are plastered with hiragana versions of the station name so that children who have not yet learned kanji can see where they are. Station names are usually (but not always) posted in Roman script as well, but not always as obviously. Katakana is useful in that it is used to transliterate foreign words. Western-style restaurants often simply list the foreign names for the dishes on their menus in katakana. Listed in the table below are the two syllabaries.

Pronunciation: With its small number of simple and unvarying vowel sounds, the pronunciation of Japanese should be easy for those who speak Western languages, which are rich in vowel sounds. The consonants should also present few problems (with the possible exception of l/r, ts and f – the only way to learn these is to have someone demonstrate them for you), and Japanese has nothing like the dreaded tonal system of Chinese to frustrate the student.

Vowels have but one sound, much like Spanish. Don't be sloppy with their pronunciations.

a – between fat and the u in but
e – like the e in egg
i – like the i in ink *
o – like the o in orange
u – like the u in butcher *

* When they occur in the middle of words, i and u are often almost silent. For example, *Takeshita* is really pronounced *Takesh'ta* while *sukiyaki* sounds more like *s'kiyaki.*

In spite of the seemingly simple pronunciation of Japanese, a lot of foreigners manage to mangle the language into a form which is almost impossible for the native speaker to understand. It is mainly intonation that is responsible for this. It would be fallacious to claim that the Japanese language has no rise and fall in pitch – just listen to a group of schoolgirls conversing on the train to confirm this

– but it is certainly "flatter" in character than Western languages.

It is important to avoid stressing syllables within words; whereas an English speaker would naturally stress either the second or third syllable of *Hiroshima*, for example, in Japanese the four syllables should be stressed equally. Another problem lies in long (actually double) vowel sounds. These are often indicated by a line above the vowel, or simply by a double vowel, e.g. *Iidabashi*. To pronounce these long vowels properly, it is simply necessary to give the vowel sound double length. However, many publications, including this book and most English newspapers in Japan, ignore these long double vowels.

The following list is designed simply to start you off in Japanese. Several courses and lengthy phrase books are available for those who wish to study the language more deeply.

Greetings

Good morning/*Ohayo gozaimasu*
Hello (afternoon)/*Konnichiwa*
Good evening/*Kombanwa*
Good night/*Oyasumi nasai*
Goodbye/*Sayonara (Shitsure shimasu* for formal occasions)
How do you do?/*Hajime mashite?*
How are you?/*Ogenki desuka?*
It's good to see you again./*Shibaraku desu* (informally,*domo* is enough.)
My name is.../*...to moshimasu*
I'm American/*Amerika-jin desu*
I'm British/*Igirisu-jin desu*
I'm Australian/*Osturaraia-jin desu*
I'm Canadian/*Kanada-jin desu*

Asking for Directions

Excuse me, where is the **toilet**?
Sumimasen. ***Toire*** *wa doko desu ka?*
Excuse me, is there a **post office** near here?
Sumimasen. Kono chikaku ni, ***yubinkyoku*** *wa arimasu-ka?*
Bakery/*Pan-ya*
Meat shop/*Niku-ya*
Fish market/*Sakana-ya*
Greengrocer's/*Yao-ya*
Stationery store/*Bumbogu-ya*
Pharmacy/*Kusuri-ya*
Barber shop/*Toko-ya*
Bookshop/*Hon-ya*
Supermarket/*Supa-Maketto*
Department store/*Depato*
Restaurant/*Restoran*
Hotel/*Hoteru*
Station/*Eki*
Taxi stand/*Takushii noriba*
Bank/*Ginko*
Hospital/*Byoin*
Police Station/*Koban*

Out Shopping

This one/*Kore*
That one (near the other person)/*Sore*
That one (near neither of you)/*Are*
Do you have...?/*...(wa) arimasu-ka?*
Could you show me that one please?
Sore o misete kudasai.
How much is it?/*Ikura desu-ka?*
Don't you have anything cheaper?
Mo sukoshi yasui no arimasen-ka?
Can I try it on?
Shichaku shite mo ii desu-ka?
Do you accept (credit) cards?
(Kurjitto) kado tsukaemasu-ka?
I'll take this./*Kore o kudasai.*
Three of these, please.
Kore o mittsu kudasai.

Boarding the Train

Ticket (office)/*Kippu (uriba)*
A single ticket to Sendai, please.
Sendai made, katamichi ichi-mae kudasai.
Two returns to Nikko, please.
Nikko made, ofuku ni-mae kudasai.
Reserved seat/*Shitei seki*
Unreserved seat/*Jiyuseki*
First class car/*Guriin* (Green) *sha*
Which platform does the train for Nagoya leave from?
Nagoya yuki wa namban sen desuka?
Thank you (very much)/*(Domo) arigato gozaimasu* (informally, *domo* is enough)
Don't mention it./*Doitashimashite*
Thanks for the meal.
Gochisosama deshita.
Here you are./*Dozo*
After you./*Dozo*
Sure, go ahead./*Dozo* (in answer to "May I...?")

Days/Time

(On) Sunday/*Nichi-yobi (ni)*
(Next) Monday/*(Raishu no) Getsu-yobi*
(Last) Tuesday/*(Senshu no) Ka-yobi*
(Every) Wednesday/*(Maishu) Sui-yobi*
(This) Thursday/*(Konshu no) Moku-yobi*
Friday/*Kin-yobi*
Saturday/*Do-yobi*
Yesterday/*Kino*
Today/*Kyo*
This morning/*Kesa*
This evening/*Konya*
Tomorrow/*Ashita*
What time is it?/*Nan-ji desu ka?*

In the Restaurant

Water/*Mizu*
Beef/*Gyuniku*
Pork/*Butaniku*
Chicken/*Toriniku*
Fish/*Sakana*
Beer/*Biiru*
Grilled/*Yaite*
Boiled/*Nite*
Fried/*Itamete*
Raw/*Nama*

Numbers

Counting is very complicated in Japanese! Counting up to ten on their fingers, the Japanese will go: *ichi, ni, san, shi (yon), go, roku, shichi* (or *nana*), *hachi, ku* (or *kyu*), *ju*. If they are counting bottles, they will go: *ip-pon, ni-hon, sam-bon, yon-hon,go-hon, roppon, nana-hon, hap-pon, kyu-hon, juppon*. Depending on what is being counted, the suffix will change. You will be fairly safe with numbers that don't need suffixes:

One/*Hitotsu*
Two/*Futatsu*
Three/*Mittsu*
Four/*Yottsu*
Five/*Itsutsu*
Six/*Muttsu*
Seven/*Nanatsu*
Eight/*Yattsu*
Nine/*Kokonotsu*
Ten/*To*

If you want five of something, simply point at it and say, *Itsutsu kudasai.*

Studying Japanese

As with most languages, the best way to learn Japanese is in context with the culture and society, and with native speakers as teachers. Those living in urban areas of Japan can take regularly-scheduled classes at their leisure – schools are everywhere in Tokyo, for example – mixing in their studies with work and play.

For those who don't live in Japan, but want to seriously study Japanese, there is a superb option, quite unique and worth considering.

The **Shibusawa International School** offers intensive (6 hours daily), live-in Japanese language studies at an elegant old estate in the town of Fukaya, outside of Tokyo. A student finishing a single three-month term will have a good foundation in conversational grammar, and some basic reading and writing skills. After six months, enough competence is obtained to do most anything, whether working in a Tokyo office or bumming around the country on tour.

There are four terms per calendar year. The full course is five terms, or 15 months. Many people come for six months or a year, then go on their way. Others come for three months at a time, returning again to continue the full course, or to brush up. Students come from all over the world, and at any one time, there are half a dozen nationalities represented among the 20–30 students attending. Classes are small, three to ten per class.

The school has modern private rooms or group dormitory rooms, with laundry and, yes, western toilet and shower facilities. In addition to the language classes, there are aikido, calligraphy, and culture classes.

It is in the country, half an hour by bicycle (which the school provides) or ten minutes by taxi to the train station. From there, it's a little over an hour to downtown Tokyo. Some may find the isolation a bit too much, but it helps keep one's mind on the studies. The school has a television room and a cafeteria with a delicious menu of Japanese, Asian and western meals.

The school is part of the legacy of Shibusawa Eiichi, who was pivotal in bringing Japan into the modern economic and industrial world at the turn of the century. His great-granddaughter, Shibusawa Takako, started the school on a family estate in 1985.

Prices are actually on the economical side, considering the amount of language studies offered and the excellent facilities. Per month, fees include: tuition, ¥60,000; private room, ¥20,000; meals, 3/day, ¥54,000 or pro-rated depending on meals consumed. It's probably one of the best bargains in the country, and unquestionably time well spent.

Shibusawa International School, Tokyo Office, 3-5-4 Shiba-koen, Minato-ku, Tokyo 105, tel: (03) 3433-5984, fax: (03) 3432-0561.

Further Reading

History and Culture

Barr, Pat. ***The Coming of the Barbarians: A Story of Western Settlement in Japan 1853–1870***. Penguin Books. 1988.

Borton, Hugh. ***Japan's Modern Century***. The Ronald Press. 1955.

Dunn, Charles J. ***Everyday Life in Traditional Japan***. Charles E. Tuttle Company, Ltd. 1987.

Frederic, Louis. (Translated from the French by Eileen M. Lowe) ***Daily Life in Japan at the Time of the Samurai***. Charles E. Tuttle. 1972.

Fukutake, Tadashi. ***The Japanese Social Structure: Its Evolution in the Modern Century*** (2nd ed.). University of Tokyo Press. 1989.

Kaempfer, Englebert. ***The History of Japan***. (3 volumes). James MacLehose and Sons. 1906.

Meech-Pekarik, Julia. ***The World of the Meiji Print: Impressions of the Meiji Print***. Weatherhill. 1986.

Neary, Ian. ***Political Protest and Social Control in Prewar Japan: The Origins of Buraku Liberation***. Manchester University Press. 1989.

Reischauer, Edwin O. & Fairbank, John K. ***East Asia: The Great Tradition***. Houghton Mifflin Co. 1960.

Sansom, Sir George B. *Japan*, ***A Short Cultural History***. Appleton-Century-Crofts, Inc. 1943.

Sansom, Sir George B. ***The Western World and Japan***. Alfred A. Knopf, Inc. 1950.

Schiffer, Robert L. (Text). Cooke, Jerry (Photographs). ***The Exploding City***. St Martin's Press. 1989.

Seidensticker, Edward. ***Low City, High City: Tokyo From Edo to the Earthquake***. Charles E. Tuttle Company. 1983.

Tanizaki, Jun'ichiro. ***In Praise of Shadows. (In'ei Raisan)***. (Translated by Thomas J. Harper and Edward G. Seidensticker. Charles E. Tuttle Co. 1984.

Tsunoda, de Bary and Keene. ***Sources of the Japanese Tradition***. (2 volumes).

Yazaki, Takeo. ***Social Change and the City in Japan: From earliest times through the Industrial Revolution***. Japan Publications, Inc. 1968.

General

Condon, Camy & Nagasawa, Kimiko. ***Kites, Crackers and Craftsmen***. Shufunotomo 1974.

Elkin, Judith. ***Japanese Family***. A. & C. Black 1986.

Gunji, Masakutsu. ***The Kabuki Guide***. Kodansha International 1987.

Kenny, Don. ***A Guide To Kyogen***. Hinoki Shoten 1968.

O'Neill, P.G. ***A Guide To No***. Hinoki Shoten 1953.

Popham, Peter. ***Tokyo: The City at the End of the World***. Kodansha International Ltd. 1985.

Waley, Paul. ***Tokyo: City of Stories***. Weatherhill, New York 1991.

Walters, Gary D.A. ***Day Walks Near Tokyo***. Kodansha International 1988.

Japan Travel Bureau. ***Japan In Your Pocket*** (series).

Tokyo: A Bilingual Atlas. Kodansha, Tokyo 1990.

Japan: A Bilingual Atlas. Kodansha, Tokyo 1990.

Other Insight Guides

Art/Photo Credits

All photography by Scott Rutherford except for:

Alain Evrard 107, 282
Allen F Grazer/Apa Photo Agency 116, 215, 238
Apa 38, 40, 41, 60/61, 71L, 207, 208, 216
Ben Nakayama/Apa Photo Agency 119, 260, 196, 310/311, 318R
Blair Seitz/Apa Photo Agency 269
Courtesy of Chinzan-so 122/123
Carol Jopp/Globe Press Agency 56, 95R, 99, 138/139, 148, 175, 218, 219, 222, 229, 230/231, 236, 266, 267, 280, 290L, 315
Carol Purcell 191
Catherine Karnow 47, 128, 178, 185
Charlotte Anderson 23, 220/221, 278L
Dallas & John Heaton/Apa Photo Agency 184, 247L, 275
Douglas Corrance 127
G Peter Richelt/Apa Photo Agency 258
Guy Fisher 69R, 134L, 134R, 137
Gorazd Vilhar 16/17, 58/59, 72, 81, 82, 83, 89, 95L, 96, 105, 108, 109 110, 124, 125, 126, 156/157, 182, 186, 194, 206, 211, 248, 250, 259, 268, 278R, 281, 291, 294, 295, 298, 314, 317, 322
Hans Höfer 225
Hiroshe Isobe 217
Jean Kugler/Apa Photo Agency 102/103, 111, 129, 146, 158, 174, 187, 189L, 193, 212/213, 240, 244, 252/253, 256, 264/265, 270, 272, 284/285, 292
Joseph Zanghi 32, 92, 100L, 236, 189R, 197
Ken Straiton 112/113, 142/143, 290R, 304, 330, 334
Lyle Lawson 161, 163 289
Michael Webb 254, 257, 283
Miguel Rivas-Micoud 71R, 181, 188, 198, 202
Mainichi Shimbun 42, 43
Nik Wheeler/Apa Photo Agency 200, 204L, 245
Patrick Nagaishi Lucero 44
Paul van Riel 86/87, 93, 209L, 237, 249R, 320/321
Photobank 36, 45, 115, 183, 190, 192L, 192R, 263
Robert McLeod 97, 114, 130/131, 194R, 195, 199, 203L, 205, 214, 224, 226, 227, 228L, 228R, 246, 247R, 249L, 318L
Ron Kucera 100R, 117
Sam Davis 241
Stuart Atkin 35, 133, 201, 203R, 204R, 209R, 235, 262
Tadashi Matsumoto 118
Tokyo National Museum 24/25, 26, 27, 28, 29, 30L, 30R, 33, 34L, 34R, 37, 39, 69L, 84/85, 88, 90, 91, 94, 274
Wah 223
Wayne Graczyk 46, 120, 121

Index

A

B

C

D

E

S

T

U

V

W